"In this beautifully crafted and timely work, the aptly named Church... makes clear that the tangled historic links between religion and politics were built into American history from the start and are unlikely to be dissolved. This is an important work that delights and informs."
—*Publishers Weekly* (starred review)

"Well researched and written, this lively book will appeal to students of American religious history." —*Library Journal*

"[A] fascinating and subtle study...An important, nuanced book, likely to overshadow titles like David Holmes's *The Faiths of the Founding Fathers*."
—*Kirkus Reviews*

"[Church] provides a wide-angled view of the whole history of the early republic...[*So Help Me God* is] both solid and scintillating."
—Edwin S. Gaustad, author of *Sworn on the Altar of God:
A Religious Biography of Thomas Jefferson* and *Faith of the Founders*

"How fortunate we are to have Forrest Church tell the story of our nation's historical encounters with God and culture...With a keen historian's eye for detail and also an informed theologian's perceptions, Church serves as a skillful guide through this fascinating wilderness of ideas."
—Peter J. Gomes, author of *The Good Book*

"Forrest Church has given us an engaging account of the role our first presidents played in the contest between authority and liberty, fraught with the ambiguity with which we still debate these matters today."
—Timothy George, senior editor, *Christianity Today*

SO HELP ME GOD

THE FOUNDING FATHERS
AND THE FIRST GREAT BATTLE
OVER CHURCH AND STATE

FORREST CHURCH

A HARVEST BOOK

HARCOURT, INC.

Orlando   Austin   New York   San Diego   London

Requests for permission to make copies of any part of
the work should be submitted online at www.harcourt.com/contact
or mailed to the following address: Permissions Department,
Houghton Mifflin Harcourt Publishing Company,
6277 Sea Harbor Drive, Orlando, Florida 32887-6777.

www.HarcourtBooks.com

The Library of Congress has cataloged the hardcover edition as follows:
Church, Forrest.
So help me God: the Founding Fathers and the first great battle
over church and state/Forrest Church.—1st ed.
p. cm.
Includes bibliographical references.
1. United States—Church history—18th century.
2. United States—Church history—19th century.   3. Christianity and
politics—United States.   4. Church and state—United States.
5. Presidents—United States—Religion.   I. Title.
BR515.C523   2007
322'.1097309033—dc22   007007363
ISBN 978-0-15-101185-8
ISBN 978-0-15-603487-6 (pbk.)

Text set in Adobe Garamond
Designed by Liz Demeter

Printed in the United States of America

First Harvest edition 2008
A C E G I K J H F D B

To the congregation of All Souls,
for three decades of loving kindness

CONTENTS

SO HELP ME GOD

INTRODUCTION

ONE WEEK after the Union debacle at Bull Run in July 1861, the Reverend Horace Bushnell ascended his Hartford, Connecticut, pulpit to issue a lament: "Our statesmen, or politicians, not being generally religious men, take up with difficulty conceptions of government...that suppose the higher rule of God." Bushnell traced this failure of moral imagination back to the founders. In his view the nation's story opened blasphemously. Where a faithful citizen would expect to find "In the beginning, God...," the story read, "In the beginning, Thomas Jefferson...."

The differences between Bushnell and today's political preachers are as intriguing as the similarities are obvious. Recognizing how profoundly Enlightenment influences shaped the Declaration of Independence and American Constitution, Bushnell called on the people to *reject* the founders' vision. His modern-day counterparts beseech their fellow Americans to *return* to the founders to resurrect America. And Bushnell was at heart a liberal Christian, whereas most of today's thunder comes from the Religious Right. But the foundation for their shared concern is more basic than any differences that may separate them. In sum, "The Christian people of America deserve and demand a moral, God-fearing government."

Bushnell's quest to save America by reestablishing the nation on sounder religious footing was by no means novel. As early as 1800, in the first hotly contested presidential campaign, Federalist Party preachers carried a like standard into political battle against Jefferson.

From the outset of our experiment in government, in fact, the founders fought tooth and nail in a contest over American values, a vigorous, sometimes savage, yet nearly forgotten thirty-year conflict to redeem the nation's soul.

Bushnell had a keen ear for the contrapuntal themes sounded by the opposing factions in early American politics. Two distinct elements informed America's experiment in government, he said. First was "the historic element represented more especially by the New England people"; these were "church ideas," establishing government on a scriptural foundation. "God was the head of authority and the rulers were to have their authority from Him." Competing with this "churchly" ideal was the Enlightenment commitment to liberty and equality "represented in Mr. Jefferson, a man who taught abstractly, not religiously, and led the unreligious mind of the times by his abstractions." In Bushnell's view, America's founders failed to raise their sights high enough to perceive the "throne of order and law above the range of mere humanity." In short, they desacralized the United States government. At the outset of our nationhood, they stripped the state bare of any explicit "moral or religious" authority. "You will thus perceive," he concluded, "that two distinct or widely different constitutional elements entered into our political order...struggling in the womb of it, like Jacob and Esau, from the first day until now."

To resolve this fraternal conflict, Bushnell called for the creation of a Commonwealth of God. Jefferson spoke as wistfully of establishing an Empire of Liberty. Both visions arose from spiritual first principles—call them *divine order* and *sacred liberty*. Cast in terms of the nation's motto, *"E pluribus unum"* ("Out of many, one"), the advocates of divine order believed that to uphold one nation under God, the secular and sacred realms must rest on a single foundation. Without a united sense of purpose and clear moral vision, they argued, liberty would lapse into license. Champions of sacred liberty believed that to promote liberty and justice for all, the secular and religious realms must be kept autonomous. Government attempts to impose religious (or moral) values suppress religion instead, they claimed, by violating individual freedom of conscience.

However vividly Bushnell presented the fraternal struggle that gave birth to these conflicting ideals of who we should be as a people, he was mistaken in lumping the founders together in secular opposition to their Puritan forebearers. The early nation's pastors were divided as well. In league with many Presbyterians and Quakers, church leaders accustomed to operating under state aegis (old-school Episcopalians, Congregationalists, and Unitarians) believed that the nation would not survive independent of a strong Christian government. An equal majority of sectarian Protestants (Scots Presbyterians, Baptists, Methodists, etc.) together with Jews, Roman Catholics, and a smattering of influential Deists championed strict church-state separation as a guarantor of the religious liberty they long had labored to secure. When political parties emerged at the turn of the nineteenth century, their constituencies mustered for battle across the same spiritual divide. Pitting order versus liberty, England versus France, the established church versus champions of church-state separation, and America's original Puritan versus its new Enlightenment inheritance, the first great culture war in American political history—waged from George Washington's inauguration in 1789 to the outset of James Monroe's presidency (1817–1825)—is the subject of this book.

☙

Like any good story, this one is full of surprises. Did you know, for instance, that George Washington was so opposed to religious lobbying that he cursed church interference in government affairs even when he *agreed* with those who were trying to reverse national policy? His successor, John Adams, deemed the church essential to government, even if Christian theology happened to be false (which he suspected it was). Thomas Jefferson, who built a famous "wall of separation between church and state," worshipped on Sundays at a chapel set up in the Capitol and dreamed that one day all Americans would subscribe to a single, "national faith." Departing from life-long principle, James Madison declared a record four national fast days as president. Later, in a blistering attack on his own policies, he recommended that the offices of congressional and military chaplain be abolished and urged future administrations to tightly regulate religious corporations, lest their unchecked wealth and growing political power undermine the government. And James Monroe, a nonbeliever who steered clear of religion, became a clergy favorite. He won kudos from many of the same preachers who earlier insisted that unless the president was a professed Christian eager to mount his bully pulpit and lead the nation in prayer, God would bring down His hammer on the United States.

The clerics who grace this tale are as central to its drama as are the statesmen they aspired to influence or leapt to defame. You will meet Baptist, Congregational, Episcopalian, Quaker, Presbyterian, Methodist, Unitarian, Jewish, and Roman Catholic clergy members and lay people whose faith instructed their politics and whose politics, in several instances, helped turn the tide in crucial national elections. The father of American geography, Jedidiah Morse; the "pope" of Connecticut, Timothy Dwight; the Quaker moralist and self-appointed ambassador, George Logan; the mad Jeffersonian millennialist, David Austin; and the Baptist pit bull, John Leland, are but five of the many divines who, endowed with political and spiritual heft in equal measure, competed for American votes as vigorously as they did for American souls. To highlight but a few of the tantalizing facts that jump from the colorful pages of early American pulpit politics:

- Virginia's Baptists, not a reluctant James Madison, spearheaded the drive to supplement the Constitution with a Bill of Rights. The Baptist passion for freedom of conscience led directly to the First Amendment.

- In the early Republic, even as most Baptists stood on the religious left as champions for church-state separation, an equal majority of Unitarians lined up on the religious right to demand a seat for God in government.

- Most politically active Presbyterians and Congregationalists rejected the Declaration of Independence as subversive to Christian values. They wore black rosettes ("the American cockade") on the Fourth of July, while defaming as sacrilegious the red, white, and blue brandished by an equal majority of Baptists, Methodists, and Deists.

- Congress subcontracted Christian denominations to aid in educating Native Americans, the first instance of today's "faith-based initiatives."

- When the government moved to Washington, D.C., Christian worship took place not only in the House of Representatives but also in the Supreme Court, War, and Treasury Buildings (where Scots Presbyterians served Communion).

- American clergymen were taken to court by partisan state and federal prosecutors on both sides of the aisle and occasionally jailed for their politically charged preaching.

- Early in Jefferson's tenure, Alexander Hamilton (a nonpracticing Christian and lukewarm fan of the Constitution) dreamed of establishing a "Christian Constitutional Society" to lobby for a Constitutional ban prohibiting non-Christians from standing for national office.

- The Second Great Awakening, an evangelical wildfire that swept the country during the first three decades of the nineteenth century, was powered, in part, by the political collapse of New England's Congregational Church establishment, inspiring a new, more democratic mission to redeem the nation from the grass roots up, not the presidency down.

- The Monroe Doctrine was above all a moral manifesto, designed to frustrate the ambitions of the "Holy Alliance," a European royal cabal founded ostensibly to establish Christ as the cornerstone of international governance. To halt the drift of Christian imperialism into the Western Hemisphere, Monroe invoked the republican ideals of self-determination and sacred liberty.

From the moment the new government opened for business, the question of whether the young country should take on the cultural trappings of its English past or fashion itself on the French Enlightenment model spurred heated debate. Initial discussions exploded into fierce animosities, pitching absolutists on both sides into a war of conflicting ideals that threatened to tear the country in two. At the presidential level, these contests took on the character of religious crusades. The apostles of divine order were victorious first, then the champions of sacred liberty. Competing claims by today's secular humanists on the left and Christian activists on the right that the U.S. government was erected on a secular or Christian foundation are, in a sense, both correct. John Adams presided over a Christian federal authority, Jefferson over a secular one. From the first contested national election onward, avatars of sacred liberty and defenders of divine order hurled imprecations at each other that would make a modern talk-show host blush.

The religious political divide came perilously close to sundering the nation during the War of 1812. But then something remarkable happened. In 1817, with the inauguration of President Monroe, followed shortly thereafter by the disestablishment of the state church in Connecticut, an armistice was struck. Preachers on both sides of the political aisle muted their partisan trumpets, and, against much of the prevailing wisdom, religion flourished. During the so-called Era of Good Feelings the executive branch became, for the first time in the young nation's history, incontestably secular, and yet American churches grew and prospered. After decades of religious-political turbulence, the ship of state was steadied, liberty protected, religion fostered, and order served.

This drama, which at times threatens to become a tragedy, plays out in five acts, corresponding to each president's tenure. No précis can do justice to the subtleties of a story as shaded as this one, but a brief synopsis of its plot and principal protagonists might read as follows:

ACT I

Whether the new Republic was Christian or not agitated Congress the moment it convened. Should Christian worship be part of the inauguration ceremony? Should the president and senators be endowed with lordly titles? In short, how closely should the U.S. government pattern itself on the state liturgies of England? Questions such as these dominated the early work of the first Congress. Although George Washington was as secular in temperament as all but a handful of his successors, many Americans worshiped him as being greater than any king, complicating efforts to establish presidential leadership on any other than the British royal, divinely sanctioned model. Washington viewed the United States as a religious (not Christian) commonwealth, to be directed by a morally grounded governmental authority. One thing he would not abide was sectarian interference in the affairs of state. More wary of disunion than he was careful of liberty, he slowly gravitated toward order as the nation's top priority, with one notable exception: religious freedom. His deep sense of duty to all Americans made him scrupulous to avoid the slightest hint of religious favoritism. Religion was one sturdy pillar of the temple of government he helped design and construct, but Christ, about whom he was deafeningly silent, was absent from the temple's architecture. By the end of his second term, leaders of the established churches had grown openly restive toward Washington's ambiguous religious posture.

ACT II

The raucous, anticlerical French Revolution heightened tensions between Jeffersonian Democratic-Republicans, who reveled in the growing storm in France, and American Federalists, whose sympathies lay squarely with Christian England. Representing roughly half the electorate, the Federalists found a champion in Vice President John Adams, who, on his elevation to the presidency, acted openly on his conviction that the United States was, by definition, a Christian country with a Christian government. Adams distrusted the letter of Christian theology, yet he composed his national fast day proclamations in the orthodox language of Puritan covenant theology. His fasts divided the electorate. He later claimed they cost him re-election. Public grumbling that Adams was a Presbyterian president who dreamed of establishing a state church doubtless robbed him of as many votes among sectarian Christians as his opponent lost by being demonized in high-steeple churches from New York to Boston as an infidel whose election would forfeit God's favor and rip America's moral fabric to shreds.

ACT III

Although their theological views were nearly interchangeable, John Adams prized order over liberty in his quest to establish a republic of virtue; conversely, Thomas Jefferson worshiped progress and proselytized for freedom as essential to his own and the people's happiness. Jefferson's "Revolution of 1800" ushered in the Empire of Liberty, no less sacred a construct than Adams's Christian Republic. His narrow victory, over howls of outrage from the New England clergy, inaugurated twenty-four years of Republican rule. His very presence in the presidential chair further polarized establishment and dissenting Christians, the former warning of a coming Apocalypse, the latter proclaiming the advent of the millennium. Supported by a new religious cast, Jefferson's "secular" presidency wore as numinous a halo as did the Christian administration of his predecessor. Even as he implemented a doctrine of church-state separation, he regularly attended congressionally sanctioned worship in the U.S. Capitol and was lionized as the nation's savior by libertarian Baptists. The Jeffersonian revival paralleled the explosion of democratic Christianity on the American frontier, known to history as the Second Great Awakening. Doctrinally, Jefferson could not have stood further from his most avid religious allies. Believing that a universal, liberal faith would arise from the spread of knowledge, he modeled his approach to religion and politics on Enlightenment doctrine. If Adams was a Puritan skeptic, Jefferson was an Enlightenment priest.

ACT IV

With the battle for America's soul rising toward a climax, President James Madison defended Jefferson's Empire of Liberty against England abroad and New Englanders at home. Madison was liberty's most dedicated scribe. He shared Jefferson's commitment to church-state separation, but lacked his mentor's dream-struck temperament and was not as doctrinaire in his humanism. His tenure saw American pulpit politics soar to a fever pitch during the War of 1812. Partisan pressure to marshal support for the war by reinstating national fast days (in essence, state-sponsored worship) beguiled him to betray his fidelity to the principles of sacred liberty, which barred all government interference in matters of religion. Paradoxically, by invoking God to support American arms against Great Britain, Madison drove the antiwar New England clergy, whose sympathies lay with Christian England, to defy his religious directives. They, in turn, showered God's judgment down on the nation and its leaders. Some Federal Christians toyed with the idea of secession. In a final plot twist, American victory in the War of 1812 branded the Christian commonwealthmen as traitors. Despite the success of his religious ploys, Madison emerged from his years in office firmly convinced that the government should forswear all future entanglement with organized religion.

ACT V

In the denouement of this drama, after three decades of fractious sloganeering and open religious strife, leaders of the established church removed themselves from national politics. In a surprising turn of events, rather than diminish Christian influence in the nation's moral life, the defeat of those who had championed Christian government freed the church from political manipulation instead and extended its moral authority. Far from vanquished, the Standing Congregational Orders of New England redirected their prodigious organizational talents from electoral contests to Bible and tract societies designed to redeem the nation from the grass roots up, not the presidency down. Their withdrawal from the federal political stage allowed the recipient of this détente, the resolutely secular President James Monroe, to achieve, for a time at least, Washington's goal of national amity. Secular governance was confirmed, yet the religious nation prospered. America's churches burgeoned in number and spiritual power during Monroe's Era of Good Feelings. Adams, Jefferson, and Madison joined in hailing his accomplishments. The hard-fought contest to fashion America on either the Puritan model of Christian Commonwealth or the Jeffersonian vision of an Empire of Liberty ended with the fulfillment, temporary to be sure and strained severely by the continuing specter of slavery, of *E pluribus unum*.

⌘

In framing this narrative, I define religion broadly. I shall certainly explore the presidents' theological beliefs to the extent that we are privy to them, but, beyond this, I view moral and religious values as basically interchangeable. Jefferson's wise (and, in part, self-incriminating) observation—"It is in our lives and not from our words that our religion must be read"—is as good a litmus test as any. His insistence that we not confuse a person's religion with his or her rhetoric applies with particular force to public figures. Successful politicians are rhetorical masters, and none but their most private words can be taken at face value, even as their actions may speak volumes.

The protagonists of this story are in some ways oddly cast as religious actors. At their most pious, the nation's first five presidents offered little to commend themselves to the sensibilities of a proper New England Trinitarian parson like Horace Bushnell. Only Adams was a church member, and they all doubted the divinity of Christ. Their wives, including Dolley Madison, who left her piety in Philadelphia when she was excommunicated by the Quakers for marrying outside the fold, were more conventionally devout than their husbands, but only Martha Washington was orthodox in her beliefs. As for James Monroe, throughout his compendious literary remains there is no inkling that he entertained a single religious notion during his entire adult life. Yet Adams, Jefferson, and Madison were thoughtful students of religion, and all five founding presidents freely made ritual accommodations to satisfy the expectations of their religious constituencies.

Among the moral quandaries that these five remarkable, if inevitably flawed, leaders tackled or avoided, Native American rights and the slavery of African Americans (the overarching moral dilemmas of the first few decades of U.S. history) cast the longest shadows. But science and religion's contesting claims provoked presidential comment and controversy also, as did arguments over the role religion should play in American education. All five presidents, in seeking to construct and defend a principled foreign policy, wrestled with matters of war and peace, inevitably provoking spirited religious debate. The culture of the White House and reputation of the First Lady, a public figure in her own right, drew concentrated fire from American moralists as well. And, finally, as we might expect in a nation with a dominant, if diverse, Christian population and a secular Constitution, questions arose during each administration over where to draw the line between church and state.

The biography of a nation is vastly more encompassing than the story of its leaders, of course. Our first presidents ignored or adapted themselves to the people's moral and religious urgings decidedly more than they shaped them. Yet how each president addressed religious questions etched its imprint on the nation's soul.

———

I take from this study a number of things I did not bring to it. From my days as a doctoral student, I have been drawn to the romance of early American history. In recent years, I introduced the latest edition of "Jefferson's Bible," wrote a biography of the Declaration of Independence, and annotated a collection of the founders' writings on church and state. Yet, until I tackled early pulpit politics head on, I, too, harbored a few easy illusions about religion and the founders. What surprised me most is how large religion loomed in their electoral fortunes. Today's Christian campaigners and their secular critics seem almost timid compared to the warring American dreamers and would-be saviors who battled for votes in the early Republic. It is impossible to pore over this material without developing a keener awareness of how explosive religious politics can be. Henry Kissinger memorably said that academic politics are so fierce because the stakes are so *small*. Religious politics draw their ferocity from how *cosmic* the outcome seems. Its practitioners are religious crusaders. Salvation is their goal, and almost any means can seem to justify so lofty an end. American electioneering is brutal to begin with; throw salvation into the mix and, if people aren't careful, it can become toxic. During the first struggle for America's soul, normal political rhetoric, however heated, paled in comparison to the language employed by politicized priests and sanctimonious politicians.

Balancing this caveat, I walk away with a deeper appreciation for the saving grace of Christian politics. If God's banner had been removed from early American discourse, the counter gospel of sovereign individualism would have taken full possession of the nation's soul. The early apostles of religious governance succumbed too easily to authoritarian persuasion, yet they checked the drift toward amoral relativism. Washington's refusal to sanction moral lobbies and, more ominously, the Jeffersonian recourse to states' rights as a libertarian stopgap against Christian attempts to legislate morality greased evil wheels. In the early Republic, liberty and slavery walked hand in hand down the road to the Civil War.

Also of note, the most spirited combatants on both sides of the cultural divide imperiled their own first principles by their unquestioning devotion to them. The imposition of order triggered rebellion even as unchecked liberty invited repression. The first law of history might well be "Pick your enemies carefully, for you will become like them." As exclusive absolutes, sacred liberty (the essence of Jefferson's empire) and divine order (the foundation stone of a Christian commonwealth) led their devotees to opposite banks of the same brink.

Another insight I garnered along the way is this: The effect of a president's civic faith is greater than the influence of his personal religious beliefs. That none of the first presidents was an orthodox Christian had little bearing on where each stood on the religious-political spectrum. Christian activists of the time understood this instinctively. How else can we make sense of the adoration born-again Baptists felt for the Deist Jefferson or the equally avid support orthodox Presbyterians lavished on the Unitarian Adams?

Finally, in America's early politics, religion, even when it entered the halls of government freely, wound up being manipulated for political gain. When church and state tucked into bed together, it was the church that ended up asking, "Will you respect me in the morning," and the answer was almost always "No."

American citizens will continue to argue over where to draw the line between church and state, even as religion will bedevil and enlighten governmental policies and electoral politics for years to come. The ideals of liberty and order will coexist in tension as they have in the nation's womb from the beginning. And champions on both sides (*unum* people and *pluribus* people) will claim the words and actions of the founders as proof texts for the righteousness of their moral, political, and religious agendas. The historical record reveals how deeply grounded this practice is, emerging at the very outset of the nation's story. The founding presidents believed in the United States as a repository for the highest human values. To betray those values was, in each of their eyes, to commit national sacrilege.

Their civic agendas arose not only from competing ideologies but also from competing visions of how "America might," as Martin Luther King Jr. dreamed, "rise up and live out the true meaning of its creed."

Of equal moment to today's divided body politic, the interplay of religion and statecraft during the nation's first half century reveals the possibility of a both/and not either/or solution to the religious-political equation. The founding presidents each wrestled to balance the ideals of liberty and order to meet the challenge of *E pluribus unum* and fulfill its promise. How they defined and finally struck this balance is the story I tell in *So Help Me God*.

ACT I

GEORGE
WASHINGTON

I

⮞⮜

OUT OF MANY, ONE

Fame stretched her wings and whither her trumpet blew,
Great Washington is near. What praise is due?
What title shall he have? She paused—and said
"Not one—his name alone strikes every title dead."

—A POEM INSERTED IN THE WASHINGTON
INAUGURAL BIBLE BY ST. JOHN'S LODGE
(FREEMASONS) OF NEW YORK CITY

A CANNONADE from old Ft. George on Manhattan's Battery saluted the sun as dawn broke on April 30, 1789. Born on the Fourth of July thirteen years before in Philadelphia, this was the day that the United States of America would come of age. Civilians donned their Sunday best. Revolutionary War veterans resurrected their proud old dress uniforms, and young militiamen brushed their new ones. On the stroke of nine, ringing in the first act of a sovereign people, all across the city church bells chimed.

Thousands made the pilgrimage from their homes to waypoints along the parade route down Wall Street, to the heart of lower Manhattan. People bedecked their eaves with bunting and their stoops with flowers. On the avenues leading up to and flanking Federal Hall, open windows overspilled with expectant onlookers. Parents held their children up to catch a glimpse of General Washington as he passed.

To the accompaniment of rolling drums, the presidential coach, its lone occupant riding with no company but his thoughts, inched down cobblestone streets through the press of humanity crowding lower Manhattan. At the end of the parade route, an honor guard of horse, light infantry, and grenadiers cordoned off a passageway for the president-elect and joint inaugural committee. They disembarked from their carriages to deafening applause, passed through the protective gauntlet, climbed the steps to Federal Hall, and entered the doorway leading to the Senate chamber.

At one in the afternoon, much to the delight of the expectant crowd, the portico doors swung open. Watching with wide eyes amid the crush of spectators was one of Washington's many namesakes, a six-year-old boy born at the end of the war. Seventy years later, near the end of his long life and distinguished literary career, this boy, Washington Irving, would recall that magical moment when General Washington emerged onto the portico to greet the crowd.

> His entrance on the balcony was hailed by universal shouts. He was evidently moved by this demonstration of public affection. Advancing to the front of the balcony, he laid his hand upon his heart, bowed several times and then retreated to an armchair near the table. The populace appeared to understand that the scene had overcome him and were hushed at once into profound silence.

Dressed in a homespun suit, his shoulder-length hair powdered white and swept back in a neatly tied queue, Washington took his place in the center of the balcony under a crimson canopy. Rising to administer the presidential oath was Chancellor Robert Livingston, the highest sitting judge in New York State. The president-elect placed his left hand on an exquisite red vellum Bible as Chancellor Livingston administered the oath of office as prescribed in the Constitution. In response, the father of his country declared, "I do solemnly swear that I will faithfully execute the Office of President of the United States, and will to the best of my ability, preserve, protect and defend the Constitution of the United States."

Tradition has it that, before bending his stately frame to kiss the Bible, Washington added a sacred codicil to this secular oath. "I swear," he avowed, "so help me God." (I defend this tradition in an appendix.) By all accounts, the nation's first great ceremony lavished the Almighty with reverence and praise.

Cast by Providence, the Actor Awaits His Call

Postponed more than a month by Congress's inability to scrape together a quorum, inauguration day was late, and Washington didn't wait well. His mind couldn't "bear a vacancy," James Madison said. The limbo between Election Day and the inauguration invited what Thomas Jefferson called his "gloomy apprehensions." Colonel David Humphreys bore the brunt of these. Lodged at Mount Vernon to write the general's authorized biography, the convivial Humphreys served Washington, as he had during Revolutionary days, in the flattering role of official shadow. He would run with the hounds by his side on horseback as happily as he would accompany him to church, though foxhunting was a more certain weekly ritual than worship for Washington during his Mount Vernon years.

Washington had been agonizing over the call to lead. "I feel very much like a man who is condemned to death does when the time of his execution draws nigh," he sighed. "If my appointment & acceptance be inevitable, I fear I must bid adieu to happiness." Maybe he shouldn't accept the office, Washington fretted aloud to Humphreys. What if people mistook his motives? He did, after all, say after the war that he was retiring for good from public service. Would people now take him for a hypocrite? To this monologue, Humphreys offered the response Washington needed to hear. "The very existence of the government will be much endangered, if the person placed at the head of it should not possess the entire confidence of both its friends and adversaries," the young man assured him. "You ought sometimes, Sir," Colonel Humphreys reasonably suggested, "to look upon the bright side of the picture; and not always to be pondering the objects you find on the reverse."

A Virginia gentleman was judged on appearances. The negative print image of a good New England Calvinist, trained not to care a whit for life's trappings as long as his or her conscience was clear with God, for Washington appearances were everything. Virtue proved itself by deeds apparent to all, not by a contrite heart or spotless soul. This made him no less moral. On the contrary, his attentiveness to outward propriety protected him from moral embarrassment as readily as the dread of guilt in the eyes of God might impel a devout Puritan to resist temptations that could lead to sin. To Washington, virtue and honor coalesced into a single overriding aspiration. "My only ambition," he told Humphreys, "is to do my duty in this world as well as I am capable of performing it, & to merit the good opinion of all men."

Practicing virtue to achieve a good name was a hallmark of ancient Stoicism. Succinctly defined as "frugality, simplicity, temperance, fortitude, love of liberty, selflessness, and honor," Roman virtue demanded fidelity to a fixed set of moral rules as illustrated in the treatises of Seneca and Cicero, which Washington admired in English translation. Cicero's thoughts on reputation capture Washington's principal obsession almost perfectly: "We are afraid not only of what we may openly be reproached with, but of what others may think of us in secret. The slightest rumors, the most improbable tale that can be devised to our prejudice, alarms and disconcerts us. We study the countenance, and the looks, of all around us. For nothing is more delicate, so frail, and uncertain, as the public favor." A Virginia planter himself, Madison understood Washington's dilemma: "To forsake the honorable retreat to which he had retired and risk the reputation he had so deservedly acquired manifested a zeal for the public interest that could, after so many and illustrious services, scarcely have been expected of him."

Washington was elected president by acclamation; he received every electoral vote. New Englanders couldn't help but think of "election" theologically. In the canons of Puritan theology, the saved were God's "elect." Viewing himself (if in a very different light) among the chosen as well, Washington, too, would honor his election by striving to prove himself worthy of it. In so doing, his thinking was Roman, not Christian; duty called, not God; and honor, not salvation, would be his reward. Yet his destiny, he was certain, was written in the stars. Washington felt anointed as the protagonist in a divine drama. The entire country, in fact, was cast to play a providential role. "The citizens of America," he said, were "the actors of a most conspicuous theatre, which seems to be peculiarly designated by Providence for the display of human greatness and felicity."

"Strew Your Hero's Way with Flowers"

While waiting for Congress to convene, Washington penned a letter to his nephew George Steptoe Washington full of avuncular advice. In the many letters he wrote to his wards over the years, the only allusion to religion, a brief commendation of reverent appearances, occurs here. Following the glum disclaimer that, contrary to his wishes, duty was about to thrust him back onto the public stage, he offered his namesake "some advisory hints, which, if properly attended to will, I conceive, be found very useful to you in regulating your conduct and giving you respectability not only at present but thro' every period of life." After instructing his nephew to beware the sins of indolence, profligacy, and idleness, Washington commended "constantly improving your manners," choosing good company over bad, and attending to "decency and cleanliness" in personal hygiene. Finally, he stressed the importance of appropriate attire, balancing the imperatives of fashion, frugality, and propriety. It is here that he speaks of religion: "You should always keep some clothes to wear to Church or on particular occasions, which should not be worn every day."

Ever conscious of appearances, Washington practiced what he preached. While awaiting official word of his nation's call, he devoted lavish attention to procuring the proper outfit for a republican leader to wear to his own inauguration. He sensed, quite rightly, that British finery would be inappropriate for so American

an occasion and was therefore delighted to chance upon an advertisement for "Superfine American Broad Cloth," spun at a woolen
manufactory in Hartford, Connecticut. Commissioning thirteen
and a half yards of brown Hartford, he arranged to have a suit cut
and sewn to his precise specifications. To make it less plain and
more patriotic, he ordered a set of American-made gilt buttons
embossed with eagles, wings outspread, modeled after the eagle
depicted on the Great Seal. Complemented by a brown, trim-
brimmed tricorn beaver hat manufactured in Philadelphia and the
necessary accessories (white silk stockings, silver shoe buckles, and
a formal sword with steel scabbard and hilt), Washington's inaugural uniform was complete.

On April 14, 1789, Irish-born Charles Thompson, secretary of
the Congress from its beginnings in 1774, arrived at Mount Vernon
to present official notice of the nation's call. He had already aided
the president-elect by fashioning the American eagle that emblazoned the buttons of his inaugural suit. In 1782 Congress had asked
Thompson to codesign a great seal for the new nation. Thompson's
classical knowledge suited him for the task. So did his faith. He was
a devout Quaker and careful student of the scriptures. Late in life,
he produced a celebrated four-volume translation of the Bible.

National seals are symbolic, evoking the country's essence in a
few bold strokes. Imagine how different our country's self-image
might have been if the great seal of the United States had incorpo-
rated Benjamin Franklin's preference for national bird, the turkey,
rather than a proud eagle with arrows in its talon. Several early suggestions for the seal's iconography, though ultimately rejected,
evoke the founders' eclectic sources of inspiration. Jefferson tapped
the Old Testament (the parting of the Red Sea) and England before
its pristine laws were corrupted by the church and crown (two legendary Saxon chieftains) to hold up the banner of liberty. Adams
turned to Greek mythology, picturing mighty Hercules insensible
to sloth, personified by an alluring female. Thompson and his committee settled instead, in addition to the eagle, on an olio of arcane

motifs, from the all-seeing divine eye to the Egyptian pyramid, accompanied by phrases from Roman literature charged with divine portent. *Annuit coeptis* ("Providence has favored our undertaking"), his great seal reads; and, from Virgil's *Messianic Eclogue,* long interpreted as prophesying the birth of Christ, *Novus ordo seclorum* ("a new order of the ages").

Washington's secular pilgrimage to the presidency, a triumphant journey to New York with Humphreys and Thompson by his side, was laden with sacral overtones. At Gray's Ferry Bridge, Pennsylvania (a makeshift flank of logs tied together over a small stream), he received an elaborate welcome designed by the artist Charles Willson Peale. Twenty-foot-high triumphal arches twined with laurel rose before him on both ends of the bridge. Recalling his revolutionary days, in front of the bridge stood a twenty-five-foot liberty pole flying a banner inscribed with the now nostalgic but no less insistent libertarian motto "Don't Tread on Me." As he passed under the first arch, Peale's white-robed fifteen-year-old daughter Angelica turned a winch, which lowered a laurel wreath upon Washington's forehead as he patiently reined in his horse to receive the at-once embarrassing and flattering crown. At Trenton, New Jersey, site of his surprise attack in late December, 1776, that overpowered a garrison of Hessian soldiers and provided the country a ray of light amid the gathering storm, an even more ornate triumphal arch awaited him, emblazoned with words of hope: "The defender of the mothers will be the protector of the daughters." Classically sheathed in matching white gowns, their hair embroidered with ivy and chaplets of flowers, mother and daughter alike hymned his advent and scattered petals in his path.

Not all the festivities drew their inspiration from pagan antiquity. At the College of New Jersey (later Princeton College), where Jerusalem was honored above ancient Rome, its Scots Presbyterian president, John Witherspoon, played host to his old congressional colleague, offering public prayers for the nation and its president-elect. The only clergyman to sign the Declaration of Independence,

Witherspoon coined the term "Americanism," and fashioned a graduate program designed specifically to "fit young gentlemen for serving their country in public stations." Princeton boasted more than seventy graduates who served during the war, many as chaplains, which is why the Chaplain Corps was dominated by Presbyterians. Witherspoon was an uncompromising champion of religious liberty. Among his students, James Madison would take liberty as his watchword, advocating a strict separation of church and state.

Shortly after leaving Princeton, Washington breakfasted with another friend from Revolutionary days, Representative Elias Boudinot. Also a Presbyterian, but of Huguenot (French Calvinist) descent, Boudinot was a staunch conservative, dedicated to the preservation of order and numbering Alexander Hamilton among his protégés. With Boudinot and Witherspoon as their mentors, Hamilton and Madison would emerge as two of the most effective spokesmen for divine order and sacred liberty. Washington, who valued the advice of all four men, would seek as president to balance the claims of their competing civic ideals.

The most lavish festivities were saved for the end of Washington's grand pilgrimage. At Elizabethtown Point, New Jersey, to carry the president-elect and his party across the Hudson there awaited a forty-seven-foot barge resplendently festooned with the requisite patriotic symbols. A nautical parade of tiny civilian craft accompanied the presidential barge, the flotilla growing in number and variety as new boats spontaneously appeared to participate in the festivities. Porpoises gamboled alongside Washington's barge. "The very water," Boudinot extolled, appeared "to rejoice in bearing the precious burden over its placid bosom." Instrumentalists and choirs crowded the decks of several larger ships, including a mixed chorus that serenaded General Washington with an ode set to the tune "God Save the King." Approaching Murray's Wharf on the lower tip of Manhattan island, Washington's boat rounded the Battery to a thirteen-gun federal salute. At this prearranged signal, in a brilliant flourish of nautical choreography the accompanying parade of sloops and schooners ran American flags up their masts. He disembarked to ascend a carpeted stairway through a third and final triumphal Roman archway, its white columns twined with ivy.

Yet not every voice was cheering. The first hint of what would become a rising chorus of democratic discontent about the royal trappings surrounding the new government arrived in the form of a caricature printed shortly before Washington's entry to New York. It pictured Washington "mounted on an ass & and in arms of his mulatto man Billy—[David] Humphreys leading the jack and chanting hosannas and birthday odes." This irreverent cartoon flaunted the scriptural couplet "The glorious time has come to pass/ When David shall conduct an Ass." The Bible would furnish partisans of every stripe with ammunition over the years ahead. For now, the crack of negative reports was all but lost in the din of praise.

Naming the Animals in America's New Ark

Washington knew he was scripting history. "We are a young nation and have a character to establish," he declared after his victory over England. He already had established his own unmistakable character; to do the same for an entire people was more daunting. "We are in a wilderness without a single step to guide us," he confided to his young Virginian sounding board, Representative James Madison. "As the first of everything in our situation will serve to establish a precedent, it is devoutly wished on my part, that these precedents may be fixed on true principles." In this same spirit, Washington appended a cautionary note to his request for Vice President John Adams's counsel on establishing a protocol for executive etiquette. "Many things which appear of little importance in themselves and at the beginning, may have great and durable consequences from their having been established at the commencement of a new general government," he warned. "It will be much easier to commence the administration upon a well adjusted system, built on tenable grounds, than to correct errors or to alter inconveniences after they shall have been confirmed by habit."

Proper etiquette was high on Congress's agenda as well. If it took six years to hammer out an acceptable great seal, perhaps it should come as no surprise that Congress devoted much of its energy during its first six weeks to resolving heated controversies over how much pomp and circumstance should attend the new government and its leaders. These debates form the opening chapter in what would become a developing story concerning the extent to which the U.S. government would honor its British patrimony. One theme recurring throughout this tale concerns America's religious inheritance from England: Would the fledgling nation continue to show a decent respect for religious custom or would it march to the irreverent French beat of Rousseau and Voltaire?

As vice president, Adams's only constitutional responsibility was to preside as president of the U.S. Senate. By design the more aristocratic of the two houses, when the Senate finally opened for business its distinguished members quibbled over everything from the inaugural ceremony itself to what titles would best befit the high stations and republican principles of their executive leaders. Senators Richard Henry Lee of Virginia and William Maclay of Pennsylvania contributed most colorfully to the chaotic scene, the former as Adams's spear-carrier, the latter as leader of the chorus that bemoaned the vice president's pet experiment with precedent setting, a spirited campaign to elevate the status of the executive offices by investing them with loftier titles. To refer to Washington as "president," Adams pleaded, would leave the nation open to ridicule by putting "him on a level with a governor of Bermuda." Remarking that the clergy in his part of the country distinguished themselves from the populace by painting their gates red, he reminded the Senate that "Religion and government have both been used as pageantry." Senator Oliver Ellsworth of Connecticut invoked religion, too, to make the case for titles. "*Fear God and honor the King,*"

Ellsworth reminded his fellow senators, was an essential rubric for civilized governance.

Sincerely convinced that so pedestrian a title as "president" would tempt foreign soldiers and sailors in particular to "despise him to all eternity," Adams entertained a number of alternatives. "His Elective (or Most Benign) Highness" was one, "His High Mightiness" another. Although he cut these titles out of sturdy republican cloth (importing them from Holland, whose governors, by no means monarchs, were invested with such honorifics), they strike the modern American ear, as they did many of Adams's contemporaries, as laughable. The Constitution seemed clear. It said, "No title of nobility shall be granted by the United States."

A towering, ruddy-complexioned, backcountry lawyer of Scotch Irish descent and strict republican principle, Senator Maclay accused Adams of attempting to smuggle "contraband language" into American writ. With but two fellow contrarians seconding Maclay's dissent (Senator Charles Carroll of Maryland, a Roman Catholic, and cantankerous Ralph Izard of South Carolina), the congenially minded Senate Title Committee that Adams had convened finally settled on "His Highness, the President of the United States, and Protector of their Liberties." When Madison, writing in code, dropped word of this particular compromise into a information-packed yet slightly catty letter addressed to his political big brother in France, Thomas Jefferson deemed it "the most superlatively ridiculous thing I ever heard."

With a united Senate, which he very nearly had, Adams might well have carried the day. He certainly was nothing if not earnest in his proposal. Recommending the speedy appointment of a "Chamberlain (or Gentleman in Waiting)" and "Master of Ceremonies" as necessary additions to the tiny executive staff, Adams presented his case for lofty titles to Washington directly. He pleaded to the chief executive, "Neither dignity nor authority can be supported in human minds, collected into nations or any great numbers, without a *splendor and majesty* in some degree proportioned to them."

In Adams's opinion, no "other name can with propriety be given [the new government], than that of a monarchical republic, or if you will, a limited monarchy." Apart from this idiosyncratic reading of American writ, his concerns were highly personal. In his role as president of the Senate, it was only appropriate that that the senators should address him accordingly. If Washington should pay a visit, there would be two presidents in the chamber. "When the President comes in to the Senate, what shall I be?" Adams plaintively asked. "I wish, gentlemen, to think what I shall be." From the peanut gallery in Philadelphia, Benjamin Franklin couldn't resist speculating, "His superfluous Excellency?" Senator Izard proposed a more descriptive and disparaging epithet: "His rotundity."

To modern ears, much of the weeks-long debate has an *Alice in Wonderland* twist to it. Should, for instance, the Senate install a raised, canopied throne to be reserved for the president on his visits to its chamber, as Senator Lee proposed? Would the title "honorable," unless plumped to "right honorable," insult senatorial dignity, as Adams insisted it would? (In Adams's mind, titles flowed to chief executives and senators alone, not to members of the House.) Adams went so far as to propose that the Senate sergeant at arms be named "Usher of the Black Rod." An exasperated Senator Maclay found himself praying to "the Goddess of Etiquette" for counsel as the Senate invested the better part of a month (from April 23 to May 13) wrestling over how they should address each other and their leader.

Although the title debate and those associated with it may seem silly to us now, the symbolism of titles carried enormous portent. Popular respect would evaporate, Adams argued, if the people's leaders did not demand for themselves and receive in return a modicum of popular obeisance. Maclay, in turn, saw Senator Lee and Vice President Adams conspiring to create "a new monarchy in America."

Maclay never fit into the smug Senate, missed his children and wife terribly, and was ill throughout his brief tenure. "Many a culprit has served two years at the wheelbarrow without feeling half the pain and mortification that I experienced in my honorable station," he said in leaving. He translated this pain into dyspeptic prose, indiscriminately lampooning almost every star on the early American stage. Yet, if this vigilant sentinel for republican ideals had not stood his ground, a royal title might have crowned the nation's president. Instead, insisting on no titles beyond those authorized by the Constitution, the House held firm and, at Maclay's dogged insistence, the Senate proposal languished on the table. On titles, thrones, and the Usher of the Black Rod, Maclay and Madison won the day.

Arguably the most dedicated public servant in a young nation that boasted more than its share of born leaders, John Adams was devastated. To Maclay he questioned the government's future viability. Well into the summer, he continued to insist that even "His Highness" was too lowly an honorific, himself preferring "the title of Majesty"—"even King, Sir!" he wrote, before prudence instructed him to edit out that most offensive of all words to American ears.

What had happened to this towering champion of liberty, who shortly before the Revolution had declared, "Formalities and ceremonies are an abomination in my sight. I hate them in religion, government, science, life." For one thing, Adams had spent a decade calling on the courts of Europe. For another, as his political philosophy matured, he had grown more conservative. But the simple answer is that back in the 1770s Adams was urging the people to topple their king; now, he was struggling to build a republican government strong enough to keep these same people from toppling themselves. With the government but a few days old, the title debate was the first standoff between divine order and sacred liberty. Adams would go on to carry the banner of order throughout his tempestuous career.

"Put and Carried by the Churchman"

During the week preceding Washington's inauguration, the question of British patrimony arose once again with the appointment of congressional chaplains and the subsequent debate over the part, if any, worship should play during the inaugural ceremony itself. Although Madison stood in opposition, naming chaplains raised few congressional hackles since earlier congresses had established precedent. Yet each of these matters hinted at the debate that loomed on the nation's political horizon and would break out in full force once Washington retired from public life: the proper role of religion in the rites and duties of American statecraft. "How much external sanction does the new American government need?" was the underlying question, a question of authority. As colonists, Americans had sworn allegiance to the crown and bowed to the legislative power invested in Parliament. In the Revolutionary War, aspiring to self-governance, they fought to liberate themselves from this allegiance. Nonetheless, the only experience most American citizens had of an overarching governmental authority derived from a lifetime spent living under the British royal parliamentary system. Given the union of church and state in England, the ceremonial role the clergy played in the British governance, and the reverence such a system engendered in the people toward the royal monarch, installing America's new executives with the pomp of borrowed ritual held real as well as symbolic portent.

Congress may have held fast to Constitutional guidelines on the title question, but when it came to penciling in a line of separation between church and state regarding chaplaincy and inaugural worship many senators deemed the lack of any mention of religion in the Constitution irrelevant. To them, the imperative to secure Divine favor and provide moral and spiritual uplift superseded any lesser concern that might be raised concerning the "Englandization" (in both the royal and churchly sense) of the United States.

Blaming him for perpetuating "all the fooleries, fopperies, fineries and pomp of Royal etiquette," Maclay held Senator Lee of Virginia almost criminally accountable for "this whole silly business" of fashioning American civil ceremony on the British royal and priestly model ("pompous titles, strong efforts after religious distinctions,...oaths, etc. etc."). Madison, too, shook his head at Lee's surprising emergence in the vanguard of aristocratic apologists. For him the shock was personal; earlier that same year, Lee had defeated Madison in a tightly contested Senate race by challenging Madison's fidelity to republican principle.

Hazarding to intuit an early American lawmaker's religious views from his political ideology is more difficult than one might imagine. Nor does the question "Will religion trump politics or politics, religion when the two interests collide?" admit a ready answer. Lee, with aquiline features and an Anglican pedigree, yet as severe in his faith as the most rigid Presbyterian, presents the perfect case in point. A dashing character—he swathed his left hand in a black kerchief to veil three missing fingers lost in a hunting mishap—the master of Chantilly Plantation in Virginia's Westmoreland County was as radical in his politics as he was pious in his devotions. His passion for public ceremony sprung from his religious not his political creed.

Adams came to know and admire this tall, spare figure in the Continental Congress, where he seconded Lee's motion to declare independence from the crown. Lee so hated slavery that he openly fantasized abandoning Virginia for Massachusetts, where together he and Adams could literally lock arms in the battle for liberty and establish a "wise and free republic in Massachusetts Bay." He dreamed of living out his remaining years there, mistaking deferential Massachusetts for a libertarian Eden. "The hasty, unpersevering, aristocratic genius of the South suits not my disposition," Lee confessed. "It is inconsistent with my ideas of what must constitute social happiness and security." Although destined to take his place in the Upper Chamber, he fretted that the Senate and president together wielded "a most formidable combination of power" capable of "unbalancing the Constitution."

Religiously, however, this otherwise radical statesman was an arch traditionalist, punctilious in his Christian devotions. When Madison and Jefferson were campaigning to disestablish religion in

Virginia, Lee fired off to Madison a tart, dismissive "Nay": "Refiners may weave as fine a web of reason as they please, but the experience of all times shows religion to be the guardian of morals." On the matter of titles, he argued, "all the world, civilized and savage" could not do without them, but Lee's loyalties to the Anglican system of church-state interdependence ran deeper than that. Adams surely recognized as much in urging his appointment as cochair of the Joint Committee on Ceremonies and by ensuring him a place on the three-member Title and Chaplain Committees as well, trusting that, in the various matters that these three bodies must police, his religious scruples would take precedence over his republican sensibilities. Back in Virginia, rumors of Senator Lee's political apostasy fomented rebellion among his republican-minded constituents, but, for the time being, he was content to serve as America's master of ceremonies.

The Senate finally mustered a quorum with Lee's arrival on April 6; by April 7, he had emerged as a most interested participant on the committee selected "to take under consideration the manner of electing chaplains." Without Constitutional mandate, his committee quickly resolved,

> That two chaplains, of different denominations, be appointed to Congress for the present session, the Senate to appoint one, and give notice thereof to the House of Representatives, who shall, thereupon, appoint the other, which chaplains shall commence their services in the Houses that appoint them, but shall interchange weekly [a practice deemed unwieldy and dropped]."

On April 25, at the committee's unanimous recommendation, the Senate ratified Lee's choice for chaplain, the Anglican bishop of New York, Samuel Provoost.

Two days before the chaplaincy vote, Lee was appointed chair, as well, of the Senate committee charged, together with its House counterpart, with planning the inauguration. The Joint Committee on Ceremonies met with General Washington to receive any instructions he might have. It is unlikely that he provided much direction. Of the man he uncomfortably served under for eight long years, Adams would say, "he possessed the gift of silence."

Many inaugural details were hammered out in private, but one issue sparked sufficient controversy that it had to be brought to the floor. The House members on the Committee on Ceremonies had rejected Senator Lee's recommendation that holy worship be included in the inauguration. Pulling rank, the Senate ignored them. On April 27, Lee's committee submitted for Senate approval its proposal that the inaugural ceremonies conclude with "divine services" to be conducted by "the chaplain of Congress already appointed" and take place at St. Paul's Anglican Chapel.

St. Paul's opened for worship in 1766, one of two chapels built to accommodate the overflow from Trinity Church, an Anglican bastion at the corner of Wall Street and Broadway. When Trinity fell victim to the great fire that torched one quarter of New York during Washington's chaotic retreat before a vastly superior British force in the fall of 1776, St. Paul's became the central house of Anglican worship in the city, which it remained until Trinity's reconsecration in 1790. Bishop Provoost had begun his American career two decades before when the Archbishop of Canterbury, Thomas Secker, dispatched him to the colonies to serve as assistant rector of Trinity Parish. His first tenure there was brief, Provoost's vocal Whig politics provoking Trinity's Tory-dominated vestry to drive him from the pulpit in 1771. When the British abandoned New York in 1784, he rode the shifting winds of political fortune back into office, first as Trinity's rector and shortly thereafter as the first bishop of New York.

In 1786, Adams played a significant role in advancing Provoost's career. As American minister to the Court of St. James, he brokered Provoost's consecration (and that of Bishop William White of Pennsylvania), acting at the behest of then president of Congress Richard Henry Lee. Lavishing Congress's esteem on the touchy diplomat for his "liberal regard for the religious rights of all men,"

Lee begged Adams to convince British sacral authorities that American bishops could coexist with split loyalties, both to their country and their archbishop.

The Anglican Church arose out of the English Reformation in the sixteenth century. During the reign of King Henry VIII, a majority of English Catholics shifted their loyalty, at royal bidding, from the pope to the crown. Inextricably woven into the warp of British secular authority, Anglican Church polity was hierarchical, with ordinations emanating from the Archbishop of Canterbury, who buttressed the authority of the royal monarch. James I summed up Great Britain's church-state partnership neatly: "no Bishop no King, no King no Bishop."

The question of consecration was a thorny one for American Episcopalians. A split developed between those who wished to retain ecclesiastical ties with England and those who preferred to establish an independent American Episcopal Church. After lengthy deliberation, the Episcopal governing body voted to reestablish communion with England. John Jay informed the Archbishop of Canterbury, in a letter entrusted to Adams, "We have neither departed, nor propose to depart from the doctrines of your church," avowing that the American faithful "were anxious to complete our Episcopal system, by means of the Church of England."

Benjamin Franklin winked at the need for British royal sanction for American bishops. "When people are more enlightened," he astutely prophesied, "it will be wondered at that men in America, qualified by their learning and piety to pray for and instruct their neighbors, should not be permitted to do it till they had made a voyage of 6000 miles, going out and home, to ask leave of a cross old gentleman at Canterbury." For now, the cross old gentleman had to be appeased. On July 4, 1786, Archbishop Moore officially informed the American Episcopal Convention that Parliament had passed a bill conceding the American church's independence from the king, while maintaining ecclesial authority over it as a subject body operating under Anglican jurisdiction. Having fulfilled his mission, Adams melodramatically recalled, "There was no part of my life in which I look back with more satisfaction than the part I took, bold, daring and hazardous as it was to me and mine, in the introduction of the Episcopacy in America."

Two years later, Lee and Adams joined forces again to elevate Provoost's fortunes, this time subduing external House and internal Senate opposition to including state worship as a part of Washington's inauguration ceremonies. When "Lee offered a motion to the Chair that after the president was sworn...the Congress should accompany him to Saint Paul's Church and attend divine service," the ever-vigilant Senator Maclay tried to object, but as he rose to contest the proposal, "The Vice President hurried the question and it was put and carried by the churchman [Senator Lee]." With this, the first inauguration of an American president moved one step closer to Lee's apparent model: a British coronation.

The most recent coronation had taken place in 1761, when Archbishop Secker crowned George III king of England. After placing his left hand on the Bible and repeating a solemn oath, the new monarch added these traditional words: "The things which I have here before promised, I will perform and keep. So help me God." King George III then bent over and kissed the open Bible; Archbishop Secker offered prayers petitioning Divine guidance and protection for the monarch and the people; the king addressed Parliament, with lavish genuflection to the deity. And, shortly thereafter, when the king mounted his throne, the archbishop pledged to him his fealty.

Compared to the sumptuous liturgy for that state occasion, the Constitutional script to which the Joint Committee turned for guidance could not have been more chaste. Addressing the inauguration of a president, Article II, Section 1, of the United States Constitution reads as follows: "Before he enters on the Execution of his Office, he shall take the following Oath or Affirmation:— 'I do solemnly swear (or affirm) that I will faithfully execute the Office of President of the United States, and will to the best of my Ability, preserve, protect and defend the Constitution of the United States.'" The framers made explicit allowance for those with religious scruples to "affirm" and not "swear" their pledge faithfully to execute the presidential office. With their only telling detail bearing on the rights of conscience, the Constitutional instructions stand in unornamented contrast to the religious pomp of regal coronations.

Despite Hamilton's reputed jocular response to the Presbyterian minister who lamented the Constitution's lack of "suitable recognition" of the Almighty ("I declare we forgot it!"), God's absence in the nation's code of laws was by no means unintentional. In acknowledgment of America's diverse religious folkways, the framers designed the Constitution as a secular document, its only explicit reference to religion (apart from the date, "in the Year of our Lord 1787") occurring in the religious antidiscrimination clause respecting candidates for federal office. Article VI includes the stipulation "no religious test shall ever be required as a Qualification to any Office or public trust under the United States." The titles they chose (president, Senate, Congress) were carefully selected as well, retrofitting the new government's political nomenclature to that of the Roman republic. Washington extolled the Constitution to a New England clergyman as "a new phenomenon in the political and moral world," deeming it "an astonishing victory gained by enlightened reason."

That God's exclusion from the Constitution was deliberate made it no less controversial. As recently as 1783, the peace treaty with England had opened, "In the name of the holy and indivisible Trinity," language familiar to British statecraft and congenial to the orthodox ear of John Jay, the principal American draftsman. Catholics, Jews, and dissident Protestants welcomed the separation of church and state, but the established churches had trouble reconciling their loss of governmental sanction. Their concern was as much doctrinal and moral as pecuniary. New England Congregationalists and Presbyterians (as establishmentarian in church-state doctrine as Scots Presbyterians tended to be libertarian) were quick to sound the dangers inherent to any government not erected on a firm scriptural foundation. In congratulating Washington on his inauguration as president, the ministers and ruling elders of the Presbytery of Massachusetts and New Hampshire confessed, "[W]e should not have been alone in rejoicing to have seen some explicit acknowledgment of THE TRUE ONLY GOD, AND JESUS CHRIST whom he has sent, inserted somewhere in the Magna Charta of our country." Washington was forthright in expressing his disagreement: "I am persuaded, you will permit me to observe, that the path of true piety is so plain as to require but little political direction. To this consideration we ought to ascribe the absence of any regulation respecting religion from the Magna Charta of our country."

The question remained, as it does today, open for debate: *Is* the path of true piety so plain as to require but little political direction? To Vice President Adams and Senator Lee the answer to this question was a ringing "No."

Inauguration Day

On inauguration day, the Senate reconvened at 11:30 A.M. to continue debate over questions of inaugural etiquette. How stark the contrast was between the high-strung Adams and Washington (the latter seemingly carved from a mighty block of ice) was never more clearly on display than when the two men stood together on a ceremonial platform, where appearances were everything. The man who eight years later would say of his own pending inauguration, "I am a being of too much sensibility to act any part well in such an exhibition," was completely atwitter over such vexing questions as whether to sit or stand on the president-elect's entrance into the chamber. "Gentlemen, I wish for the directions of the Senate. How shall I behave?" Adams pleaded. "Shall I be standing or sitting?" Senator Lee carefully spelled out the British parliamentary precedent. Members of the House of Lords sat in the royal presence; those in the Commons stood to honor him. Senator Carroll reminded his colleagues that this was America not England, only to find himself again in the minority. Washington's inauguration was delayed a full hour while Lee defended British protocol and the president-elect rocked on his heels, awaiting the committee's escort.

Opening his door at last to Senator Lee and the six-member congressional delegation, the president-elect, majestic in both stature and mien, bowed respectfully. The more austere for never smiling (to disguise his false teeth and also to avoid leaving false impressions of intimacy), Washington had as little use for the new-fangled democratic fashion of shaking hands as he did for aristocratic wigs, which he was too proud to wear. The committee escorted him to the carriage Congress had requisitioned for the occasion, one less congenial than his sleek coach and six, canary yellow with emerald green appointments and murals of the four seasons painted on the doors.

On entering the Senate, Washington progressed at a stately pace through the chamber, with everyone standing like commoners (which the Senate finally deemed proper) and him bowing in acknowledgment (which was his custom) as he approached the chair. Rendered speechless, a stammering Adams was rescued by Senator Lee, who, knowing the script by heart, seized the stage and introduced the president-elect to Congress. Having collected his composure, Adams recited his next assigned passage from the newly minted inaugural liturgy without a hitch: "Sir, the Senate and House of Representatives are ready to attend you to take the oath required by the Constitution. It will be administered by the Chancellor of the State of New York."

Except Quakers and Mennonites, who followed Jesus's injunction from the Sermon on the Mount to "Swear not at all," Americans were accustomed to swearing public oaths on the Bible. One scrupulous Christian had recently claimed that, in contrast to those "bound by the oath taken on the Holy Evangelists of Almighty God, the candid Deist feels not bound by the oath he takes on a book, the contents of which he openly professes to believe to be nothing but priestcraft." Although a Deist, Washington held the Bible in polite esteem. Any oath he swore on it would be equally sincere.

The sea of humanity flooding the square and overflowing into every adjacent thoroughfare remained hushed as the president-elect took the oath of office. From his great height—he stood almost 6'3"—and with august flourish, General Washington leaned down and kissed the open Bible. To those gathered on the portico, Chancellor Livingston then pronounced, "It is done." Facing the people, he proclaimed in his most stentorian voice, "Long live George Washington." As one the people echoed in joyous accord, "Long live George Washington!" Cannons reported from the Battery and, all but lost in the din of celebration, again the church bells chimed.

On inauguration morning, indicating how irrelevant he had already become to the workings of government, Vice President Adams wondered aloud, "The president, I suppose, will address Congress?" He did indeed, and memorably so. After taking the oath of office, Washington reentered the Senate chamber to deliver the first inaugural address. Several times during its brief course he invoked the aid of Providence. In closing, he said,

> I shall take my present leave, but not without resorting once more to the benign Parent of the human race, in humble supplication that since he has been pleased to favor the American people with opportunities for deliberating in perfect tranquility, and dispositions for deciding with unparalleled unanimity on a form of government for the security of their union and the advancement of their happiness; so the divine blessing may be equally *conspicuous* in the enlarged views, the temperate consultations, and the wise measures on which the success of this government must depend.

To craft his words, Washington followed his established custom, entrusting the drafting of important addresses to an aide or valued advisor, in this instance, James Madison, who deserves principal credit for framing Washington's first inaugural. Madison did have a text of sorts to work with, the sprawling seventy-three-page draft that Washington had composed with the ready though not necessarily able assistance of Colonel Humphreys. On receiving it in mid-February, Madison discarded the entire text, delivering his own version, less florid and dramatically shorter, one week later.

About a third of the Humphreys draft has resurfaced over the years. It contains views that are recognizably Washington's, albeit cast in the baroque style of which Humphreys was unjustifiably so proud. Among the religious passages that Washington's audience was spared is one that read, "if the blessings of Heaven showered thick around us should be spilled on the ground or converted to curses through the fault of those for whom they are intended, it would not be the first instance of folly or perverseness in short-sighted mortals." The young man's Puritan upbringing jumped more eloquently from the page when he wrote that "The blessed religion revealed in the word of God will remain an eternal and awful monument to prove that the best institutions may be abused by human depravity." Madison recast this declamation into language consonant with Washington's nondoctrinal temperament, omitting all scriptural and theological admonitions while maintaining a sharp moral focus. In its lapidary restatement, President Washington envisioned a government built on moral bedrock—the American people themselves: "The foundations of our national policy will be laid in the pure and immutable principles of private morality," he states. He balances this ideal with its libertarian counterweight: "The preservation of the sacred fire of liberty, and the destiny of the republican model of government, are justly considered as *deeply,* perhaps as *finally,* staked on the experiment entrusted to the hands of the American people."

Order and liberty: These two themes recur, variously shaded, at critical moments throughout Washington's presidency. They are at the heart of his vision for America: that the essence of the Republic, "the sacred fire of liberty," can be preserved solely in conjunction with the maintenance of morality and public order.

Washington's first inaugural may lack explicit Christian reference, but, with the exception of Lincoln's second, no subsequent inaugural address strikes a more religious tone. Washington offered his "fervent supplications to that Almighty Being who rules over the universe, who presides in the councils of nations, and whose providential aids can supply every human defect, that his benediction may consecrate to the liberties and happiness of the people of the United States." He tendered "homage to the Great Author of every public and private good." And he averred that "No people can be bound to acknowledge and adore the invisible hand, which conducts the affairs of men more than the people of the United States." In 1776, the Scottish Enlightenment philosopher Adam Smith depicted "the invisible hand that rules the universe" as an economic instrument driven by the underlying engines of finance and instructed by the distribution of capital. Washington's invocation of "the invisible hand" alludes to the Almighty in more familiar guise.

If his first inaugural (accented by Madison's lifelong conviction that matters of conscience fall strictly within the private domain) offers a liberal spin on his political philosophy, Washington's Farewell Address (hammered into shape by Alexander Hamilton, who had few qualms about subordinating liberty to order) will sound a more conservative note. Yet both fall comfortably within the same broad, morally instructed compass. To Washington, liberty was the be-all and end-all of the American Republic, and social peace was its guarantor. His philosophical priorities (liberty, knowledge, and happiness) complemented his religious ones (morality, order, and charity).

According to congressional plan, the benediction with which the president closed his speech marked a waypoint, not the end, of the day's formal ceremonies. With the full House and Senate in train, through a vortex of saluting militiamen he walked roughly half a mile to St. Paul's Chapel to attend inaugural worship. The service was brief and to the point. With de facto master of ceremonies Senator Richard Henry Lee worshipping beside Washington in the presidential pew, the liturgy Dr. Provoost performed followed the revised Episcopal *Common Prayer Book* and concluded with a sung *Te Deum*.

When darkness fell, New York reawakened and a citywide party brought the inaugural celebration to a jubilant close. Many residents whitewashed or soaped their windows, illuminating stenciled eagles and patriotic messages with candlelight. Washington's face and name were ubiquitous; transparencies of his profile brightly illuminated home and storefront alike. At the Inaugural Ball, the ladies in attendance would carry home his silhouette on delicate Parisian ivory fans. To commemorate his ceremonial role in one of history's great transitional acts, Chancellor Livingston ordered a fine set of dress buttons, embossed with the words "Long live the President." By far the most elaborate transparency appeared on the marquee of the John Street Theater, a majestic scene depicting the goddess of fame descending from the heavens to place on President Washington's head the crown of immortality. If fated not to be the nation's king, George Washington remained the people's demigod.

The Deist-in-Chief

Just how religious *was* George Washington? The short answer is "Not very." If Richard Henry Lee was an avid religious Anglican, Washington contented himself with being a cool, political one. Baptized into the Church of Virginia by his vestryman father, the father of our country stemmed from a long line of adherents to the Church of England. His Anglican pedigree receives notice on a wall plaque in the cloister of Durham Cathedral:

Remember in these cloisters
Which were finished in his day,
John Washington of Washington in
This County, prior of this
Cathedral church
1416–1446
Whose family has won an everlasting
Name in lands to him unknown.

Two centuries later, with the end of the English civil war, George's great-great-grandfather, Lawrence Washington, an English cleric ensconced in a benefice courtesy of Archbishop William Laud, was listed ninth among the first hundred "scandalous, malignant priests" whom the victorious Puritan Parliament stripped of their livings (in his case for cleansing Oxford of Puritans). Lawrence died in disgrace, and his son John took to the sea. In 1677, when his ship went down in the Potomac River, John opted to remain in Virginia, a Royalist sanctuary, to seek his fortune growing the tobacco he had been carting. For the better part of seven decades, the Washington family adorned the fringe of Virginia high society as small plantation owners. Like his father and grandfather before him, Augustus Washington served on the twelve-member Vestry of Truro (later Fairfax) parish, a position his son George would grow into in 1763.

Among the scant memorials to Washington's youth is his carefully hand-copied reproduction of "The Rules of Civility and Decent Behaviour in Company and Conversation" from Francis Hawkin's then-popular etiquette manual, *Youth Behaviour*. For an ethic in which appearance, reflected in society's mirror, carries much of the moral load, manners, deportment, address, and civility are paramount. Although the list was compiled by Jesuits in the late sixteenth century, God is mentioned in only half of one of its 110 citations, leaving the ratio between instructions on proper table manners to those prescribing religious observance at roughly forty to one. The lone reference to God falls near the end of the list, immediately following number 107 (which closes, "talk not with meat in your mouth"): "When you speak of God or his attributes, let it be seriously & with reverence."

George received seven years of formal schooling. He took no pride in his defective education, yet the practical thoroughness of his early training served him well. Washington learned by rote. Every page of his surviving workbooks testifies to his discipline and orderliness. He filled one binder after another with painstaking exercises in mathematics and geometry, the building blocks of account management and surveying. When he put his knowledge into practice, his surveys were elegant as well as accurate, his financial records thorough and neat.

Washington's education and imitative style of learning continued long after he finished school. As a young officer in General Edward Braddock's service, he noted his superiors' bearing with care and faithfully copied each morning's order of the day into his private journal. He also painstakingly polished his handwriting and diction, purchasing *The Royal English Grammar* and poring over British periodicals for pointers on style. To smooth his rough edges, he signed up for music and fencing lessons and dipped into *The Young Man's Companion* (the *Emily Post* of its day). His finishing school took place on horseback and the dance floor. Washington won plaudits as an effortless rider and a graceful dancer, badges of distinction for an aspiring Virginia gentleman. During the Revolution, French officers marveled that he adorned a ballroom better than the finest dancers at Versailles. Upon mastering his final and most important lessons (to rein in his temper and tame the passions of youth) Washington emerged from his diligent self-schooling tempered like steel: a graceful, aloof gentleman, amiable within the limits of his reserve and as prudent as he was ambitious. Others among the nation's founders were better educated than he, but none was more studied.

Washington's reputation was forged in the furnace of war. King George II shook his head in wonder at this rash young American who reputedly loved to hear the bullets sing and who made his name at twenty-two by massacring a French diplomatic party and thereby (or so the instant legend reads) single-handedly igniting the French and Indian War. In battle, where he courted glory and won her hand, he could appear reckless to the point of vanity. He flirted almost contemptuously with death at first, but what began as derring-do he steadily refined into a disciplined gallantry.

George's most influential mentor was his next-door neighbor, William Fairfax. In 1757 the seasoned twenty-five-year-old began his quest for office with Colonel Fairfax's full backing, standing for an assembly seat in sparsely populated Fairfield County, where he owned a parcel of land. After placing third for one of the county's two seats in the House of Burgesses, he studied the system and stood again when the seats fell vacant the following year. This time he comfortably outdistanced the competition, gaining three-quarters of some 400 votes cast. Washington lubricated his victory—one wag called it "swilling the planters with bumbo"—by plying his prospective constituents with more than 150 gallons of wine, beer, rum punch, and brandy. Although liquoring up the electorate was a traditional electioneering ploy, at half a gallon of spirits per vote he went to considerable lengths to escape the embarrassment of being defeated a second time. From the poll sheets we know that all three clergyman who voted for the assembly seat (an Anglican, Baptist, and Presbyterian) cast their ballots for Colonel Washington.

From that day forward, his political fortunes began to glow as brightly as his military reputation. His marriage at twenty-eight in 1759 to the fabulously rich widow Martha Dandridge Custis led to Washington's election to the vestry. Typical of many ecclesiastical hierarchies, pillars of the church in Colonial Virginia were made of gold. Washington dutifully subscribed to forward pews in both the Falls Church and Old Pohick parish churches, paying the expected premium. Election to the vestry put him in line for a local assembly seat as well, which he snared easily at the next election. In the House of Burgesses, Washington served on the Religion Committee beside fellow Anglicans Patrick Henry, Richard Henry Lee, and Robert Carter Nicholas. One memorable sketch of his developing character comes courtesy of a fellow assemblyman: "He is a modest man, but sensible, and speaks little, in action cool, like a bishop at his prayers."

Vestrymen in Virginia were political officers. Religious fervor, or church membership for that matter, was not a prerequisite for service in the vestry. His election smoothed Washington's way in Virginia politics, but it did not oblige him to join the church. To the end of his days he would stand with the other noncommunicants (often a majority of worshipers) during prayers and leave following the sermon right before the service of the Lord's Supper on Communion Sundays, while Martha kneeled with the faithful and remained to partake of the Eucharist. Typical of the vow Washington might have sworn on taking his seat, one Virginia vestryman oath unambiguously invests its occupant with great latitude: "As vestryman for this parish, I will well and truly perform my duty therein, being directed by the laws and customs of this country and the Canons of the Church of England, so far as they will suit our present capacity."

It requires no great effort—and many have done so—to string together an impressive series of pious-sounding phrases from Washington's writings to certify that the first president was a true believer. He was culturally Christian, to be sure, but throughout volumes of correspondence, public and private, Washington mentions Christ by name only once, in a 1799 address to the chiefs of the Delaware Indians composed almost certainly by an adjutant. Contrasting him with fellow Deists Thomas Paine and Thomas Jefferson, both of whom expressed sincere admiration for Jesus, the most fastidious student of Washington's religion calls his muteness concerning Jesus "truly remarkable."

Deism, which grew out of the Enlightenment, attracted believers who found it easier to divine the Creator's signature from nature itself than from the biblical record. The best-known Deist in America during Washington's day was Paine. His politically inflected beliefs would eventually cause widespread offense, but the credo he included in his controversial book, *The Age of Reason,* eloquently encapsulates Deism's first principles: "I believe in one God, and no more; and I hope for happiness beyond this life. I believe in the equality of man and I believe that religious duties consist in doing justice, loving mercy, and endeavoring to make our fellow-creatures happy."

Washington was what might best be called a "warm Deist." In good Deist fashion, he worshiped Providence gratefully and from afar, but the "Providence" he spoke of was by no means an absentee landlord. On multiple occasions he acknowledged the Almighty's intervention, expressing an unswerving faith that Providence had watched over and protected both him and his country during their times of trial. Somewhat shy about employing the word "God," Washington cast his appeals to the Almighty in universal religious terms, employing, in addition to Seneca's favorite divine appellation, "Providence," such Deist and Masonic circumlocutions for God as "Grand Architect" or "Author of all Good."

On those rare occasions when he expressed an opinion about Christianity, Washington placed himself outside the fold. "Being no bigot myself to any mode of worship," he told Marquis de Lafayette shortly before taking office, "I am disposed to indulge professors of Christianity...that road to Heaven, which to them shall seem the most direct, plainest, easiest and least liable to exception."

In unguarded moments, Washington made light of his piety. He jokingly chastised Martha's brother-in-law for writing him a letter on the Sabbath day. "Could you but behold with what religious zeal I hie me to Church on every Lord's Day, it would do your heart good, and fill it, I hope, with equal fervency." His brother-in-law knew perfectly well that Washington relaxed on most Sundays, reconciling his books and catching up with his mail. Even when attending to his mail, should religion intrude he could be irreverently dismissive. Speaking of a sermon received by post, he joshed, "I presume it is good coming all the way from New Hampshire, but do not vouch for it, not having read a word of it." As of 1783, when a catalog was made of his Mount Vernon library, Washington did not possess a Bible. The three recorded in his collection shortly before he died all appear to have been presidential gifts.

As it was for many Virginia planters, Sunday was the most convivial day of Washington's week. When he attended worship, he mixed politics in the churchyard and followed services with pleasure at home, often in the form of evening entertainments with abundant food and neighborly good cheer. He was known for "sending the bottle about pretty freely." At once amiable and proper—in Virginia it was proper to be amiable—he closed his entertainments by toasting each person around the table. He ordered his wine by the pipe (in 110-gallon kegs) and drank like a gentleman, downing as much as he could without embarrassing himself.

Real man as much as true gentleman, Washington swore with relish, hunted, bet on cards, cocks, and horses, and charmed the ladies, each to the edge of excess during his youth but continuing in tempered, tightly disciplined ways throughout his life. He carefully recorded his gambling winnings and losses in his account ledger and took the name of God in vain to powerful effect, leaving Jefferson, Hamilton, and his other cabinet members speechless. He would "By God them," Jefferson recalled—Washington once exclaiming to his querulous cabinet, "By God, I would rather be in my grave,...I would rather be on my farm than made Emperor of the World." When on his farm, he may not have attended church every Sunday, but for years he answered the fox horn religiously every Saturday. "He was always in at the death," reported his grandson, George Washington Custis, "and yielded to no man the honor of the brush."

If far from being devout, Washington took his duties as a vestry-man seriously. In addition to overseeing the church's finances and ministries, the vestry, part moral constabulary and part charitable foundation, sat in judgment on everyone living in the parish, from tax scofflaws who undercounted their slaves to white women who gave birth to mixed-blood children. With equal attentiveness, vestry members offered neighborly assistance to help feed, house, and clothe the local poor. Even when absent from Mount Vernon, Washington instructed his family to maintain the spirit of generosity, handsomely setting aside some forty or fifty pounds per year ($2,000–$2,500 today) to clothe and feed visiting panhandlers. "Let no one go hungry away," he beseeched his nephew George Augustine Washington. "Let the hospitality of the house, with respect to the poor, be kept up."

The spirit of George Washington's faith rests here: an enlightened liberalism tempered by proper conduct. "Nothing but harmony, honesty, industry and frugality are necessary to make us a great and happy people," he told Lafayette on the eve of his presidency. "Happily the present posture of affairs and the prevailing disposition of my countrymen promise to co-operate in establishing those four great and essential pillars of public felicity." Next to countless variations on Shakespeare's "All the world's a stage," Washington's favorite all-purpose metaphor was a classical temple, its roof supported by four essential pillars, which he renamed as need would serve. In constructing the temple of liberty, he carved each pillar with moral uplift foremost in his mind.

"His Name Alone Strikes Every Title Dead"

Vice President Adams reconvened the Senate after worship on inauguration day to transact a final piece of important inaugural business: composing the official message of gratitude to the president for his "most gracious speech." His language was by no means accidental. These were the very words that Parliament reflexively employed to express its humble appreciation for any speech delivered by its king.

Maclay shot to his feet. "We have lately had a hard struggle for our liberty against kingly authority," he reminded the vice president. "The minds of men are still heated. Everything related to that species of government is odious to the people." Adams was unmoved. To scorn formal protocols "taken from the practice of that government under which we have lived, so long and so happily, formerly" was childish. He begged the distinguished senator from Pennsylvania to please remember that the president of the Senate was among the first to enter the lists in the late contest. "Had I known it would come to this," Adams huffed, "I never would have drawn my sword."

Senator Maclay would win this particular challenge handily. On further reflection, his colleagues found Adams's sanctimonious echo too distasteful to swallow and dropped the offensive language from their text. "If our new government does well," Adams sighed shortly thereafter, "I shall be more surprised than ever I was in my life." Senator Maclay was more confident. "Every error in government will work its own remedy among a free people," he assured the vice president.

From beginning to end, the Republic's first great state occasion—people referred to it as a "coronation"—was imbued with an air of consecration. Declaring Washington so near to being perfect that he straddled the boundary separating "human from divine," one national newspaper gushed in anticipation, "Tomorrow is the day of her espousals, when in presence of the King of Kings, the solemn compact will be ratified between her and the darling object of her choice." This same spirit spilled over to the ceremony itself. One eyewitness was deeply moved by the event's religious solemnity, reporting that "The impression of [Washington's] past services, the concourse of spectators, the devout fervency with which he repeated the oath, and the reverential manner in which he bowed down and kissed the sacred volume—all these conspired to render it one of the most august and interesting spectacles ever exhibited on the globe." In a letter to Philadelphia's *Federal Gazette,* this spectator confessed that he found himself "under an awful and religious persuasion that the gracious ruler of the universe was looking down at that moment with peculiar complacency." God's tangible presence so affected him that, when the throng echoed Livingston's "Long live the president," he was rendered speechless and could do no more than wave his hat.

The people's reverence cast a regal and sacred glow on Washington's person, giving his office, royal title or no, an aura reminiscent of that which, by definition, anointed the King of England with divine favor. Yale's president, Dr. Ezra Stiles, an otherwise sober clergyman and scholar, set the bar of reverent exclamation particularly high. "O Washington," he extolled, "thy fame is of sweeter perfume than Arabian spices. Listening angels shall catch the odor, waft it to heaven and perfume the universe!" One spectator caught a different smell in the air: "the odor of incense," beguiling his countrymen to go "through all the Popish grades of worship."

The trappings surrounding President Washington (less a cult of personality than a cult of personage) would send tremors through republican precincts for years to come. In presidential entertainment, he cast a particularly regal shadow. The hour-long levees Washington grudgingly hosted in the Presidential Mansion every Wednesday afternoon, starchly dubbed by Vice President Adams "Visits of Compliment," took on a courtly glow, the statuesque president costuming himself in black satin suits, accessorized with silver knee and shoe buckles, a white hilted sword in a white leather scabbard, and canary gloves. Respectable dress and introductions were required for entry to these exclusively male gatherings. Cradling his hat under his right arm so that shaking hands would be out of the question, and standing erect before the fireplace in a room stripped of furniture lest anyone inadvertently sit in the great man's presence, the president ceremoniously bowed as each visitor filed by to stammer his respects. Colonel Humphreys, who was happily weaned on royal levees at the Palace of Versailles, added to the drama of the first such occasion by importantly announcing to the guests as the doors swung open, "Gentlemen, THE PRESIDENT OF THE UNITED STATES!" But Washington would have none of that. Jefferson approvingly passed along hearsay of how the president dressed his majordomo down the moment the levee ended. "Well, you have taken me in once," Washington swore, "but by God, you shall never take me in a second time!"

His dilemma epitomized by the crab-apple walking stick Benjamin Franklin had given him—at once radical in its symbolism and exquisite in its manufacture, it was topped by a solid gold handle in the shape of a Greek slave's liberty cap—the president wrestled over how he might escape "too free an intercourse and too much familiarity" without indulging in "an ostentatious show of mimicry of sovereignty." Washington admitted that "To draw such a line for the conduct of the president as will please *every* body, I know is impossible." Not that he didn't try. Even Senator Maclay, who branded Washington an "eastern lama," was forced to concede, "The president is a cold, formal man, but I must declare that he treated me with great attention."

Fighting her husband's losing cause, Abigail Adams addressed the president as "Your Majesty" the first evening that she and John dined at the Presidential Mansion. She concurrently sketched an artful portrait of Washington's amiable reserve—"a dignity that forbids familiarity, mixed with an easy affability that creates love and reverence." Chastened by experience without quite finding his sea legs, her husband directed his almost limitless attention to selecting a politically correct honorific for Mrs. Washington. He finally concluded that "Her Presidentess" had a more republican ring than "Lady Washington." This time, though, the British title stuck; Lady Washington she remained.

The aspirations Madison, Jefferson, and Maclay harbored to establish the new government on a firm republican footing were sorely tested by the people's reverence toward Washington. As long as he remained in power, their efforts would be muted by the protocol that surrounded his person, rendering criticism unseemly. The one person who would protect the nation from returning naturally to its British orbit was the president himself. As faithful to liberty as he was comforted by order, throughout his first term Washington would balance the two, employing his authority, not least in church-state relations, in such a manner that the principles on which the nation was founded would outlast the British trappings that adorned his inaugural rites.

The aura surrounding the first inaugural festivities lingers to this day. On the bicentennial of Washington's inauguration, New York again pulled out all the stops. Dozens of tall ships, naval and civilian, crowded the harbor. President George H. W. Bush visited the Federal Hall National Memorial, where he witnessed a dramatization of the first inaugural ceremony and went on to attend an ecumenical commemorative worship service conducted at St. Paul's Chapel. One spectator captured the spirit of the occasion in words that rang with a two-century-old echo. Hearkening "to the chorus of ships' horns ringing through the harbor," she mused, "kind of sounds like church bells, doesn't it?"

ᗧᗧ

WITH LIBERTY AND
ORDER FOR ALL

Proceed, great chief, with virtue on thy side,
Thy ev'ry action let the goddess guide.
A crown, a mansion, and a throne that shine,
With gold unfading, WASHINGTON! Be thine.

—PHILLIS WHEATLEY, "TO HIS EXCELLENCY
GENERAL WASHINGTON"

THE AMERICAN people held their collective breath as the one man they trusted to lead them lay wracked with fever and gasping for air. Twice during the first year of his presidency, his doctors gave George Washington up for dead: Two months after taking office he battled a sepsis following surgery to remove an ulcerated tumor from his left thigh; the following spring he courted death again, prostrated by a combination of pneumonia and a ruthless influenza that swept its scythe across the eastern seaboard.

Washington had prophesied an early death. His father, Augustus, died at 49, an age four of George's brothers failed to reach. In 1783, Washington confided to Lafayette that, stemming as he did from short-lived stock, he "might soon expect to be entombed in the dreary mansions of my fathers." He expressed no regrets about this. "I will not repine," he told his old friend. "I have had my day."

Ready as he was to let go of this life, Washington placed no particular stock in the promised life to come. He invested his hopes in the bank of earthly immortality, resting content to "sleep with my fathers." Not that he was dogmatic on this, or any other, theological score. He cast the afterlife in Greek shadow, speaking of "the world of spirits," "the shades of darkness," and "the shades below," while readily suspending his disbelief, by rote when writing letters of condolence and occasionally (to intimate correspondents) with verve. Annis Stockton was Elias Boudinot's sister. A gifted poet, she stood prominent among the white-gowned matrons who hymned Washington's triumphant arrival in Trenton and numbered also among the handful of fearless women who knew how to melt his icy veneer. To Mrs. Stockton, Washington teasingly confessed, "respecting [Cicero's] belief of the immortality of the soul, I will say, if I am in a grateful delusion, it is an innocent one, and I am willing to remain under its influence."

Delusion or not, he paid his place in heaven little mind. All that concerned him was his reputation here on earth, which a dignified death would no doubt burnish. When Washington fell ill the following May, Martha, mindful of her husband's dignity, cordoned off the Presidential Mansion to discourage merchants of death from peddling their commemorative wares beneath his open window. She further instructed her staff of fourteen hired white servants and seven slaves to insulate the streets around their home with hay to mute the racket of daily commerce, a cacophony of cowbells, street vendors, and groaning carriages.

Martha Custis Washington was a generously proportioned woman with dancing hazel eyes. She stood five feet at a stretch, more than a full foot shorter than her husband. "A fine healthy girl," she called herself, "cheerful as a cricket and busy as a bee." Whatever house he might occupy, and "George Washington slept here" was a sign with wide currency, he was at home only in her company.

Protective as she was, Martha could not shield her husband from death. She could, however, admire his courage in facing it. Washington again betrayed no fear when he fell deathly ill for the second time in less than a year, leading her to observe, "He seemed less concerned himself as to the event than perhaps any other person in the United States."

The American people had cause to worry. However unfashionable it may be these days to invest a single individual with history-shaping powers, to them the fate of their young republic hung suspended in the balance. How this stolid, two-dimensional figure could make the difference he so manifestly did is difficult for us to imagine. It was difficult for his storied contemporaries to imagine as well. Other leading founders, better book educated than he, quicker and suppler of mind, found it easy to condescend to Washington, though rarely with his knowledge and never in his presence. To be charitable, their judgments may have evolved in self-protective compensation for his withheld intimacy; none save Madison would number him a friend, and even Madison could be tart regarding his superior's limited talents.

Whatever its source and however guardedly they confined its expression, the bitterness such disparate figures as Hamilton, Adams, and Jefferson harbored toward the president ran deep. In moments of frustration, they lampooned him as either an imperious galoot or the perfectly wrapped package without a gift inside, "too illiterate, unread, and unlearned for his station," in Adams's blunt summation (or, as he put it more tersely, "Old Muttonhead"). For all his majesty and acclaim, indeed because of them, Washington offered a generous target. Yet his dance with death threw a reputed infidel, Thomas Jefferson, to his knees and shot legitimate panic through the heart of John Adams, his constitutional successor. They were not pretending. Adams, who later called Washington "the central stone in the geometrical arch," no doubt agreed with his wife Abigail's assessment that "the union of the states and consequently the permanency of the government depend under Providence upon his life."

"A Kind Destiny Has Thrown Me upon this Service"

The leadership model Washington brought to the presidency was perfected during his eight-year service as commanding general of the Continental Army. Act One of the nation's sacred political drama was staged in dress rehearsal in the theater of war.

Revolutionary War legends passed down by hagiographers hail Washington as a saint in arms, whose Christian devotion inspired Quaker pacifists to battle and God to answer his fervent prayers. One tale pictures Washington firing at an officer who dared to interrupt his daily communion with God. Without rising from his knees, he shot safely wide of his impious target, reholstered his pistol, and completed his devotions. Even stripped of such folderol, the picture is stirring.

Settling into his Cambridge headquarters, his singular uniform festooned with a royal purple sash, General Washington faced the daunting task of shaping willful bands of independent militia—one incredulous Frenchman described them as "a flock of ducks in cross-belts"—into a functioning army. *E pluribus unum* received its first test in the Continental Army, where Washington fashioned one set of rules for a culturally incongruous, unruly band of citizen soldiers. That he succeeded in this task and proceeded to outlast the world's best disciplined army was, he admitted himself, nothing short of miraculous.

Washington built his command on four sturdy pillars: "the favor of divine Providence, exactness of discipline, alertness when on duty and cleanliness in their arms and person." Given that eight times as many soldiers died of disease than from wounds, cleanliness was of no less practical concern than discipline and alertness, but worship, too, held up its corner of the tent. From the moment he arrived in Cambridge on Sunday, July 2, 1775—he did so without fanfare because of Sabbath day restrictions—General Washington strictly enforced Sunday worship for all troops not on guard duty. Anyone "making a disturbance in the time of public worship" received a public whipping.

The Sabbath day presented more than the challenge of mustering reluctant troops to worship. Washington told his brother that he found himself "incessantly, Sundays not excepted, employed in throwing up works of defense" and drilling his soldiers. In other words, military exigencies compelled him to trespass the Sabbath day commandment, a sacred prescription revered by New England divines. Washington didn't scorn their scruples. As soon as it was practicable, he ordered that "No fatigue parties to be employed on Sundays till further orders." By banning drills and other military exercises following worship, he was officially honoring religious convictions that he neither shared nor understood.

New England militiamen and regiments from the middle Atlantic and southern states were accustomed to dedicating their day of rest to contrasting pursuits. That made Sunday potentially the most contentious day of the week. Washington solved this dilemma by taking everyone's half out of the middle. The balancing act is evident on the three occasions he proclaimed a combined day of thanksgiving and feast day to usher in a "season of general joy." After the victory at Saratoga in 1777, to commemorate the alliance with France in 1778, and to celebrate the British surrender at Yorktown in 1781 he appointed, in addition to solemn thanksgiving services, hearty afternoon and evening festal celebrations. Washington maintained the same delicate give and take throughout the campaign. Admonishing his officers that "Gaming of every kind is expressly forbid as the foundation of evil and the cause of many gallant and brave officer's ruin," without missing a beat he continued, "Games of exercise, for amusement, may not only be allowed of, but encouraged." Washington's halfway covenant won few full-throated advocates. More soldiers than not chafed at mandatory worship, while chaplains sanctimoniously groused that "the Sabbath was a high play day." Given the inherent tensions, their commander in chief showed disciplined sensitivity in harmonizing the dissonant customs of his divided religious constituencies.

Throughout the war, Washington fought to maintain a large, responsive, and well-paid Chaplain Corps. When his chaplains disappeared en masse during winter quarters, he issued an order that "no furloughs will be granted," but he also lobbied Congress to expand the chaplaincy and pay better wages. Washington was mindful of the doctrinal minefield that accompanied his Christian soldiers into battle. A scarcity of chaplains heightened the danger by forcing some of his men to worship in ways alien to their accustomed practice. To limit this necessity, he successfully lobbied Congress to maintain at the very least one clergyman for every two regiments, rather than economize by appointing a single chaplain for each six-regiment brigade. A shortage of chaplains "has a tendency to introduce religious disputes into the Army, which above all things should be avoided, " he pointed out in pressing his suit. To "compel men to a mode of worship which they do not profess" violated sound military as well as sound republican principle.

A more widespread threat to religious freedom was bigotry in the ranks, especially against Roman Catholics. Washington took direct action against anti-Catholic animus by banning the then-popular New England festival Pope's Day, the American version of Guy Fawkes Day in England, where drunken Protestant revelers would torch effigies of the pope and devil. His sharp displeasure was motivated by pragmatism as well as by principle.

> As the Commander in Chief has been apprized of a design formed for the observance of that ridiculous and childish custom of burning the effigy of the pope, he cannot help expressing his surprise that there should be officers and soldiers in this army so void of common sense as not to see the impropriety of such a step at this juncture, at a time when we are soliciting...the friendship and alliance of the people of Canada, whom we ought to consider as brethren embarked in the same cause; the defense of the general liberty of America. At such a juncture and in such circumstances, to be insulting their religion...is not to be suffered or excused.

He voiced like concerns to General Benedict Arnold, back when the future traitor was still working on his pedigree as a prospective American hero. Arnold's assigned task was to take Canada. Launching him on this ill-fated campaign, Washington's parting instructions include a moral blandishment and rare theological observation: "While we are contending for our own liberty, we should be very cautious of violating the rights of conscience in others, ever considering that God alone is the judge of the hearts of men, and to him only in this case, they are answerable."

With American casualties multiplying, the churches played a key role in the national war effort. Religious meetinghouses, none excluded on the basis of denominational favoritism, were requisitioned as needed and transformed into military hospitals. Not all ministers greeted the seizure of their congregational homes with patriotic understanding. One such parson, in protesting the loss of his sanctuary, got a taste of his own brimstone. "I need not explain to you how necessary establishments of this kind are to the welfare of the army," Washington sternly admonished, "and you must be sensible that they can be placed nowhere without occasioning inconvenience to some set of people or other."

The British, in contrast, played religious favorites. In New York City, the Moravians, Anglicans, and Methodists (each with strong British ties) were spared when the occupying army converted all other churches into prisons, storehouses, or barracks. As a consequence, the British high command attended services at St. Paul's during winters in New York. In American encampments such as Morristown, New Jersey, where the churches were otherwise occupied, Washington and his officers worshiped with their troops outdoors in the freezing cold.

A decade later, Washington returned to New York City and St. Paul's Chapel as president of the United States.

Leading the Nation in Prayer

Washington brought the religious protocol he had hammered out in the army with him to the presidency. On his watch, the government was by no means Christian, but neither was it constructed on a purely secular foundation. As long as the language employed was inclusive, Washington had no qualms about calling his fellow citizens to prayer.

On September 26, 1789, one day after the House of Representatives passed the First Amendment to the Constitution avowing that "Congress shall enact no legislation respecting the establishment of religion or the free practice thereof," it pivoted on its heels and, at Representative Boudinot's instigation, recommended that the president proclaim a National Day of Prayer and Thanksgiving to honor God for "affording them an opportunity peacefully to establish a constitutional government for their safety and happiness." Following the armistice with England (a stretch of six years), all such proclamations had been suspended. Boudinot thought it high time to redirect the nation on a more reverent course.

Two thirds of the House voted in favor of his resolution over the spirited objection of two South Carolina congressmen. Representative Thomas Tucker presented the secular argument, characterizing Boudinot's bill as "a business with which Congress has nothing to do; it is a religious matter, and as such is proscribed to us." Aedanus Burke expressed religious as well as republican reservations, appalled at the prospect of Congress "mimicking...European customs, where they make a mere mockery of Thanksgiving." A legislative juggernaut swept Tucker's and Burke's objections aside, and a week later Washington submitted the proclamation as requested, marking November 26, 1789, as the first national thanksgiving to be celebrated under the new Constitution.

Although without internal warrant, the Constitutional grounding for such proclamations was founded on strong congressional precedent. From 1774 onward, the Continental Congress appointed "Congress Sundays" (alternating fast days and days of thanksgiving recommended to Christians of all denominations) every spring and fall. Freighted with symbolism, congressional prayer days performed two distinct nontheological functions. First, they consolidated public support for the Continental cause, while exercising a form of moral intimidation against those who chose to exclude themselves from the circle of worshipers. Second, they implicitly confirmed Congress's usurpation of the crown's prerogative to direct the people's spiritual observance by kingly decree. Adapting New England custom, Congress codified its independence from royal British sacral authority while at the same time donning the ecclesiastical mantle long worn by Puritan divines.

Thomas Jefferson's eager participation in the first legislatively sponsored fast day to be employed as a weapon against British policy reveals the political subtext of these purportedly religious acts. No founder expressed a higher degree of principled disdain toward the political abuse of religion, yet Jefferson's education in how cynical and effective such proclamations could be was self-taught. Near the end of his life he was still crowing about how he "cooked up" a fast day resolution in the Virginia House of Burgesses in 1773. Jefferson drafted the act, but, "to give greater emphasis to our proposition," called on Robert Carter Nicholas ("whose grave and religious character was more in unison with the tone of our resolution") to move it. Because the most conservative delegate was reluctant to vote against God and the most radical was delighted to press Him into service, the motion passed without dissent.

Jefferson's proclamation declared a colonywide "Day of Fasting, Humiliation and Prayer devoutly to implore the divine interposition for averting the heavy calamity which threatens destruction to our civil rights." As a piece of guerrilla theater, the gambit proved gloriously successful. The governor disbanded the House of Burgesses, further radicalizing its members. When the Assembly convened for prayer at Williamsburg's Bruton Parish, the cooperative rector dropped "God Save the King" from the liturgy. His proclamation worked "like a shock of electricity," Jefferson said, "arousing every man and placing him erect and solidly on his center." Washington dutifully fasted and, for the first time in his life, attended church twice in a single day.

When the practice become commonplace as a revolutionary tactic, not every New England divine was pleased by the flattery. One

flinty Puritan, Dartmouth College president Eleazar Wheelock, refused to participate in all legislatively sponsored worship, arguing
that "making such a solemn offering to God as had been proposed,
purely and only out of respect and obedience to the advice of Congress, would be an open affront to the King of Zion... expressive of
a principle abhorred by all Protestants." The thanksgiving that
Boudinot proposed in 1789 revived an additional specter. By revert-
ing the authority to make such a proclamation to the president and
therefore tacitly resubscribing to the British royal model, Congress
flipped its earlier symbolic diffidence on its head.

As he demonstrated during the course of the war, Washington
was by no means averse to declaring a prayer day. It was one thing
to marshal his army for worship, however, and something else entirely to muster the whole citizenry. His first presidential thanksgiving met a polite yet cool reception. The president dutifully put
in an appearance at St. Paul's, but the church, for this particular
state occasion, was half empty. To more practical effect, he returned
thanks by purchasing beer for the unfortunates languishing in
debtor's prison. Not until three years later, when Congress would
reject recommending that the president proclaim a national fast, explicitly because it recalled royal presumptions to sacral authority,
did the divide on the propriety of such proclamations begin to
widen. In 1795, at Hamilton's behest and purely for political gain,
the executive itself would seize the initiative to declare a national
thanksgiving. Subsequent declarations during the Adams and
Madison administrations had similarly partisan subtexts.

For the proclamation he issued in response to Congress's call,
the president won lavish praise from the Presbyterian Church General Assembly for "devoutly acknowledging" the Almighty's divine
governance. Actually he stopped short of making such an acknowledgment. Washington recognized no governmental authority beyond that sanctioned directly by the people.

These same Presbyterians would soon be murmuring that Washington's thanksgiving proclamations lacked "a decidedly Christian

spirit." Whether they did lack a Christian spirit or not is debatable, but they certainly steered too clear of the Christian letter to be considered decidedly Christian. In fashioning their language, he bent over backward to accommodate diverse viewpoints and express his balanced appreciation for reason and religion. Washington's first such proclamation includes something for everyone save perhaps the avowed atheist, who at the time, if demonized from the pulpit, was conspicuously absent from the population. In an epitome of his guiding civil religious principles, he expressed gratitude to

> that great and glorious Being, who is the beneficent author of all the good that was, that is, or that will be, that we may unite in rendering unto him our sincere and humble thanks for the great degree of tranquility, union, and plenty which we have since enjoyed; for the peaceable and rational manner in which we have been enabled to establish constitutions of government for our safety and happiness, and particularly the national one now lately instituted; for the civil and religious liberty with which we are blessed, and the means we have of acquiring and diffusing useful knowledge; and, in general, for all the great and various favors which he hath been pleased to confer upon us.

Washington's thanksgiving proclamations avoided explicit Christian language, a scruple that certainly did not pass unnoticed by American Jews. The world, too, took note of the new nation's official stance toward its Jewish citizens. America was demonstrating, one British commentator observed, "that to admit Jews to all the privileges of natural born citizens is far from being a dangerous experiment."

The Jewish population in the United States was tiny. In 1790 there were six synagogues in the United States (in New York, Philadelphia, Charleston, Savannah, Richmond, and Newport) serving a population of 1,243 Jewish citizens (according to the 1790 census). Yet, of Washington's nineteen letters on the rights and obligations of religious groups, he addressed five of the six Hebrew congregations in three separate communiqués. His response to Congregation Jeshuat Israel (Truro Synagogue) in Newport was published in the Newport *Herald* and reprinted in papers across the land by editors who recognized its significance. In it, Washington moved intentionally beyond the condescending virtue of tolerance to express true respect:

> All possess alike liberty of conscience and immunities of citizenship. It is now no more that toleration is spoken of, as if it was by the indulgence of one class of people, that another enjoyed the exercise of their inherent natural rights. For happily the Government of the United States, which gives to bigotry no sanction, to persecution no assistance, requires only that they who live under its protection should demean themselves as good citizens.

Washington closed this letter with the one bit of scripture that obviously delighted him (and the only passage from the Bible he would ever quote directly), the lovely vine and fig tree metaphor from the Book of Micah: "May the children of the stock of Abraham, who dwell in this land, continue to merit and enjoy the good will of the other inhabitants while every one shall sit in safety under his own vine and fig tree and there shall be none to make him afraid."

Freedom of Conscience and the Baptists

For himself and others alike, George Washington had only one religious test: Actions count, words don't. "With me," he said, "it has always been a maxim rather to let my designs appear from my works than by my expressions." His bookplate boasts the motto emblazoned on the Washington family crest of arms. Topped with a raven nesting in a crown and dating to fourteenth-century England, it reads, "*Exitus Acta Probit*" ("The act is proof of the deed").

In good Virginia fashion, to validate his deeds Washington consulted his reputation. The trouble was, the court of public opinion could not render a fair verdict as long as partisan ideology or religious conviction insinuated subjective factors—"Is he a true republican?" "Is he saved?"—into its assessment of his moral performance. Washington's acute intolerance for faction springs from this fact. Those who placed creed over deed, whether in politics or religion, violated his cherished rules of honorable engagement.

From this simple yet exacting worldview arose the president's philosophy toward church and state: Religious freedom would be honored fastidiously as long as the church behaved. "In politics, as in religion," he said, "my tenets are few and simple: the leading one of which, and indeed that which embraces most others, is to be honest and just ourselves, and to exact it from others; meddling as little as possible in their affairs where our own are not involved." Following this dictum, Washington saw no earthly reason for the church to meddle in government. Any divine, clerical or lay, who would presume to trump the laws of state with a "higher" law taxed his limited patience to the hilt.

As president, Washington had no difficulty embracing the principle of church independence from governmental authority. Virginia's traditional pathway to power, which he followed dutifully, led through the Anglican vestry, but he harbored no lingering affection for the notion of a state church. As a young man Washington bristled against Virginia's church establishment for economic reasons. When his brother Lawrence attempted to lure a group of German Brethren to work uncultivated family lands, they refused. Anglican Virginia was famous for its official unfriendliness to other religions, whose members were taxed to support the established church. "Restraints on conscience are cruel," Washington lamented at the time. He felt this cruelty in his pocketbook. States without religious establishments, like Pennsylvania, attracted sectarian immigrants and migrants, whereas Virginia's population "increased by slow degrees," he rued, "except [for] Negroes and convicts." A decade later, in the 1760s, the specter of the Virginia state church dissuaded yet another group of potential religious émigrés from indenturing themselves to work his holdings. Washington had hoped that shifting to white indentured servants might slowly wean Mount Vernon from its dependence on slaves.

Washington was remarkably free from religious prejudice. The exceptions to this rule are so trivial as to hardly bear mentioning. When first sworn in as a civil servant, he took the religious oath required by Virginia law forswearing the Catholic interpretation of Holy Communion. As one who forsook the Eucharist altogether, whether he had qualms about making this vow is unknown, but he would never again evince a trace of anti-Catholic bigotry. The presidential letter he addressed to America's Catholics near the end of his first year in office contains his most confident affirmation of religious freedom: "As mankind become more liberal, they will be more apt to allow that all those who conduct themselves as worthy members of the community are equally entitled to the protection of civil government. I ever hope to see America among the foremost nations in examples of justice and liberality."

When his emotions or self-interest were not in play, Washington acted decisively. Within months of assuming national command he had established a clear protocol for dealing with the nation's religious constituencies. From his letters to religious bodies, we can tease out three interlocking imperatives: 1) a national commitment to defend individual freedom of conscience; 2) absolute governmental neutrality with respect to religion; and 3) the obligation of religious bodies to uphold the law by supporting the constitutional powers invested in their government and its representatives. In the main, this protocol followed the military model he developed as commander in chief of the Continental Army, with one new wrinkle. Soldiers *take* orders from their commanding officer; citizens in a democracy also *deliver* them.

Among those most eager to instruct their new president were America's Baptists. On major points of doctrine, apart from the precedence they placed on adult baptism, most Baptists were theologically indistinguishable from the Congregational stalwarts who inherited the Puritan mantle as overseers of the Standing Orders of New England. Where they differed from their Congregationalist counterparts was in their approach to church and state. When the Puritan Commonwealth of Massachusetts expelled Roger Williams from its borders in part for his Anabaptist beliefs, he founded Rhode Island on an explicit foundation of complete religious freedom. Employing the very language that Jefferson would famously popularize ("a wall of separation" between church and state), Williams enshrined what he called "soul freedom" on the altar of religious separationism. By the late eighteenth century, leading Baptist theologians had discreetly removed a brick or two from Williams's wall, but without exception they remained dedicated to freedom of conscience and opposed all church establishments. At the outset of the Republic, the Baptists were as democratically inclined as any sect in American Christendom.

Petitioning on behalf of the General Committee of Baptist Churches in Virginia, Elder John Leland, sacred liberty's most tireless advocate, demanded a bill of rights the moment Washington became president. "We as a society had unusual strugglings of mind, fearing that the *liberty of conscience,* dearer to us than property or life, was not sufficiently secured," he wrote. Leland then exercised his considerable guile to flatter the president into a favorable disposition:

> If religious liberty is rather insecure in the constitution, the administration will certainly prevent all oppression, for a WASHINGTON will preside. According to our wishes, the unanimous voice of the union has called you, Sir, from your beloved retreat, to launch forth again into the faithless seas of human affairs, to guide the helm of the states. May that Divine munificence which covered your head in battle make you yet a greater blessing to your admiring country in time of peace.

Washington told his Baptist neighbors not to worry. "If I could have entertained the slightest apprehension that the Constitution framed in the Convention, where I had the honor to preside, might possibly endanger the religious rights of any ecclesiastical society, certainly I would never have placed my signature to it." Then he made the following vow: "I beg you will be persuaded that no one would be more zealous than myself to establish effectual barriers against the horrors of spiritual tyranny and every species of religious persecution—for you, doubtless, remember that I have often expressed my sentiment, that every man, conducting himself as a good citizen and being accountable to God alone for his religious opinions, ought to be protected in worshipping the Deity according to the dictates of his own conscience."

While declaring his "opposition to any kind of restraint upon religious principles," Washington never lost sight of a second priority, "quiet to the state." He would uphold religious freedom, but religion had no business intruding itself in government affairs. In this first of nineteen letters to religious bodies, Washington stated emphatically that religious groups must conduct themselves as pliant citizens. Knowing his Baptist petitioners to be "firm friends to civil liberty," he returned their flattery with the confidence that they would also remain "faithful supporters of a free, yet efficient general government."

Tolerant of Slavery, Intolerant of Quakers

If one religious group put a thorn under Washington's elegant saddle, it was the Quakers. Founded in the mid-seventeenth century by George Fox, the Society of Friends, first in England and then in America, was for a time the most radical and reviled sect in Christendom. Quakers were pacific in temper and neighborly in affection. Dispensing with church and clergy alike, this principled lay movement democratized the religious spirit. At their peak in the mid-eighteenth century, the Society of Friends had become the third largest denomination in the colonies. Their self-described "holy experiment" took civic root in America largely due to the efforts of

William Penn, who founded the Commonwealth of Pennsylvania. Whereas Puritans were guided by an abiding conviction of human sinfulness, Friends espoused as deep a faith in natural goodness, which they called "the inner light." The inner light led those who followed it to the creation of a more tolerant society. Pennsylvania prospered, economically as well as spiritually, in large measure due to the diverse group of religious immigrants who sought peace and freedom there.

As dedicated as the Friends were to religious toleration, they were more devoted to fulfilling the divine truth that their inner light illuminated. Mediated through a process of consensus (which is how the inner light becomes a beacon), one Friends meeting after another came to the divinely inspired conclusion that slavery was an evil that must be eradicated from society. No Constitutional shadow could extinguish this conviction. When it came to legislating morality, the Quakers stood at the opposite pole from John Leland, who anchored the hard left flank of America's Baptists. "Conscience," Leland said, "has nothing to do with another man's conduct." As avid in their championship of social justice as Leland was protective of individual liberty, the Quaker conscience held others' conduct very much accountable. Powered by holy certitude, America's leading Quakers set out to enlist the nation's new president as an agent of the Divine will.

During the Revolution, the Friends' principled pacifism had bewildered and aggravated General Washington. At the outset of his presidency, however, the issue they divided on was one that otherwise would appear to unite them: the question of slavery. In his record book, amid drafts of other position papers, Colonel Humphreys includes a précis of Washington's thoughts on slavery during the months immediately before he took office. "The unfortunate condition of the persons, whose labor in part I employed, has been the only unavoidable subject of regret in [my] life," he acknowledged, adding that "to lay a foundation to prepare the rising generation for a destiny different from that in which they were born afforded some satisfaction to my mind & could not, I hoped, be displeasing to the justice of the Creator." This entry hints that Washington may have been entertaining a call for gradual emancipation. If so, his flirtation with an act to facilitate the nation's moral redemption was brief.

Washington had nothing good to say about slavery. "There is not a man living who wishes more sincerely than I do to see a plan [for abolition] adopted," he declared. While certainly not untainted by the prevailing racism, Washington couched his prejudice in the cradle of his ideals, which pivoted on the virtue attached to a sterling reputation. "Blacks are capable of much good labor," he said, "but having—I am speaking generally—no ambition to establish a good name, they are too regardless of a bad one." Acknowledging exceptions to this rule, he also honored them. When Phillis Wheatley, a Massachusetts slave ambitious to establish her good name and given the rare opportunity to do so, extolled General Washington in a fine, celebratory ode, he was quick to extend his respect, along with the invitation that she pay him the further compliment of a visit to his Cambridge headquarters, where he might thank her in person. Jefferson, in contrast, was more condescending. "Religion produced a Phillis Wheatley," he dismissively said, "but it could not produce a poet."

One distinguished denominational leader testified to the tension between Washington's words and actions over this "very troublesome species of property." Francis Asbury, the first Methodist bishop in America, sailed from England as a missionary in 1771. By the end of his ministry four decades later, sacrificing his health but never his spirit, he had traveled 270,000 miles and ordained 4,000 Methodist clergy. An offshoot of Anglicanism founded by Charles and John Wesley in early eighteenth-century England, Methodism came to America in the 1750s in the person of George Whitefield, a pulpit star of the First Great Awakening. In Methodist (so-called Arminian) theology, people could place themselves freely in the way of salvation—no child of God was born to be damned. Its adherents also believed in direct conversion through the agency of the Holy Spirit as opposed to the agency of the established priesthood. Following the war, Bishop Asbury institutionalized the Whitefield magic by creating a powerful grassroots organization of itinerant evangelists who planted churches to the very edge of America's ever-expanding frontier. Their Jesus was no less eager and more likely to embrace a half-literate backwoodsman than a Virginia planter or powdered Yale divine.

Unlike John Leland and other radical Baptists, Bishop Asbury was hardly a political firebrand. In 1784, he was appalled to read "a late publication by a Baptist preacher, in which he has anathematized the whole race of kings from Saul to George III." The apolitical bishop concluded, "His is republicanism run mad." Being social outsiders, American Methodists tended to favor church-state separation and therefore drifted naturally toward Jefferson's Democratic-Republican Party when the country divided into political camps, but their republicanism came nowhere close to running mad.

The one issue that could lure a Methodist off his knees to beat the political pavement was slavery. In the company of Reverend Thomas Coke, Bishop Asbury visited Mount Vernon in 1785 to lobby the renowned general for an emancipation bill then pending in the Virginia House. During the course of their conversation, Washington registered "his opinion against slavery," but refused to take a public stand on the matter. "He informed us that he was of our sentiments, and had signified his thoughts on the subject to most of the great men of the state," Coke recalled. "He did not see it proper to sign the petition, but, if the Assembly took it into consideration, would signify his sentiments to the Assembly by letter." Lacking Washington's imprimatur, when the Methodist petitions reached the Assembly they were, as Madison reported to Jefferson, not exactly thrown under the table, but nonetheless "treated with all the indignity short of it."

Washington sincerely hoped that a plan would emerge by which slavery would be abolished "by slow, sure, & imperceptible degrees."

Slow and imperceptible are the operative words here. As president, he expressed frustration with any troublemaker who would dare press the government to take meaningful action to loosen slavery's stranglehold. When their modest efforts failed in Virginia, most Methodists politely returned to their prayers, making them, in Washington's eyes, ideal religious citizens. The same could not be said for America's Quakers.

In early October 1789, a delegation of Friends called on President Washington to present their case for humane government, including the belief that "Unfeigned righteousness in public as well as private stations is the only sure ground of hope for the divine blessing." In reply, Washington coolly stated his "wish and desire that the laws may always be as extensively accommodated to them as a due regard to the protection and essential interests of the nation may justify and permit." The Quakers' moral absolutism—they beseeched him to proscribe "vice, infidelity and irreligion and every species of oppression on the persons and consciences of men"—was foreign to Washington's understanding of the presidential office. In his judgment, the Friends had no place imposing their morality on others, only a moral duty to behave and uphold the social contract. The conscience-driven Quakers, who answered to a greater authority than the president of the United States, would have none of that. Their moral duty required that they attack social conventions when directed to do so by a higher law.

Washington's mention of his interview with the Quaker delegation was the sole substantive entry in his diary for October 13, 1789: "At two o'clock received the Address from the people called Quakers." He would receive a second call from the people called Quakers three months later. Foremost in the mind of their spokesperson, Warner Mifflin, were provisions in the U.S. Constitution that, judging by the comments recorded by Humphreys in his record book, Washington must have considered no less "displeasing to the justice of the Creator" than the Quakers did. Mifflin had been a slave master once. He freed his slaves for the same reason that he tossed the rum bottles out of his larder: God told him to. Armed with a divine mandate, he entered Washington's study to lobby in favor of a Quaker petition "promoting the abolition of slavery, and discouraging every species of traffic in slaves."

Mifflin's petition, sponsored by the Pennsylvania Society for Promoting the Abolition of Slavery, arrived on Washington's desk under the impressive imprimatur of non-Quaker Benjamin Franklin, who vilified slavery as "an atrocious debasement of human nature." What may fairly be called Franklin's dying wish was that Congress would "promote mercy and justice toward this distressed race, and that you will step to the very verge of the power vested in you for discouraging every species of traffic in the person of our fellow-men." He died a month later, by which time any opportunity for action on his plea had been tabled indefinitely. Following a furious debate along sectional lines, Congress agreed to accept the petition (and a second one, as well, from the New York Society of Friends) but danced around its demands, citing the Constitutional provision that the slave trade might continue until 1808 and expressing for the first time the states' rights argument that would serve as the linch-pin for slavery until the Union finally fractured seven decades later.

The House debate was chaotic, three or four members speaking at once, the air acrid with "base invective." Congressman James Jackson of Georgia argued that both the Bible and nature endorsed slavery. He also wondered aloud who would serve as field hands on southern plantations if it were abolished. In reply, Franklin fired off a mischievous little satire, the final salvo from the pen of America's most celebrated scrivener, cast in the voice of the Bey of Algiers. Arguing that the Koran sanctions slavery, Franklin's mouthpiece defended the North African traffic in white Christian slaves by echoing Mr. Jackson's quandary: "If we forbear to makes slaves of their people, who in this hot climate are to cultivate our lands?"

The House of Representatives did not dismiss the Quaker concerns lightly. Mustering a narrow majority, including Representative Madison, who parted ranks with his fellow Virginians, it pledged that Congress would endeavor to "exercise [its power] for the humane objects of the memorialists, so far as they can be promoted on the principles of justice, humanity, and good policy" and, further, would encourage state legislatures to "revise their laws from time to time, when necessary, and promote the objects mentioned in the memorials." On another close decision (Madison again voting with the North), these same memorials were entered into the *Congressional Record Book*. Such consolation aside, the Quaker petitioners were dismissed in language that Madison decried as "shamefully indecent." Deploring the harsh tone taken by the petitions' opponents in the House, Senator Maclay wondered whether those representatives who were warning that the nation would break asunder actually hoped that it might.

Washington considered the debate indecent also, but for a different reason entirely. When Mifflin solicited his personal support, the president washed his hands of all responsibility, noting in his diary that since it "might come before me for official decision, I was not inclined to express any sentiments...on the merits of the question before this should happen." That may have been the official line; in fact, he was livid. To a friend in Virginia he dismissed the Quaker intrusions into government business as "very *mal-apropos*," sighing in relief that the issue agitating their consciences would be "put to sleep" and not "awake before the year 1808," when the importation of slaves would lose Constitutional sanction. A follow-up letter finds Washington still steaming: "The introductions of the memorial respecting slavery, was to be sure, not only an ill-judged piece of business, but occasioned a great waste of time. The final decision thereon, however, was as favorable as the proprietors of that species of property could have expected considering the great dereliction to slavery in a large part of this Union."

Washington was not alone in dismissing the Quaker memorials' propriety. Unlike the House, the Senate refused to hear them. "The Senate have met with great applause for not taking notice of the Quakers' Memorial," a Virginia constituent needled Representative

Madison, "and people find great fault with your House for wasting so much time and expense in a frivolous manner." What little notice the Senate did take was disrespectful in the extreme. Vice President Adams received the petitions "rather with a sneer," Senator Maclay reports. Senator Izard donned his southern cloak and branded their authors "fanatics." Although Maclay twice rose on the Senate floor to defend the petitioners' "benevolent intention," it was to no avail. He cleared his spiritual palate two weeks later by attending worship at a black church. Of the pastor, he reported, "It would be in favor of religion in general if preachers manifested the same fervor and sincerity that were apparent in his manner. He declared himself untutored, but he seemed to have the Bible by heart." Maclay then cited an old adage: "The times are changing and we must change along with them."

The Quakers were by no means prepared to return to the silence that so eloquently adorned their meetings. In 1791, Warner Mifflin's cousin, Pennsylvania governor Thomas Mifflin, petitioned Congress to redress the continuing grievance Pennsylvania had with Virginia over slave snatchers crossing state lines to recapture runaways. His plea opened an old wound. When the Society of Friends first pressed legal action several years before, Washington lost his storied temper. "This Society is not only acting repugnant to justice so far as its conduct concerns strangers," he raged, "but, in my opinion extremely impoliticly with respect to the state...without being able (but by acts of tyranny & oppression) to accomplish their own ends." This sentence tells us everything we need to know about Washington's view of the Quaker social activists: They were moral absolutists with no respect for the law; far from being just, they had no respect for justice; these self-styled champions of freedom were, in fact, tyrants; and the stranger whose plight his heart went out to was the slaveholder, not the slave.

Washington's approach to the civil questions slavery posed was founded on principle, not spun from rationalization or erected as a cover for hypocrisy. He believed that if individuals or self-sanctioned groups should attempt to impose their moral or political agenda on society at large, the nation would be beset by faction. Included in his ban were the democratic clubs, which would soon spring up in sympathy with the French revolutionary call for "liberty, equality, and fraternity." Whether moralistic in their judgments (like the Quakers) or libertarian (like the democratic clubs), such groups or individuals, unsanctioned by law, set off his most sensitive alarms. Not that the slavery statutes should not gradually and judicially be reformed, when the proper moment arrived. About this Washington was consistent. But when divisive groups, religious or otherwise, challenged constitutionally established authority, social order, in his eyes, was fatuously compromised. Without a social contract, "There is no avoiding the snares of individuals, or of private societies," he declared, "whatever my opinion of the law may have been." He may have been untainted by the bigotry that fired extreme southern passions during the first congressional debate over abolition of the slave trade, but Washington surely empathized with the frustration expressed by Representative Jackson, who scornfully demanded to know whether the Quakers were the only moral people in America.

The Worshipper in Chief

In mid-October 1789, shortly after his meeting with the Quaker delegation, Washington set off for Puritan New England. In a ceremonial tour reminiscent of the king's progress across England, he traveled from one town to the next, leaving his carriage at the outskirts of each to ride on horseback into the village green. Six evenings a week for almost a month he was lavished with expressions of reverence, including those offered by the local clergy; on Sundays, as was the prevailing custom, he attended church twice. By November 10, Washington's patience with the rituals associated with his presidential progress and the social regulations specific to New England Congregationalism had worn thin. Marooned one

Sunday in tiny Ashford, Connecticut, he experienced the frustration of being forbidden to spirit himself homeward due to religious strictures against travel on the Sabbath day. One Boston paper reports that a local tithingman (the religious constabulary assigned to police Sabbath infractions) took active measures to detain the president when he attempted to flee town. It is unlikely that Washington would so offend custom, but that evening the sourness of his mood seeped into the pages of his diary. Noting archly that, being Sunday, it is "against the law to travel," he recorded his acute displeasure with the town's only inn ("not a good one") and derided his visits to church, where he suffered through two "very lame discourse[s] by a Mr. Pound."

Accustomed as he was to relaxed Virginia society, it is not surprising that Washington was ready for a respite from his official duties after a month in New England. One evening after returning to less morally defended ground, he attended his favorite local haunt, New York's John Street Theater. Like most Virginia gentlemen, Washington adored the theater, this at a time when clergymen to the north could still be heard harping on it as the devil's playground. (Legislation banning stage plays for promulgating "immorality, impiety and a contempt for religion" remained on the books in Boston until 1791.)

During the war in the depths of winter at Valley Forge, Washington had staged a production of Joseph Addison's *Cato* to lift his officers' spirits. In this lofty paean to liberty, humanized by a sentimental love story, Addison's goal, perfectly suiting Washington's sensibilities, was "to enliven morality with wit, and to temper wit with morality." In nonattributed paraphrase, Washington cited *Cato* as often as he did the scriptures, including two short passages that he knew by heart, perhaps because they spoke his heart's abiding story: "'Tis not in mortals to command success"; and "The post of honor is a private station." Rather than sacrifice his honor, Cato brings down the curtain by committing suicide, by the canons of Stoic morality a noble act, to Christian theologians, a mortal sin. Washington's staging of *Cato* for his soldiers took place in 1778, the very year that John Adams and his fellow New Englanders importuned Congress into passing a law banning theatrical entertainments as an impious diversion from the work at hand. In Washington's estimation, *Cato* summed up the work at hand admirably.

Washington enjoyed lighter entertainment as well. When he took respite from the severe moral climate of New England at St. John Theater, the playbill featured a lively farce. In response to a bit of verbal fun aimed at puncturing Washington's presidential balloon, he went so far as actually to laugh out loud, marking the only occasion where the press would catch him enjoying a moment of unguarded levity.

Outside the theater, if anything could tease forth the president's deficient wit it was religion. The only joke Washington is recorded telling makes light of a sanctimonious New England parson, who comically lost his wig in a river. A singular witticism in his diary touches on religion as well. Shortly before following the government from New York to Philadelphia, President Washington worshiped one Sunday at the Dutch Reformed Church in New York. "Being in the language not a word of which I understood," he quipped, "I was in no danger of becoming a proselyte to its religion by the eloquence of the preacher." Truth be told, he stood in no such danger when the sermon was in English. Yet Washington found his way to church during his presidential years more easily than his Virginia successors did. Viewing worship as part of his presidential duties, he considered it a requisite of national stewardship to strengthen the moral sinew that binds society together. He was performing a public rather than personal role by attending church, but he wasn't misrepresenting himself. Adapting the Anglican civic model, Washington served on the nation's vestry as chief warden, presiding over an elite tribunal of citizens entrusted with moral and fiduciary stewardship for their neighbors' prosperity, security, and general happiness.

When the capital moved from New York to its temporary home in Philadelphia in the fall of 1791, George and Martha Washington regularly attended either Christ Church, where Pennsylvania's Episcopal bishop William White held forth, or St. Peter's Episcopal Church, to hear storied pulpiteer Dr. James Abercrombie. At St. Peter's, Washington's lifelong practice of ducking out before the celebration of the Eucharist earned him a severe dressing-down from the pulpit. One Communion Sunday, with the president in attendance, Reverend Abercrombie lit into, as he phrased it, "those in elevated stations, who uniformly turned their backs on the Lord's Supper." This clerical attack hit its target squarely, at least according to the preacher, who was quite full of himself for his display of principled bravado. He reported hearsay of Washington confessing later that same week that he had received "a very just reproof from the pulpit, for always leaving the church before the administration of the Sacrament... [But] as he had never been a communicant, were he to become one then, it would be imputed to an ostentatious display of religious zeal, arising altogether from his elevated station." Apocryphal or not, this explanation failed to satisfy the rector of St. Peter's. Asked later to describe the president's faith, Abercrombie dismissed Washington as a Deist.

Abercrombie's immediate superior was more admiring of the president. Yet he, too, would assess Washington's faith guardedly. "I do not believe that any degree of recollection will bring to my mind any fact which would prove Gen. W. to have been a believer in the Christian revelation," Bishop White confessed. "Although I was often in the company of this great man, and had the honor of often dining at his table, I never heard anything from him which could manifest his opinions of the subject of religion."

William White was a conservative Low Church Episcopalian whose dedication to the Episcopal Church was matched by his fidelity to interfaith amity and national union. Temperamentally opposed to all expressions of enthusiasm, he preached orderly obeisance to state authority. Moral without being moralistic, while ab-

staining from dancing himself he was quick to reassure his cultivated Episcopal clientele, "I am by no means opposed to others
learning, if they like to dance." The most colorful incident from his
early life found the future bishop and fifty-six-year-old Benjamin
Franklin in the dead of night holding a ladder outside the window
of painter Benjamin West's eloping bride. Against her father's wishes,
they secreted her on a ship in Chester Harbor that spirited her off
to join her betrothed in Italy. About his role in this adventure, to
the end of his days the broad-minded prelate displayed not a twinge
of regret.

White became presiding bishop of the American Episcopal
Church during Washington's second term. His leadership could
only have impressed the retired vestryman. Bishop White spearheaded prison reform in Philadelphia and participated actively in
the Magdalene Society, created to aid fallen women. Balancing
works of faith with an interest in contemporary science, he also
served as vice president of the American Philosophical Society,
which Thomas Jefferson led from 1797 to 1814. Free of the wariness
toward scientific advancement typical of New England's religious
establishment, White was immune to the anti-intellectual virus that
would infect the Christian polemic against Jefferson.

Washington supported Bishop White's ministry. Generous as always with charitable donations "for the comfort of the needy," he
contributed the then-handsome sum of $250 on New Year's Day
1794 to advance the church's mission, requesting anonymity. White
was also one of several eyewitnesses to testify that Washington never
knelt during prayer (one witness to the contrary is John Adams,
who admired seeing Washington on his knees during the prayer
that opened the Continental Congress). "His behavior in church
was always serious and attentive," Bishop White allowed, but, "on
the point of kneeling during the service, I owe it to the truth to declare that I never saw him in the said attitude." As for Abercrombie's public taunt, one upshot of the good reverend's bluntness does
seem clear. From that day forward, George Washington appears

never to have darkened the door of any church where the Eucharist was being served.

As Washington's first term in office came to a close, he had more pressing matters to worry about than his parson's theological scruples. Growing tension between the friends of order and the champions of liberty was about to break into the open, creating a chasm that even George Washington could not bridge.

UNUM VERSUS PLURIBUS

Oh, God, the source of light supreme,
Shed on our dusty morn a gleam,
   To guide our doubtful way!
Restrain, dread pow'r, our land from crimes!
What seeks, tho' blest beyond all time,
   So querulous an age?

—DAVID HUMPHREYS,
"MOUNT VERNON: AN ODE"

ON MARCH 4, 1793, in a private noonday ceremony hosted by Congress in Philadelphia's Federal Hall, George Washington took his presidential oath a second time. He performed the Constitutional rite without fanfare before a joint session of the legislature. There was no inaugural parade. No worship service followed the ceremony. His inaugural address (with no mention of the Almighty) lasted precisely a minute. And he didn't bother dressing down for the occasion. Instead, he donned his finest imported black velvet suit fringed with silver lace trim and a vest spun of fine white satin, his shoe buckles and the hilt of his ceremonial sword bejeweled with diamonds. To add a splash of color to this elegant study in black and white, the president slipped on his favorite canary yellow kid gloves.

Six months after his second inauguration, in the roughed-out dusty streets of his namesake city, Washington exchanged his inaugural formal wear for a Masonic apron. On September 18, 1793, in full Masonic regalia and carrying a silver trowel, fraternal brother George Washington led the members of his home lodge (Lodge 22

of Alexandria), together with two Maryland lodges and an assortment of actual stonecutters, mechanics, and masons who would raise
the Capitol up from its foundation, on a grand procession from the
bank of his beloved Potomac River along the cow path that would
become Pennsylvania Avenue to the top of Capitol Hill. Included
in the Order of March were "wardens with truncheons," "stewards
with wands," "treasurers with their jewels," "two sword bearers,"
and "Bibles on grand cushions." On reaching Capitol Hill, Washington clambered into the builder's trench and ceremonially laid a
silver commemorative plaque (inscribed with the date, "in the year
of Masonry, 5793") on the foundation stone. The assembled fraternity performed chanting honors as Washington tried the stone, employing the ancient tools of the mason's craft (level, plumb line,
compass, and square), and offered libations of oil and wine and a
stock of corn to sanctify the new house of government. The colorfully bedecked brethren, each Mason wearing the apron and sash
appropriate to his rank, then retired to a capacious tent where they
devoured the barbecued delights of a 500-pound ox.

In Washington's blessing of the Capitol, apprentice Masons understood the corn, oil, and wine to be symbols of nourishment, re-
freshment, and joy; to Masons who had graduated to higher orders
of understanding, they stood for Freemasonry itself, science and
virtue, and universal benevolence. The level, plumb line, compass,
and square, which he employed symbolically to test the integrity of
the cornerstone, represented equality, judgment, self-mastery, and
rectitude. To this day, we speak of being "square" with each other
and "on the level." By symbolically evoking the Masonic virtues,
which could not have been more congenial to his worldview, Washington was emulating, even standing in for, the Grand Architect
himself. Tracing their founding to the head builder of Solomon's
Temple and drawing meaning from the tools of the ancient masonic guild and craft, the Brotherhood of Freemasons—which he
praised as "founded in benevolence, and to be exercised only for the

good of mankind"—built their symbolic temples of individual character, fraternal brotherhood, and civil community according to the Grand Architect's design.

A male fraternity emerging from the European Enlightenment, Freemasonry had its American beginnings in Philadelphia at St. John's Lodge, chartered in 1731. Its growth was impressive, approaching 40 lodges in 1776 and ten times that number (with approximately 25,000 members) by the turn of the century. Benjamin Franklin, Marquis de Lafayette, and one third of the Constitutional Convention were Masons. Franklin was inducted into the notoriously anticlerical Masonic Lodge in Paris, arm in arm with the *philosophe* Voltaire.

Freemasonry's easy translation to American soil and luxuriant growth during and immediately following the Revolution make perfect sense. Although ostensibly drawing on ancient schools of occult philosophy in quest of secret wisdom passed down through the ages, Masonic teachings in fact fostered a meld of Christian and republican virtues. The four Masonic pillars of individual and public happiness were charity, harmony, order, and moderation. With sound moral character and neighborly love as the building blocks of wisdom and community alike, active Masons would graduate from one order to the next, progressing by degrees from darkness (ignorance) to light (knowledge). In American Masonry, Christianity was honored but sectarian proselytizing was forbidden for the sake of amity. The Masonic constitutions required brothers to "leave their particular opinions [on religion] to themselves."

In his presidential correspondence with Masonic temples, Washington permitted himself an intimacy absent from his Christian correspondence, even when writing to leaders of the Anglican Church. "I receive your kind congratulations with the purest sensations of fraternal affection," Washington told the members of Pennsylvania's Grand Lodge. "At the same time, I request you will be assured of my best wishes and earnest prayers for your happiness while you remain in this terrestrial mansion and that we may hereafter meet as brethren in the eternal Temple of the Supreme Architect." Addressing the King David's Lodge in Newport, he abandoned his vaunted distance almost entirely. Professing his belief that "a just application of the principles on which the Masonic order is founded must be promotive of private virtue and public prosperity," the president declared, "I shall always be happy to advance the interests of the society and be considered by them a deserving brother." Washington is speaking here fraternally, one Mason to another. He identified himself with the Brotherhood of Freemasons as he never would with the Christian church.

For a clear view of the basic elements that constituted Washington's moral philosophy, we need look no further than the Masonic Lodge in Fredericksburg, Virginia, where as a young man he received instruction in any number of "mysteries" that would have made perfect common sense to him. Combining the Christian virtue of charity, the Stoic virtue of self-control, the Enlightenment virtue of knowledge, and the Republican virtue of liberty (including religious liberty), his fraternal teachers would have had at the ready all the pillars Washington would need to construct the temple of his character and fashion the temple of his government, erected "for the benefit of the whole" to serve "the public good" and dedicated to "the aggregate happiness" of the American people.

The Perils of Order

The United States, at least on paper, began as a one-party state. There was no official opposition, loyal or otherwise. Parties emerged only after Washington left office. Yet, however much Washington scorned them, factions did exist, with tempers between them growing shorter throughout his tenure. Since faction was a four-letter word in early American politics, champions of liberty and order alike were quick to pin its tag on their opponents, each "antifactional" party bidding to preserve the peace by eliminating the other.

In Connecticut, where the lack of a state constitution gave the ruling clerical party free rein to perpetuate its holy franchise, Yale president Timothy Dwight taught the gospel of one party, one church. Even in the heart of New England, however, fissures were appearing in the establishment bedrock. In 1790, the peripatetic John Leland appeared in Hartford on the State House steps to proclaim that Connecticut's "rulers run without bridle or bit." With clergymen like Dwight and Leland investing divine order and sacred liberty with competing holy imprimaturs, the devotees of each principle found it difficult to imagine the nation achieving its destiny until all advocates of the other were either converted or silenced. Even when the Democratic-Republican and Federalist Parties finally came out of the closet in the electoral wars between Adams and Jefferson, both sides still forswore the sin of party. They each existed for one purpose only: to eliminate the other and restore the nation to a prefactional (Edenic) state.

At the outset of his second term, with growing evidence to gird his anxieties, Washington saw disorder everywhere. He no longer enjoyed the moral luxury of pinning the label of divisiveness on external enemies alone, for discord had broken out in his own cabinet. He nonetheless persisted in viewing the disruptions in American politics as a foreign import, this time from France, where the revolution that drew inspiration from Lady Liberty's triumph in America was running amok. As one brief generation of liberal reformers after another proved insufficiently orthodox in its radicalism, idealistic French heads (alongside those of the king and queen) piled up in baskets beneath the purists' guillotine. Washington must have cringed when, shortly after the king's head rolled, a Philadelphia troop staged a commemorative run of Addison's *Cato,* inaugurating each performance by singing "Le Marseilles."

Washington's growing apprehension about the course liberty was taking did not want for sponsors. Principal among them was Alexander Hamilton, the chamberlain of his court and, as the most brilliant and powerful treasury secretary in American history, architect of his domestic agenda. Apart from their graying red hair, Hamilton shared virtually nothing with his principal antagonist in the cabinet, Thomas Jefferson. Scorning his distinguished foe for having "a womanish attachment to France and a womanish resentment against Great Britain," Hamilton did everything within his considerable power to seduce Washington into sharing his animus for his rival, who in turn esteemed Hamilton as little and caricatured him as mercilessly. Hamilton was so enamored by the charms of English statecraft, Jefferson said, that his every act aimed "a fatal stroke at the cause of liberty."

The president gravitated slowly toward Hamilton as the schism in his cabinet widened, but the two men, for all their years of proximity, were never close. If Jefferson and Washington had their differences, at least they came from the pages of the same book. Hamilton's story could not have been more alien to the world of cavalier Virginia, literally as well as figuratively. Born poor and illegitimate in the British West Indies, he reinvented himself on moving to New York and attending King's College (Columbia) at seventeen to become the poster child for the American meritocracy. The mission of his life was to impose order on chaos, beginning with the chaos of his upbringing. Despite having grown up among them, Hamilton harbored no affection for the poor. A power politician, he was beguiled by the American machine, how to make it run smoothly and well, not by the romance of equality, which he considered a fairy tale for grown-ups. He especially despised those who, born to a life of ease, declared themselves on principle eager to sacrifice the very power that he, beginning with nothing, had worked so assiduously to attain.

Hamilton, who confessed to never liking Washington, was calculating in his attempts to gull the president into adopting his policies. "It has aptly been observed that Cato was the Tory, Caesar the Whig of his day," he seductively let drop in 1792, tugging adroitly at the sentimental hem of Washington's moral foundation. "The former frequently resisted, the latter always flattered the follies of the people."

Tireless in his efforts to build a strong federal authority, Secretary Hamilton refused to leave a single trick on the table. As America's first director of symbolism, in his compendious "Report on the Establishment of a Mint" he slipped in a proposal to strike the Goddess of Liberty from American coinage and replace her with a bust of the president. "Far from being matters of indifference," the symbols with which we emboss our coins "may be made the vehicles of useful impression," he argued. Minting a set of prototypes and distributing them to Congress, he lost this battle on a split decision. If Washington's head would not yet be embossed on American coinage, at least Liberty's tresses could be trimmed. With Jefferson in retreat at Monticello and the mint (supervised by the secretary of state) under the dependably conservative oversight of its new director, Elias Boudinot, the goddess Liberty lost her republican cap and the coins their Liberty Poles. Sympathetic artist Gilbert Stuart boasted that he had tamed "Liberty's hair with a bow," thereby stripping all symbols of revolution from American coinage within a decade of final victory in the War of Independence.

The Perils of Liberty

By 1794, Hamilton's most persuasive, if unwitting, allies in his relentless campaign to fortify the president against libertarian fancies were a ragtag assortment of still owners in western Pennsylvania who rebelled at the government tariff on whiskey and rum. More chaotic than effectual, their protests nonetheless led to accidental bloodshed and the terrorizing of a government tax collector, finally prompting the president to call out the guard in the fall of 1794. He mounted his horse as commander in chief and led the march, with Secretary Hamilton at his side, toward rebellious Washington County (named after him by its once faithful residents), where the insurrection was throwing up the greatest amount of dust. The entire adventure, leading to two convictions—one was a simpleton, the other certifiably insane—and as many presidential pardons, took slightly more than a month.

In fashioning Washington's campaign against the whiskey rebels, Hamilton could justifiably claim to be acting on moral principle. The excise on whiskey was in part a sin tax. Early federal excises were assessed either on luxuries such as loaf sugar and carriages or discretionary substances like whiskey and snuff. With yearly alcohol consumption at a staggering 6.2 gallons per capita, three times the current national level, Hamilton was not exaggerating when he pronounced the unbridled distribution of spirituous liquor dangerous to the nation's "health and morals." Anticipating the temperance movement that would swing its sharp ax against American immorality, the Federalist press picked up Hamilton's refrain, bemoaning "the pernicious effects of spirits on the under classes of society" and beseeching "government to check [their] immoderate use."

Excise taxes served a second, more immediate purpose. They greased government wheels, suiting the designs of those who, like Hamilton, favored a strong, well-financed federal authority. They also drove libertarians, a fierce majority among the hardy souls who were setting down stakes on the Western frontier, absolutely mad. "Those who make bad laws and attempt to subvert liberty are certainly very bad men and very unfit to hold the reins of authority any longer," declared one populist in the Pennsylvania House. The Federalist answer to anyone irresponsible enough to champion "the wild liberty of an individual" was that "voluntary obedience and a love of order are among the most distinguished honors in the character of a...citizen." As the rebels grew cockier, the government became more belligerent. Before long, the friends of liberty and friends of order were headed for a showdown in front of a Pennsylvania saloon.

The population of the four Pennsylvania counties west of the Allegheny Mountains—fully half hailed from Scotland, Ireland,

and Germany—was not only irreverent toward the government but also noticeably indifferent to the gospel. With the Second Great Awakening, which would bring Jesus to the frontier, still in incubation, Washington's Virginia neighbor Arthur Lee, during a visit to the region in the 1780s, saw "not a priest of any persuasion, nor church, nor chapel, so that they are likely to be damned *without the benefit of clergy.*"

They were damned *with* the clergy's benefit as well. Some ministers on the near side of the mountains were delighted by the president's show of force. On the first Sunday of October in Carlisle, Pennsylvania, where some 15,000 troops had mustered, Washington attended worship at the Presbyterian Meeting House. He recounted hearing "Doctor Davidson preach a political sermon, recommendatory of order & good government." This kind of "political sermon" Washington could tolerate. Robert Davidson raised his church's rafters the previous Sunday, too, holding the "sinners" and their moonshine grievously at fault. "If they will *resist,* and involve themselves in the *guilt* of rebellion," he fulminated, "they deserve not to be pitied nor spared."

By the time Washington's army marched, however, there was no one to march against. During the buildup to battle, one child was accidentally shot and killed; a local resident raised his glass to "the Whiskey boys" and during the resulting scuffle was bayoneted to death; and a Liberty Pole flaunting the seditious boast "Liberty and Equality" was hacked down. That was it. In Jefferson's wry summation, "An insurrection was announced and proclaimed and fought against, but could never be found."

If anything, Washington's attempt to restore order stoked the engines of liberty instead. On arriving in force in western Pennsylvania, "the army of the Constitution," as Washington grandly dubbed his federal militia, randomly rousted 150 local citizens from their beds and marched them half naked down the road toward Pittsburgh. The victims swept up in this dragnet, in addition to satisfying thousands of underemployed soldiers' martial ardor, were taken on a forced march onward to Philadelphia where, in shackles, they were paraded in humiliation down Broad Street and then incarcerated, without the courtesy of an indictment, for four to six months apiece. When the federal prosecutors failed to come up with any evidence that would hold up in court, they finally won their release. Educated in the arts of government, they returned to western Pennsylvania with their democratic ardor locked and loaded.

The wonder is that Washington's so-called watermelon army, treating the campaign as a holiday and free with the whiskey he was trying to tax, did not accidentally incite a real rebellion. One Pennsylvania resident who won the confidence of both parties while trying to broker a peaceful settlement warned the president that if he did not rein in the rowdier elements of his command, "there is no law, divine or human, to oblige people tamely to submit to being skewered, hanged, or shot in cold blood, and this was for some time the declared object of such [troops] as made the noise."

Bidding farewell to his army, Washington's rhetoric (courtesy of Hamilton) soared higher than its new occasion warranted, but he did close with a solemn civil religious vow. "The essential principles of a free government confine the provinces of the military to these two objects," the commander in chief declared. "First, to combat and subdue all who may be found in arms in opposition to the national will and authority. Secondly, to aid and support the civil magistrate in bringing offenders to justice. The dispensation of this justice belongs to the civil magistrate, and let it ever be our pride and our glory to leave the sacred deposit there unviolated."

More agitated than quieted by his success in quashing the "enemies of order," the president became less attentive to freedom's requirements. His principal new obsession was the Francophile Democratic Societies, founded to advance the revolutionary gospel of "liberty, equality, and fraternity." Some thirty-five associations, ranging from a handful of activists to upward of 300 members, sprang up in cities across the country. Viewing themselves as patriots, their members gathered to keep the revolutionary spirit of '76 alive.

The president viewed the society members in a very different light: as rabble-rousing anarchists, dangerous antibodies in the nation's body politic. The democratic clubs, he sincerely believed, represented "the most diabolical attempts to destroy the best fabric of human government and happiness that has ever been presented for the acceptance of mankind." In point of fact, the Democratic Society of Pennsylvania, founded on the Fourth of July the year before, had officially condemned the insurrection (although denouncing the excise tax on whiskey as "hostile to the liberties of this country").

Like politicized churches, American voluntary associations that dared to intrude in government affairs unbalanced Washington's republican mind. There is no doubt that the democratic clubs were party seedlings dedicated to advancing the principle of sacred liberty. It was this that elicited the president's ire and not alone their "self-created" status. Marking one of the rare times that he would place his legendary temper on public display, in his 1794 annual address to Congress Washington indulged himself with a double-barreled diatribe that fairly crackles with incendiary rhetoric: "Fostered and embittered by the artifice of men…certain self-created societies assumed the tone of condemnation…fomented by combinations of men, who, careless of consequences…have disseminated…suspicions, jealousies, and accusations, of the whole government…Legal process was therefore, delivered to the marshal against the rioters and delinquent distillers."

Washington's frontal assault on the democratic clubs and whiskey rebels paid one unexpected dividend. The fracas marshaled, for the first time since the Revolution, a sizable cadre of New England clergymen into the front ranks of American political discourse. The Black Regiment was back, but not in freedom's name to strip a repressive regime of its presumed moral authority, as New England's Standing Orders had done two decades before. This time they stood tall in their pulpits for precisely the opposite reason: to defend the government from swarms of democratic Huns.

The Black Regiment Changes Sides

Philip Freneau was a Jeffersonian journalist and noted poet. One of his literary characters, the stocking weaver Robert Slender, chances on an open letter in the newspaper written to the president by a clergyman. "It must be good," Slender thinks to himself, "and a sacrilege not to read it." To his dismay, what he finds himself reading is not a spiritual sermon aimed at uplifting the meek and downtrodden (which Slender's father had taught him Christianity was all about) but rather a political polemic designed to advance elite interests. The irony of America's clergy honoring their president as if he were a king was not lost on Freneau.

Two decades before, as America was girding for revolution, Governor Thomas Hutchinson of Massachusetts had blamed the New England clergy—the Black Regiment, he called them—for stirring up the populace against their rightful leaders, the parliament and crown. The Reverend Gad Hitchcock was one of many Standing Order preachers to equate "the cause of liberty" with "the cause of God." In response, Loyalist preachers understandably downplayed liberty as a Christian virtue, invoking "the God of order" instead. One student of American providential thought notes that, in the American Revolution, the "God of Order" squared off against the "God of Liberty," and the "God of Liberty" won.

By the mid-1790s, with independence secured and a new government in place, the established clergy had returned to their original object: to fortify and defend the status quo. The Black Regiment looked back on the Revolution more as a Restoration, fought to restore rights that their Puritan forebearers had established on first coming to America. This conservative viewpoint stood in marked contrast to that of the democratic clubs, for whom the Revolution represented not the end of an isolated injustice but the beginning of an international movement of liberation that promised to usher in an Age of Reason and secure the Rights of Man.

Nowhere did the democratic clubs and Black Regiment divide as sharply as they did on France. New England's Standing Congregational Orders had initially welcomed the French Revolution, because it undercut Catholic authority. But as embers from the French bonfire began wafting back across the Atlantic to spark a democratic revival in America, an overwhelming majority of the established clergy began to think better of their erstwhile enthusiasm for the French Revolution. What stirred their concern was less the creeping anarchy in France than the looming danger of a socially disruptive, leveling movement here at home. To make matters worse, as if cast by an evil spell, democratic reform was walking magically across the water from France hand in hand with atheism and Deism, scourges so terrible that few moral sentries wasted any effort in trying to differentiate them.

The Reverend Jedidiah Morse personifies the emergent clerical politics of the newly reactionary New England church establishment. A striking, dark-complectioned figure with intense brown eyes, Morse cut at least a few of his political teeth at Mount Vernon. The young geographer was a guest there in 1787 when Shays' Rebellion in Massachusetts was the talk of the country. This earlier taxpayer revolt, in some ways a precursor of the Whiskey Rebellion, wrenched from Washington both a hearty oath and the express fear that, God forbid, the Tories may have been right. He surely was more discreet around his young guest, but Morse proudly reported home to his father how the two entered into animated conversation on the matter, with the general expressing concern over how the insurrection would be resolved. Less a scholar or theologian than an organizer, Morse placed his work as a geographer at the service of his values and his class. In the first edition of *The American Geography*, he tipped his future hand by commending the Connecticut Standing Order, from which he hailed, "as a check upon the overbearing spirit of republicanism."

Ready and eager to enlist the clergy in the great debate over American values was Alexander Hamilton. "Opinions, for a long time, have been gradually gaining ground, which threaten the foundations of religion, morality and society," he wrote in 1794. Hamilton's interest in religion was political. Yet his logic proved irresistible to the pillars of New England's Standing Orders. Implicit in his reflections on the progress of revolution in France was a parallel scenario for the collapse of responsible government in America:

An attack was first made upon the Christian revelation, for which natural religion was offered as the substitute. The Gospel was to be discarded as a gross imposture, but the being and attributes of a God, the obligations of piety, even the doctrine of a future state of rewards and punishment were to be retained and cherished. In proportion as success has appeared to attend the play, a bolder project has been unfolded. The very existence of a Deity has been questioned, and in some instances denied. The duty of piety has been ridiculed, the perishable nature of man asserted and his hopes bounded to the short span of his earthly state....Irreligion, no longer confined to the closets of concealed sophists, nor to the haunts of wealthy riot, has more or less displayed its hideous form among all classes....A league has at length been cemented between the apostles and disciples of irreligion and of anarchy. Religion and government have both been stigmatized as abuses, as unwarrantable restraints upon the freedom of man, as causes of the corruption of his nature, intrinsically good, as sources of an artificial and false morality, which tyrannically robs him of the enjoyments for which his passions fit him, and as clogs upon his progress to the perfection for which he was destined. As a corollary from these premises, it is a favorite tenet of the sect that religious opinion of any sort is unnecessary to society; that the maxims of a genuine morality and the authority of the magistracy and the laws are a sufficient and ought to be the only security for civil rights and private happiness...so wild and fatal a scheme, every modification of which aims a mortal blow at the vitals of human happiness.

Morse, for one, was poised to heed Hamilton's warning. In 1794, ruing how the foundations of deference were eroding, he began preaching against democracy with a vengeance. Morse wouldn't give up all hope that the French revolutionaries would eventually find their manners until 1798, but by late 1794 he was all in arms against the encroaching dangers posed by American democracy. Drawing the most radical card from the French revolutionary deck, Morse and his fellow churchmen summed up the democrats' religious and political sins in a single epithet: "Jacobin."

The threat democracy posed to the New England status quo made for strange political bedfellows. Beginning in the mid-1790s and continuing for almost two decades, New England clergymen at opposite ends of the theological spectrum locked arms to defend the cultural establishment. The Reverend Jeremy Belknap of Harvard, an unabashed Unitarian, told the Massachusetts Congregational Clergy Association, "I consider politics as intimately connected with morality, and both with religion." Of one mind with Belknap on this point alone, Morse could boast with confidence, "Very few of the clergy in the circle of my acquaintance seem disposed to pray for the success of the French, since they have so insidiously & wickedly interfered in the management of our political affairs."

Trumpeting the Black Regiment back into battle in the autumn of 1794 was none other than George Washington himself. In lambasting the democratic clubs, he spoke from the heart, and the heart of old New England beat more quickly in response. In Morse's estimation, "nine out of ten" preachers gave the president a ringing "amen" for bringing his hammer down on democracy.

One sermon in particular, preached by Morse's closest friend, the Reverend David Osgood of Medford, caught the public fancy. "I love your plain speaking ministers," one New York partisan enthused on reading Osgood's jeremiad. "They do good and will become more useful if encouraged by our federal rulers." They were so encouraged. In fact, Federalist operatives mustered a willing Black Regiment into the front ranks of the political campaign to alert the public against the dangers of democracy. They bankrolled multiple printings of Osgood's sermon and distributed it throughout the country, endowing it with the luster of antidemocratic holy writ. The prayer with which Reverend Osgood closed summed up the revived Black Regiment's new political gospel: "May the God of order and peace preserve us from such dreadful calamities!" Morse made sure Osgood's sermon came to the administration's attention, begging Controller of the Treasury Oliver Wolcott to put it "into the hand of our most worthy president." It would, he said with confidence, "add to his satisfaction and...certainly to our honor in his view."

Religious attacks against the democratic clubs led republican spokesman Tunis Wortman of the New York Democratic Society to counterattack, pronouncing religion as detrimental to liberty. "Ambition and tyranny have always been fond of assuming the masque of religion and making instruments of judges and divines," he proclaimed. "Superstition in religious creeds and despotism in civil institutions bear a relation to each other."

Fearing to challenge the president directly, most opponents of Washington's campaign to squelch the democratic clubs were less forthright. Privately, they bit their tongues in frustration and anger. Future Treasury secretary Albert Gallatin sarcastically confessed to his wife, "I hate treason, and you know that it would be less sacrilegious to carry arms against our country than to refuse singing to the tune of the best and greatest of men." For Jefferson, this same tune had lost its remaining sweetness. "The denunciation of the democratic societies is one of the most extraordinary acts of boldness of which we have seen so many from the fraction of monocrats," he mourned. "It is wonderful [i.e., incredible] indeed that the President should have permitted himself to be the organ of such an attack on the freedom of discussion, the freedom of writing, printing and publishing."

Jefferson fixed his guns on Hamilton. Although "double delicacies," he would plead, "have kept me silent," he called for a swift, merciless counterattack, which he directed from his preferred distance. Shortly before, he had beseeched Madison, "For God's sake, my dear sir, take up your pen. Select the most striking heresies and cut [Hamilton] to pieces in the face of the public." Betraying his acute susceptibility to the demonic logic possessing revolutionary France, Jefferson deemed his foe worthy of execution. Being guilty of "high treason," he told Madison, Hamilton should "suffer death accordingly. This is the only opposition worthy of our state, and the only kind which can be effectual."

If lacking his inquisitorial temper, Madison shared his compatriot's doctrinal scruples. Dutifully, if oddly, he followed Jefferson's instructions to skewer Hamilton by choosing to lambaste "the foreigners and degenerate citizens among us who hate our republican government and the French revolution." In the American oven there were foreigners for every political chef to burn; Hamilton, who had emigrated from the Caribbean, proved an inviting target for patriotic American Francophiles like Madison and Jefferson.

By the middle of 1795, the battle lines between the friends of order and friends of liberty had been drawn. Although Hamilton and Jefferson marshaled their respective forces secretly as long as Washington remained in office, the fight for America's soul was set to begin.

Hamilton Calls the Nation to Prayer

With concord foremost on his increasingly agitated mind, Washington closed his 1794 address to Congress with what has been dubbed "an American psalm." "Let us unite," he beseeched, employing Hamilton's ready pen, "in imploring the Supreme Ruler of nations, to spread his holy protection of these United States: to turn the machinations of the wicked to the confirming of our constitution: to enable us at all times to root out internal sedition, and put invasion to flight: to perpetuate and to verify the anticipations of this government being a safeguard to human rights."

Extending the invocation of Providence, on New Year's Day 1795 the president declared a second National Day of Thanksgiving to celebrate the federal suppression of the Whiskey Rebellion. Drafted by Hamilton and beseeching "the kind Author of these blessings...to diffuse and establish habits of sobriety, order, morality, and piety," Washington's proclamation slated the national thanksgiving for February 19, strategically placing it three days before the nationwide celebration of his birthday. Attentive to ecclesial propriety, a few dour New Englanders muttered under their breath that the president had inverted the Christian order of things by declaring that thanksgiving be celebrated in the middle of Lent. Washington's least favorite Episcopal bishop, Samuel Seabury—he pompously dubbed himself "Samuel, Bishop of Connecticut"—refused to celebrate the federal thanksgiving in New London for that very reason. But most New Englanders placed governmental sanction over theological scruple and fulfilled their national religious obligations dutifully.

There was nothing surprising about where the established pulpits came down in the contest between social stability and free speech, but the evangelical zeal with which their occupants met the challenge posed by Francophile democrats had grown exponentially over the past twelve months. Puritan faith was deferential at its very core, and Washington's condemnation of the democratic clubs was all the provocation most establishment preachers needed to begin sounding the alarms.

Inspired by Osgood's earlier success as a Federalist evangel, one partisan prayed that Washington's national prayer day would "afford an opening for other clergymen to seek glory." And so indeed it did. Timothy Dwight wailed that radicals were vomiting heresy across the Atlantic. Jedidiah Morse decried Boston's democratic club members as "grumbletonians," agreeing with Washington that such self-created societies presented "the greatest danger which, at present, threatens the peace and liberties of our country." In Philadelphia, Bishop William White hammered home the "reciprocal influence of civil policy and religious duty," decrying the "'madness' of popular tumult and insurrection" and offering religion as a "counterpose to the basest passions of our nature."

Amid the calls for stability in the face of chaos emerged a theological subtext that soon would take on weighty political portent. Morse cited the pernicious effect of Thomas Paine's newly published *Age of Reason,* lamenting, "We have too many among us who are deeply affected with the contagious disease both in their politics and religion." In Morse's mind, the two enterprises were inextricably intertwined. The hated democrats were challenging the sanctity of federal power; and infectious libertine, Deist, and atheistic germs imported from France by pests like Paine were infecting the pure Christian air of America. The Constitution itself was called into question, with one conservative Massachusetts clergyman saying that the American people were deifying a godless document.

Reviewing the latest spate of thanksgiving day sermons, the New England establishment's leading paper, the Boston *Columbian Centinel,* comfortingly concluded that, taken together, they composed "a political Bible, in which might be found the most invincible arguments in favor of good order, peace, and Federalism." With dismay, the opposition paper made the same observation. Declaring it "remarkable that so many of the clergy appear in favor of the British," the republican editor of the Massachusetts *Chronicle* deemed it high time "for the clergy of United America to renew their former spirit of love and friendship to the *rights of men* and no more throw their weight into the scale of aristocracy, as many of them have done." He was urging the Black Regiment to remount their revolutionary pulpits, but the regiment would henceforth be fighting on behalf of order, not liberty.

Not everyone preached Washington's antidemocratic gospel on thanksgiving day. Among the renegades was Bishop James Madison of Virginia, who shared his cousin and namesake's republican politics and Thomas Jefferson's Enlightenment faith. In response to Washington's call for law and order, Madison dared to celebrate the

triad of French revolutionary virtues—liberty, equality, and fraternity. "In vain had reason, the hand-maid of pure religion, long attempted to convince men of the reciprocal duties which equality
and fraternity impose," he sadly acknowledged. In a footnote to his
published text, Madison further rued that "the term, *equality,* seems
to be in the wane; it has its enemies even in America... [but] it is
the only basis on which universal justice, order, and freedom can be
firmly built."

In New England, renegade Congregational minister William
Bentley made much the same point, but his paean to freedom was
lost in the clamor for obedience. One liberal pastor mourned the
obvious: "The clergy are now the tools of the Federalists and
Thanksgiving sermons are the order of the day." With Washington's
birthday and his national thanksgiving occurring back to back, the
third week of February 1795 proved to be a very good week for the
government. Washington and Hamilton could take comfort from
reports that, this time, the churches were packed.

Washington won his battle against the democratic clubs. Extinguished by his long shadow (together with a growing suspicion that
the French Revolution offered a problematic model for American
statecraft), one by one they disappeared from the political map.
From their ashes, however, would arise the phoenix of Jeffersonian
Republicanism. Under the banner of sacred liberty, America's democratic movement would not rest until it had marshaled sufficient
force to toss the friends of order from their seats of power.

The Pillars of Morality and Religion

Back near the end of his first term, weary to the bone of the indig-
nities attendant on public service and holding open the option to
retire from office when his term expired, Washington had asked
Madison to draft his farewell letter to the American people. The
president's personal contribution to this exercise (including a text-

book example of the rhetorical device litotes, where the speaker says precisely what he tells you he has chosen not to say) exhibits the unbridled passion of an unsent letter.

> As this address, fellow citizens, will be the last I shall ever make you, and as some of the gazettes of the United States have teemed with all the invective that disappointment, ignorance of facts, and malicious falsehoods could invent—to misrepresent my politics and affections, to wound my reputation and feelings, and to weaken, if not entirely destroy, the confidence you have been pleased to repose in me—it might be expected at the parting scene of my public life that I should take some notice of such virulent abuse. But, as heretofore, I shall pass them over in utter silence.

He buried this lament for historians to ponder, while squirreling away Madison's more tempered farewell for another day.

Four years later, in May 1796, with his second term at long last lumbering to a close, Washington forwarded Madison's draft, buttressed by a few new paragraphs of his own, to Hamilton, inviting him to amend, correct, or, should he so wish, recast it entirely. The result is a masterpiece. Next to Lincoln's remarks at Gettysburg, it is perhaps the most often quoted presidential address. Then and today, the most frequently cited passage from Washington's Farewell is his elegiac testament to morality and religion as central pillars for upholding the public good. Constituting an ethical will of sorts bequeathing to posterity an inheritance of moral value, taken alone it is easy to see how the temple Washington constructs here might be mistaken for a church.

> Of all the dispositions and habits which lead to political prosperity, religion and morality are indispensable supports. In vain would that man claim the tribute of patriotism, who should labor to subvert these great pillars of human happiness, these firmest props of the duties of men and citizens. The mere politician, equally with the pious man, ought to respect and to cherish them. A volume

could not trace all their connections with private and public felicity. Let it simply be asked where is the security for property, for reputation, for life, if the sense of religious obligation desert the oaths, which are the instruments of investigation in courts of justice? And let us with caution indulge the supposition that morality can be maintained without religion. Whatever may be conceded to the influence of refined education on minds of peculiar structure, reason and experience both forbid us to expect that national morality can prevail in exclusion of religious principle.

These strong, declarative sentiments, though by no means alien to Washington's view of religion and society, appear uniquely here, with abiding consequence on how he would be remembered.

When he first set out to construct his final public memorial, religion was the furthest thing from Washington's mind. His initial instructions to Madison, the Madison draft, Washington's enlargement of that draft, and his cover letter to Hamilton overlook the subject almost entirely. But Hamilton could not resist the opportunity to employ his favorite new rhetorical tool: touting Christian morality as a bulwark against the invasion of French ideas into American politics.

While underscoring Washington's dedication to social stability, Hamilton ignored another Washington pillar, education, which balanced his thought with a strong Enlightenment tilt. The president complained to Hamilton about the education gap in his draft. "I have regretted that another subject (which in my estimation is of interesting concern to the well-being of this country) was not touched upon also," he chided. "I mean education *generally* as one of the surest means of enlightening & giving just ways of thinking to our citizens, but particularly the establishment of a university; where the youth from *all parts* of the United States might receive the polish of erudition in the arts, sciences & Belle Letters."

Washington dreamed of establishing a national university. At the time, all America's institutes for higher learning were sectarian religious colleges dedicated principally to the preparation of clergy-men. Washington envisioned a national school of arts and sciences drawing its student body from every state to create a deeper pool of prospective leaders ("the future guardians of the liberties of the country"). "There is nothing which can better deserve your patron-age than the promotion of science and literature," he exhorted Congress at the outset of his presidency. "Knowledge is in every country the surest basis of public happiness." An almost evangelical Enlightenment spirit kindled his passion to spread the very knowl-edge he so deeply regretted having never received. In no description of his national university did Washington introduce religion into its curriculum.

In response to Washington's critique and plea, Hamilton fi-nessed the question, arguing that this was not the proper forum for Washington to share his views on education. The president none-theless interpolated two concise sentences into a text he feared was already too long: "Promote then, as an object of primary impor-tance, institutions for the general diffusion of knowledge. In propor-tion as the structure of a government gives force to public opinion, it is essential that public opinion should be enlightened."

For all his tinkering, in its final form Washington's Farewell Ad-dress lacks the balance familiar to his trademark equation of reason and religion. Routinely he counterpoised his philosophical first principles (knowledge, liberty, and happiness) with his religious first principles (morality, order, and charity) to strike a pleasing equilibrium. Hamilton tilted this equation in favor of religion. As a result, to borrow a Masonic notion, Washington's Farewell Ad-dress is not on the level. It stands on two pillars, not on four.

"The Old Fox Was Too Cunning for Us"

If he inaugurated his presidency by holding up "the sacred fire of lib-erty" and ended it with a call to "sacred union," one thing did not change during Washington's eight years in office: his personal faith.

As he prepared to leave the public stage, among those who queued up to offer their respects were the local clergy. Bishop White paid his compliments to the president on behalf of the Christ Church Vestry. "In his answer," White confessed, "he was pleased to express himself gratified by what he had heard from our pulpit; but there was nothing that committed him relatively to religious theory."

How frustrating Washington's gracious yet noncommittal posture must have been for the Christian clergy. He shied clear of employing the word "Christian," even in his Christian correspondence. It pops up only three times in the sixteen letters Washington wrote to Christian ecclesiastical bodies during his presidency. When he did name his correspondents' faith directly, it was to remind them of their civic duties. He told the Episcopal General Convention, "It affords edifying prospects indeed to see Christians of different denominations dwell together in more charity." To the General Assembly of the Presbyterian Church, he defined a good Christian in strictly moral and civic terms. "No man who is profligate in his morals," he said, "or a bad member of the civil community, can possibly be a true Christian or a credit to his own religious society."

One clergyman professed himself content with leaders who, unable to believe in Christ, nonetheless supported the church. New Hampshire Congregational minister Stephen Peabody acknowledged that "many professed Deists contribute with cheerfulness and liberality to public teachers of morality. They are patrons to the worship of God in gospel order. They have considered it as a measure wisely adapted to uphold government, and in this they deserve an encomium." If Peabody didn't have Washington in mind when he spoke these words, they are uncannily apt and capture the president's civil religious practice to a tee.

Peabody's clerical brethren in Philadelphia took a less generous view of Washington's theological diffidence. In fact, in their final communication, they appear to have attempted to cajole him to declare himself for Christ. Two days after bringing his vestry's good wishes, Bishop White addressed the president again, this time bearing greetings from twenty-four of his colleagues in a formal letter penned by Philadelphia's most avid political clergyman. House chaplain Ashbel Green was minister of Second Presbyterian Church, a future president of Princeton College and, on all matters political, Jedidiah Morse's comrade-in-arms. Lauding Washington for the "just and pious" sentiments concerning religion in his Farewell Address, the pastors affirmed that "in our special character as ministers of the gospel of Christ, we are more immediately bound to acknowledge the countenance which you have uniformly given to his holy religion." In response to this curious misstatement of fact—Washington had never testified to a belief in the Christian gospel—the president abandoned his usual ploy of parroting his correspondent's sentiments in his formal reply. In its place, he politely expressed the "unspeakable pleasure" with which he viewed "that harmony and brotherly love which characterizes the clergy of different denominations as well in this, as in other parts of the United States; exhibiting to the world a new and interesting spectacle, at once the pride of our country and the surest basis of universal harmony."

This exchange gained in historical significance by resurfacing in Jefferson's posthumously published *Anas* ("jottings") three decades later, leading to a furious bit of orthodox spin-doctoring to redeem Washington's holy name for Christ. In his entry for February 1, 1800, Jefferson had recorded a story whispered to him by Dr. Benjamin Rush (who shared Jefferson's republican politics but despaired of his dear friend's lack of Christian conviction).

> [Rush] had it from Asa Green, that when the clergy addressed General Washington on his departure from the government, it was observed in their consultation that he had never on any occasions said a word to the public which showed a belief in the Christian

religion and they thought they should so pen their address as to force him at length to declare publicly whether he was a Christian or not. They did so. However, he observed, the old fox was too cunning for them. He answered every article in their address particularly except that, which he passed over without notice.

Jefferson adds that he heard from a dependable Federalist, Gouverneur Morris (who shared Jefferson's skeptical take on Christianity but abhorred his politics), that Washington was no more a believer in Christ than Morris himself was.

Very much alive at the time, Ashbel Green vigorously disputed the Jefferson hearsay. Bishop White backed up his old colleague. Weighing in on the other side, a clergyman who had worked for the Philadelphia Presbytery thirty years before did indeed recall Green telling the group following their meeting with Washington that "the old fox was too cunning for us." Cunning he wasn't, but when it comes to entering the seemingly empty inner sanctum of Washington's theological temple, his private thoughts on religion remain even more elusive than the foxes he once so loved to chase and corner every Mount Vernon Saturday, when he ran with the hounds.

Willing Freedom to His Slaves

Fantasies of retirement and departures from public service found the otherwise prosaic Washington waxing poetic. When a cabal of competing generals were plotting to unhorse him from his command during the darkest days of the Revolution, he wrote the Reverend William Gordon to thank him for his words of warning. "I shall quit the helm with as much satisfaction and retire to a private station with as much content as ever the wearied pilgrim felt upon his safe arrival in the Holy Land or haven of hope." Years later, when Washington took his final military bow and left the field to thunderous applause, he addressed his beloved Lafayette and unveiled the ambitions of a hero who, his duty accomplished, may retire from the world's stage and dwell in peace, beyond demand and without regret, safe within the fortress of his heart.

I am become a private citizen on the banks of the Potomac and under the shadow of my own vine and my own fig tree. Free from the bustle of a camp and the busy scenes of public life, I am solacing myself with those tranquil enjoyments of which the soldier who is ever in pursuit of fame, the statesman whose watchful days and sleepless nights are spent in devising schemes to promote the welfare of his own, perhaps the ruin of other countries (as if this globe was insufficient for us all); and the courtier who is always watching the countenance of his prince, in hopes of catching a gracious smile, can have very little conception. I am not only retired from all public employments, but I am retiring within myself and shall be able to view the solitary walk and tread the paths of private life with heartfelt satisfaction. Envious of none, I am determined to be pleased with all, and this, my dear friend, being the order for my march, I will move gently down the stream of life until I sleep with my fathers.

Unsentimental to a fault, Washington got dewy only when on stage at the close of a scene or in contemplating his Arcadia on the Potomac, for him an earthly paradise and the final destination of his dreams. It was here, to quote a phrase that would echo through his correspondence, that he could contemplate existence "in the calm lights of mild philosophy." If good New England Puritans set their hearts on heaven, praying to escape this earthly prison with their souls unsullied, Washington's ambition was to dress the earth and keep it: to cultivate its fields, harness its rivers, chart its forests, and name as his own as much of its bounty as he could amass. Deemed by Thomas Jefferson the finest horseman in Virginia, he could have imagined no finer accolade.

The problem with sentiment is that it misconstrues reality. Washington couldn't escape the grind of daily performance, nor did he wish to. During his final retirement, if age had finally taken the joy out of hunting and disinclination ended his attendance in church—he worshiped six times during his last three years—Mount Vernon remained a tavern, with Washington entertaining high and low alike with indiscriminate graciousness. He fled the opportunity for introspection by surrounding himself with company and working harder than ever. Plunging into the daily grind of his farm, he wondered aloud whether the next book he would find leisure to read would be the "Doomsday Book."

This not particularly gloomy meditation was interrupted when war clouds from France became visible on the Atlantic horizon. In fulfillment of every retired actor's dream, Washington began receiving calls for an encore. For all his complaining, these summonses were a godsend. He fairly leaped into his old government saddle and became preoccupied by the hundred tasks requisite to cobbling together an army from used parts—assembling his high command, chafing at the incompetence of his successor, and doing everything in his power to get a crisp new uniform ("with cockades and stars for the epaulettes") cut and made to his elaborate specifications. Soon, however, due almost singlehandedly to the prudence and principled obduracy of President John Adams, the war that everyone was waiting for ended before it began. Washington's new uniform never arrived, and within a year he was dead.

On July 9, 1799, five months before he died, Washington completed his Last Will and Testament. "I possess a good and clear estate," he had told his secretary several years before, acknowledging but a single exception that troubled his peace of mind. One matter remained to be addressed, inspired by a motive "more powerful than all the rest": "to liberate a certain species of property which I possess very repugnantly to my own feelings, but which imperious necessity compels, and until I can substitute some other expedient by which expenses not in my power to avoid (however well disposed I may be to do it) can be defrayed." Washington finally felt free to settle the one debit to his character and good name that he still considered open: his obligation to his slaves. "Upon the decease of my wife, it is my will and desire that all the slaves which I hold in *my own right* shall receive their freedom."

Suggesting that liberty was utmost in his mind when he set out to revise his will, Washington prepared a special watermark for that very purpose: His name encircles an image of the goddess of agriculture sitting on a plow; Demeter holds a sprig of laurel in one hand; and, in the other, she holds a staff, atop which rests a liberty cap. Liberty caps were taboo among partisan Federalists, suggesting that the rising antidemocratic tide had not bleached Washington of all his Revolutionary spirit. How much the radical act of liberating his slaves revitalized that spirit we will never know, but the liberty cap on his final watermark offers a tantalizing clue.

To liberate his slaves, Washington had to risk offending the sensibilities of his neighbors and complicate his wife, Martha's, widowhood, which indeed his action did. Given that her life was the only thing standing between them and their freedom, enlightened self-interest or simple fear inspired her to fulfill her husband's mandate to free his slaves—her own remained in bondage—*before* she died, lest she perish prematurely at one of their hands.

Entering the Mansions of Rest

In late September 1799, Washington mused, "I was the *first* and am now the *last* of my father's children by the second marriage who remain. When I shall be called upon to follow them is known only to the giver of life. When the summons comes, I shall endeavor to obey it with a good grace." Less than three months later, in mid-December 1799, the summons came. No clergyman was called; no prayers spoken. Shortly before midnight on December 14, 1799, less than twenty-four hours after the crisis commenced, as he reached to take his own pulse Washington's hand fell from his wrist. His final words, spoken shortly before, sum up a lifetime of dutiful obedience to whatever Providence might hold in store for him: "'Tis well."

According to scripture, on the third day after he died Christ rose from the tomb. Deathly afraid of waking up alive there, Washington made his loved ones promise to wait until the third day following his own death before placing his body in the family vault. His funeral on December 17 was ceremonially grand but liturgically spare. At three o'clock on a gray afternoon, cavalrymen and foot soldiers, musicians "playing a solemn dirge with muffled drums," remnants of the Fairfax clan along with other close neighbors, and sixty aproned Masonic brothers led the entire Mount Vernon household in a procession around the mansion, family members and slaves alike clad entirely in black. Eleven cannons had been carted to Mount Vernon from Alexandria and a schooner lay off shore in the Potomac, from which minute guns made their mournful report. The general's horse, led by two groomsmen, accompanied its master one last time.

In his will, Washington left explicit instructions for his funeral. "It is my express desire that my corpse may be interred in a private manner, without parade or funeral oration," he declared. These dutifully self-deprecating instructions were imperfectly followed. At graveside, the Anglican clergyman who read the service for the dead from the *Book of Common Prayer* added a brief, extemporaneous eulogy. The Masons then took command of the interment and buried their fraternal brother with full honors and due ceremony according to the Masonic rite.

Pews across the nation were draped in black, including the presidential pew at Christ Church in Philadelphia, where "Light-Horse Harry" Lee famously pronounced Washington "first in war, first in peace, and first in the hearts of his countryman." Some three hundred less immortal eulogies would follow, delivered from pulpits and lecterns across the land. Most memorialists built their tributes around the morality and religion paragraph in the Farewell Address, which had come to epitomize Washington's civic creed. "Bind it in your Bible next to the Sermon on the Mount," William Cunningham instructed the citizens of Lunenburg, Massachusetts, "that the

lessons of your two saviors may be read together." Seizing on the former president's death to sound alarms against the double threat that
"irreligion" and "disorder" posed to the "national honor and prosperity," the Reverend Joseph Buckminster, a Congregational clergyman
from Portsmouth, New Hampshire, tidied Washington's Farewell
into an easily remembered syllogism: "Without a prevalence of virtue
republics cannot exist; without religion virtue cannot prevail."

Jedidiah Morse's eulogy testified to the Virginian's hope for
earthly immortality: "He has left behind him, to be transmitted to
posterity, that *good name which is better than precious ointment.*"
While making the best of Washington's silence concerning Christ—
his "secret devotion," Timothy Dwight called it—Morse and Dwight
were both theologically honest enough to celebrate Washington's
"immortal name," not his "immortal soul." This distinction paid
him the honor he sought. During Washington's darkest nights, his
abiding fear was that his name, not his soul, stood in jeopardy.
David Humphreys got it right when he flattered Washington with
the glittering prospect of his fondest dream come true. "And indeed, my dear General, it must be a pleasing reflection to you amid
the tranquil walks of private life to find that history, poetry, painting, & sculpture will vie with each other in consigning your name
to immortality."

All but unnoticed in the sanctimonious din, a singular black eu-
logist played more telling changes on the Washington mystique.
The Reverend Richard Allen was America's most prominent black
clergyman. Preaching to his Philadelphia congregation, the founder
of the African Methodist Episcopal Church pointed out a little
known yet essential fact about the nation's fallen hero. Ratifying the
integrity of his liberation of America by liberating his own slaves,
America's Moses actually lived the role he played to the world's acclaim. Of this man, "who broke the yoke of British burdens 'from
off the neck of the people of this land,'" Allen asked, "by what
name shall we call him who secretly and almost unknown emancipated his 'bondwomen and bondmen,' became to them a father,

and gave them an inheritance?" His answer: "our father and friend." Only by his final act, Allen suggests, did Washington earn full title to being "father of his country."

The most succinct précis of Washington's faith was written half a century after his death by the Reverend Theodore Parker: "He had much of the principle, little of the sentiment of religion." Washington's religious principle came straight from the book, not the Bible but the books of his childhood and young manhood: elementary primers establishing the importance of correct behavior; the canons of Freemasonry, a sacrosanct oral tradition hinting at the building plans of the Great Architect; his favorite play, Addison's *Cato*, which gave him a republican champion after whom to model his civic deeds; and, classical treatises setting forth the austere Stoic morality of ancient Rome. An adage penned by John Randolph, prominent early member of the Virginia aristocracy, might serve as Washington's epitaph: "Life is not so important as the duties of life." Observing that "He was more moral than pious," Theodore Parker was guilty only of understatement.

George Washington may not have been religious in the traditional sense of the word, but he perfected his role to suit the part he believed Providence had appointed for him. He chiseled his character out of ancient marble and, once it was struck, held his pose, winning his countrymen's admiration by never forgetting how he would appear in the mirror of their eyes. One begrudging competitor was not beguiled, however. Near the end of his long, tempestuous life, John Adams wistfully pronounced Washington, if "not the greatest President...the best actor of the presidency that we have ever had."

ACT II

❦

JOHN ADAMS

4

A CHURCHGOING ANIMAL

Mark his majestic fabric; he's a temple
Sacred by birth, and built by hands divine;
His soul's the deity that lodges there;
Nor is the pile unworthy of the god.

—JOHN DRYDEN

AFTER FIRST laying eyes on General Washington, to voice her unqualified awe Abigail Adams drew a John Dryden stanza from her beloved trove of poetry. Her wonderment at this American George who "moved with a grace, dignity, and ease that leaves Royal George far behind" continued unabated for years. When she first dined with "his Majesty" and Lady Washington at the presidential mansion, stars pooled in her eyes. But then, one by one, the stars flickered out. By Washington's death in December 1799, her praise had lost its luster. The words fell into place as she confirmed the nation's loss, but mechanically and edged with understandable resentment that her husband, who was very much alive, seemed more dwarfed by his predecessor's memory than he had been even by his presence.

By the time Washington died, Mrs. Adams had had her fill of divine kingship American style. The national paroxysm over the fall of its godlike leader exhausted her earthly patience. What's more, it offended her religious sensibilities. What irritated her most was the bombast echoing from American pulpits. "Those who deify Washington's character degrade that of their country," she protested. "To no man in America belongs the epithet of Savior."

Fallen back to earth, Mrs. Adams found herself in perfect sync with her self-regarding husband, who so little breathed the incense of Washington idolatry that, midway through the Revolution, he had openly rejoiced at the general's ambivalent war record. Its mediocrity, Adams hoped, would free America to adjudge him "wise, virtuous and good, without thinking him a deity or a savior."

Her own mourning was sincere, Abigail insisted to her sister-in-law, as if trying to convince herself that this was so. Preaching to an almost empty choir, she went on to add an important piece of forgotten civic information: "We ought not to lose sight of the blessings we have enjoyed and still partake of, that he was spared to us, until he saw a successor filling his place, pursuing the same system which he had adopted, and in times which have been equally dangerous and critical."

In one significant respect, her husband didn't, in fact, pursue the same system that Washington had. Drawing on his New England heritage, Adams took the civil religious temple he inherited from George Washington and put a steeple on it. Federal bells began to chime and, just like that, the United States of America became a Christian state.

Christian Governance

John Adams brought to the presidency a set of firm convictions regarding the interdependent relationship of church and state. Three Sundays before the publication of Washington's Farewell Address in September 1796, he returned from church one Sunday to sum up a lifetime's reflection on public faith.

> One great advantage of the Christian religion is that it brings the great principle of the law of nature and nations—love your neighbor as yourself, and do to others as you would have that others should do to you—to the knowledge, belief and veneration of the whole people; children, servants, women, and men are all profes-

sors in the science of public and private morality. No other institution for education, no kind of political discipline could diffuse this kind of necessary information so universally among all ranks and descriptions of citizens. The duties and rights of the man and the citizen are thus taught from early infancy to every creature. The sanctions of a future life are thus added to the observance of civil and political as well as domestic and private duties, prudence, justice, temperance and fortitude are thus taught to be the means and conditions for future as well as present happiness.

Adams codified this approach to Christian governance in the Massachusetts State Constitution in 1780, which he drafted during a three-month hiatus from his diplomatic service in Europe. In good Enlightenment fashion, it opens by shifting the contractual equation from a pact between God and His people (bound by covenant into a Christian commonwealth) to one between the people themselves, joined in "a social compact by which the whole people covenants with each citizen, and each citizen with the whole people, that all shall be governed by certain laws for the common good." But Adams also drew deep from the wellsprings of his New England heritage. While doubting the key tenets of historical Christianity, he embraced the Christian church as a godsend to the state.

In addition to a Christian requirement for state office and provisions to underwrite the church with direct governmental support, in his initial draft Adams insisted that a belief in God, God's government, and "a future state of rewards and punishments" are "the only true foundation of morality." This article prompted heated debate on the convention floor, leading to compromise language, slightly watered down from the author's original. Yet his intent, twice-stated lest anyone miss it, remains: "the happiness of a people and the good order and preservation of civil government essentially depend upon piety, religion, and morality; and...these cannot be generally diffused through a community but by the institution of the public worship of God and of public instruction in piety, religion, and morality."

The final word on Adams's 1780 constitution belonged to Elder John Leland, who deemed it "as good a performance as could be expected in a state where religious bigotry and enthusiasm have been so predominant." The same might be said of Adams's entire public witness on matters of church and state. Until he converted to strict separationism late in life, Adams was doggedly consistent. He believed that the government 1) had no business interfering with people's religious beliefs, and 2) was responsible on a statewide level for supporting the church financially and on a national level for prescribing occasional religious observance as dictated by the commonweal. That these positions might collide seems only to have occurred to him long after it was too late to undo the damage that the accident of their inevitable collision would inflict on his political fortunes.

How did Adams, theologically a unitarian and skeptical toward almost every tenet of orthodox Christianity, come to personify the American religious-political ideal of divine order? The answer, which tests many common assumptions about religion and politics, beats at the heart of this story.

Frigid John Calvin and Hot-Blooded John Adams

Adams is the most vivid American founder. He broods, snorts, and pouts his way into the history books, as critical of his own performance as he is ruthless in his assessment of the world's failure to appreciate it. However complex he may have been, little about him is mysterious. He probed his every thought and act so unguardedly, and with such childlike relish, that those who accept his invitation to view the world as he experienced it may soon know him better than they know themselves. Everything Adams touched bore the imprint of his nature: petty, querulous, rigid, ambitious, vindictive, jealous, and vain; yet also loyal, candid, playful, valiant, indefatigable, curious, and sage. We don't have to guess at these things; we know them, because he invites us to horn in on the lifelong conversation he carried on ostensibly with others but essentially with himself. Adams was nothing if not endlessly fascinated by the stimulating emotional and intellectual contortions of his own tortured company. He said so himself: "When a man is hurt he loves to talk to his wound."

Adams elevated self-scrutiny into an art. His diary ("a self-examination at once severe and stimulative," his son John Quincy called it) drips with Puritan angst. Its earliest entries find him pining over his slacker ways. John procrastinates. John lusts. John drinks and idles away his hours. Ruing three lost days, he summed up the prosecution's case against what was left of his immortal soul: "All spent in absolute idleness or, what is worse, gallanting the girls." A bit of a hypochondriac and a penitent enthusiast for moral perfection, over one eighteen-month stretch he forswore "all meat and spirits and lived upon bread and milk, vegetables and water," only to be reformed to a less presumptuous regimen by his temperate father's ridicule. Nothing he accomplished satisfied him for long: It never would. "What am I doing?" he asked himself impatiently, "Shall I sleep away my whole 70 years?" Half a century later, he pronounced himself guilty of having done precisely that.

Born in 1735 in Braintree, Massachusetts, into the fourth generation of the "sober, industrious, frugal and religious" Adams clan, John grew up on his parents' farm. Deacon John Adams—shoemaker, farmer, and archetypal "churchgoing animal," as his son described New Englanders—was the moral beacon John would ever be guided by. Sternly facing the congregation with eleven other pillars, he presided on the deacons' bench below the pulpit of North Precinct Church and took his regular turn as tithingman, policing local Sabbath day offenders. For one whose guileless ruminations on titles would open him to the charge of being sweet on monarchy, Adams had no taste for luxury and boasted his humble ancestry over the most distinguished lineage. "I should think a descent from a line of virtuous, independent New England farmers for a hundred and sixty years was a better foundation for [pride] than a descent through royal and noble scoundrels ever since the flood," he said. Few could match John's filial piety, but the church stood one rung higher in his hierarchy of values. "What has preserved this race of Adamses in all their ramifications, in such numbers, health, peace, comfort and mediocrity?" he asked, armed as always with a ready answer. "I believe it is religion, without which they would have been rakes, fops, sots, gamblers, starved with hunger, frozen with cold, scalped by Indians, &c., &c., been melted away and disappeared."

Adams even toyed with entering New England's most esteemed vocation, the learned ministry. He certainly was weaned on religion; he learned his ABCs in a primer that ran from "In Adam's fall/We sinned all" to "Zebediah served God." There was only one problem—"Frigid John Calvin" held no allure for hot-blooded John Adams. He nonetheless remained dedicated to the forms and fascinated by the concepts, both moral and theological, of his inherited faith. For every epithet he hurled against dour preachers and hidebound doctrine, the subsequent page in John's diary finds him on bended knee. These entries reflect an attentive, reverent mind, fascinated by metaphysical puzzles and highly susceptible to the blandishments of New England morality.

The light of the stars drew Adams to God, not the logic of Christian theologians, yet he came down adamantly on the Puritan side of the theological ledger in his assessment of human nature. With moral roots twisted deep in New England's rocky soil, Adams viewed natural men and women as creatures of unbridled passion, who must, for their own sakes and the good of society, be protected from themselves and each other. Christianity's purpose was to create not "good riddle solvers or good mystery mongers," he said, but rather, "good men, good magistrates and good subjects, good husbands and good wives, good parents and good children, good masters and good servants." Although he didn't believe in Christ, Adams had an abiding faith in Christendom.

When he moved to Worchester, Massachusetts, after Harvard, John fell in with a clique of aspiring young philosophers ("great readers of Deistical books and very great talkers"). In their company he devoted many an alcohol-drenched hour to poring over "original sin, origin of evil, the plan of the universe." That John found himself defending the church in mixed theological company over a schooner of ale in Worchester's taverns is confirmed by his diary. But his head also nodded in frequent agreement with his skeptical friends. "Mystery is made a convenient cover for absurdity," young Adams groused. "Where do we find a precept in the Gospel requiring Ecclesiastical Synods? Convocations? Councils? Decrees? Creeds? Confessions? Oaths? Subscriptions? And whole cartloads of other trumpery that we find religion encumbered with in these days?"

In Worcester, the word on the street was that Adams was an Arminian. Later popularized by Methodists, Arminianism put moral choice on the theological menu. No longer fated at birth to be saved or damned, on their own volition people could act in a godly manner, resist temptation, and open their hearts to receive God's grace. People also whispered that Adams took his faith on trust from Congregational preacher Jonathan Mayhew. An outspoken champion of liberty, Mayhew challenged the crown and parliament to keep their paws off New England's free institutions. Though perhaps the most radical and independent-minded Boston cleric, Mayhew was not, however, a Deist. He grounded his faith in scripture. But he considered reason a necessary supplement to revelation, found no evidence in the Bible for a triune God, and dismissed many of the fine points of Calvinist theology as slurs against God's loving goodness.

Whether he brought his doubts to Worchester or found them there, Adams fell several tenets short of the basic requirements of

Christian orthodoxy. For starters, he rejected original sin. "To damn the whole human race without any actual crimes committed by any of them" struck him as unworthy of the Deity. The Calvinist doctrine of predestination he also deemed "a strange religious dogma," dismissing it out of hand as "detestable" and "invidious." Electing children to be saved or selecting them to be damned at birth placed the world "under the government of humor or caprice," he said. His liberal critique of Christian doctrine was wide-ranging. The Atonement—"Christ died for our sins"—fit nowhere in Adams's theological lexicon. Later in life, he dismissed Christ's deity as "an awful blasphemy." And, in response to claims that God would not have permitted Christianity to hold sway over human souls for 2,000 years if its teachings were not true, he asked himself, "may not this question be asked of the Mohometan, the Chinese, in short of every religion under the sun, and will not the argument equally prove them all to be true?" He also defended scientific advancements against Christian diehards who believed that vaccination played havoc with God's preordained mortality tables or that the erection of a lightning rod "was an impious attempt to rob the almighty of his thunder, to wrest the bolt of vengeance out of his hand."

For all his irreverent sputtering, Adams was a poster child for the very faith whose tenets he spurned. The Protestant ethic—*all play and no work makes John a damned boy*—was bred in his bone. He didn't think like a true believer but he felt like a true believer. A life-long churchgoing animal like his fathers and mothers before him, to Adams the Bible was the best book in the world and Christianity the one indispensable guarantor of public morality.

Salvation by Martyrdom Alone

Recognizing how poorly her excitable son would fit into the cloth, John's mother agreed that he should hang his shingle elsewhere than above the door of a parsonage. His disappointed father succumbed to the inevitable, and their young man set off in quest of the law. Adams's allergy to dogma is but one part of the story behind his vocational decision. Acquaintances whose praise he lapped up like a puppy flattered his oratorical manner and told him "I should make a better lawyer than divine." Also, the solidly built yet physically far from prepossessing youth (squat and firmly packed, with a plump, round face and beady eyes) must have cringed at the prospect of wearing a dress on Sundays. Contemporary clergymen struck him as "effeminate" and "unmanly." In contrast to the New England clergymen of his acquaintance, the ancestors he worshiped were men of "steady, manly, pertinacious spirit." Manliness to John was next to godliness. Contemplating his forbearers, he obsessed that he had "degenerated from the virtues of the house so far as not to have been an officer in the militia," a blot against his manhood that would haunt him for decades. During his years of service in the Continental Congress, he read deeply in the arts of war and volunteered for every task that had any bearing whatsoever on military preparedness. Hoping to impress Abigail (and convince himself), he styled himself a modern-day Cincinnatus, the very sobriquet his fellow citizens would reserve for the gentleman farmer commanding their armies in the field.

Adams persuaded himself, against already established prejudice, that "The study and practice of the law, I am sure, does not dissolve the obligations of morality or of religion." Once that matter was resolved, the law fit his ambition like a glove. While wistfully peeping up at Washington from his lowly vice-presidential perch, "*Glory*," Adams would muse, "attends the great actions of lawgivers and heroes, and the management of the great commands and first offices of state." Yet, courtesy of his religious upbringing, Adams also knew that the number one sin was pride. "The love of fame naturally betrays a man into several weaknesses and fopperies that tend very much to diminish his reputation, and so defeats itself," he reminded himself. Unlike his Virginian contemporaries, for whom outward appearances were paramount and virtue indistinguishable from public esteem, Adams would never confuse honor with virtue. "If virtue was to be rewarded with wealth, it would not be virtue," he said. "If virtue was to be rewarded with fame, it would not be virtue of the sublimest kind." The only sure guarantor for virtuous felicity was "an habitual contempt of fortune, fame, beauty, praise, and all such things."

Seeking glory while avoiding pride kept Adams slightly off kilter his entire adult life. Yet he was less negligent in his aspirations for glory than the American people would prove to be in satisfying them. Near the height of his political ascent, he offered a clearer peek into the recesses of his soul: "The desire of the esteem of others is as real a want of nature as hunger; and the neglect and contempt of the world as severe a pain as the gout or stone."

The Stamp Act of 1765 established Adams's name and fixed his course. On December 25 that same year, the staccato notes of his diary give voice to a new state of mind: "Christmas. At home. Thinking, reading, searching, concerning taxation without consent." Over the succeeding decade, his life flowed with the political tides out into uncharted waters and then back into the safety of his private haven, where he would vow to remain, only to be shaken from his moorings by a new parliamentary storm. The watershed moment of his legal career fell in 1770, when he boldly defended in court the British officer and soldiers who fired into a boisterous mob with fatal consequence in what colonial propagandists instantly branded "the Boston Massacre." He won both cases, generating a buzz in the legal community without alienating the affections of his cousin Samuel Adams or other leading radicals. A lawyer is duty-bound, he said, "to hold himself responsible not only to his country but to God, the ultimate source of all justice."

The same occasion opens a window on the gnarled workings of Adams's psyche. Inspired by the liniment of his Puritan upbringing and growing naturally out of his penchant for self-scrutiny, Adams permitted himself the luxury of fully crediting his accomplishments only when a whiff of martyrdom was attached to them. Magnifying his sacrifice at the time and squaring it again years later in his *Autobiography,* he reckoned the cost he paid for his defense of the British soldiers with mathematical grandiosity. He had hazarded, Adams recalled, "a popularity very general and very hardly earned, incurring a clamor and popular suspicions and prejudices, which are not yet worn out and never will be forgotten as long as [the] history of this period is read."

The martyr's role that Adams found so becoming to his rectitude was less evident to his constituents. For all his talk of the people's obloquy, six months later the town of Boston elected him to the legislature by a 4-to-1 margin, honoring him with 418 of 536 votes cast. If anything, his sacrificial defense of the soldiers added to his stature as a leading citizen. The radicals didn't shun him. On the contrary, they sought his advice and assistance more assiduously.

For all their many differences, the contrasting ways in which Washington and Adams rationalized their ambition distinguish them more clearly than perhaps any other. Both men sacrificed to serve their country and each was obsessed by his reputation. "Reputation ought to be the perpetual subject of my thoughts and aim of my behavior," Adams reminded himself at the outset of his career. "How shall I gain a reputation! How shall I spread an opinion of myself as a lawyer of distinguished genius, learning, and virtue?" The conundrum he faced, which wouldn't have occurred to Washington, arose from a moral suspicion of popularity and a wariness of his motivations in seeking it. The tension between ambition and pride would never cease to bedevil Adams. Ultimately he inverted this conundrum into a masochistic paradox: He could take honest pride only in abasement. In good Virginia fashion, Washington won honor by doing his duty, in order to enhance his good name. Adams's name was not secure (in his own eyes and, by extension, the eyes of God) unless trampled almost beyond recognition by the ungrateful mob. To shine on the inside Washington had to shine on the outside. With profound consequence to their respective spiritual complexions, in this regard Adams was Washington's ideal opposite. He couldn't be certain he had acted with integrity until he lost every-thing in exchange for doing what was right. For his conscience to be clear, he had to convince himself and posterity that he not only risked but also immolated his reputation on the pyre of justice and truth.

Adams summed up half a century of political wars by saying, "I have constantly lived in an enemies' country." With fateful conse-quence to American sacred politics, he thrived, and only thrived, on opposition, even to the point of exaggerating it in order to rouse himself from his imagined torpor into concerted action. "The times alone have destined me to fame," he said at the end of his political life, "and even these have not been able to give me much. Yet some great events, some cutting expressions, some mean hypocrisies have at times thrown this assemblage of sloth, sleep and littleness into rage a little like a lion."

The Perfect Soul Mate

If he was seeking a true biblical "helpmeet," in Abigail Smith John made the perfect match. Abigail grew up in the parsonage of the North Church Parish in Weymouth, Massachusetts, where her fa-ther, the Reverend William Smith, served for almost half a century. Under the kind, strict tutelage of her nondoctrinaire but conven-tionally pious, Harvard-educated father and strong, nurturing mother, Elizabeth Quincy (the granddaughter of two clergymen and born into one of Boston's first families), she developed into an opinionated yet obedient, well-read yet devout young woman. In-dependent by nature and nurtured by the deferential Puritan ethos of her upbringing, she mirrored John's dual nature as a liberty-loving traditionalist, at once open-minded and moralistic, free-spirited but also easily discomfited by the slightest blush of moral chaos.

In his diary, John boasted that "thinking women" caught his fancy, in particular those well enough versed in the classics to ask such important questions as "What do you think of Hector?" He met his wish and more by marrying Abigail. She would famously hector her important husband to "Remember the ladies" as he was designing a new government; observe that "No man ever prospered in the world without the consent and cooperation of his wife"; and have her prestigious family coat of arms painted on the door of their coach when he became president. For his part, John forgot the ladies, luxuriated and languished alike while brooding through his days, and "totally obliterated" her presumptuous handiwork from their carriage door. As dedicated to order as her husband was, Abigail would forget the ladies, too, as she and her husband bridled together at the prospect of permanent rebellion. At the slightest hint of democratic presumption, she reverted to as prim a stance toward the gospel of social equality as her husband held. The government's rein had been "so long slackened," Abigail said, "that I fear the people will not quietly submit to those restraints which are necessary for the peace and security of the community."

For John and Abigail alike, morality without religion was inconceivable. Describing "Religion as the most perfect system, and the most awful sanction of morality," he told her, "I have no confidence in any man who is not exact in his morals." The pair also shared the same prejudices. Neither harbored much sympathy for Jews or Roman Catholics. John thought nothing of describing an acquaintance as "a perfect viper, a fiend, a Jew, a devil," and dismissed Catholics as "poor wretches, fingering their beads." Initially at least, their bigotry grew out of almost complete ignorance. "A native of America who cannot read and write is as rare an appearance as a Jacobite or a Roman Catholic, that is, as rare as a comet or an earthquake," Adams stated with characteristic certitude in his first major work. His attitude toward Quakers—"dull as beetles," he called them—which Abigail would adopt, was more an acquired prejudice, dating from his years in Philadelphia. Both partners most knowingly disdained a religious type with which they were all too familiar: the disputatious, fulminating, censorious Puritan divine.

"Deliver me from your cold phlegmatic preachers, politicians, friends, lovers and husbands," Abigail teased her husband.

With respect to the preachers, at least, he was able to oblige. He had no more patience than she did for ministers, "whose noise and vehemence is to compensate for every other deficiency." The clergymen Adams did admire were religious liberals with a low Christology and a high regard for public virtue. Theologically most comfortable just within the outer fences of the established Massachusetts Standing Order of Congregational Churches (somewhere in the left forty where his mind could wander free from the constraints of dogma), he gravitated naturally to the Brattle Street Meeting House, where the theatrical pulpiteer, Samuel Cooper, would remind his congregants on a weekly basis that God had called them unto liberty. He also frequented Boston's First Church, whose stout, formidable pastor Charles Chauncey was laying the foundation for the rational Unitarian faith that a mature Adams would embrace as the most sensible approach to the cosmic mystery. Some Sundays he caught both preachers in action, on one occasion pondering Chauncey's morning disquisition on righteousness and later that afternoon admiring Cooper pronouncing "harmoniously upon the deceitfulness of sin."

Adams was a preacher's dream. He went home after services, pondered the sermons he had heard, and examined the state of his soul. On any given Sunday, he could decode the logic of two well-crafted hour-long sermons with the same delight that Washington derived from a perfect Saturday afternoon on horseback chasing down a cagey fox.

Religion and Politics in Philadelphia

When he went to Philadelphia to join the Continental Congress, Adams remained a churchgoing animal. He championed national fasts and thanksgivings and served on the three-man committee that drafted language for the first such proclamation. He also kept his eye out for religion when he drew up the Naval code.

Religion was to blame for the first congressional tussle. Speaking to the proposal to hire a chaplain, the correct Anglican John Jay argued that "we were so divided in religious sentiments, some Episcopalians, some Quakers, some Anabaptists, some Presbyterians, and some Congregationalists" that to "join in the same act of worship" would simply be "impossible." What Jay found impossible got easier to envision when the Massachusetts delegation, who were Congregationalist to a man, floated an Anglican cleric's name for the chaplaincy position. With the encouragement of Benjamin Franklin—he cared too little about religion to get agitated over who should do the praying—and a generous second from the strict Puritan Samuel Adams, Congress invited the Reverend Jacob Duché, assistant rector of Christ Church in Philadelphia, to consecrate its deliberations. Intoning the Thirty-fifth Psalm, a befitting collect for the day that Adams first thought a happy "accident" before quickly correcting himself by deeming it "providential," Duché girded the loins of this legislative David to face the mighty Goliath, Great Britain.

> Plead my cause, O LORD, with them that strive with me:
> Fight against them that fight against me.
> Take hold of shield and buckler,
> and stand up for mine help.
> Draw out also the spear,
> and stop the way against them that persecute me:
> Say unto my soul, I am thy salvation.

The Reverend Duché followed this politically correct psalm with a prayer that launched Adams's soul into orbit. "Go on, ye chosen band of Christians," the soon-to-be-elected chaplain commissioned his employers. Adams then knew that his mission must be blessed. "Dr. Cooper himself never prayed with such fervor, such ardor, such earnestness, and pathos, and in language so elegant and sublime, for America, for the Congress, for the Province of Massachusetts Bay, and especially for the town of Boston," Adams breathlessly reported home. "It had an excellent effect upon everybody here." Shortly thereafter, Congress's godsend was ruing the war as a national punishment for national guilt—Calvinist words in the mouth of an Anglican priest that took on political portent when he showed his true colors two years later and defected to the crown.

On balance, Duché's story is one familiar to Anglican divines during the Revolution. Caught between conflicting loyalties, they would finesse their ongoing Christian responsibilities as best they could until events forced them to betray either their country or their church. In Virginia, twenty of some one hundred Virginia Anglican ministers remained loyal to Canterbury and the crown. If this "zealous friend of liberty," as Adams first described him, was now "an apostate and a traitor," Duché was an apostate in the political sense only, a distinction that forever will complicate the calculus of sacred politics.

A letter from Philadelphia's six Anglican ministers to the Bishop of London in June 1775 dramatically underscored the political bind that hamstrung the Anglican priesthood. "Our people call on us and think they have a right to our advice in the most public manner from the pulpit," they explained. "Should we refuse, our principles would be misrepresented and even our religious usefulness destroyed among our people." Avowing themselves "His Majesty's most dutiful and loyal subjects in this and every other transaction of our lives," the clerics nonetheless conceded that "our consciences would not permit us to injure the rights of the [colonies]." Upon Duché's defection, William White was named rector of Christ Church and St. Peter's. "I continued, as did all of us," White remembered, "to pray for the King, until Sunday before the 4th of July, 1776."

When clergymen began doing the nation's business, not simply praying over it, Adams expressed his patent skepticism. The Reverend John Zubly, a Georgia Presbyterian émigré from Switzerland, was "the first gentleman of the cloth who has appeared in Congress," he reported to Abigail. "I cannot but wish he may be the last." Not until the Reverend John Witherspoon of Princeton arrived would a minister stand as tall in the chambers of government as he did in the pulpit.

Adams Takes on the Baptists

Adams viewed state religion in modern Massachusetts as the epitome of enlightened toleration. The doughty Baptist church historian Isaac Backus disagreed. A *Mayflower* descendent born in Norwich, Connecticut, in 1724, Backus served his Middleborough, Massachusetts, parish for sixty years until his death in 1806. Over the half-century span of his ministry, he reckoned that he had traveled some 70,000 miles, taking nearly a thousand trips of ten miles or more on horseback, a reminder that the term "circuit rider" can be taken literally. Backus was a prepossessing figure, with the muscular build of a yeoman farmer and endowed with a toughness that would serve him well throughout a lifetime of combat on behalf of religious freedom. Throughout the early years of his ministry, his congregants were fined, whipped, and jailed repeatedly by the Commonwealth of Massachusetts for faith-related offenses. Backus took his turn behind bars for refusing to pay the annual assessment imposed to support the established Congregational clergy. He was also a fine scholar, served as trustee of the Baptist College of Rhode Island (now Brown University), and was a delegate to the Massachusetts Ratifying Convention. The scriptures convinced Backus that Christ's Kingdom is not of this world. America could never become a Christian nation until full religious freedom was secured.

Backus championed the American Revolution, which he hailed as "the new Reformation." Yet, as a Baptist lobbyist, pestering first the authorities in London and then those in Philadelphia, he petitioned for his people's rights. The crown proved sympathetic, but at home Backus met with a chorus of patriotic jeers. How dare he petition the king to reform American laws, people asked? Backus replied bluntly. If you chafe at a three-pence tax on tea, he argued, you can free yourself from its burden by drinking something else. But if you chafe at a state assessment to support a church establishment whose tenets you don't share, you can't salve your conscience without sacrificing the freedom of your soul. Branded a traitor, Backus remained unrepentant. A cry went up to send him to the gallows.

Undeterred from his mission, in the fall of 1774 Reverend Backus conspired with the Philadelphia Quakers to win an audience with members of the Massachusetts congressional delegation. Adams recalled this encounter as a trap, a religious conspiracy designed to embarrass the Massachusetts delegates, which in part it surely was. The Quakers and Anabaptists were natural allies in the struggle for religious freedom. Both had long been persecuted by state church authorities for their faith, with Quakers put to death and Baptists banished from Massachusetts in the early days of the settlement. Rhode Island and Pennsylvania, the colonies founded under Baptist and Quaker auspices, sanctioned full religious liberty, a struggle their coreligionists were still fighting in the Bay Colony.

Called without stated pretext, Adams arrived at Carpenters' Hall early in the evening of October 14 to be greeted by Backus and a Quaker tribunal. Complaints, they charged, had been raised by "some Anabaptists and some Friends in Massachusetts against certain laws of that province restrictive of the liberty of conscience, and some instances were mentioned in the General Court and in the Courts of Justice, in which Friends and Baptists had been grievously oppressed." Adams suspected that the Quakers—they were not only pacifists but also, in many instances, pro-British—had seized on this pretext to provoke sectarian infighting and thereby forestall the gathering revolutionary storm.

Adams was practiced at defending his colony for its imputed religious sins. Exacerbating matters, he excused his Puritan ancestors for hanging Quakers. "The very existence of the colony was at that time at stake," he gamely explained, "surrounded with Indians at war, against whom they could not have defended the colony, if the Quakers had been permitted to go on." How nonplussed his Quaker auditors were by this specious argument is easy to imagine, but Adams was not about to be distracted by another man's religious scruples, not in times like these. Unless they could be employed against the crown, the niceties of complete religious freedom were luxuries too costly for his already overtaxed attentions.

Adams wouldn't forget the Quakers' cheek, on this occasion or any other. His acquired animus may help explain the sneer Senator Maclay observed on the vice president's face when the Society of Friends presented their petition on slavery to the Senate. Later, though a majority of Quakers likely supported him in his campaigns against Jefferson, he nonetheless nursed a grudge against those who did not, grumbling in his *Autobiography* that in "the late elections for president, some of the Quakers were heard to say, 'Friend, thee must know that we don't much affect the name of Adams.'"

During the 1774 Philadelphia meeting, after the Quakers presented their brief demanding that Massachusetts Friends and Baptists be placed on the same legal and financial footing with their privileged Congregational neighbors, Backus stood to address the defendants. He doubtless posed the question, as he would later that year before the Massachusetts Provincial Assembly, "Is not all America now appealing to Heaven against the injustice of being taxed where we are not represented?" Adams, already apoplectic at being baited into a trap, informed his nettlesome constituent that he could expect the heavenly bodies to spin out of their orbits before Massachusetts would strip the Standing Order of its historic privileges.

Shortly thereafter, Adams did drop into a local Baptist church for worship. The preacher, he told Abigail, was uncouth. All he could think of was how surpassingly excellent the Massachusetts preachers were, apparently forgetting that Backus, endowed with a

New England pedigree more venerable than Adams's own, also called Massachusetts home.

Strange Revolutionary Bedfellows

In Philadelphia, the productive alliance between Puritan Massachusetts and Cavalier Virginia—the nation's two largest states led the fight for independence—made for mixed company. Adams viewed his fellow Massachusetts stalwarts as the true revolutionary party, more egalitarian and therefore better suited to republican rebellion than the aristocratic Virginians could ever be. The southern planters were "habituated to higher notions of themselves and the distinction between them and the common people than we are," he said. "This inequality of property gives an aristocratical turn to all their proceedings."

Adams freely acknowledged his bias. Home, church, and family, he told Abigail, are "often so powerful as to become partial, to blind our eyes, to darken our understandings and pervert our wills. It is to this infirmity in my own heart that I must perhaps attribute that local attachment, that partial fondness, that overweening prejudice in favor of New England which I feel very often, and which, I fear, sometimes leads me to expose myself to just ridicule."

That history would cast Adams as an aristocratic apologist and Jefferson as a republican hero would become his life's most perplexing irony, but it unfolded naturally. The deferential religious culture in which he was raised shaped Adams's penchant for order as profoundly as Jefferson's Enlightenment faith infused his lordly existence with a passion for liberty. Remove faith from the equation and, in the political wars of the 1790s, Adams might well have been manning the siege engines while Jefferson pulled up his drawbridge. As it was, within a decade the son of a farmer and shoemaker was defending the sanctity of hierarchical government while the scion of privilege was waving a proverbial pitchfork.

In the halls of Congress, Adams found Jefferson's posture toward

Christianity inconceivably irreverent. On one occasion, the two men got into a spat over whether Congress should hold Sunday sessions. Jefferson argued (in hushed words, as always, for when he raised his voice, it disappeared) that scruples against work on the Sabbath day were antiquated. Adams shot to his feet to trumpet his astonishment at this impiety. He was "sorry to hear such sentiments from a gentleman whom [he] so highly respected and with whom [he] agreed on so many subjects, and that was the only instance [he] had ever known of a man of sound sense and real genius that was an enemy of Christianity." According to their mutual confidant, Dr. Benjamin Rush, having witnessed to his faith Adams at once began to fret. Had his forwardness in branding Jefferson an infidel cost him a friend? A bit later, Jefferson shambled over and slouched amiably into the seat next to his, assuaging Adams's fears.

No record remains of Adams's celebrated speech that sealed the case for rebellion three days before the storied Fourth of July, 1776. He recalled being "'carried out in spirit,' as enthusiastic preachers sometimes express themselves." It should have remained in common memory as his proudest hour. But it did not. At Adams's own behest, it was Jefferson who would commemorate the occasion with the words posterity would remember. When Congress published the Declaration of Independence on July 8, "the bells rang all day and almost all night," Adams reported to Abigail. "Even the chimes chimed away." Those same bells would peal again to commemorate the fiftieth anniversary of independence on the day both men died, one half forgotten, the other an American icon.

"They Do Not Believe in Christianity"

In February 1778, with eleven-year-old John Quincy in tow, Adams sailed for Europe. Although he took every honey-coated compliment at face value—the Spanish ambassador made his day by calling him "Le Washington de la Negotiation"—Adams clocked eight mostly miserable years as an American diplomat. Most depressing of all was the state of the American diplomatic corps, to Adams's mind a revolving circle of egoists placing knives in each other's backs.

His greatest disappointment was the celebrated dean of American diplomacy. By his moralistic estimation, old Benjamin Franklin (charming, secretive, exasperating, and, not infrequently, effective) had, morally at least, all but gone over to the dark side. "The falsest character I have ever met with in life," Adams called him. While begrudgingly acknowledging his famed superior's shimmering talents, he saw clearly only Franklin's turpitude. To languish in the shadow of a man who appeared to have broken at least nine of the Ten Commandments added richly to Adams's martyrology. While forced to concede that his "fulsome and sickish" charm worked the occasional diplomatic miracle, "The life of Dr. Franklin was a scene of continual dissipation," he glowered. "[His] very statue seems to gloat on the wenches as they walk the State House yard."

As little as there was to do during long stretches of his exile, Adams viewed himself as doing nearly all of it, while receiving none of the credit and most of the blame. Alternating between bouts of mental and physical exhaustion, for months at a stretch he cut off everyone, including Abigail. She cajoled, begged, prayed for, and finally demanded his attentions. "For God's sake, never reproach me again with not writing," he exploded. "Your wounds are too deep." For all his accomplishments (securing loans from the Dutch, protecting New England fisheries in peace negotiations with the British), if ever Adams's pertinacious spirit was in danger of being broken, it was during the six years when he and Abigail were separated. Barring one three-month visit home, John was left, save for the lifesaving presence of young John Quincy, with no company he trusted, including his own. "I believe I am grown more austere, severe, rigid and miserable than ever I was," he reported to Abigail, which was scarcely news to her.

He thought he found a worthy friend when Jefferson joined him in France. By all accounts, the two men got on famously. Adams gave his heart to Jefferson. Though never less than gracious, Jefferson guarded his own affections more closely. His colleague's behavior bewildered him. "He hates Franklin, he hates Jay, he hates the French, he hates the English. To whom will he adhere?" Jefferson wondered aloud to Madison. "His vanity is a lineament in his character which had entirely escaped me. His want of taste I had observed. Notwithstanding all this," Jefferson was forced to admit, "he has a sound head on substantial points, and I think he has integrity."

Over time Jefferson grew fonder of Adams, and even more so of his wife. When they packed off for London, in a rare display of unvarnished sentiment he confessed, "The departure of your family has left me in the dumps." He maintained the friendship from afar, especially with Abigail, procuring her silk stockings (exquisitely woven by a French order of hermits) and, with express inadequacy, shopping for corsets for Nabby, their teenage daughter. After seven weeks at Adams's side in Paris and as many in London, Jefferson penned a fair assessment of his New England colleague. "He is vain, irritable and a bad calculator of the force and probable effect of the motives which govern men," he reported to Madison, quickly adding, "This is all the ill which can possibly be said of him. He is as disinterested as the being which made him; he is profound in his views; and accurate in his judgment except where knowledge of the world is necessary to form a judgment. He is so amiable that I pronounce you will love him if ever you become acquainted with him." But Madison despised Adams on making his acquaintance, and Jefferson's affections soon cooled. From that date forward until they reconciled three decades later, Adams and Jefferson, different by almost every measure, would fatefully grow ever more estranged.

When Abigail joined him in France, John took furlough from his sacrificial existence. She balanced his mood swings, gave balm to his wounds by honoring their significance, and offered instant gratification to his prejudices. Before long she, too, was merrily skewering Franklin and his grandson, William Temple Franklin (illegitimate son of Franklin's illegitimate son, William), as "wicked unprincipled debauched wretches, from the old deceiver down to the young cockatrice." Abigail was at once shocked and titillated by the French. "To be out of fashion," she confided to her sister Mary, "is more criminal than to be seen in a state of nature, to which the Parisians are not averse." She blushed at the exposed garters and diaphanous costumes on wanton display at the theater and then rushed back for another peek. Her moral critique extended well beyond fascinated prudery. She also visited the orphanages of Paris. Half the children in the city were born out of wedlock. Writing home, she memorialized her Christian compassion in verse: "Where can they hope for pity, peace or rest/Who move no softness in a parent's breast?"

One day she and Nabby accompanied Jefferson to the convent where, to Abigail's horror, he was educating his daughters. The occasion, a ceremony in which postulants rose to the status of novitiates, replete with head shaving, prostration, and the sprinkling of holy water, was affecting and chilling, a fair summation of her take on European Catholicism in general. Jefferson boasted highly of the convent school until his elder daughter, Patsy, announced suddenly that she had decided to become a nun. Without a moment's hesitation, her father plucked her from school and swept her home in his phaeton.

Adams pondered the state of religion in the old countries with fascination and horror. He was appalled at the wealth of the Catholic Church. No less offensive to his Puritan sensibilities, libertinism ran rampant among the soulless French elite. Agape at one unembarrassed French *ménage à quatre,* as bereft of "the delightful enjoyments of conscious innocence" as it was rife with "mere brutal pleasure," he confessed himself "astonished that these people could live together in such apparent friendship and indeed without cutting each other's throats." When sin and religion met, Adams lost what little patience he possessed for behavior less regular than his own. At a bishop who openly kept a mistress ("with some compensation to the husband") and the private abbess who domiciled lavishly under noble sponsorship, he took justifiable umbrage.

> These ecclesiastics, one or more of whom reside in almost every family of distinction, I suppose have as much power to pardon a sin as they have to commit one or to assist in committing one. Oh Mores! said I to myself. What absurdities, inconsistencies, distractions and horrors would these manners introduce into our republican governments in America. No kind of republican government can ever exist with such national manners as these. *Cavete Americani.*

In London, Abigail found the churches large yet crowded and was surprised to discover how faithfully the people there honored the Sabbath. John gravitated naturally toward the Unitarian pulpits of Joseph Priestley and Richard Price, each a prominent friend of the American Revolution. Both men would play bit roles as ex-friends in future Adams melodramas: the scientist and theologian Priestley as a candidate for prosecution under the Alien and Sedition Acts; the philosopher and political scientist Price as one of several apologists for the French Revolution whose naïveté Adams demolished in his little-read, three-volume masterwork, *Defense of the Constitutions of Government of the United States of America.* Having first admired and then deplored both men, he arrived at a more balanced assessment late in life: "Price and Priestley were honest enthusiasts carried away by the popular contagion of the times."

Adams's conservative philosophy matured in counterpoint with the French Revolution. Part of his critique was religious in nature. In his view, by supplanting the worship of God with the worship of humanity, the reigning *philosophes* were lowering humanity, not uplifting it. "Is there a possibility that the government of nations may fall into the hands of men who teach the most disconsolate of all creeds, that men are but fireflies, and that this all is without a father?" he asked. "Is this the way to make man, as man, an object of respect? Or is it to make murder itself as indifferent as shooting a plover?" He summed up his fears for a godless America by quoting an old duchess he met in France before the terror swept away her family: "They do not believe in Christianity, but they believe in every conceivable foolishness."

As his revolutionary contemporaries were tearing down old castles and the French *philosophes* were busy building new ones in the clouds, Adams sketched blueprints for an enduring republic. Good government comes in many forms, he concluded; there are good and bad monarchies, even as there are good and bad republics. The best government is one that "produces a love of law, liberty, and country, instead of disorder, irregularity, and...faction," he wrote in *Defense of the Constitutions*. Adams never lost his faith in liberty; he conditioned it, however, on strong governmental authority. Jefferson identified liberty with the restraint of power; for Adams, liberty hinged on power. To abrogate power was to sacrifice liberty to the circling vultures of tyranny that prey on disorder. Like New England's Black Regiment, Adams viewed the Revolution as a Restoration. Lending his authority to this interpretation, in an early edition of his famous dictionary, Noah Webster, like Adams a New Englander protective of the church's governmental prerogatives, offered as an alternative definition for the word *revolution:* "the restoration of the constitution to its primitive state."

"Order Is Heaven's First Law"

When Adams returned to the United States after eight years abroad in the diplomatic corps, critics like William Maclay were quick to observe that the courts of Europe had corrupted him. He did, in fact, develop a taste for royal ceremony while living in Paris and London. Reflecting on rites he had admired at the Palace of Versailles, he confessed, "These ceremonies and shows may be condemned by philosophy and ridiculed by comedy with great reason," and yet, not only did people welcome them, he argued, but their elevating grandeur, in marked contrast with the leveling principles of democracy, could uplift, even save, lost souls. Public ceremony emits "a degree of sublimity and pathos which has frequently transported the greatest infidels out of themselves," Adams fancifully maintained long after the Puritan battle for America's soul appeared to have been lost.

After his comical reappearance in the Senate as the new government's self-appointed protocol officer, Vice President Adams found himself cast in the familiar role of martyr. Spurred into literary combat by the catcalls that greeted his campaign for titles, he cranked out, periodically, an intemperate philosophy of government with the arcane, if accurate, title *Discourses on Davila*. Even as his enemies—the list grew daily—were worshiping at the shrines of democracy, reason, and progress, Adams, in *Davila* (based on the writings of an obscure Renaissance historian), set out to correct their flawed assumptions. He drew his epigraph for *Davila*'s tenth installment from Alexander Pope's "Essay on Man": "Order is heaven's first law."

That *Davila* offended Jefferson and his Republican following is scarcely surprising. Placing the two men firmly on opposite sides of the great divide between divine order and sacred liberty, in its pages Adams dismissed reason, liberty, and the pursuit of happiness as bromides. "This world was not designed for a lasting and a happy state, but rather for a state of moral discipline," he wrote as a young man. That early insight had now forged itself into a creed. Spelled out in *Davila,* the same hard-edged view of human nature surfaced to mock every ideal that the doctrinaire Virginian held sacred.

The world grows more enlightened. Knowledge is more equally diffused. Newspapers, magazines, and circulating libraries are making mankind wiser. Titles and distinctions, ranks and order, parade and ceremony, are all going out of fashion. This is roundly and frequently asserted in the streets, and sometimes on theaters of higher rank. Some truth is in it.... But, on the other hand, false inferences may be drawn from it, which may make mankind wish for the age of dragons, giants, and fairies. If all decorum, discipline, and subordination are to be destroyed, and...anarchy and insecurity of property are to be introduced, nations will soon wish their books in ashes, seek for darkness and ignorance, superstition and fanaticism, as blessings, and follow the standard of the first mad despot, who, with the enthusiasm of another Mahomet, will endeavor to obtain them.

In a republic where "limited monarchy," which Adams fondly touted, was an oxymoron, the conclusions he drew in *Davila*—aristocracy is essential and inevitable and social inequality not a problem, but rather the only possible solution for a stable state—were anathema.

Mrs. Adams summed up her partner's temperament with admirable concision: "Beds of roses have never been his destiny." On returning to the United States and arriving in New York to assume his vice-presidential perch, Adams nonetheless settled comfortably into the next closest thing, an Episcopal pew. (Back home in Massachusetts, he still worshiped in his ancestral meetinghouse, a mainstream Congregational church that would become more liberal over the years, affiliating with the Unitarians when the two Congregational factions split after the War of 1812.) At the time, the leading Puritan churches in New York were Presbyterian. "There is something more cheerful and comfortable in an Episcopalian than in a Presbyterian Church," he said. "It is very humane and benevolent, and sometimes...affecting: but rarely gloomy, if ever." John's beliefs were no longer those of his parents. He had long since translated his Calvinist inheritance from his religion to his politics.

About his choice of churches, his wife couldn't agree more. When the two took up residency in New York in 1789, Abigail—who freely acknowledged, "I am not made of a gloomy nature"—could not abide the local Calvinist clerics. Preferring "liberal good sense...true piety without enthusiasm, devotion without grimace, and religion upon a rational system," she railed at the preachers' "solemn phiz and gait...flaming, loud speaking, working themselves up into such an enthusiasm as to cry." And so it was that at least two true-blue New England churchgoing animals found themselves worshiping with President and Lady Washington in the high Episcopal pews of St. Paul's Chapel and Trinity Church.

BLACK COCKADES AND TRICOLORS

So shall our nation, form'd on Virtue's plan
Remain the Guardian of the Rights of Man.

—PHILIP FRENEAU,
"ON MR. PAINE'S RIGHTS OF MAN"

In vain thro' realms of nonsense ran
The great Clodhopping oracle of man.

—TIMOTHY DWIGHT,
"THE TRIUMPH OF INFIDELITY"

WHEN PRESIDENT-ELECT John Adams rolled into Phila-delphia in March 1797, one local broadsheet fifed his arrival with the mocking headline TRIUMPHAL ENTRY OF HIS SERENE HIGH-NESS OF BRAINTREE INTO THE CAPITAL. Even this tribute would have been denied him, if one electoral vote in Virginia and another in North Carolina had flipped to Jefferson in the coin toss of the 1796 election. "I am heir apparent, you know," John told Abigail, yet the heir's victory over Jefferson was so breathtakingly close that appear-ances came within a whisker of being upset by reality. In one of his-tory's small ironies, under the yet to be amended Constitution Jefferson's second-place finish made him Adams's vice president.

As the election hung in doubt, John bravely told Abigail, "I have a pious and a philosophical resignation to the voice of the people,...which is the voice of God." Yet even as he parroted, oddly, the Jeffersonian adage of the hour, he doubted his own words. "*Vox populi vox dei,* they say, and so it is sometimes, but it is sometimes the voice of Mohamet, of Caesar, of Catiline, the Pope and the Devil." John Jay put the case against popular democracy in a nutshell: "The wise and the good never form the majority of any large society, and it seldom happens that their measures are uniformly adopted." Adams agreed. "If the majority is 51 and the minority 49, is it certainly the voice of God?" he asked. "If tomorrow one should change to 50 vs. 50, where is the voice of God? If two and the minority should become the majority, is the voice of God changed?" Adams's God was anything but a majoritarian. On reading Rousseau's boast that "The general will is always for the party which is most favorable to the common good," he sniffed, "The majority is not so fond of justice."

With but a few exceptions (politicians, journalists, and the regrouping Black Regiment among them), most of America was paying so little attention to the 1796 presidential election that the voice of God could barely be discerned. The Republican *Aurora* made the choice easy for any interested voter: People could support either "the uniform advocate of equal rights among citizens [Jefferson]" or "the champion of rank, titles, and hereditary distinctions [Adams]." On the other side of the aisle, Federalist preachers found an apt text in Exodus 18:21: "Thou shalt provide out of all the people able men, such as fear God."

Of his formal procession into office, despite marching down the path cast by his predecessor's long shadow, Adams proudly observed, "The sight of the sun setting full orbit and another rising no less splendid was a novelty." The president-elect didn't do himself any favors by wearing an oyster gray, unornamented broadcloth suit and buckleless shoes. Next to Washington in his shimmering black velvet formalwear, Adams looked like a retainer.

From afar, Mrs. Adams blessed her agitated husband with a solemn prayer. "You have this day to declare yourself head of a nation," she wrote. Then she cracked open her Bible to the third chapter of the Book of Kings to anoint John with scriptural balm.

"And now, O Lord, my God, thou has made thy servant ruler over the people. Give unto him an understanding heart, that he may know how to go out and come in before this great people; that he may discern between good and bad. For who is able to judge this thy so great a people?" These, she reminded John, "were the words of a royal sovereign [Solomon]; and not less applicable to him who is invested with the chief majestracy of a nation, tho he wear not the crown nor the robes of royalty."

In one variation from young custom, the sixty-one-year-old president-elect delivered his inaugural address before taking the oath of office. Being practiced in forensic oratory, Adams was in his element. His formal prose, in contrast to his ebullient epistolary style, was tortuous as always. But unlike Washington, who plodded, Jefferson who whispered, and Madison who mumbled their way through their public addresses, Adams possessed the stamina and zeal of a public defender. He might easily have wowed his audience completely if a severe case of pyorrhea contracted five years before had not deprived him of several teeth and left him, though still eloquent, with a noticeable lisp and the tendency to whistle when he spoke. By any fair measure, however, he put in a solid performance, presenting the joint session of Congress with sturdy Federalist doctrine indistinguishable from his predecessor's and displaying a respect for the Constitution and nonbelligerent tone that temporarily assuaged Republican skeptics.

Little of substance distinguished Adams's inaugural address from his predecessor's, save one small but not insignificant innovation. After roundly condemning "the spirit of party" and just before his generic Washingtonian closing prayer for the protection of Providence, Adams capped off a three-minute sentence (the longest in inaugural history) by professing his faith. "I feel it my duty to add," he declared, "if a veneration for the religion of a people who profess and call themselves Christians, and a fixed resolution to consider a decent respect for Christianity among the best recommendations for the public service, can enable me in any degree to comply with your wishes, it shall be my strenuous endeavor that this sagacious injunction of the two Houses shall not be without effect." Unlike Washington, whose formalistic nods to Providence were sincere but cool, Adams was speaking from the heart. He told himself that the nation's second president "must be armed, as Washington was, by integrity, by firmness, by intrepidity—these must be his shield and his wall of brass—and with religion, too, or he will never be able to stand sure and steadfast." Adams could offer at least one thing that his stately predecessor lacked. He carried with him to the presidential office the sword of faith.

Their new president's Christian solidarity did not pass unnoticed by the clergy. The Reverend Joseph Lathrop spoke for the entire Black Regiment when he extolled Adams for the openness with which he testified: "It is a happiness, especially at a time like this, that there's at the head of our government a magistrate who is not ashamed to profess himself a Christian." As for Jefferson, one Litchfield, Connecticut, clergyman offered up a brief, facetious prayer: "O Lord! Wilt thou bestow upon the vice president a double portion of Thy grace, for *Thou knowest he needs it.*"

The Hated Red, White, and Blue

Adams began his presidency in a time of religious turmoil. "Since our late Revolution," Lathrop lamented, there has "been a visible tendency toward infidelity and an observable growth of impiety and immortality." In his *Observations upon the Present State of the Clergy of New England,* the Reverend Peter Thatcher agreed. "The late contest with Great Britain, glorious as it hath been for their country, hath been peculiarly unfortunate for the clergy," he said. "Perhaps no set of men, whose hearts were so thoroughly engaged in it, or who contributed in so great a degree to its success, have suffered more by it." Liberty, it seems, was catching. Set free from their king, uppity Americans were liberating themselves from the authority of their parsons. "Having emancipated themselves from the

British government and felt their competence to carry every point they chose," the American people, Thatcher mourned, "have been too ready to suppose that their declaration and authority were sufficient to dissolve the most solemn engagements, and that *the people could do no wrong*."

David Daggett was a proud Connecticut Congregational layman, destined, in the U.S. Senate, to become a steadfast critic of godless government. As early as 1787, he was mourning the demise of a "perfect aristocracy" and the accompanying "loss of the happy influence of the clergy." Others drew a different conclusion from the same evidence. Jean Pierre Brissot de Warville approvingly reported during his 1791 visit to Boston, "Universal tolerance, the child of American independence, has banished the preaching of dogmas, which always leads to discussion and quarrels. All the sects admit nothing but morality, which is the same in all, and the only preaching proper for a great society of brothers." This turn of affairs would have suited Brissot's confrere Jefferson, but tolerance and international brotherhood ranked no higher on the list of Puritan virtues than theological indifference did. If their churches were hardly teetering on the brink, the alarm felt by leaders of the established churches was palpable. Given their position in society, it contributed to an atmosphere of creeping ruin.

As it had been since the beginning of Washington's second term, the problem was France. In the first wave of revolutionary euphoria that welled across the Atlantic, American Protestants hailed the demise of French Catholicism. By now, these same preachers were trembling at the triumph of Jacobin infidelity. In the darkest days of the Revolution, Dr. Benjamin Rush exclaimed before Congress, "We look only to Heaven and France for succor." Two decades later, for many Americans, heaven and France could no longer appear together in the same sentence without defying all logic. "Dragons' teeth have been sown in France," Adams said, "and come up as monsters."

Resurfacing in this changed atmosphere, the Declaration of Independence assumed new political portent. In 1776, Congress had instructed that it be read aloud at public gatherings. In Massachusetts, the church became the principle venue for its proclamation. The governor declared that a copy "be sent to the ministers of each parish of every denomination within this state and that they severally be required to read the same to their respective congregations." Preachers who intoned Jefferson's words back then as if they were holy writ were now more wary. With France as their new stomping ground, in conservative American precincts liberty and equality were losing their allure. In the Declaration's preamble, Jefferson had introduced four radical principles: the right to liberty; God-given equality; popular sovereignty; and the people's authority to overthrow their government. Federalist and republican alike viewed Jefferson's rights-based philosophy interchangeably with the radical Jacobin motto of "liberty, equality, and fraternity."

In the epithet "Jacobin," the Federalists summed up their two greatest nightmares: atheism and democracy. The hated Jacobin colors were red, white, and blue, familiarly flaunted in the form of a tricolor cockade (a knot of ribbons pinned onto the side of a cocked hat) in saucy contrast to the more formal, less frivolous cockade emblematic of the American rebellion against Great Britain. Officially designated by Congress, the American cockade was a black rosette, perfectly suited to adorn a clergyman's formal beaver tricorn hat. Attempting to influence the 1796 election, the French agent to the United States instructed all French citizens in America to sport a tricolor cockade, a style that soon caught on among republican sympathizers. By the time Adams was inaugurated, the infestation of tricolors had spread as far as New England.

The shift in mood was sudden. In 1793, a year before Washington sounded his alarm against the democratic clubs, Yale's president, Ezra Stiles, had seized the occasion to do what would seem natural. He celebrated liberty. He even named its author (a fact few

Americans were privy to back then) and lavished Jefferson with praise, memorably saying that he "poured the soul of the continent into the monumental act of Independence." Scarcely had Dr. Stiles brought the Declaration of Independence back to public notice before his successor (and Daggett's uncle), Dr. Timothy Dwight, was voicing his dismay over the so-called rights of man that the Declaration so shamelessly proclaimed.

Was America going to fritter away its moral capital in a presumptuous pursuit of happiness or would it return instead to the Puritan pursuit of godliness that sanctified the government of its Bible-toting forebearers? This was the question dividing America. What, for instance, should its patriotic citizens be celebrating on the nation's birthday? Was it the restoration of American rights, as most Federalists argued, or the inauguration of international revolution, which was the general republican view? To Federalist eyes, American Jacobins had taken the Fourth of July hostage and were desecrating it for their own nefarious purposes. And not the Fourth alone. For a time tricolors, liberty poles, and liberty caps were brought out for Bastille Day and other French revolutionary holidays as well. When a great thunderstorm washed out the Independence Day festivities in Philadelphia one year, festival organizers pushed the celebration forward to July 14, which they happily pointed out was "the anniversary of the French Revolution." With American city folk aping French custom and addressing each other as "citizen" and "citess," one prominent Federalist bemoaned, "Our greatest danger is from the contagion of levelism. What folly is it that has set the world agog to be all equal to French barbers?"

At the height of America's French fever, Independence Day in Philadelphia might as well have been Bastille Day as far as the local Federalists were concerned. Boycotted by proper Philadelphians, nary a black cockade was to be seen on the anniversary of the nation's birth; many church bells remained silent; and revelers throughout Independence Square indecently festooned themselves in heretical red, white, and blue. A French tilt pervaded the South, as well. Radical Episcopal Bishop James Madison told his flock of Virginia Episcopalians that "the voice of Heaven itself seems to call to her sons, go ye forth and disciple all nations, and spread among them the gospel of equality and fraternity." Noah Webster, who subscribed to the gospel of peace and propriety instead, called the tricolor cockade, far from honoring liberty, in truth "a badge of despotism," uniting "the littleness of boys with the barbarity of Goths." Looking for the perfect word to describe faithless France, he came up with "demoralized."

The split over France divided neighbors into opposing camps. Across New England, separate tricolor and black cockade Fourth of July celebrations came into fashion. In their Independence Day orations, Federalist preachers presented a negative print image of Jefferson's original script, critiquing the un-American, anti-Christian dogma he had so impudently inserted into the nation's founding writ. One Fourth of July, Puritan pillar John Lowell warned his Boston listeners to beware "the seductive doctrines of 'Liberty' and 'Equality.'"

The hardening of New England opinion was epitomized at Yale College by the contrasting presidencies of Ezra Stiles, who died in 1795, and his successor, Timothy Dwight. Of tolerant temperament and generous in his affections, during his pastorate in Newport, Rhode Island, Stiles befriended the local Roman Catholic priest and studied Hebrew at Truro Synagogue. At Yale, he found the courage to introduce an avowed republican into the faculty and a French text into the curriculum. "There is so much pure Christianity among all sects of Protestants, that I cheerfully embrace all in my charity," Stiles graciously said. "There is so much defect in all, that we all need forbearance and mutual condescension. I don't intend to spend my days in the fire of party."

His successor's faith was forged and purified in the fire of party. The grandson of the country's greatest theologian, Jonathan Edwards, and Aaron Burr's first cousin, Dwight was nothing if not zealous. He read himself almost blind as a young student, and among his followers in the Connecticut clergy he inspired an equally blind devotion. Dwight's sacred politics were by no means subtle. "The same principles, which support or destroy Christianity, alike support or destroy political order and government," he declared. Yale's president for twenty-two years and Connecticut's leading spokesman for what one scholar calls "Godly Federalism," "His Holiness Pope Timothy" Dwight was anointed by republican critics "the grand pabulum and fountainhead of political and religious orthodoxy." "Connecticut is almost totally an ecclesiastical state," one republican bemoaned, "ruled by the president of the college as a monarch," whose dual authority encompassed the "united power of an ecclesiastic and politician." Dr. Dwight once boasted that one ordained preacher outweighed a thousand votes, and, according to the peculiarities of the Connecticut electoral system, a Congregational clergyman did indeed wield sufficient power to keep the reins of government in proper Christian hands. At town meetings, ministers of the Standing Order routinely placed prospective office holders' names into nomination, their election guaranteed by open ballot, conducted under the clergy's watchful eyes.

None of this blatant favoritism bothered Dwight. When a 1795 tax bill to underwrite Congregationally run schools and meetinghouses in sparsely settled parts of the state elicited squeals of protest, he was astounded that any religious person could oppose such sacred work, blaming sectarians for fostering "complete disorganization . . . to our ancient system of order and peace." That same year, he likened the nation's leaders to fathers responsible for the welfare of their children. While protesting that "Religion has nothing to do with politics or, in other words, with government," Dr. Dwight's practice supported the opposite presumption. So did the majority of his cascading words.

From its Yale headquarters and under Dwight's generalship, the Standing Order of Connecticut defended America's Christian fortress more vigorously than any other band of clerics, but Adams's old teachers and proto-Unitarian religious fellow travelers at Harvard were no less disconcerted by the threat liberty posed to the social order. If more liberal in its curriculum—Harvard offered French to its students as early as 1787, nearly four decades before Yale condescended to allow the language of Catholics and infidels into its hallowed halls—when it came to upholding the Christian establishment Arminian Harvard, whose moral philosophers deemed it the "right and duty for government to provide for the support of religion by law," was as old school as Calvinist Yale.

The Reverend William Ellery Channing, who would become America's most renowned Unitarian minister, attended Harvard during the mid-1790s. He deplored the "French mania" that intoxicated his classmates, recalling the "infidel and irreligious spirit" that then prevailed. Harvard "was never in a worse state," he recalled, "with the tendency of all classes to skepticism." To curb the spread of infidelity, the Harvard Corporation distributed Richard Watson's *An Apology for the Bible* to all its students in 1796. Two years later, John T. Kirkland instructed Harvard's Phi Beta Kappa chapter to beware "the poison of the skeptical and disorganizing philosophy, which is now perverting and corrupting man." Kirkland reframed the preamble of the Declaration of Independence to suit the purposes of his class, turning Jefferson's ringing affirmation of equality into an endorsement of the status quo. American equality, he said, is "an equality which secures the rich from rapacity no less than the poor from oppression" and "proclaims peace alike to the mansions of the affluent and the humble dwellings of the poor." Looking back on the turbulent final decade of the eighteenth century, a prominent Harvard Unitarian, Henry Ware Sr., boasted that his faculty had "sided with the friends of order and government in opposition to the popular following which then broke out in insurrections."

Loyal alumnus Adams had no difficulty seconding the motion for law and order. "Statesmen may plan and speculate for liberty," he said, "but it is religion and morality alone, which can establish the principles upon which freedom can securely stand." What little sympathy Adams harbored for the French Revolution had long since

evaporated. "I know not what to make of a republic of thirty mil-
lion atheists," he sniffed, bantering to make a serious point: "I am
willing you should call this the Age of Frivolity...Folly, Vice,
Frenzy, Fury, Brutality, Demons, Bonaparte, Tom Paine, the Age of
the Burning Brand and the Bottomless Pit: or anything but the Age
of Reason."

"I Like a Little Rebellion Now and Then"

It is uncertain whether Adams and Jefferson tested their friendship
when together in Europe by interjecting political philosophy into
their conversations—Adams would later claim they didn't—but
Abigail Adams and Jefferson exchanged words over how much
liberty was actually desirable in the land of the free. The gentle-
mannered Virginian had a sweet spot for rebels. When Shays' Rebellion broke out in western Massachusetts in 1786, he invoked
the Almighty. "God forbid that we should ever be 20 years without
such a rebellion," he said. In contrast, Mrs. Adams verbally scorched
its perpetrators. The feisty cabal of mountain men and farmers, who
resented paying taxes for a government whose services they felt they
didn't need, were, in her eyes, "ignorant, restless desperados, without
conscience or principles." She asked her idealistic friend to answer
one simple question: "Will my countrymen justify the maxim of
tyrants, that mankind are not made for freedom?"

Jefferson preferred flirtatious Abigail to dyspeptic John, but this
particular bit of apostasy doubtless reinforced his steadfast conviction that, when the discussion turned to politics, women should be
seen and not heard. His only quarrel with the French Revolution
pivoted on that very issue. He shuddered aloud that his friends in
France were permitting women to meddle in government. To Abigail's voiced concerns, Jefferson took gentle exception. "The spirit
of resistance to government is so valuable on certain occasions that
I wish it to be always kept alive," he replied. "It will often be exercised when wrong, but better so than not to be exercised at all."

With sweet insouciance, he continued, "I like a little rebellion now and then. It is like a storm in the atmosphere."

Jefferson left France the week the Bastille fell. Far from cause to tremble, for the author of the Declaration of Independence a head or two was small price to pay in exchange for liberty. Reminiscent of the early Christian father Tertullian, who celebrated the blood of the martyrs as the seed of the church, Jefferson coolly noted that "The tree of liberty must be refreshed from time to time with the blood of patriots and tyrants." People shouldn't make too much of his friend's flights of rhetorical fancy, James Madison suggested. "Latitude ought to be made for a habit in Mr. Jefferson, as in others of great genius, of expressing in strong and round terms impressions of the moment." Unfortunately, because of the delay in transatlantic correspondence, expressions of the moment were swiftly outdated, and Jefferson's valiant efforts to maintain his revolutionary ardor cast him unwittingly in a macabre light. "May Heaven favor your cause," he wrote Lafayette as his old friend was being trundled into exile and an Austrian jail. Even as his cheery congratulatory letters to Condorcet and Brissot were crossing the Atlantic, the two men lost their heads to succeeding generations of revolutionaries. With surpassing understatement, Jefferson confessed that "all my friends there have been turned adrift in the different states of the progression of their Revolution."

As liberty got ugly in France, people grew less patient with its partisans here at home. In 1799, one republican complained that his town's Fourth of July was vandalized the night before when "some infernal Federal incendiary or incendiaries...disgracefully sawed down" its liberty tree. The rising antirepublican Fourth of July spirit is captured in a 1798 Independence Day toast: "John Adams: may he like Sampson slay thousands of Frenchmen with the jawbone of Jefferson."

With neither man displaying a gift for balance, what the author of American liberty couldn't permit himself to question, Adams as steadfastly refused to honor. He pronounced the "nonsensical" flaunting of liberty, equality, and fraternity "a swindle," sarcastically adding, "Liberty flattered the natural savage; equality flattered all the pride and vanity of civil life, but fraternity added the moral, the Christian feeling, and melted all into tears." Life, liberty, and the pursuit of happiness may have invested the American rebellion with thrilling rhetorical sanction, but, in Adams's estimation, they wouldn't stand the sober test of constructive statecraft. Penning a tribute to the orderly virtues of Christian monarchy in the margin of an essay by Rousseau (while serving as president or very shortly before), he mourned how in Enlightenment thought "The state of nature, the savage life, the Chinese happiness, have all been falsely celebrated and cried up, in order to lessen the reverence for the Christian religion and weaken the attachment to monarchical government." When Rousseau shifted his utopian eye from egalitarian individualism to collectivism and the nation state, the president, now nearing the end of his term, found his conclusions more palatable. "Every citizen," Rousseau was now saying, "should live in perfect independence of all the others and in the most complete dependence on the state." Adams deemed this authoritarian formula "an admirable maxim of government and liberty."

"We Have Gospel Light, and Political Light"

In June 1789, the then vice president gazed into his crystal ball and accurately predicted, "We shall very soon have parties formed—a court and a country party—and these parties will have names given them. One party will support the president and his measures and ministers; the other will oppose them." By the outset of his presidency growing bands of political partisans did indeed have names given them just as Adams had predicted, especially by their detractors. One side colorfully defamed their opponents as Monocrats, Anglomen, and the Anglican Party—Jefferson dubbed it the "anglo-monarchico-aristocratic party." The other band of partisans branded their political foes Jacobins, Infidels, and Democrats—

Abigail Adams favored the four-letter epithet "Demo." The two groups naturally gravitated respectively into Adams's court party, the government-friendly Federalists (defending divine order, government authority, and Christian virtue), and Jefferson's Democratic-Republican country party (championing sacred liberty, freedom from governmental restraint, and church-state separation). With the nation's architects in opposing camps, each faction could authoritatively curse the other for betraying the founders' original intent and present itself as the embodiment of true Americanism and its opponents as shills, either for the British or the French.

In this charged political atmosphere, religion was both a target and a weapon. In the best Enlightenment fashion, the Jeffersonians cried foul at the political designs of conniving churchmen. Had the great Voltaire himself not warned that "theologians who, having begun by aiming at being heads of a sect, soon aimed at being heads of a party?" Just such a bait and switch, they feared, was well under way in New England.

Right on cue, Dr. Timothy Dwight mounted his pulpit. For his 1798 Fourth of July address, Dwight expressed his horror that the "Age of Reason" and "Rights of Man" were being whispered in pagan Masonic temples even as they were being trumpeted in sacrilegious Independence Day festivals by the democratic mob. He called the character and conduct of his fellow Americans into question. "For what end shall we be connected with [such people]?" he asked, unleashing a torrent of invective that a yellow journalist might aspire to emulate but could never surpass:

> Is it that our churches may become temples of reason, our Sabbath a decade [the new French calendar had a 10-day week], and our Psalms of praise Marseilles hymns? Is it that we may change our holy worship into a dance of Jacobin frenzy and that we may behold a strumpet personating a goddess on the altars of JEHOVAH? Is it that we may see the Bible cast into a bonfire, the vessels of the sacramental supper borne by an ass in public procession, and our

children, either wheedled or terrified, uniting in chanting mock-
eries against God, and hailing in...the ruin of their religion and
the loss of their souls? Is it that we may see our wives and daughters the victims of legal prostitution?...Shall our sons become the
disciples of Voltaire, and the dragoons of Marat, or our daughters
the concubines of the [Masonic] Illuminati?

Where Dr. Dwight saw myriad dangers, the consummate political strategist Alexander Hamilton recognized a golden opportunity.
Beyond its political utility, Hamilton harbored scant interest in the
church. Adams, who despised the de facto leader of his own political party, would later scorch Hamilton's memory for how freely
he employed religion as a political tool. "The pious and virtuous
Hamilton," he sarcastically recalled, "began to teach our nation
Christianity and to commission his followers to cry down Jefferson
and Madison as atheists in league with the French nation." He remembered well. Fashioning Jefferson "an atheist, [and] a modern
French philosopher," Hamilton determined to seed the clouds for a
Christian hailstorm. If Jefferson and the Republican insurgents were
going to tip their tricolor cockades to the goddess of liberty, the government should not hesitate to respond in kind by mustering the
Black Regiment to its aid. In an anonymous pitch to the faithful,
Hamilton avowed that, should morality be overthrown, "(and
morality *must* fall without religion), the terrors of despotism can
alone curb the impetuous passions of man and confine him within
the bounds of social duty." If Hamilton recognized the utility of
these words, Adams believed them with all his heart. "Our constitution was made only for a moral and religious people," he preached
to an assembly of the Officers of the Massachusetts Militia in the fall
of 1798. "It is wholly inadequate to the government of any other."

The churches were certainly poised to act. One Republican
provocateur (or naïf) attended Philadelphia's Congregational Church
one Sunday sporting a red, white, and blue cockade. When he seated
himself in the balcony, the maddened congregation lost its Chris-

tian head, ripped off his hat, plucked the cockade from its brim, and threw it into the nave below.

The religious divide ran largely along sectional lines. "We want no *Southern lights* in these parts," Timothy Dwight's brother Theodore editorialized in the *Connecticut Courant*. "We have Northern lights—we have gospel light, and political light, sufficient to exterminate Jacobinism." The Federalists could field no better army to win the battle for America's soul than New England's Black Regiment. After all, the Jacobin opposition had confected liberty and equality into a witches' brew. To exorcise America, President Adams must declare a day of prayer.

Adams Calls the Nation to Prayer

The Presbyterian Church was the first to issue a public call for a day of fasting and repentance to enlist God's aid in calming the winds of anarchy, sedition, and French belligerence. In their summons to prayer, the Presbyterian General Assembly averred that "formidable innovations and convulsions in Europe" posed a real and present danger to American godliness, should the people not heed the warnings posted by their religious watchmen. Contemplating this call, Hamilton could not but remember how effectively Washington's second national prayer day had served his overall campaign to clip the wings of the noxious democratic clubs. With the Republicans vulnerable to the charge of sedition for having pledged their troth so wantonly to the French, charging the loyal clergy to muster their congregations for a national fast would not only separate the saved from the damned but also generate a wave of positive publicity for the government.

In February 1798, Hamilton commissioned one of his moles in the cabinet, Secretary of War James McHenry, to set the wheels in motion for a presidential proclamation. Adams's first mistake as president had been to reenlist Washington's cabinet secretaries, few of whom felt any personal loyalty to him. Secretary of State Timothy

Pickering would later pronounce it a cabinet officer's duty "to prevent, as far as practicable, the mischievous measures of a wrongheaded president." Hamilton instructed McHenry to convince Adams to declare a national fast. "On religious grounds this is very proper—on political, it is very expedient. The government will be very unwise, if it does not make the most of the religious prepossessions of our people—opposing the honest enthusiasm of religious opinion to the frenzy of political fanaticism." Describing such a fast day as critical to the nation's well-being, Hamilton pressed his agents in the Cabinet to act with alacrity.

To hear Adams tell it, Hamilton's efforts were wasted. He remembered settling on a national fast day well before its meticulously briefed advocates began knocking down his door, not for political reasons but because "there is nothing upon this earth more sublime and affecting than the idea of a great nation all on their knees at once before their God, acknowledging their faults and imploring his blessing and protection, when the prospect before them threatens great danger and calamity." Such a vision truly did raise goose bumps whenever Adams contemplated it. As a young revolutionary serving in the Continental Congress, he conjured up the same vision in 1775, when advocating the first national prayer day: "Millions will be on their knees at once before their great creator, imploring his forgiveness and blessing, his smiles on American councils and arms." He would later claim, "I mix religion with politics as little as possible," but Adams's New England blinders directed him down a perilous political path even when he thought he was following a safe religious one.

On March 23, 1798, President Adams appointed May 9 as a national day of fasting and repentance. In the logic of covenant theology, God made a compact with His people, which when honored would ensure divine favor and when breached call down a double dose of punishment. Drawn in this spirit, the wording of Adams's fast day proclamation was Puritan to the core. In this "season of difficulty and danger," the president somberly declared,

All religious congregations [ought to] with the deepest humility, acknowledge before God the manifold sins and transgressions with which we are justly chargeable as individuals and as a nation; beseeching Him, at the same time, of His infinite grace through the Redeemer of the world, freely to remit all our offences and to incline us, by His Holy Spirit, to that sincere repentance and reformation which may afford us reason to hope for his inestimable favor and heavenly benediction.

The rhetoric of covenant theology was second nature to Adams. In the Continental Congress he told his colleagues that "the people in America have now the best opportunity and the greatest trust in their hands that Providence ever committed to so small a number since the transgression of the first pair." Break this trust, he warned and "their guilt will merit even greater punishment than other nations have suffered." The Puritan God was harsh with his people in equal measure to the preference He bestowed on them. To Adams, the covenant his forebearers made with their God in establishing a Christian commonwealth anticipated a yet more momentous compact—that between God and the new republic. When George Washington spoke of Providence favoring America, his words were generic and theologically inclusive. Adams uttered them with a strong New England accent.

The president's motivations for declaring a national day of repentance were both moral and martial. It could "scarcely fail to have a favorable effect on [people's] morals in general," Adams predicted, "or to inspire them with warlike virtues in particular." Hamilton's ambitions were more partisan. What gave *him* goose bumps was to imagine America's Federalist clergy hailing the government and damning the Jacobins and then rushing their tracts into print. The religiously nonchalant New Yorker understood the political power of the pulpit. He knew, as one wag put it, that,

> Some sought for votes by praying;
> To church they went,

On prayer bent,
To see what the priest was saying.

During the Revolution, Adams lamented a lesson from history: As long as the government, however oppressive, privileges the church, the clergy will support the government. The very law that had disadvantaged his cause then was now working in its favor. The tall-steeple clerics stepped up to the plate just as Hamilton trusted they would. The lion of the Philadelphia clergy, Ashbel Green, intoned every verse of the Christian Federal anthem. American piety and morality had declined since the Revolution, he preached. God was allowing France to fall into chaos in order to chastise "this guilty age—this age of *infidel reason*." No Christian nation can become pagan without losing God's favor. To save themselves, the people must reject "the idea that 'morals can be separated from religion.'" Grateful that the nation was blessed with a bold Christian leader, Green thanked God for giving America Adams in her hour of need:

> Be warned, that without religion and morality, harmoniously united, we are an undone people; without these our civil liberty and social happiness cannot possibly be preserved. Let us esteem these our principal and most essential defense at the present hour and let us be thankful to God that he has given us a chief magistrate who, in looking to the defense of the country, has seen this important truth in its just light—has seen that we must implore and obtain the favor of God, or all other means will be ineffectual.

Green's covenant theology and Federalist politics echoed from establishment pulpits across the land. Presbyterian Samuel Miller of New York confessed that he wasn't accustomed to drag politics into the pulpit, but did so anyway. Several preachers compared Adams to King Hezekiah, who withstood the Assyrians by enlisting the people of Jerusalem to pray for God's intervention on their behalf. Another text that commended itself to fast day preachers was Romans 13:2: "Whosoever resisteth the power, resisteth the ordinance of God; and they that resist shall receive themselves to damnation." Among the Jacobins who popped up on preachers' hate lists were Cain and Satan.

As he had at the height of the democratic club controversy, the Reverend David Osgood fulfilled Alexander Hamilton's robust hopes. He hysterically told his parishioners (and subsequently, with the aid of the Federalist propaganda machine, a much vaster readership) that henceforth any success the French might enjoy "will sweep away all your liberties, gradually wrest from you your possessions, strip you of your virtue and religion, and after transforming you into French demons will give you up to be tormented through successive generations under the yoke of a foreign despotism."

But it was Jedidiah Morse who took the Federal prize. Supplying Dwight and countless other partisans with ammunition that would arm their polemics for years to come, in addition to heaping praise on "our respected and beloved president" Morse added an element of conspiracy to the pulpit paranoia running rampant in New England. Courtesy of John Robison's book on the Bavarian Illuminati, a fringe movement in European Freemasonry founded in 1776, Morse employed Adams's fast day to publish word of a democratic underground festering under the cover of America's Masonic institutions and secretly laboring to destroy church and government alike.

Morse's sermon was only the first salvo in his campaign to cleanse America of Illuminists. The following month, he prevailed on the Massachusetts Convention of Congregational Ministers to affirm their loyalty to Adams by pledging their support of his effort to expunge disorganization and atheism from the land. Recognizing Morse as the perfect new shill for their political gospel, Massachusetts Federalists George Cabot, Otis Ames, and their friends in the so-called Essex Junto leapt to extend his voice. They published his fast day sermon with a lengthy appendix and distributed 400 copies to every clergyman in New England. By early the following year, Morse had identified France as the Antichrist and fingered American

Republicans as Satanic agents. Through the channels of the Illuminati, they were already hard at work, he claimed, systematically endeavoring "to destroy not only the influence and support, but the official existence of the clergy."

Unable to resist being caught up in the hysteria he was fomenting, on a lobbying trip to Philadelphia where he also huddled with Secretary of State Pickering and Ashbel Green, Morse told Oliver Wolcott that he was now "convinced that the *Jacobins,* like their father, the first *Disorganizer,* can transform themselves into any shape, even into that of an angel of light, in order to accomplish their purposes, prejudices, vices—in a word, all that is wrong in human nature, against all good." As soon became evident to anyone who was paying reverent attention, Morse's Luciferian angel of light was none other than Thomas Jefferson.

A Christian Government

Both as a unifying holiday (Adams's hope) and as a popular marshaling of "honest enthusiasm of religious opinion" in answer "to the frenzy of political fanaticism" (Hamilton's stated intent), Adams's national day of fasting, humiliation, and prayer ended up embarrassing the Federalists as much as it chastened the Republicans. For the most part, the Republicans laid low. Bemoaning "the disposition of the age to sermonize," Jefferson hunkered down in Monticello to wait out the storm. One wit excused himself from national worship, explaining that he was "not of the opinion that in Adams's fall, we sinned all." An isolated Republican cleric in Massachusetts mourned that the Federalists had "stripped liberty of its ascendancy."

As for the Federalists, the fast galvanized their base to be sure, unified the progovernment faction, and kept plenty of local printers working overtime. But it also raised populist hackles. Any hint of collusion between the old church and the new state found few friends in some of America's most vital spiritual precincts. Adams's fast day alienated untold numbers of American Baptists and Methodists, whose churches were not languishing as New England divines complained theirs to be, but flourishing and multiplying, lifted on the wings of religious freedom.

Adams's fast day proclamation sent tremors across the land. Some of these tremors were not metaphorical. He retained haunting memories of protesters mobbing the streets of Philadelphia. Twenty years after the fact, Adams revisited that wild fast day evening in a letter to Jefferson.

> I have no doubt you was fast asleep in philosophical tranquility, when ten thousand people, and perhaps many more, were parading the streets of Philadelphia on the evening of my Fast Day; when even Governor Mifflin himself thought it his duty to order a patrol of Horse and Foot to preserve the peace; when Market Street was as full as men could stand by one another, and even before my door; when some of my domestics, in frenzy, determined to sacrifice their lives in my defense; when all were ready to make a desperate sally among the multitude and others were with difficulty and danger dragged back by the others; when I myself judged it prudent and necessary to order chests of arms from the War Office to be brought through bye lanes and back doors, determined to defend my house at the expense of my life and the lives of the few, very few domestics and friends within it.

Awash with pathos, this letter is vintage Adams. Not that his fast didn't provoke a melee. A gang of Republican thugs sporting tricolor cockades did indeed haunt Philadelphia's alleyways on the prowl for black cockades. Governor Mifflin called out the cavalry to patrol the streets and guard the president's residence, as Adams correctly remembered. He was wrong, however, to presume that Jefferson slept through the fracas. His vice president offered this eyewitness account to Madison:

> Some of the young men who addressed the president on Monday mounted the black cockade. The next day numbers of the people appeared with the tri-colored cockade. Yesterday being the fast day,

the black cockade again appeared, on which the tri-color also showed itself. A fray ensued, the light horse were called in, and the city was so filled with confusion from about 6 to 10 o'clock last night that it was dangerous going out.

A week later, tricolors had disappeared from the streets, "but the black is still frequent," Jefferson reported from the front, adding matter of factly, "The president received 3 anonymous letters announcing plots to burn the city on the fast day."

Given his acute aversion to controversy, Jefferson likely suffered more than Adams did from the effects of the political gang warfare incited by the federal fast. Acting on rumors that Jacobin terrorists were intending to torch the capital, 1,200 spirited young partisans, many sporting black cockades, streamed into Market Square to "address the president" and place themselves at his service. Not only did they raise a raucous cheer for Adams, but a gang of Federalist rowdies proceeded to gather under Jefferson's window to serenade him with the "Rogue's March." "You should know the rancorous passions which tear every breast here," he lamented to his daughter, Martha, fastidiously adding, "even of the sex which should be a stranger to them. Politics and party hatreds destroy the happiness of every being here. They seem, like salamanders, to consider fire as their element."

In the American South, the president's call to prayer was honored in the breach more than in the pews. Ever the contrarian, Bishop James Madison distributed a prayer to be read in every Episcopal parish in Virginia, calling on his people to fast instead in solemn protest against the government's abandonment of "Christian liberty." As for the president himself, if he cherished any hope of hearing himself praised he went to the wrong church. As Ashbel Green was extolling him to the heavens across town at Second Presbyterian, Adams was seated in the congregation of First Presbyterian, whose preacher, Dr. Samuel Blair, while following the party line concerning "our bounden duty to accommodate ourselves to the decision of those who legislate for us," gave equal and refreshing emphasis, "as good Christians," to "our bounden duty to consider, and to treat with charity and candor the political opinions of those who may differ with us."

Most of the political damage Adams suffered would not kick in until two years later at the height of his campaign for reelection, when unwarranted fears that he was flirting with imposing a state religion neutralized Federalist efforts to turn the nation's Christians against Jefferson on account of his "infidelity." In the meantime, never one to leap to the conclusion that a position he had taken might be wrong, Adams, apparently having learned nothing from his first experience, proclaimed a second national fast day the following spring, to enforce "the sacred duties of religion in public and private" and to inoculate the citizenry "from unreasonable discontent, from disunion, faction, sedition, and insurrection."

Inspired perhaps by the laudatory sermon he missed, Adams turned to Green to draft the second fast day declaration. One can only imagine Dr. Green's joy. Presented a more golden opportunity than the one President Washington had denied him, he later boasted that he intentionally imbued Adams's text with an "evangelical character." No truth, it proclaims,

> is more clearly taught in the Volume of Inspiration, nor any more fully demonstrated by the experience of all ages, than that a deep sense and full acknowledgment of the governing providence of a Supreme Being and of the accountableness of men to Him as the searcher of hearts and the righteous distributor of rewards and punishments are conducive equally to the happiness and the rectitude of individuals and the well-being of communities.

At long last, Green had just what his soul had been pining for—a Christian government.

"ORDER IS HEAVEN'S FIRST LAW"

> O happy State! the state, by Heaven design'd
> To reign, protect, employ, and bless mankind.
>
> —TIMOTHY DWIGHT, "GREENFIELD HILL"

TIMOTHY DWIGHT was not the Connecticut Wits' finest poet. That honor would go to Joel Barlow, a future player in our drama. But unlike Barlow, Dwight remained faithful to their creed. The Connecticut Wits, a Yale cabal of neoclassical moralists featuring Barlow, the Dwight brothers, and David Humphreys, began sharpening their pens against the folly of their fellow mortals shortly after the war. One early joint effort, "The Anarchiad," reveals in its title everything we need to know about their convictions. Humphreys helped construct its witty pastiche of antidemocratic dogma. "For God, a God of order, ne'er designed/Equal conditions for the human kind," he elsewhere said, pronouncing the reactionary young Turks' guiding mantra.

When he wasn't on the attack, Dwight wrote some really quite touching poems, among them "Greenfield Hill," a deftly crafted 200-page millennial eclogue considered by literary critics to be his finest effort. Inspired by the town where he conducted his first pastorate, Dwight celebrates in its gentle pages the New England embodiment of Christian commonwealth. His evocation of unadulterated American "unum," unfraught by faction and uncomplicated by difference in faith or opinion, prefigures the promised

Kingdom of God on earth, the so-called postmillennial 1,000-year reign of peace that would usher in Jesus's Second Coming. To Dr. Dwight's reverent eye, for the advent of the millennium all signs pointed to America.

In 1777, pondering the Revolution's hidden meaning, Dwight perceived God's handiwork: The Lord intended to liberate America in order to complete the Divine plan. "This land was settled by Christians," he said. "God brought his little flock hither and placed it in this wilderness for the great purpose of establishing permanently the church of Christ in these vast regions of idolatry and sin, and commencing here the glorious work of salvation." Connecticut's leading theocrat then foresaw the extension of his commonwealth's godly government all across America. "This great continent is soon to be filled with the praise, the piety, of the Millennium."

> One blood, one kindred, reach from sea to sea;
> One language spread, one tide of manners run;
> One scheme of science, and of morals one;
> And, God's own Word the structure, and the base,
> One faith extend, one worship, and one praise.

As placid as "Greenfield Hill" seems on its surface, a sharp polemic simmers just beneath. Written in 1788, shortly before the great American divide rent the nation into warring political camps, in it Dwight upholds the virtues of God's commonwealth ("with order, peace and harmony, adjusted all its weal") against the fanciful visions of pagan philosophers, whether they be Greek or French. If all the world were as perfectly ordered as Greenfield, Connecticut,

> Soon would politic visions fleet away,
> Before awakening truth! Utopias then,
> Ancient and new, high fraught with fairy good,
> Would catch no more the heart....
>
> ...would'st thou for these exchange
> Thy sacred institutions? Thy mild laws?

Thy pure religion? Morals uncorrupt?
Thy plain and honest manners? Order, peace,
And general weal?

The correct answer to Dwight's rhetorical question was, of course, "No." But since people wouldn't necessarily arrive at this answer on their own, until Christ returned they needed proxies to help them order their lives in a fit manner—civic-minded pastors, say, and good Christian governors to cultivate God's earthly garden in its restored, Edenic state.

Still, as of yore, in church, and state, elect
The virtuous, and the wise; men tried, and prov'd
Of steady virtue, all thy weal to guide;
And HEAVEN shall bless thee, with a parent's hand.

Where were his readers to find such leaders? As always, Dwight was prepared to serve as their political guide. He dedicated "Greenfield Hill" to the one American statesman who knew this poem by heart even before he read it: John Adams.

Defending Greenfield Hill

Shortly after Adams proclaimed his first national fast in the spring of 1798, a lurid tale of French skulduggery dominated the American press. Under cover as "X," "Y," and "Z," three French intermediaries attempted to extort large cash payments from America's diplomatic representatives as a condition for further talks between the two governments. At this shocking piece of news, the American people were rightfully indignant. By early summer, what remained of the Jacobin bubble had burst, Federalist chests swelled, and the Republican opposition in Congress vanished.

With the XYZ Affair topic number one in the nation's barbershops and taverns, by the time the jeremiads unleashed from the pulpit on May 9 had been published, the sentiments they expressed jibed with the prejudices of the hour so perfectly as to lose not a little of their prophetic urgency. There would be no red, white, and blue cockades on this particular Fourth of July. Boston's largest paper announced that authorities would not tolerate "improper" symbols on Independence Day. Its Republican counterpart cautioned local democrats to avoid brandishing the tricolor, lest they attract unwanted attention from the local police.

The Republican press wasn't silenced. Jefferson's journalistic voice, Philip Freneau, cleverly twisted the headlines of the hour, slipping X, Y, and Z out of French Republican into Federalist Christian dress.

> Do you know, said my neighbor, any wicked men who are rich? Yes, says I, there is X, Y and Z. They are very rich and everybody knows they are great rascals. Well, says my neighbor, are they excommunicated? No—I protest, said I, now when I think of it, the Rev. Mr. W. dined with X on————, and with Y on————, and six or seven clergymen dined with Z a few days ago. God preserve us, I said, where shall we look for help; in the *great,* depravity is permitted, some kinds of wickedness counted laudable, and every species winked at.

Where, Freneau asked, were the nation's self-proclaimed moral watchdogs? Mired in corruption was his answer. If the failed French bribery of American ministers of government could spark so great an outcry, why shouldn't the successful Federalist seduction of American ministers of Christ provoke equal outrage?

In the summer of 1798, Congress passed four measures designed to eliminate all lingering sources of domestic unrest. Known to history as the Alien and Sedition Acts, they tarnish Adams's legacy to this very day. The Naturalization Act extended residency requirements for citizenship from five to fourteen years; the Act Concerning Aliens granted the president absolute power to banish any resident alien deemed "dangerous to the peace and safety of the United States"; and the Sedition Act (passed into law by the Senate on the Fourth of July) criminalized individuals who might dare speak or publish "any false, scandalous, and malicious" attack against the government. Only the noncontroversial Alien Enemies Act was conditioned on the nation actually being at war. That the Federalists overreached in forcing this Draconian legislation through Congress is evident from the closeness of the division. The Naturalization Act carried by one vote, the Sedition Act by three, and the Alien "Friends" Act by six votes in the House, narrow victories indeed at a time when the stars were perfectly aligned in their favor.

The acts were drafted so broadly that they could easily have swept up most any political activist in their dragnet, should he dare to express his opposition to the government in terms unacceptable to the federal watchdogs. Enforcement was sporadic, but that takes nothing away from the intent of these laws, which was to quash all French-inflected Republican criticism of the Adams administration and return the nation to a one-party state.

While damning the Alien Act as "a monster that must forever disgrace its parents," liberty's most faithful scribe, James Madison, got right to work. His comprehensive "Report of 1800" on the Sedition Act's "palpable and alarming infractions of the Constitution" forthrightly challenged the presumptions of power. "The right of freely examining public characters and measures [is] ... the only effectual guardian of every other right," Madison declared. Citing his own handiwork, Madison reminded his fellow citizens that freedom of press and religion were "both included in the same amendment, made at the same time, and by the same authority." In the First Amendment, Madison exclaimed, "Liberty of conscience and the freedom of the press were equally and completely exempted from all authority whatever of the United States."

Jefferson, too, remounted his charger, filled with holy purpose. His campaign against the Alien and Sedition Acts was a sacred crusade. At the height of the furor, he told a young disciple, "To preserve the freedom of the human mind & freedom of the press, every spirit should be ready to devote itself to martyrdom, for as long as we may think as we will & speak as we think, the condition of man will proceed in improvement." He pronounced the Alien and Sedition Acts "worthy of the eighth or ninth century." He even sought a *premunire* injunction in Virginia, hearkening back to English legal proscriptions against papal interference with the state. If Madison hadn't rushed to Monticello and stuffed a sock in Jefferson's blunderbuss, the Kentucky Resolutions Jefferson drafted to challenge the Alien and Sedition Acts' constitutionality might well have included language asserting a state's right to nullify federal legislation. Jefferson deemed nullification "a natural right" decades before John Calhoun raised the same specter in his battle to preserve slavery. As it was, in distancing their states from the federal authority, Jefferson's muted Kentucky Resolutions and another set of anti-Alien and Sedition Act resolutions passed by the Virginia legislature at Jefferson's urging were every bit as radical as the federal legislation they were crafted to thwart. To Madison, Jefferson declared himself ready "to sever ourselves from that union we so much value, rather than give up the rights of self government which we have reserved, and in which alone we see liberty, safety and happiness."

The president received a copy of the Kentucky Resolution with an anonymous note attached. "Take care, John Adams," it threatened. "An evil day is approaching. Traitors will be punished." For his part, Jefferson took special care to lay low. He knew he was baiting the bull. If his sponsorship of these truculent resolutions had come into the light of day, the vice president might conceivably have been impeached for treason.

The Best of Enemies

At the beginning of their tenure as the nation's chief executives, the president and vice president kept up appearances. One evening, they dined together alone. Ruffling the very feathers the meeting was doubtless intended to smooth, Adams's monologue on liberty and order confirmed Jefferson's belief that his erstwhile friend was truly a lost cause. "Trusting to a popular assembly for the preservation of our liberties," Adams lectured over supper, "was the merest chimera imaginable." If we can accept Jefferson's word—and the quote does ring true—he then went one step further, preposterously claiming "that anarchy did more mischief in one night than tyranny in an age."

Adams had also lost the affections of his cherished friend Benjamin Rush. The dapper, dedicated physician—the two met in the Continental Congress—struck him on first meeting as "an elegant, ingenious...sprightly, pretty fellow...too much of a talker to be a deep thinker. Elegant not great." With growing acquaintance, Rush soared in his estimation and the two became fast friends. Both were devout liberal laymen. Their religious bond and Adams's transparent openness engendered an intimacy that Rush would never feel with Jefferson. But politics intervened and the Philadelphia doctor now found himself allied with the opaque Virginian. Sacrificing their intimacy for the remainder of Adams's political career, Rush provocatively flaunted "a conversation that passed between Mr. Jefferson and myself...of which you were the principal subject. We both deplored your attachment to monarchy and both agreed that you had changed your principles since the year 1776."

Rush had additional cause for his disillusionment: the artless letter his friend sent him to defend his views on government. Declaring himself "as much a republican as I was in 1775," Adams took the witness stand and demolished his own case.

I do not consider hereditary monarchy or aristocracy as "rebellion against nature;" on the contrary I esteem them both institutions of admirable wisdom and exemplary virtue in a certain stage of society in a great nation, the only institutions that can possibly preserve the laws and liberties of the people—and I am clear that America must resort to them as an asylum against discord, seditions, and evil wars, and that at no very distant period of time—I shall not live to see it but you may. I think it therefore impolitic to

cherish prejudices against institutions which must be kept in view
as the hope of our posterity....I am by no means for attempting
any such thing at present, but our ship must ultimately land on
that shore or be cast away.

It is hard to imagine how Adams could possibly have been less
politic. "There have been many times in my life," he sheepishly
conceded years later, "when I have been so agitated in my own
mind as to have no consideration at all of the light in which my
words, actions, and even writings, would be considered by others."
This was one of those times.

Looking back on the tumult of his presidency, Adams absolved
himself of all culpability for the Alien and Sedition Acts. Yet his ac-
quiescence to the will of Congress was not as passive as he remembered. Adams's penchant for exaggeration led him to magnify the
danger "seditious" editors posed to the peace of society. "This country never appeared to me to be in greater danger," he said at the
time. "Philosophers, theologians, legislatures, politicians, and moralists will find the regulation of the press is the most difficult, dangerous, and important problem they will have to solve." Having
worked himself into a lather, Adams lapsed effortlessly into the
spirit of the new laws.

Mrs. Adams, too, believed that, "until Congress passes a Sedition Bill" nothing would curb "the stirrer up of sedition, the writer
or printer of loose and unfounded calumny." Understandably tired
of seeing her husband lampooned as the "old, querulous, bald,
blind, crippled, toothless Adams," she lashed out at the "mad
democratic style" adopted by his "Jacobin" and "Jesuitical" (atheist and Catholic) foes. One noted Federalist editor, John Fenno, recommended that the Republican editor Benjamin Franklin Bache be
treated "as we would A TURK, A JEW, A JACOBIN, OR A DOG."
Infected by the savage spirit of the times, Abigail embraced the logic
of Inquisition. "Perdition catch them," she cursed. "Bache has the
malice and falsehood of Satan, and his vile partner the [Boston]

Chronicle is equally as bad. An abused and insulted public cannot tolerate them much longer. In short they are so criminal that they ought to be presented by the grand jurors." She esteemed the Alien Act no less highly, praying that it would pass "without being curtailed and clipped until it is made useless."

As patriotic tributes began pouring in from around the country, Abigail cheered. "They breathe one spirit," she said, "approving the measures of government and expressive of full confidence in the wisdom, virtue, and integrity of the Chief Magistrate." Adams succumbed to his vanity and responded to each favorable petition with intemperate enthusiasm. To Federalist memorialists in Hartford, Connecticut, he congratulated himself for having "awed into silence the clamors of faction and palsied the thousand tongues of calumny." To a group of smitten Dartmouth students, he rhetorically asked, "Is the republic of the United States a fief of the republic of France?" Madison called Adams's official replies to his partisans' encomia "the most grotesque scene in the tragicomedy acting by the government." The Federalist press thought otherwise, investing the president's "patriotic addresses" with the authority of scripture, one paper running them serially under the headline "SACRED TRUTHS."

As a young patriot, Adams had rallied his contemporaries not to be intimidated "by any terrors from publishing with the utmost freedom whatever can be warranted by the laws of your country; nor suffer yourselves to be wheedled out of your liberty by any pretences of politeness, delicacy, or decency." When Governor Hutchinson called for "an abridgement of what are called English liberties," Adams railed that no art or subtlety would be sufficient to "vindicate or excuse that expression." Adams expressed equal disdain for clergymen preaching against populist uprisings. Writing to Abigail in the summer of 1774, he harrumphed, "Mobs are the trite topic of declamation and invective among all the ministerial people far and near." As late as 1788, he deemed a free press "that great barrier and bulwark of the rights of mankind." A scant decade later, his rejection of such liberties was all but complete. Adams now believed that, unless constrained by "the balance of a well-ordered government," unshackled liberty would degenerate "into dangerous ambition, irregular rivalries, destructive factions, wasting seditions, and bloody civil wars."

"Acting '*in terrorem*'"

Whenever they were prosecuted, the rarely invoked Alien and Sedition Acts (a grand total of twenty-five indictments, fourteen trials, and ten convictions) embarrassed the government. The loudest such embarrassment followed the fortunes of Congressman Matthew Lyon from national laughingstock to libertarian hero. Before being immortalized by federal prosecutors, the dedicated, uncouth Vermont Republican, who found himself in one embarrassing scrap after another, had long been denigrated as no better than an animal by elitist House colleagues, partly on account of his Irish ancestry. As future generations would discover, being Irish in New England, the most homogenous section of the country, presented endless opportunities for abasement. "I have seen many, very many Irishmen, and with a few exceptions they are," one proper New Englander declared, "the most God-provoking Democrats on this side of Hell."

Far from being an innocent victim, Lyon contributed colorfully to the case that was building against him. He was dubbed "the spitting Lyon" for expectorating in the face of a colleague who unmanned him by charging that he played soldier during the Revolution with a wooden sword. Two weeks later, following the chaplain's invocation, on the floor of the House, Roger Griswold of Connecticut retaliated by caning Lyon (who defended himself with fire tongs), giving the nation's cartoonists a field day. Mrs. Adams chided the House for not expelling "the wretch" the way people sweep "impurities and filth from their docks and wharves."

Lyon gave as good as he got, boasting that his ancestors didn't drown witches or hang Quakers. "When I shall see the sacred name of religion employed as a state engine to make mankind hate and persecute one another," he dared to write, "I shall not be their humble advocate." Statements such as this one—among his listed crimes was calling Adams "pompous"—were deemed seditious, and Lyon was indicted and convicted in October 1798. The Federalist press rejoiced, one editor praying, "May the good God grant that this may be the case of every Jacobin."

Denied permission to collect a coat or blankets from home, Lyon was shackled and unceremoniously dumped in a twelve-by-sixteen-foot unheated cell reserved for runaway slaves, where he outlasted the stench and cold until his release four months later. Justifying Madison's and Jefferson's paranoia—they wrote to each other in code—the local Federalist postmaster rifled through Lyon's mail, made public the names of his correspondents, and returned his packages and letters, unsealed, to their senders.

Lyon found a champion in itinerant Episcopal clergyman John C. Ogden, whose shoestring ministry he had supported financially during Ogden's years as a supply preacher in Vermont. Ogden was the epitome of an unsettled minister. He patched together a subsistence out of odd clerical jobs and the occasional interim pastorate, in one year alone clocking 5,000 miles preaching the gospel through northern New England and southeastern Canada. An avid Republican, he applied his full energies to right the injustice perpetrated against Congressman Lyon. Armed with thousands of Vermont signatures, in late 1798 Ogden set foot for Philadelphia to meet with the president. Adams favored Reverend Ogden with an interview, but on learning that Lyon himself was not begging the president's pardon, he refused to receive the petition and dismissed the Episcopal plaintiff with words memorable enough to return and haunt him. "Penitence," the president primly declared, "must precede pardon."

Ogden was hardly a luminary in the American ecclesial firmament. Yet, at a time when outspoken advocacy invited unwanted government attentions, he had the grit to pen a lively series of articles on Lyon's behalf, which Benjamin Franklin Bache happily published in the *Aurora*. "Col. Lyon has been generous, respectful, and hospitable to religionists of every name, at home and elsewhere," Ogden testified. "Catholics, Episcopalians, Baptists and Methodists experience equally his respect and favors." Lyon's only crime, he said, was "his unshaken opposition to a humiliating and degrading system of empty pomp and degrading ceremony."

Standing for reelection from jail, Lyon brokered his martyrdom into a landslide at the polls. Not only was he rewarded by his constituents for poking the government in the eye, but he became a Republican hero. The victory parade that followed him into the streets of Philadelphia to reclaim his seat in Congress ran for twelve miles. Lyon's clerical champion was less fortunate. In apparent retribution for his impertinence, Jedidiah Morse's confidant, now Secretary of the Treasury, Oliver Wolcott, put out a warrant out for Ogden's arrest. He was seized passing through Litchfield, Connecticut, unfriendly territory to evangelical democrats during the gentlest of seasons, and jailed on the opportunistic if legitimate charge of bankruptcy. Lampooned in the Federalist press as "The Rev. Gaolbird" and "High Priest of Sedition," Reverend Ogden relived Representative Lyon's experience. He, too, spent four months in an icy cell.

Elevated by his sacrifice on behalf of freedom, Ogden peppered the nation's leaders with dramatic pleas from prison, eliciting the sympathy of Madison and Jefferson, but little more. Ogden's plight didn't end on his release. Dragooned by a platoon of soldiers as he tried to escape town, he was paraded back through the streets of Litchfield to the accompanying jeers of "Damned Democrat" and "Jacobin." Ogden didn't leave the state without drawing a conclusion about its most powerful citizen. Of Timothy Dwight he said, "Connecticut is more completely under the administration of a Pope than Italy." Debt-ridden and unemployable, the pesky minister nonetheless scraped together sufficient backing to publish a Jeffersonian tract and spent the final year of his life campaigning for the Republican ticket in Maryland. It would be his last hurrah.

Four months before he could savor the joy of victory, Ogden died. "One great sin alone was sufficient to draw down the wrath of abused power," the *Aurora* wrote in its obituary, "the sin of avowing DEMOCRACY in a democratical government."

Other cases provoked no less pronounced a backlash, in part because their pretexts were so laughable. Luther Baldwin made every Republican editor's day when he was charged in New Jersey for drunkenly praying that a patriotic cannonball might smack President Adams in the rump on the Fourth of July. David Brown of Dedham, Massachusetts, got cited for abetting sedition by holding a ladder while his accomplice tacked an anti-Federalist poster to a makeshift liberty pole (not to mention that the same poor fellow, a day laborer and ne'er-do-well, was overheard extolling Paine's *Age of Reason*). The latter indictment, which led to an eighteen-month sentence, inspired hardliner Representative Fisher Ames of Massachusetts to hail the government for acting "*in terrorem*" ("in [order to incite] fear in the hearts of potential offenders"). "Acts *in terrorem* [are] not justifiable," Jefferson persuasively argued. "[They] leave everyone at the mercy of a bigot." Ames had no particular fear of bigots. What terrified him were liberty mongers. "The devil of sedition is immortal," he warned, "and we, the saints, have an endless struggle to maintain with him."

The Heralds of Liberty

The sharpshooters enforcing the Alien and Sedition Acts soon discovered that their targets packed a ricochet. They did manage to bag several of the nation's cheekiest scriveners, but, true to the history of martyrdom, the blood of the editors seeded the press.

In the most noted case, Benjamin Franklin Bache, his namesake's grandson, succumbed at the age of twenty-nine to yellow fever before the case against him could go forward, but his successor at the helm of the *Aurora*, the pugilistic Irish émigré William Duane (who inherited Bache's widow along with his press), was charged with accusing the president of being in bed with the British. His farce of a trial was suspended when Duane, employing the "truth as a defense" clause sanctioned by the Sedition Act, produced a letter written by Adams himself bemoaning British influence in American halls of power.

When the dust finally settled, only two Republican papers had folded as a result of the government policies and dozens had opened to combat them. Between 1798, when the Alien and Sedition Acts became law, and Election Day 1800, the percentage of newspapers openly identified as Republican increased from 28 to 40 percent of the national press. If Congress's acts were intended to tame liberty, the mastheads of these papers tell a different story. Along with *The Republican Atlas,* among the new opposition voices to emerge were *The Herald of Liberty, The Tree of Liberty, Genius of Liberty,* and *The Rights of Man.* On the *Herald*'s masthead, an angel perched in billowing clouds blasphemously trumpets, "MAN IS MAN & WHO IS MORE."

There was a religious backlash against the government as well. Even as the Sedition Act was selling Republican papers, the Alien Act swelled Republican ranks among the culturally conservative German-speaking Lutheran and Reformed population of western Pennsylvania and other clusters of Dunkers, Mennonites, and German Brethren, who dreaded the popular hostility it was fomenting against non-English-speaking Americans. It also came within a hair's breadth of snaring America's most celebrated martyr to freedom of conscience, the Reverend Dr. Joseph Priestley. A chemist whose studies of the pulmonary system had earned him international renown, Priestley was a Unitarian minister and much published theologian. His dismissal of the Trinity on scriptural grounds had led to the burning of his library and laboratory in Birmingham, England, and eventual asylum in the United States. While serving as minister to the Court of St. James, Adams frequented London's Unitarian Essex Street Chapel to hear Priestley preach. In 1792, he wrote to express sympathy for his "sufferings in the cause of liberty."

Ironically, the year before he was accused of sedition, Priestley dedicated his *Evidences on Revealed Religion* to Adams, citing his "steady attachment to the cause of Christianity." Having the evangelical Unitarian Priestley hail him on the flyleaf of his new book presented Adams with political difficulties that orthodox Dwight's earlier dedication did not. "It will get me the character of a heretic, I fear," John joked to Abigail.

Priestley's "coconspirator" in lobbying for a revival of American liberties in face of the government crackdown was Thomas Cooper, an Oxford-trained scientist and lawyer who emigrated from England to join his hero in Northumberland, Pennsylvania, where Priestly had hung up a shingle and was preaching his "uncorrupted" gospel. Cooper, too, was an avid Unitarian. (British Unitarianism sprang from a separate theological well and had a very different political flavor than the Unitarianism percolating through the Congregational Order of Massachusetts.) The two men shared a growing dismay at the hard right turn America was taking under Adams. In response, Cooper published a series of articles in the *Northumberland Gazette* and a book-length refutation of Federalist economic policies. Jefferson so admired Cooper's book that he sent copies to his partisans in every county in Virginia.

Jefferson, predictably, was aghast at Cooper's arrest and the related charge that Priestley was a French spy. "How deeply have I been chagrined & mortified at the persecutions which fanaticism & monarchy have excited against you, even here!" he told his favorite American theologian. "You have sinned against church & king, & can therefore never be forgiven." To his son-in-law, Jefferson declared, "It suffices for a man to be a philosopher, and to believe that human affairs are susceptible of improvement, and to look forward, rather than backward to the Gothic ages, for perfection, to mark him as an anarchist, disorganizer, atheist and enemy of the government." Well aware of his sympathetic encouragement of Priestley, Cooper, Duane, and several other outspoken critics of government policy, Federalist papers perceptively called Jefferson the "chief juggler" of sedition, manipulating his "emissaries" in the press while hiding safely out of public view.

Blaming Priestley for Cooper's heresies, Abigail Adams could only "presume" that "the Demo Cooper" and "the Demo philosopher" would alike receive swift and certain punishment under the provisions of the Alien Act. Her husband leapt to agree as to the seriousness of their attack. With respect to "poor Priestley," however, he counseled against prosecution. "His influence is not an atom in the world," Adams snorted. But Cooper's crime must not go unpunished. "A meaner, a more artful or a more malicious libel has not appeared," he told Secretary of State Pickering. "As far as it alludes to me I despise it; but as I have no doubt it is a libel against the whole government, and as such ought to be prosecuted."

The pint-sized, impossibly huge- and square-headed Cooper was a gifted scientist whose talents won him election to the American Philosophical Society. He believed in freedom, and at this particular moment in American history, freedom was a dangerous creed to profess. When brought before the Federal Court, Cooper accused the government of promulgating a "new-fangled doctrine of infallibility" to silence its political opponents and countercharged Hamilton with sedition. Justice Samuel Chase ruled that, by choosing such a defense, Cooper convicted himself of the "criminal and malignant intent of persuading the public that Adams was unfit for the presidency." On April 24, he gave Cooper a six-month sentence and imposed a $400 fine. When friends proposed begging the president's mercy, Cooper refused to appeal his sentence, mouthing the very justification Adams earlier had employed in rejecting Odgen's plea on behalf of Lyon—"Repentance must precede forgiveness." He would accept no pardon from the president, "until I receive myself & hear that Dr. Priestley had received a satisfactory acknowledgement from Mr. Adams of the impropriety of his conduct to us."

Adams could have predicted the populist outcry against the Alien and Sedition Acts he so imprudently embraced, if only he had remembered the passion for liberty that had once fired his revolutionary ardor. "There is a latent spark in the breasts of the people, capable of being kindled into a flame," Adams declared at the outset of the Revolution he helped to inspire. "What is this latent spark?" he asked. "The love of liberty. *A Deo hominis est indita naturae.*" ("It has been placed in the nature of man by God.")

"THE GRAND QUESTION"

That man must have religion plenty,
Who soars from "*no* God," up to "twenty."

—THOMAS GREEN FESSENDEN,
"DEMOCRACY UNVEILED"

Equality of Right is nature's plan,
And following nature is the march of man.

—JOEL BARLOW, "THE COLUMBIAD"

DURING THE ratification debate over the U.S. Constitution, a supporter of religious tests for office direly prophesied that "a Turk, a Jew, a Roman Catholic, and what is worst than all, a Universalist, may be President of the United States." In 1800, this nightmare threatened to become a reality. Looking back on the political drama that starred his great-grandfather, the historian Henry Adams painted a colorful portrait of the Federalist Black Regiment that rushed to defend American Christendom from the infidel Jefferson. "The minister put his three cornered hat on his head, took his silver-tipped cane in his hand," mounted the pulpit, and proclaimed that "every dissolute intriguer, loose-liver, forger, false coiner, and prison-bird; every hair-brained, loud talking demagogue; every speculator, scoffer, and atheist—was a follower of Jefferson." At the height of the campaign, the *Gazette of the United States* offered the electorate a stark choice.

THE GRAND QUESTION STATED

At the present solemn and momentous epoch, the only question
To be asked by every American, laying his hand on his heart, is

"Shall I continue in allegiance to
GOD—AND A RELIGIOUS PRESIDENT;
Or impiously declare for
Jefferson—and no god!!!"

Boston's Reverend Aaron Bancroft posed the same question—would the American government welcome the embrace of the "protecting arm of Deity" or "become the sport of atheistical chance and accident" instead? To law-and-order Christians, Jefferson's elevation to office would represent "no less than rebellion against God."

During the 1800 campaign for president, reading a Federalist newspaper was a little like going to church. "GREAT GOD OF COMPASSION AND JUSTICE, SHEILD MY COUNTRY FROM DESTRUCTION," blared a banner headline in the *Connecticut Current.* "Should Jefferson prove victorious, there is scarcely a possibility that we shall escape a *Civil War,*" prophesied its editor, Timothy Dwight's brother, Theodore. "Murder, robbery, rape, adultery, and incest will be openly taught and practiced, the air will be rent with the cries of distress, the soil will be soaked with blood, the nation black with crimes." With Dwight's assistance, American journalism achieved an early nadir. Only one estate contributed as much vitriol to the new republic's political engine—the American clergy.

Federalist preachers thundered that to elect the "great arch priest of Jacobinism and infidelity" would be tantamount to incinerating Christian decency and morality. "Are you prepared to see your dwelling in flames, hoary heads bathed in blood, female chastity violated, or children writhing on the pike and the halberd?" one parson asked. "If not, prepare for the task of protecting your government. Look at every leading Jacobin as at a ravening wolf, preparing to enter your peaceful fold, and glut his deadly appetite on the vitals of your country." William Duane lampooned the confusion of religion and politics. "It is proper, I think, that the subject be discussed," he sarcastically proposed, "that we may find out whether CHRIST is a MONARCHIST, a REPUBLICAN, a JACOBIN—or WHAT!!"

Timothy Dwight certainly had no doubts on the subject. "The question is not what he will do, but what he is," he said in addressing Jefferson's candidacy in the spring of 1800. "Is he an infidel? Then you cannot elect him without betraying our Lord." Jedidiah Morse chimed in, "From all known infidels then let us withdraw our confidence & support. We are highly criminal if we knowingly contribute in any way to increase their influence or power for in so doing we contribute to our own & our country's ruin." No mention here of turning the other cheek. Dr. Dwight beseeched, "Let us hear no more, at such times, of amiability and gentleness—or candor, liberality, and moderation—of conciliating, mild and generous feeling. Such qualities are now not virtues, but vices."

The Federalist preachers' overarching concern was the threat democracy posed to authority—both moral and governmental. In an 1800 election day sermon delivered in Hartford, the Reverend John Smalley chastised those who fill "the heads of inferiors with exalted notions of the equal 'rights of man.'" Rulers "must have authority to punish treasonable lies against themselves," he argued, "otherwise, who will be afraid of them?" Like many of his Connecticut cohorts, Smalley was suspect of liberty and alert to its abuses.

> In this state, though not near so free as some, great liberties are enjoyed. We have liberty to do every thing that we ought and a great many things that we ought not. In matters of religion, our liberties are almost unbounded. We may sell, buy and read what books we please, the best or the most atheistical and blasphemous. We may worship what god we choose: a just God or one who has not justice for men to fear. Every creature has equal liberty to preach the gospel and to preach what gospel he thinks proper....How any man, on the least sober reflection, should be willing that all others should be under less restraint than they now are, appears almost inconceivable.

During the months leading up to the election, Federalist pastors published entire tracts defaming Jefferson's impiety. The first chaplain of the House of Representatives, Dr. William Linn of the Collegiate Church in New York City, assembled the most effective of these in his "Serious Considerations on the Election of a President." Sensitive to the charge of mixing church and state, Linn couched his diatribe with a disclaimer: "I would not presume to dictate to you *who* ought to be President, but entreat you to hear with patience why *he* ought not." He hastened to add that he favored no other candidate, but could not resist admitting that Adams and the other (vice-presidential) candidates were "irreproachable."

Linn drew up his indictment from the pages of Jefferson's only published book, *Notes on Virginia.* Among its feast of facts and postulations, Jefferson questioned the creation narrative in Genesis, adduced scientific evidence for the earth's venerable age, and cast doubt on Noah's flood. He defended church-state separation, arguing that religion "of various kinds, indeed, but all good enough, all sufficient to preserve peace and order" would continue to prosper without state assistance. He advocated removing the Bible from the schools. And he championed freedom of conscience by colorfully confessing that "it does me no injury for my neighbor to say there are twenty gods, or no god. It neither picks my pocket, nor breaks my leg." Finally, in his tortured ramblings on the human status of blacks, Jefferson's conviction that "all men are created equal " collided squarely with deep-seated prejudice, offering northern parsons with the same stash of ammunition against his moral character that has stockpiled an entire industry of modern-day Jefferson bashers.

Rifling through Jefferson's *Notes* for ammunition, Dr. Linn pronounced its author a self-proclaimed despiser of Christianity. Given sanction, the religiously lax Virginian's indifferent attitude toward his countrymen's beliefs would reduce the United States in no time to "a nation of atheists," ending in the same fell stroke all hope for law and order. "Let my neighbor once persuade himself that there is no God," Jefferson's inquisitor wryly said, "and he will soon pick my pocket, and break, not only my leg but my neck."

Shifting from Jefferson's infidelity to his inhumanity, Dr. Linn threw the gauntlet of nature's law back into his face. "You have degraded the blacks from the rank which God hath given them in the scale of being," he said, rendering hyperbole unnecessary by letting Jefferson speak for himself. As proof that black *isn't* beautiful, a black man, Jefferson had claimed in *Notes on Virginia,* prefers white women for sex partners even as a male orangutan prefers black women to females of his own species. With his own apparent choice of sex partners contributing the charge of hypocrisy to an already long list, rumors of "Dusky Sally" and "Mr. Jefferson's Congo Harem" ground through the nation's gossip mills, hinting (if true) at the Virginian's closely guarded sexual relationship with Sally Hemings, a house slave, his wife's half sister and the purported mother of his bastard children.

Jefferson was blindsided by the direction that the attack on his racial views took. He had wished to keep his *Notes* private in the first place, because he feared that his blanket condemnation of slavery might complicate efforts to abolish it. A complimentary Adams certainly read his words that way. "The passages upon slavery are worth diamonds," he effused in 1785, untroubled by sentiments that would galvanize his partisans a decade and a half later.

One irony in the Christian attacks against Jefferson's Enlightenment worldview is that in some instances the biblical arguments raised to counter Jefferson's scientific ones fall closer to today's scientific consensus than Jefferson's theories did. John Mitchell Mason, pastor of New York City's Scots Presbyterian congregation, offers a case in point. On both the question of shells found on mountaintops and the genesis of humankind, Mason's biblical arguments are sounder than Jefferson's antibiblical ones. Having excluded Noah's flood as a possible explanation, Jefferson was completely stumped by shells in the Andes and Shenandoahs, denying as scientifically preposterous that there could ever be such a "great convulsion of nature" as to turn the perfect order of creation upside down. Mason answered by quoting Genesis 7:11: "All the fountains of the great deep were broken up." "Was this no 'great convulsion of nature?'" he asks. "Could not this 'heave the bed of the ocean to the height at which we now find shells?'" The answer, from contemporary plate tectonics, is "Yes, it could." The same principle holds for Jefferson's misbegotten reflections on race. Superficial and perceived differences between blacks and whites led Jefferson to speculate "as a suspicion only" that blacks "are inferior to the whites in the endowments both of body and mind," because they represent "a distinct race." By this he meant "less than fully human." Quoting Genesis again, Mason pronounced this bit of speculation as blasphemous as it was, to a Virginia plantation owner, self-serving. Mason's scriptural faith in "the common origin of mankind," not Jefferson's racist postulates on multiple genesis, stands the test of time. *Notes on Virginia* shimmers with Jeffersonian brilliance, but lapses such as these, even where its author is modest in his claims, stand as reminders that science, too, is prone to purblind presumption.

In addition to mining his *Notes* for ammunition, the Federalists put to equally good use a letter Jefferson had written to his longtime friend and sometime next-door neighbor, the Florentine Philip Mazzei. Mazzei lacked the one trait Jefferson most valued in a friend—discretion. He couldn't resist telling tales out of school. To the horror of Republican partisans who were having trouble enough staunching Jefferson's self-inflicted wounds, Mazzei's published and rumored recollections fed the monster of their candidate's infidelity. Linn reports him confessing that "Mr. Jefferson is rather farther gone in infidelity than I am." He also replayed a conversation the two men purportedly had on horseback. As they rode together past a decrepit church, Mazzei expressed astonishment that this house of God should have been allowed to fall into so "ruinous a condition." Jefferson glibly replied, "It was good enough for him who was born in a manger." To Linn, "Such a contemptuous sling at the blessed Jesus could issue from the lips of no other than a deadly foe to his name and his cause." He was certain that Jefferson's elevation to the presidency would "destroy religion, introduce immorality, and loosen all the bonds of society."

In *Notes on Virginia,* Jefferson foreshadowed his own destiny when he said, "They wish it to be believed that he can have no religion who advocates its freedom." If he had elected to answer his critics, he could have drawn his most stirring defense against "the calumny of atheism" from the same source. The very text that his religious detractors were citing chapter and verse to destroy him, finds Jefferson asking, "Can the liberties of a nation be thought secure, when we have removed their only firm basis, a conviction in the minds of the people, that these liberties are the gift of God?"

The Puritan Skeptic and the Enlightenment Priest

Adams found the religious attacks on Jefferson unseemly. They triggered his disdain for faction and mistrust of religious politics. A seasoned victim of political attacks, Adams had sympathy for the defendant. "I hate polemical politics and polemical divinity," he testified. As for the sexual innuendos, slavery corrupts everyone it touches, he muttered. "There was not a planter in Virginia who could not reckon among his slaves a number of his children," he said. Adams viewed the gossip swirling around Jefferson as "a natural and almost inevitable consequence of a foul contagion in the human character, Negro slavery."

In the meantime, Adams faced his own troubles. The tempest he had stirred up years before continued to blow in Republican attacks on his *Discourses on Davila.* Few people had actually read *Davila,* but savvy Republican operatives told their neighbors that it explained everything anybody needed to know about why Adams should not be reelected president. After all, what respectable American could think, much less write, "Every man should know his place and be made to keep it?" When *Davila* compounded his political troubles rather than alleviating them, its author grandly avowed that he had uttered not a single opinion that couldn't be found in the Bible. He took moral comfort from hearsay that at least one soul had understood him. "Mr. Adams reads the scriptures and there he finds that man is as stupid as the wild ass's colt," this plucky defender explained. "He believes what he reads and infers his necessary consequences from it, that is all. Mr. Adams is not to blame. He did not write the scriptures. He only reads and believes." A quarter century later, Adams shed modesty's most intimate garments and proclaimed *Defense of the Constitutions* (to which *Davila* formed an appendix) "a book that has been misunderstood, misrepresented, and abused more than any other, except the Bible."

In fact, that honor might better be reserved for Thomas Paine. In 1796, the first volume of his *Rights of Man* (familiarly known in New England as "The Devil's Bible") arrived by profane post from Europe. Delighted "that something was to be publicly said about the political heresies which have sprung up among us," Jefferson wrote to Paine's American publisher to praise the American edition of Paine's controversial work, naively declaring, "I have no doubt our citizens will rally a second time round the standard of Common Sense." The opportunistic merchant knew a great blurb when he saw one. Being enlisted as a pitchman for "The Devil's Bible" identified Jefferson, not unfairly but to his political detriment, with the book's radical contents. It also hammered a final nail into the coffin of his friendship with Adams.

John Quincy Adams rushed to defend both his father (the apparent heretic in question) *and* free discourse. Writing anonymously under the byline "Publicola," he borrowed Jefferson's favorite hammer to drive his point home. "I have always understood, sir, that the citizens of these States were possessed of a full and entire freedom of opinion upon all subjects, civil as well as religious," he said. "They have not yet established any infallible criterion of orthodoxy, either in church or state, and the only political tenet which they could stigmatize with the name of heresy would be that which should attempt to impose an opinion upon their understandings." Seeing through Jefferson's liberal veneer, young Adams exposed his inner ideologue.

Neither champion in the battle for America's soul was whom he appeared to be. Jefferson the infidel was in fact a true believer. Adams was a thoroughgoing skeptic. Inverting New Testament iconography (and political logic), doubting John and the beloved disciple Thomas were the respective standard bearers of divine order and sacred liberty.

If Adams was skeptical about almost everything, Jefferson worshiped just as doggedly at the altar of reason and progress. Only half joking, he declared that the Republican creed "contains the catholic faith, which whosoever doth not keep whole and undefiled, without doubt, he shall perish everlastingly." Noah Webster observed, "The Jacobins differ from the clergy of the dark ages in this—the clergy persecuted for heresy in religion—the Jacobins, for heresy in politics." No less astutely, Hamilton called Jefferson's circle "popes in government...who brand with heresy all opinions but their own." Proving both men correct, Jefferson dismissed Federalism as a "sect," pronouncing those who "apostatized from the true faith" "heretics," guilty of unforgivable "blasphemies." In his illuminated world, the children of light were pitched against the children of darkness. Worshiping reason in the pantheon of modernism, Jefferson was an Enlightenment priest.

Defending Sacred Liberty

One rumor spicing Christian fears during the height of the electoral smear campaign against Jefferson was that, given the opportunity, he would ban the scriptures. A joke made the rounds that, to protect her precious Bible from government confiscation, a pious Connecticut woman asked the lone Jeffersonian in her village if he would keep it safe for her at his home.

"My good woman," he replied, "if all the Bibles are to be destroyed, what is the use of bringing yours to me?"

Because, she said, "They'll never think of looking in the house of a Democrat for a Bible."

Such humor tapped a paranoia felt by New England Federalists to which their Democratic-Republican neighbors were more legitimately entitled. New Haven's beleaguered Congregational pastor, Isaac Jones, wrote to elicit sympathy from an unlikely source. To Ashbel Green he complained that "Being the only democratical preacher in the state who dares to speak, I am, of course, the object of persecution." He was less alone than he imagined. Across New England, Republican preachers were increasingly under attack either for supporting Jefferson or for insisting that the church had no business messing in politics. Jones lost his New Haven pulpit for backing Jefferson in the 1800 campaign.

Jefferson himself could hardly step out of doors without drawing religious fire. When he attended a Sunday reception in his honor, the Federalist press pounced on his desecration of the Sabbath.

Republican propagandists were knocked on their heels by the relentless strafing of their champion's beliefs. Their first line of defense was denial. New York Republican stalwart DeWitt Clinton argued that as long as Jefferson believed in the divinity of Christ (which he did not), his theological views might be in error and even heretical, but that didn't make him a Deist. Other Republican apologists, writing in response to Reverend Linn's shopping list of grievances, offered an even less nuanced defense of his party's standard-bearer. Jefferson was *not* a Deist, but a faithful Christian. That Jefferson called Noah's flood "a wonder" only proved that he believed in miracles. The letter to Mazzei was a forgery and the stories he told suggesting Jefferson's infidelity amounted to nothing more than "hearsay of hearsay." Not a word Jefferson had written "mitigates against the Mosaic account of the creation." And he didn't exclude blacks from the human race; he simply "endeavors to prove what can't be denied: that they are inferior in complexion, beauty, and form to the whites."

In response to Democratic boasts of Jefferson's Christian fidelity, Dwight rushed to call their bluff. He demanded that the Republican candidate demonstrate his presumptive faith by publicly affixing his signature to the Apostles' Creed. Hardly muffled by such antics, rumors ran rampant that Dr. Dwight had privately beseeched President Adams to establish a national church. Speaking of Dwight and the Connecticut Standing Order—in the popular mind, Northern Presbyterians and Congregationalists were politically and theologically interchangeable—one Connecticut Republican warned, "If a national Presbyterian Church was not contemplated by them during the revolution, it is now advocated."

Speaking to such fears, John Leland lifted up Article VI of the Constitution: "It is one of the great excellencies of the Constitution that no religious test is ever to be required to qualify any officer," he said. And, in the first mock-up of a political party platform, William Duane's *Aurora* laid out among its planks the principle of "good government without the aid of priestcraft or religious politics, and justice administered without religious interference." Duane contrasted his party's fidelity to liberty with the Federalist policy of incorporating religion into government "for political purposes,...equally polluting the holy altars of religion and the seats of justice."

Fearless Connecticut Republican Abraham Bishop made the religious case for Jefferson's election most persuasively by posing what was fast becoming the real religious question of the hour: "How much has religion been benefited by sermons intended to show that Satan and Cain were Jacobins? How much by sermons in which every deistical argument has been presented with its greatest force as being part of the republican creed?" The Federalist clergy were at once undermining faith and demonstrating too little of it, he said. "The captain of salvation is not so weak as to need an army and a navy and a majority in Congress to support his cause."

The spirited Republican defense of Jefferson was far from ineffectual. It resonated in particular with America's religious minorities, already a near majority of the Christian electorate. The Baptists and Methodists together soon would eclipse the combined establishment churches in both spiritual and temporal clout. As if on political cue, the Second Great Awakening opened with a bang during the height of the 1800 campaign. Baptist, Methodist, and Scots Presbyterian ministers—"wandering stars," some called them—were coursing through the western firmament. By the thousands, seekers gathered at interfaith, evangelical camp meetings, hoping to be liberated by the gospel of freedom in Christ from all earthy authorities, including the authority of the established church.

The most dependable gauge of religious-political affiliations during the early Republic was any given denomination's insider or outsider status in society. Outgroups tended to be politically progressive, ingroups politically conservative. The established churches (Congregational, Unitarian, and to a lesser extent, Episcopalian) were predominantly Federalist in their voting patterns. Dissenting Protestants (Baptist, Methodist, etc.), along with Catholics and Jews, by and large voted Republican. The Presbyterians split North and South, with the Northern Presbyterians, predominantly of English descent, aligning with the Federalists, and the southern and western Scots Presbyterians gravitating to the Republicans. As insiders in Pennsylvania and the Delaware Valley, the Society of Friends held a unique position. The Quakers' high social status and strong civil ethic combined to forge a constituency at once supportive of order and avid for liberty. Their natural conservatism, coupled with a revulsion against slavery, drew most Quakers into Adams's camp. For all the blustering about infidelity, theology played a relatively small role in defining the nation's sacred politics. Baptists and Congregationalists, though political polar opposites, stemmed from the same Calvinist roots.

At first the clerical advantage went to the Federalists. "The clergy, who are numerous and as a body very respectable," Jedidiah Morse smugly observed, "have hitherto preserved a kind of aristocratical balance in the...government of the state which has happily operated as a check to the overbearing spirit of republicanism." Sectarian pastors maintained a greater Christian distance from worldly affairs than those in the Standing Orders, for whom politics and religion were two modalities of a single ethos. Many Christian Republicans (Moravians, German Brethren, etc.) were Quietists, and almost all practiced some form of Pietism. Few Methodist pastors took an active role in politics, and Baptists entered the lists primarily to defend freedom of conscience, but both sects could be counted on to vote the Republican Party line.

Isaac Backus is typical in this regard. New England's most influential mainstream Baptist preacher disapproved of the government action to suppress the Whiskey Rebellion and remained sympathetic with the French Revolution. Backus even read and was undaunted by Jefferson's *Notes on Virginia*. Libertarian politics forged a bond between the two men that overcame their theological differences. After the election, celebrating Jefferson's victory over Adams, Backus would say, "The man who was the chief magistrate of these United States for four years was very fond of partiality. But a man was elected into that office in 1801 who is for equal liberty to all the nation."

Establishing an equivalency between religious and political egalitarianism, Republican advocates made a persuasive connection between the ideals of the Declaration of Independence and those of sectarian Protestantism. Playing to the concerns of liberty-loving Christian minorities, the Lancaster Republican Committee in Pennsylvania targeted local sects to expand its voter base. "To religious men, Mr. Jefferson has indisputably been the most useful character since *William Penn*," they proposed, promising that his election would advance the "sound practical equality of the Quaker" and "the *equal brotherhood* of the Moravian, the Mennonist, and the Dunker." The Republican Party of New Jersey went an emotional step further, likening the persecution of Jefferson to that which had plagued their religious forebearers.

> [He is] a man against whom falsehood has raised its voice, under the garb of religion, only because he has banished tithes and an established church from his native state, and who would brand him with the name of infidel because he is not a fanatic, nor willing that the *Quaker,* the *Baptist,* the *Methodist,* or any other denomination of Christians, should pay the pastors of other sects; because he does not think a Catholic should be banished for believing in transubstantiation, or a Jew, for believing in the God of Abraham, Isaac, and Jacob.

No religious body was too small to escape the notice of competing political evangelists, not even the people of Abraham. Looking to siphon off a few Jewish votes, one overzealous Federalist partisan under the alias Moses S. Solomon ("a follower of Moses and the Old Testament") fabricated a letter to the editor defaming Jefferson as "an atheist who should receive no religious man's vote, whatever his faith may be." Benjamin Nones, a prominent citizen and leading member of the Philadelphia synagogue, easily smoked out one of the first recorded dirty tricks in American presidential politics as a ruse, "no doubt" intended for "political ends." Nones attested to just how important the strict separation of church and state was to him and his people. "I am a Jew, and if for no other reason, for that reason, I am a Republican."

Once Jefferson's faith had become a political football, the other candidates became fair game. More than one Republican apologist fairly pointed out that the unitarian Jefferson was no greater an infidel than the unitarian Adams. Federalist vice-presidential candidate Charles Pinckney came under particularly vicious fire. Republican henchmen accused him of impregnating and abandoning a "female of a respectable family" and produced unimpeachable Federalist testimony to cast doubt on his Christian orthodoxy. In his

1788 satirical poem "The Triumph of Infidelity," none other than Timothy Dwight had branded Pinckney a Deist: "I am the first of men in the ways of evil," the poem finds him boasting, "the truest, thriftiest servant of the Devil."

Adams stayed above the fray. On principle, he refused to tack his sails to the winds of partisan opinion, even those that were blowing at his back. He later chafed at political opportunists who employed whatever religious argument best served their party's advancement. "In the year 1798 the Democrats opposed the election of Mr. [James] Ross [of Pennsylvania] upon the ground of his being a Deist," he later recalled. "The Federalists either denied it or said his religious tenets had nothing to do with his qualifications for governor. In 1799 the Federalists opposed the election of Mr. Jefferson upon the ground of his being a Deist. The Democrats denied it or said his infidel principles had nothing to do with his qualifications for President!!!" Whatever we choose to make of the three exclamation points, Adams knew from long experience that "When parties run high, one side cries 'Crucify' and the other 'Hosanna.'" In 1800 both sides were crying, "Crucify."

"Great Is the Guilt of an Unnecessary War"

A popular ditty of the time lampooned the practical difficulties faced by Calvinists, who were born either to be saved or damned and could do nothing to wriggle free from their fate.

> You can and you can't,
> You shall and you shan't;
> You will and you won't.
> You're damned if you do,
> And damned if you don't.

The final couplet tells the story of Adams's presidency.

Inviting fire from both sides, Adams's monumental accomplishment as president was keeping the United States out of an unnecessary war with France. For a time, the XYZ Affair sufficiently muted Francophile sentiment and roiled patriotic passions that not to turn a diplomatic war of words into a real one required true political courage. As his successors would discover, war against an outside enemy offers the president, at least initially, useful cover against domestic political foes. Conversely, frustrated bellicosity can ricochet to wound any leader who refuses to provide an external outlet for the people's blood lust. With the "ultras" in his own party fomenting hatred of the "factious, cutthroat, frog-eating, treaty-breaking, grace fallen, God-defying [French] devils," peace was a brave thing to wage.

Adams temporized on going to war, driving Federalist ultras to their wits' end. "Assassination shall be your lot," wrote one livid constituent when the president delayed the rush to arms. Most shockingly, he unofficially countenanced the self-initiated, religiously inspired peace mission carried out by Dr. George Logan, who carried a letter of commendation to French Foreign Minister Talleyrand from Jefferson. A genuine radical, Logan adopted *Vox populi vox Dei*" as his personal motto. Here he not only tested the government's latitude but also broke ranks with his religious community, many of whom set aside their pacifism to honor their English roots. "The Quakers were the most clamorous for war," Jefferson remembered. "Their principle of peace, as a secondary one, yielded to the primary one of adherence to the Friends in England, and what was patriotism in the original became treason in the copy."

Logan's peace efforts fed the fantasies of conspiracy theorists. The Philadelphia *Gazette* ranted that this "noted and violent democrat" doubtless entertained the "infernal design" of introducing French troops to American shores "*to teach us the genuine value of true and essential liberty* by re-organizing our government through the blessed operation of the bayonet and guillotine." Noah Webster whispered that, in advance of this dread invasion, plans were already afoot for an American directorate fashioned on the French model, with Jefferson, Madison, and Monroe penciled in as its governing troika. Concerned that their loyalty might be tested in a war with France, Washington is said to have floated the idea that Republicans be screened from the army.

Upon returning from his wildcat mission, Logan had the gumption to lobby General Washington, who was in Philadelphia closeted with Hamilton hammering out the protocols for his new military command. Throughout their brief interview, the general maintained a stony silence, alone acknowledging Logan's clerical escort, while presenting the "ambassador" a cold shoulder. In telling contrast, President Adams sent shock waves through Federalist ranks by favoring Jefferson's *envoy extraordinaire* with a hearing. During the course of their conversation, Logan urged an appropriately wary Adams to crack his mind open to the possibility that the French might indeed be sincere in their desire for peace. Adams's Federalist colleagues responded less genially to Logan's mission. They drew up legislation (the Logan Act, which stands to this day) barring American citizens from appointing themselves diplomats.

Although busily planning for war, Washington was by no means eager to fight one. He opposed international entanglements on principle and counseled patience. If America's greatest warrior was reluctant to take up arms, surely the commander in chief, ever vigilant lest anyone mistake his manhood, could dismount from the charger his political cohorts had so solicitously outfitted for him. After a final bit of macho posturing—to Washington he decried the Republicans' "babyish and womanly blubbering"—Adams ended the so-called quasi-war with France by fiat, firing off his peace message to an astonished Congress on February 19, 1799 and signing the treaty of peace a year later. Drowning out the Republican crowing was a resounding chorus of Federalist catcalls. History alone would confirm that the country's second president might justly have etched on his tombstone (as he once contemplated doing) this worthy epitaph: "Here lies John Adams, who took upon himself the responsibility of the peace with France in the year 1800." At the height of war fever, he renamed his Quincy homestead "Peacefield."

Of all the attacks leveled against Adams, the most brutal and unaccountable was the act of literary terrorism sponsored by a suddenly deranged Alexander Hamilton, whose scheme for personal and national redemption hinged on building up an army (which he, under Washington, would lead) in preparation for a possible war with France. As de facto commanding general of the American forces, Hamilton was at last fulfilling his life's dream, a military command. He drew up lengthy, fastidious battle tables, recruited a full complement of officers for sixteen army battalions, and set up an elaborate set of rules and regulations fit for a modern army. With a personality perfectly tailored for epaulets, it had been years since Hamilton was so happily engaged. But then the winds of war shifted. Soon the great American Army, still little more than a dream, would be nothing but a memory. Bereft of purpose and expectation, Hamilton looked back on a lost year of strenuous preparation and forward into the void. At this juncture in his life, he could not have been more vulnerable to passion's demonic allure.

In the political equivalent of murder-suicide, Hamilton launched an eighty-page broadside in which he sadly informed the electorate that, because of Adams's "disgusting egotism," "distempered jealousy," and "ungovernable indiscretion of temper," the incumbent president did "not possess the talents adapted to the administration of government, and there are great and intrinsic defects in his character, which unfit him for the office of chief magistrate." Due to his "eccentric" imagination and "vanity without bounds," the president's every action, Hamilton sniped, contributed "to the detriment of any cause of which he is the chief." In a final spasm of tortured logic, he closed this screed by reluctantly endorsing its victim for reelection as the preferred alternative to Jefferson. To whatever extent Hamilton had not earlier bewildered his friends, delighted his foes, and damaged his reputation when he defended himself against false charges of petty malfeasance by confessing to adultery, the unguided fusillade he launched against Adams destroyed it completely.

Invigorated by Hamilton's wayward attack, Adams lashed back with all his bitter might, defaming the illegitimate Hamilton as "a bastard brat of a Scotch peddler." In his furious estimation, Hamilton had proved himself no better than "a proud-spirited, conceited, aspiring mortal always pretending to morality,...with as debauched morals as old Franklin who is more his model than anyone I know." Adams had finally found an enemy more vivid in real life than in his overheated imagination. On the bright side, which would dawn in reconciliation between the two men twelve years later, Adams hinted at the possibility of redemption for the "infinitely better" and "wiser" Jefferson. Given Adams's state of mind, being deemed better and wiser than Hamilton, even infinitely so, was a backhanded compliment. Yet, disregarding his oath never to return to the office he so despised, the president intriguingly speculated that he would prefer serving as Jefferson's vice president (a live possibility in the yet to be modified electoral system) or even as his minister to the Hague, "than be indebted to such a being as Hamilton for the presidency."

Sharing Hamilton as a common foe gave Adams and Jefferson an abiding, if for years unspoken, bond. Adams perfunctorily forgave Hamilton. Allergic even to the memory of controversy, Jefferson attempted to forget him. The concept of forgiveness was superfluous to Jefferson; he treated unpleasantness with a cup of amnesia. Adams, on the other hand, forgot nothing. If, as he once said, "The devil is no part of my faith," the Devil's servants were essential to maintaining it in fighting trim. A year after Burr struck Hamilton down in a duel, Adams placed a scripturally encrusted epitaph on the sarcophagus of their tortured relationship.

Although I have long since forgiven this archenemy, yet vice, folly and villainy are not to be forgotten because the guilty wretch repented in his dying moments. Although David repented, we are nowhere commanded to forget the affair of Uriah; though the Magdalene reformed, we are not obliged to forget her former vocation; though the thief on the cross was converted, his felony is still upon record. The prodigal son repented and was forgiven, yet his harlots and riotous living, and even the swine and the husks that brought him to consideration, cannot be forgotten. Nor am I obliged by any principles of morality or religion to suffer my character to lie under infamous calumnies, because the author of them, with a pistol bullet through his spinal marrow, died a penitent.

Adams was not, by any stretch of the religious imagination, a Jesus person. He was an Old Testament Christian: Job huddling in the corner picking at his scabs with a potsherd; Hosea declaiming the nation's harlotry; Daniel in the lion's den; Joseph wrestling with an angel. He didn't live by the ancient Hebrew *lex talionis* (an eye for an eye and a tooth for a tooth), much preferring the bitter pleasures of martyrdom to actual revenge, but he certainly *believed* in the *lex talionis*. Before he could even think of letting Hamilton rest in peace, he had to disembowel him.

The Treaty of Tripoli

Ironically, under Adams's Christian watch the executive branch would issue its most explicit rejection of any formal entanglement between Christianity and the U.S. government. This disclaimer appears in the Treaty of Tripoli, which Adams submitted to the Senate for ratification during his first year in office. In exchange for a pasha's ransom, the Kingdom of Tripoli promised, temporarily as it turned out, to constrain the pirates under its jurisdiction from intercepting American merchant ships. Drafted in Arabic, signed by Commissioner Plenipotentiary of the United States David Humphreys, whom President Washington had assigned to negotiate the treaties, and translated by free-agent diplomat Joel Barlow, Article 11 of the Treaty of Tripoli reads:

AS THE GOVERNMENT of the United States of America is not in any sense founded on the Christian Religion—as it has in itself no character of enmity against the laws, religion or tranquility of Musselmen—and as the said States never have entered into any war or act of hostility against any Mohometan nation, it is declared by the parties that no pretext arising form religious opinions shall ever produce an interruption of the harmony existing between the two countries.

Although faithful to the framers' secular intent, this article may constitute a Republican Trojan horse. Barlow was a fascinating character. He appeared on the public stage as poet, linguist, Continental Army chaplain, freethinker, and diplomat. A Connecticut Wit turned democrat, Barlow shifted his loyalty, investing it no less completely, from Christ to liberty. Barlow's panegyric on the French Revolution (plucked from a personal letter not intended for publication) received wide circulation in America when Congressman Lyon got hold of it and published its contents, thereby adding a significant count to his indictment for sedition.

Adams had no use for the mercurial Barlow, whom he branded a libertine. "Thomas Paine is not a more worthless fellow," he said, scraping the bottom of his insult barrel. In a more intimate affront, Barlow's old cohort Timothy Dwight removed his portrait from the walls of Yale, where it hung in impudent reminder that one of proud Eli's sons had unconscionably fallen from political and religious grace into wanton French arms. Barlow's defection even embarrassed his family. His proper Connecticut wife begged him to "go home and be respectable."

As an Arabist, Barlow was far from respectable, perhaps even devious. He cobbled together a translation of the original Arabic that is by no means exact, its most curious defect being the eleventh article itself, which does not appear in anything like its final form in the Arabic text. Under the loose diplomatic protocol of the day,

Barlow could easily have parked his favorite hobby (freedom of conscience) smack in the middle of his English translation with no one in America being any the wiser.

Whether the poet was guilty of invention in translating the treaty is immaterial. His translation is the document that Adams approved and the full Senate ratified, investing Article 11 with the full force of U.S. law. Distributed to papers across the land, the Treaty of Tripoli was published with the following preamble:

> Now be it known that I, John Adams, President of the United States of America, having seen and considered the said treaty do, by and with the advice and consent of the Senate, accept, ratify, and confirm the same, and every clause and article thereof. And to the end that the said treaty may be observed and performed with good faith on the part of the United States, I have ordered it to be made public.

Too much can be made of this document as a proof text that Adams believed, as the treaty says, that "the United States is by no means founded on the Christian Religion." Washington, Jefferson, and Madison certainly could have endorsed this clause, but Adams, at this point in his political career, anyway, could not. In signing the treaty, he either glossed over the eleventh article as being of no moment or read its meaning narrowly. At the time Adams expressly believed that the U.S. government could not prosper apart from a sound Christian foundation.

The Voice of the People

Electoral politics unsettled Jefferson's stomach, but they pierced Adams to the marrow. Years after their political wars were but a distant memory, in a letter to his old rival Adams damned the soul-destroying properties of electoral democracy. "Our money, our commerce, our religion, our national and state constitutions, even our arts and sciences, are so many seed plots of division, faction, sedition and rebellion," he mourned to Jefferson. "Everything is transmuted into an instrument of electioneering. Election is the grand Brama, the immortal Lama, I had almost said, the Jaggernaught, for wives are almost ready to burn upon the pile and children to be thrown under the wheel." Adams's problem with elections was fundamentally spiritual. Not only did internecine animosities bring out the worst in people, but, on a personal level, to put himself forward was to tempt the—for him irresistible—sin of pride. "Elections to offices which are great objects of ambition, I look at with terror," he confided to Jefferson in 1787. He broached the subject again in a letter to his inconstant friend a decade later, shortly before the two would first contest the presidency. "You and I shall go to the kingdom of the just, or at least shall be released from the republic of the unjust, with hearts pure and hands clean of all corruption in elections: so much I firmly believe," Adams hopefully declared. "Those who shall introduce the foul fiend on the stage after we are gone must exorcise him as they can." To whatever extent victory tamed this electoral monster in 1796, the fiend took full revenge four years later in the president's equally narrow defeat.

During the course of the campaign, Abigail Adams grew "disgusted with the world," concluding that "the chief of its inhabitants do not appear worth the trouble and pains they cost to save them from destruction." Hyperbole ran in the family. Their youngest son, Thomas Boylston Adams, likened his father to God and Hamilton to Lucifer, who "would assail the Almighty Chief of the skies to drag Him from His throne, though sure to fall by failing in the attempt." Hamilton's efforts notwithstanding, the vast majority of Federalists stood firm. Distraught at the prospect of an Adams loss, one party newspaper, inverting *E pluribus unum* to "*Pluria e Uno*" ("many out of one"), prophesied that, under the influence of democracy's moon, the "lunatic party" was hell-bent on

sacrificing the American eagle and supplanting him with a skeptical owl.

To buffer his pending fall, Adams sought the consolations of
martyrdom. "I am not about to write lamentations or jeremiads
over my fate," he stoutly said as the blade was coming down. "You
may think me disappointed [by the prospect of defeat]. I am not.
All my life I have expected it." Defeat suited the requirements of
Adams's temperament. But he was no Stoic. Nor did Christian resignation come to him naturally. From the depths of his electoral
anguish, honesty would force him to confess, "I know of no philosophy or religion…which can reconcile man to life." Given the
chance to live his life over again, he would, like his father, be a
shoemaker.

If far from the fray, in the ramp up to the election Jefferson
wasn't sitting on the sidelines. Acting as his own campaign manager
(raising campaign dollars, controlling the message, and ensuring
that it got out), he dashed off instructions to Madison. "This summer is the season for systematic energies and sacrifices," reads one
coded exhortation. "The engine is the press. Every man must lay his
purse and his pen under contribution. As to the former, it is possible I may be obliged to assume something for you. As to the latter, let me pray and beseech you to set apart a certain portion of
every post day to write what may be proper for the public. Send it
to me while here, and when I go away I will let you know to whom
you may send, so that your name shall be sacredly secret."

This time the presidential campaign did provoke heated public
interest. Due in no small measure to the religious wars galvanizing
the electorate, turnout practically doubled, with as many as 70 percent of eligible voters casting their ballots in several states. The split
decision, finally clear by late December, followed sectional lines,
with Jefferson claiming 80 percent of the southern vote and Adams
an even higher percentage in the north, with Adams edged out by
a mere eight electoral ballots.

The Republican press trumpeted Jefferson's victory. One editor from Bennington, Vermont, heralded the role played by the public rejection of the Alien and Sedition Acts in the election's outcome.

> At length election came about,
> And democrats were handy,
> They pled their skill the land throughout,
> Sing Yankee Doodle Dandy;
> Then Thomas took the seat from John,
> And dungeons lost their men, Sir,
> Through Jefferson the grace was shewn,
> Our press is free again, Sir!

With once seditious words like these chorusing through the streets, John and Abigail Adams, now ensconced in the nation's new capital city, drew their curtains on the public, rarely emerging from the President's House save for Sunday worship at practically the only church in town, the chapel that had been set up in the Capitol building, its services conducted by the House and Senate chaplains.

"An Infidel President"

To Abigail Adams, the president's white house (a name then reserved for a Washington tavern) was both palace and prison, with thirteen fireplaces and as many chilling drafts. Others marveled at its twenty-one-foot ceilings, white gold-corniced curtains, and the crimson-damask upholstered sofas and chairs in its magnificent drawing room. Although responsible for its furnishings, neither John nor Abigail required such splendor. In good Puritan fashion, both mistrusted luxury, preferring the more humble comforts of their farm in Quincy. During the long winter of 1801, they could not help but feel like prisoners in their "great castle."

Compounding the people's rejection was a more intimate anguish, the death in October of their middle son, Charles. Two of the Adams's three boys and their son-in-law as well would fall victim to alcoholism, with Charles dying from the effects of drink at the age of thirty. Abigail took strange comfort that her son, "beloved in spite of his errors" and ballooned almost beyond recognition by water retention but not red-faced, betrayed no telltale signs of the intemperance that killed him. The Adams household was a stern environment for children to prosper in. Of its asperities, John Quincy's wife, Louisa, whose American ancestors hailed from the South, would exclaim on first visiting Quincy, "Had I stepped into Noah's Ark, I do not think I could have been more utterly astonished." Everything was foreign to her, "even the Church," she exclaimed, "its forms, the snuffling through the nose." Only one presence softened the chill New England hospitality. "The old gentleman," Louisa said, "took a fancy to me."

During the old gentleman's younger years, he wasn't so sweet. Even as he aged, moral imperatives outweighed family ties in the Adams family scale of values. When his errant son-in-law, William Smith, dispatched his own son on a madcap errand to end Spanish dominion over Venezuela, Adams declared, "I had no other hope or prayer than that the ship with my grandson in it might be sunk in the Gulf Stream." Years before, Abigail assured eleven-year-old John Quincy that, if the mores of Paris should compromise his morals, she prayed he would drown on the way home to America. Adams later told him that if he didn't become president, it would be due to his own indolence. After paying the necessary tariffs, John Quincy returned uncontaminated and did become president. The other two boys drowned themselves in alcohol.

No less devastated than his wife by the moral and physical collapse of their most beguiling child—"I love him too much," he once confessed—Adams was unable to suspend judgment. Charles was no longer his son but "a madman possessed of the devil." "I renounce him," he cried. "King David's Absalom had some ambition and some enterprise. Mine is a mere rake, buck, blood, and beast." Adams's standards for his children were as impossibly high as those he blamed himself for failing to meet.

Having disowned Charles, Adams refused to visit his son as he lay dying. Yet, from the depth of his anguish, he poignantly framed his family drama in the cosmic language of atonement. "Oh!" he wailed. "That I had died for him, if that would have relieved him from his faults as well as his disease." Adams's valedictory letter to Jefferson hints at the quenched flame he carried for his lost son (and lost friend, too, perhaps). "Once the delight of my eyes and a darling of my heart," Charles had been "cut off in the flower of his days amidst very flattering prospects by causes which have been the greatest grief of my heart and the deepest affliction of my life." If Jefferson had been privy to his sorrow, Adams said, the knowledge of its burden "might have given you a moment of melancholy or at least of sympathy with a mourning father." Jefferson, who answered his correspondence fastidiously, found no reason to favor Adams with the courtesy of a reply.

After his defeat, Adams confronted his demons in the only way he knew how—by retreating into the refuge of solitude to nurse his precious wounds. Abigail, no less true to character, mounted her epistolary platform and cursed the darkness. Not given to self-pity, she narrowed "her hawk's eyes" (as pictured by one unsympathetic contemporary and in a famous Gilbert Stuart portrait) and vented her rage. In the bonfire of her memory, she torched Jefferson (the gentle-natured, shuffling, freckle-faced man, whom she had sincerely loved as "one of the choice ones of the earth") as an impious miscreant. "A patriot without religion," Abigail once said, is "as great a paradox, as an honest man without God." Being, in her eyes, without religion and godless and therefore unpatriotic and dishonest, Jefferson, she now bitterly remembered, made "no pretensions to the belief in an all wise and supreme Governor of the world." He went so far as to dismiss Christian worship in her very presence as "mere mummery." Returning to the letter of her faith, Abigail viewed the election results in apocalyptic terms. "If ever we saw a day of darkness," she bemoaned, "I fear this is one which will be visible until kindled into flames."

Still in mourning at Mount Vernon, Lady Washington shared Lady Adams's alarm. Liberated by age and the absence of her husband's imperial censor to blurt out anything she pleased, Martha pronounced Jefferson "one of the most detestable of mankind" and his election "the greatest misfortune our country has ever experienced."

Abigail did render to the president-elect the courtesy of inviting him to his new residence for dinner. They were seen arm-in-arm strolling on the garden terrace. Her pen sharper than her tongue— "I wrote many things," she confessed, "that I suppose I never could have talked"—Abigail raised the sore subject of the late election only to counsel her lost friend obliquely against the radicals in his circle who would destroy the government if given half a chance. She borrowed the quip of a clergyman, whom she had once heard preach on the text "And they knew not what to do." When the people don't know what to do, Abigail warned, "they should take great care that they do not do they know not what." Jefferson chuckled in nonreply and, with that, their interview on matters of public moment and, with it, the final hint of mutual affection, came to a close. Although their friendship would be resurrected, blossoming into the most vibrant political correspondence in the history of American letters, Jefferson and the Adamses would never meet again.

Abigail departed Washington for her home on February 13, passing through Philadelphia on the day Jefferson's election was finally certified and witnessing with unqualified disgust the sacrilege of church bells ringing for "an Infidel President." One Federalist wag commemorated the same blasphemy with a vicious bit of doggerel.

> Oh ye rascally ringers and Jacobin foes,
> Ye disturbers of all who delight in repose,
> How I wish, for the quiet and peace of the land
> That ye had round your necks what ye hold in your hands.

On arriving in Quincy, Abigail set up house and awaited the self-styled "Monarch of Stony Field's" return. The monarch himself fled Washington under the cover of darkness. At four in the morning on inauguration day, lighted by the sliver of a moon, Adams boarded a public stage and flew from the scene of young America's greatest glory, when the baton of power is ceremonially passed from one sitting president to the next in a peaceful exchange of power. In two and a quarter centuries of inaugural history, only two defeated presidents have so refused to honor not their successor so much as the office itself and the system of government it represents. The other president too proud to show up for his own political funeral was the nation's sixth president, John Quincy Adams.

"The Garrulity of Narrative Old Age"

The Reverend Theodore Parker of Boston had a gift for summing up the great men of America's storied past. Of Adams he said, "He was terribly open, earnest, and direct, and could not keep his mouth shut." After licking his wounds long enough to get a full taste of how grievously he had been wronged, Adams emerged from his den and singed the air with his grievances. "Such is the melancholy lot of humanity, that I cannot presume to promise immortality to liberty," he mourned. "The republican electorate was as unjust, tyrannical, brutal, barbarous and cruel as any king or senate."

Part of his therapeutic venting was private in nature. In his sixty-seventh year, apologizing for the historical insignificance of its subject, Adams began recording an authorized version of his life. "Having been the object of much misrepresentation," he began, "some of my posterity may probably wish to see in my own handwriting a proof of the falsehood of that mass of odious abuse of my character, with which newspapers, private letters and public pamphlets and histories have been disgraced for thirty years." In the theological sense of the term, he was writing less a memoir than an "*Apologia*" for his life and beliefs, a vigorous defense of "those moral sentiments and sacred principles which at all hazards and by every sacrifice I have endeavored to preserve through life." Adams's *Autobiography* reads a little like the saint's life of a Christian martyr.

He also commenced a manic correspondence with his old friend Mercy Warren. In her *History of the Rise, Progress and Termination of the American Revolution,* Mrs. Warren had had the impertinence to choose the wrong side—not Great Britain but Thomas Jefferson. The root of her betrayal lay deeper than a preference for Jefferson over Adams. Warren committed cultural sacrilege by refusing to buy into the New England restorationist myth. Puritanism was more an impediment than a facilitator of revolution, she said. In her history, she makes no allusion to the Puritan model for liberty and chides New Englanders, "prejudiced by the severities their fathers had experienced," for their crippling deference to authority. She upbraids them further for permitting "a tincture of superstition" to outweigh natural talent and excellence. In Warren's book, not only was the Revolution *not* a restoration of Puritan freedoms, it was a rejection of Puritan bondage. An apoplectic Adams, his foundational prejudices threatened, picked apart her history at random, until their once firm friendship had been incinerated on the self-renewing pyre of his unquenchable rage. Years later, the two octogenarians reconsecrated their ancient alliance by exchanging locks of hair.

The happiest reunion to take place during the decade following his presidency was with Benjamin Rush. Their letters are jewels of the epistolary art, second only to the effervescent correspondence Adams would later initiate with Jefferson at Rush's behest. Rush had soured on Jeffersonian democracy, giving Adams full license to vent. Although differing in the specifics of their theology, the two old political warriors shared a deep, nonsectarian fidelity to Christian universalism. "I have attended public worship in all countries and with all sects and believe them all much better than no religion," Adams said, "though I have not thought myself obliged to believe all I heard. Religion I hold to be essential to morals." Rush, who spent a lifetime church shopping, searching for the one Christian denomination that would dare to encompass them all, had found a soul mate.

At the outset of their monthly exchanges, Adams conceded that he had "a little capillary vein of satire meandering about in my soul," whose flow was enhanced by "the garrulity of narrative old age." For once he was not exaggerating. "Secrecy! Cunning! Silence! *Voila les grands sciences des temps modernes,*" Adams joyously raved. "Washington! Franklin! Jefferson! Eternal silence! Impenetrable secrecy! Deep cunning! These are the talents and virtues which are triumphant in these days." He groused that the *philosophes* had "undermined the Christian religion and the morals of the people as much in America as they have in Europe," speculating that the progress of democracy, if taken any further, would provoke an inevitable backlash. "Democracy," he told Rush, "[is] always short-lived, and its atrocious cruelties are never checked but by extinguishing all popular elections to the great offices of state."

Adding a footnote to Adams's political demise, in the fateful summer of 1812 Rush passed along word that, in "a long and interesting session," the Presbyterian General Assembly meeting in Philadelphia had entertained a motion "for petitioning the President to appoint a national fast." The "vote was lost," he lamented, because a majority of the delegates (mistakenly, as it turned out) believed that President Madison would refuse to comply. He then asked Adams, "Are we not the only nation in the world, France excepted, whether Christian, Mohammedan, pagan, or savage, that has ever dared to go to war without imploring supernatural aid, either by prayers, or sacrifices, or auspices, or libations of some kind?"

Instead of the "amen" he expected by return post, Rush received a passionate civics lesson. His allusion to the Presbyterian proposal for a national fast day opened a wound in Adams's delicate psyche that would never heal. In 1775 he had exulted from Philadelphia, "the clergy this way are but now beginning to engage in politics, and they engage with a fervor that will produce wonderful effects." He now knew too well that these effects were not always so wonderful. With twenty-twenty hindsight, he named the reason, or what he now perceived to be the reason, for his political demise. Replying to Rush, he bitterly recalled. "The national fast recommended by me turned me out of office."

> It was connected with the General Assembly of the Presbyterian Church, which I had no concern in. That Assembly has alarmed and alienated Quakers, Anabaptists, Mennonites, Moravians, Swedenborgians, Methodists, Catholics, Protestant Episcopalians, Arians, Socinians, Arminians, etc. A general suspicion prevailed that the Presbyterian Church was ambitious and aimed at an establishment as a national church. I was represented as a Presbyterian and at the head of this political and ecclesiastical project. The secret whisper ran through all the sects, "Let us have Jefferson, Madison, Burr, anybody, whether they be philosophers, Deists, or even atheists, rather than a Presbyterian president." This principle is at the bottom of the unpopularity of national fasts and thanksgivings.

Still feeling the wounds inflicted by "Dr. Priestley and his friend Cooper and by Quakers, Baptists, and I know not how many other sects, for instituting a national fast, for even common civility to the clergy, and for being a churchgoing animal," Adams added that

> If I should inculcate those "national, social, domestic, and religious virtues" you recommend, I should be suspected and charged with an hypocritical, Machiavellian, Jesuitical, Pharisaical attempt to promote a national establishment of Presbyterianism in America, whereas I would as soon establish the Episcopal Church, and almost as soon the Catholic Church.... If I should recommend the sanctification of the Sabbath, like a divine, or even only a regular

attendance on public worship as a means of moral instruction and social improvement, like a philosopher or statesman, I should be charged with vain ostentation again and a selfish desire to revive the remembrance of my own punctuality in this respect; for it is notorious enough that I have been a churchgoing animal for seventy-six years, i.e., from the cradle. And this has been alleged as one proof of my hypocrisy.

Judging from these bitter words, culled from back-to-back letters written many years after the event, one might conclude that Adams, not Jefferson, had been the principal victim of religious assassination during the months leading up to the election of 1800. And in a sense he was. Declaring a federal fast was like poking a stick into a nest of hornets. "Nothing is more dreaded than the national government meddling with religion," he finally and sadly would conclude. "This wild letter, I very much fear, contains seeds of an ecclesiastical history of the U.S. for a century to come."

Nowhere was Adams's idiosyncratic truculence more manifest than in his religious politics. Adams believed in God and believed in belief, but he never believed in believers. Believers drove him wild and broke his heart. He lamented how readily preachers "[make] themselves the willing instruments of an ignorant popularity [or] an insolent oligarchy," decrying that "some of the grossest newspaper slanders [are] trumpeted from the pulpit against the most important men in the nation." How well Thomas Jefferson knew.

With respect to the demise of religious politics, Adams proved less than a prophet; the death notice he issued to Rush was not only wild, it was also wildly premature. Stung by heartbreaking personal experience, America's second president underestimated the resolve of his fellow churchgoing animals as fully as the nation's citizens had underestimated him.

With the Republican Party in power, Adams quickly faded in the public mind. His fondness for British precedent, stubborn fidelity to

Puritan customs, and New England deference toward the established church hosted an experiment in Christian governance that, in Jefferson's coming Empire of Liberty, would swiftly be reversed. The irony, which did not escape John Adams, was that his successor's tenure in office would prove to be more doctrinaire and spiritually charged than his own.

ACT III

THOMAS
JEFFERSON

8

THE AMERICAN DREAMER

> Let foes to freedom dread the name
> But should they touch the sacred tree,
> Twice fifty thousand swords shall flame,
> For JEFFERSON and LIBERTY.
>
> —REPUBLICAN VICTORY
> ANTHEM (1801)

A LANKY, LOOSE-LIMBED stranger appeared on Margaret Bayard Smith's doorstep shortly after the 1800 election to pay a social visit. A twenty-two-year-old newlywed almost as new to Washington City as Washington itself was new, Smith was born to American politics. She would mingle with and worship beside the nation's leaders for the next four decades, forgiving their ambition and admiring their sacrifice. Her father, Colonel John Bayard, and father-in-law, Jonathan Bayard Smith, served together in the Continental Congress and performed gallantly as officers in the Continental Army. The Bayards were ardent Federalists, but Margaret married Republican and adopted the political views of her husband, Samuel Harrison Smith, who came to town at the age of twenty-eight to found what would instantly become Washington's leading Republican newspaper, *The National Intelligencer.* None of his reporters, however, could match his wife's keen eye for the ins and outs of Washington society.

A company town with politics its only industry, the nation's capital ran on gossip and power. Its doors swung on loose hinges, new visitors arriving weekly to spice the local dish. It was to one such visitor that Margaret opened her home that midwinter morning. "Carelessly throwing his arm on the table near which he sat," the stranger, she later recalled, displayed "a manner and voice almost femininely soft and gentle." Entranced by his demeanor, she found herself rapt in conversation, drawn before she knew it from "commonplace topics of the day...into observations of a more personal and interesting nature."

> There was something in his manner, his countenance and voice that at once unlocked my heart....I knew not who he was, but the interest with which he listened to my artless details...put me perfectly at my ease; in truth so kind and conciliating were his looks and manners that I forget he was not a friend of my own, until on the opening of the door, Mr. Smith entered and introduced the stranger to me as *Mr. Jefferson.*

Spellbound, Mrs. Smith blushed and said not a further word. Could this gentle, sandy-faced visitor be "the violent democrat, the vulgar demagogue, the bold atheist and profligate man I have so often heard denounced by the Federalists?" she asked herself. "Can this man so meek and mild, yet dignified in his manners, with a voice so soft and low, with a countenance so benignant and intelligent, can he be that daring leader of a faction, that disturber of the peace, that enemy of all rank and order?" If Jefferson had been privy to his hostess's bewilderment, he surely would have empathized. "There are fanatics both in religion and politics," he said, "who, without knowing me personally, have long been taught to consider me as a raw head and bloody bones."

Margaret Smith was not completely uncritical of her Republican knight. During his first term in office, the new president's almost fetishistic attachment to democratic etiquette gave her heartburn. Yet, in every other respect, the "revolution of feeling" she experienced on meeting him face to face fulfilled Jefferson's most buoyant aspirations for "the Revolution of 1800."

Gulliver Unbound

Jefferson cast himself and his Republican cohort as Gulliver, certain to break free and overpower their multitude of tiny foes. "We have only to awake and snap the Lilliputian cords with which they have been entangling us during the first sleep which succeeded our labors," he promised Philip Mazzei. When the electorate awoke in 1800 to spark what Jefferson called "as real a revolution in the principles of our government as that in 1776 was in its form," the victor punctuated his favorite Swiftean allusion with an exclamation point. To Joseph Priestley, he wrote,

> What an effort, my dear Sir, of bigotry in politics & religion have we gone through! The barbarians really flattered themselves they should be able to bring back the times of vandalism, when ignorance put everything into the hands of power & priestcraft. All advances in science were proscribed as innovations. They pretended to praise and encourage education, but it was to be the education of our ancestors. We were to look backwards, not forwards, for improvement; the president himself declaring, in one of his answers to addresses, that we were never to expect to go beyond them in real science....But it was the Lilliputians upon Gulliver. Our countrymen have recovered from the alarm into which art and industry had thrown them; science and honesty are replaced on their high ground.

In Swift's tale, the superstitious Lilliputians wondered whether Gulliver's pocket watch (to them an inconceivable mechanical marvel) might perhaps be his god, because he consulted it so often. The Deist God that Jefferson honored so respectfully was, in fact, perceived as a watchmaker, who created an intricate, perfectly synchronized world and set it ticking. A convinced if not consistent Deist, Jefferson consulted nature for clues to decipher the divine mystery; and, in good Deist fashion, he esteemed human rights and human reason as bellwethers of enlightened governance. Dr. Priestley, the nation's most famous living scientist, admired nature, too, of course, but, unlike Jefferson, he decoded God's holiest runes by consulting his Bible. What bound them together (apart from Lilliputian bonds) was an unqualified belief in human progress.

When all the votes were in, Jefferson's Democratic-Republican army was exultant. One victory party featured a skit in which Liberty appeared as a virgin amid caricatures of royalty, the church, and the Federalist Party promiscuously damning her as a Jacobin. The trump sounds, a herald announces Jefferson's election, the opposition scatters, and sixteen white-clad beauties (America's sixteen states) enact a rite of cleansing, grinding the crown under their dancing heels.

From his farm, President Adams congratulated his successor in a terse yet gracious note. "This part of the union is in a state of perfect tranquility & I see nothing to obscure your prospect of a quiet & prosperous administration, which I heartily wish you," he said. This portrait may have reflected the tranquility of his cattle, but it failed to impart the true mood of Federalist New England (not to mention his own). "Drunken frolics is the order of the day," one partisan shuddered, "and more bullocks and rams are sacrificed to this newfangled deity than were formerly by the Israelitish priests [of Baal]." Elias Boudinot was shaken to the depths of his pious soul by the election. In his apocalyptic tract *The Age of Revelation,* he solemnly warned, "Our country should be preserved from the dreadful evil of becoming enemies to the religion of the Gospel, which I have no doubt but would be the introduction of the dissolution of government and the bonds of civil society." The Reverend Job Swift, a graduate of Yale and acolyte of Timothy Dwight, dropped the customary liturgical prayer for the president from the weekly litany, refusing to pray for the chief executive during the entire course of Jefferson's presidency. And, as if reading Abigail Adams's mind, on inauguration eve a distressed congregant removed the clapper from his church's bell, lest it sacrilegiously ring an infidel into office.

Jefferson freely conceded that his quarrel with the New England clergy was "on too interesting a ground to be softened." He did some clever building on this hard ground. Accusations of infidelity provoked him to revisit Jesus's teachings, inspiring his most original religious reflections. Less happily, he had a tendency to confuse himself with the Savior. Jefferson believed that Jesus was persecuted for much the same reason that he was. In defense of sacred liberty, both prophets stood up to the worldly principalities and powers of the reigning priesthood. The clergy's hatred compounded Jefferson's own, prompting the very bigotry his Enlightenment philosophy boasted it would banish. New England's clerics, he maliciously said, "are marked, like the Jews, with such a perversity of character as to constitute, from that circumstance, the natural division of our parties." He expected no mercy: "They crucified their Savior, who preached that their kingdom was not of this world, and all who practice on that precept must expect the extreme of their wrath. I wish nothing but their eternal hatred."

Jefferson loathed the established clergy for three simple reasons. First, they returned the compliment. Second, he had concluded from history that "In every country and in every age, the priest has been hostile to liberty." And third, Calvinist theology offended every precept he held dear, from God's justice to the universal hope for happiness. Priestcraft, as he dubbed the work of the clergy, was dark magic. With smoke and mirrors, official Christendom offered up the pure and benevolent Jesus as a whole burned sacrifice on the very altar it had erected in his name. Drawing from a bottomless pool of deprecatory synonyms ("cannibals," "mystery mongers," "mountebanks," "necromancers," etc.), he avowed that the church would be better off dispensing with the clerical office altogether.

Of Jefferson's nineteen thousand surviving letters, only about a hundred touch on matters of faith, but those that do crackle with electricity. Adapted over the years, his boilerplate letter on religion attests to an ever more virulent disdain for "priestcraft," counterbalanced by a steady fondness for Jesus, whom he viewed in the mirror of his own philosophy and accordingly admired. A victim first of the Roman state and then of the Christian church, Jefferson's

228 CO THOMAS JEFFERSON

Jesus is the lamb humankind would never tire of slaughtering. Identifying with Jesus the reformer and martyr as distinct from Christ the messiah, Jefferson boasted to his friend Benjamin Rush, "I am a Christian, in the only sense he wished any one to be; sincerely attached to his doctrines, in preference to all others; ascribing to himself every *human* excellence & believing he never claimed any other."

Jedidiah Morse captured Jefferson's theology as well as anyone, scornfully dismissing it as "Reason and Nature deified and adored." God, Nature, and Reason were indeed almost interchangeable in Jefferson's cosmic hierarchy, with God not so much the ghost but rather the mind in the machine. Unlike Adams, for whom every theological proposition was open to question, Jefferson was a dogmatist when it came to matters of faith—a fundamentalist of the left, inflexible in his fidelity to rational religion.

Jefferson's ultraviolet position on the religious spectrum is manifest in the stance he took on the Masonic controversy during the late 1790s. Although not a Mason himself, Jefferson sympathized with the Masons when Morse charged them with harboring cells of "Bavarian Illuminati." He then went a significant step further. In defending the secretive Illuminist mastermind, Baron Adam Weishaupt, who founded the short-lived experiment in Enlightenment utopianism that so shook America's theological rafters, Jefferson painted a religious self-portrait:

> His precepts are the love of god & love of our neighbor. And by teaching innocence of conduct, he expected to place men in their natural state of liberty & equality. He says, no one ever laid a surer foundation for liberty than our grand master, Jesus of Nazareth.... As Weishaupt lived under the tyranny of a despot & priests, he knew that caution was necessary even in spreading information & the principles of pure morality. He proposed therefore to lead the Freemasons to adopt this object & to make the objects of their institution the diffusion of science & virtue.

To Jefferson, every religious hero was the same: a liberty-loving figure, informed by the laws of Reason and Nature, who dedicated his life to the happiness of others only to be persecuted by the religious establishment—in other words, a man very much like Jesus (or like himself).

Jefferson has been called "the most self-consciously theological of all American presidents." His scant interest in Christian doctrine notwithstanding, this assessment is correct. Spun from his fondest dreams, his vision for society was itself mythic. Jefferson was a nostalgic futurist: his Arcadia an imaginary age of stout, uninflected liberty hosted by the ancient Saxons; his Utopia established on the same eternal principle, with liberty's final triumph to be ushered in by reason. Imagining a future as free from organized religion's bonds as were the Saxon innocents of his imagination, he pictured himself and his enlightened company of natural philosophers fulfilling a divine mandate in creating their Empire of Liberty.

Carrying forward into the future four abiding lessons from his idiosyncratic myth of America's Saxon origins (the relationship of liberty to natural law, the evil of church-state collusion, the idea that right makes might, and the moral superiority of yeomen), Jefferson picked up the baton of the Enlightenment to lead the march of progress. In Jefferson's mythos, since knowledge trumps ignorance and with it every king, queen, and ecclesiastical joker whose power rests entirely on superstition and self-interest, the corrupt guardians of the past must ultimately cede their temporal authority to Liberty's legions. No one believed more devoutly in the dream of knowledge and reason triumphant, with liberty in their inevitable train, than Jefferson did.

Looking back from the early twenty-first century, with a religious revival sweeping the globe, Jefferson's optimistic faith in the coming Age of Reason is a marvel to behold. He was cocksure that, once the tonic of science had replaced the nostrums of superstition, the original design of the Creator could not help but gradually reveal itself to all. Investing his every hope in a more perfect future, Jefferson was America's bluebird.

Growing Up on Virginia's Religious Battlefield

Jefferson's Saxon romanticism and devout modernism both came to him naturally. He was born on the spiritual boundary line between the genteel new world of plantation Virginia, courtesy of his mother's Randolph clan, and the wilds of Northern Wales, the Jefferson family ancestral home. Jefferson touted the notion of a natural not inherited aristocracy, inviting others to ascribe whatever faith and merit they might wish to accidents of birth. Yet those same accidents fixed the stars in his firmament. Spiritually his kinship was to the rough-hewn Saxons of the old country rather than the planter aristocrats, whom he politely disdained. But it was the latter who bequeathed the boons of his worldly inheritance, refined his exquisite tastes, and defined his desires.

Jefferson's earliest memory finds him plumped on a pillow in the careful arms of a slave carrying him on horseback from one plantation to another. Family legend also pictures young Thomas, hungry as a bear, chanting the Lord's Prayer ("Give us this day our daily bread"). This early snapshot contains the full record of Jefferson as a biblical literalist.

When he turned nine, Thomas's intellectual precocity prompted his father, Peter, to enroll him in a tiny Latin academy under the supervision of the Reverend William Douglass of Goochland's St. James Parish, an unexceptional teacher whom Jefferson remembered without affection or gratitude. Remaining loyal to the crown, Douglass was stripped of his pulpit by an angry vestry in 1777. On his father's death, fourteen-year-old Thomas was fortunate to study under the Reverend James Maury, a fine classicist of Huguenot descent. From 1751 to his death in 1769, Maury served Albemarle's Fredericksville parish. He also marshaled the locals, with limited

THE AMERICAN DREAMER ∞ 231

success, to exterminate the spreading infestation of Anabaptists. He complained that these itinerant preachers, often uneducated, had the gall to suggest that "Everyone had the right to preach by virtue of the inspiration of the spirit." Like the good Anglican he was, Maury branded their presumption "disturbing the peace."

With profound consequence for Jefferson personally and to the unfolding story of the disestablishment of the church in Virginia, Maury played a conspicuous role in the most heated local religious controversy of the day. In the case that made him famous, Patrick Henry faced off against Maury and two other Anglican parsons who were demanding back pay from the state. Crushed by Henry's arguments, though winning their suit, they were awarded legal damages of one insulting penny.

The matter turned, strangely to our ears, on the price of tobacco, the medium of exchange by which tax assessments to support the clergy were determined. Since 1662, clerical stipends had fluctuated with the market. In drought years, the price of tobacco soared and, with it, the clergy's fortunes rose. At times of great duress, clerical "livings" might increase as much as threefold. In response to the complaints of aggrieved taxpayers, whose suffering reaped a windfall for their pastors, in 1755 the Virginia Assembly passed a bill (The Two Penny Act) standardizing clergy support by fixing the tax at two cents per pound of tobacco per year regardless of the market price. After fierce lobbying, the king yielded to Anglican ecclesiastical pressure and countermanded the Two Penny Act, without specifying whether his decision was retroactive. Seizing on this ambiguity in the law, Reverend Maury petitioned the courts for back assessments.

When Maury's suit was finally brought to trial in 1763, Henry, colorfully branding Maury and his coplaintiffs "rapacious harpies snatching from the hearth of their honest parishioner his last hoecake, from the widow and her orphan children their last milk cow," seduced the jury even as he underscored the moral contradiction implicit in any law that taxed parishioners more heavily for clergy support when economic times were hard. By overruling the Two Penny Act, the king drove Henry to flirt with treason. "From being the father of his people," he declaimed, the sovereign had "degenerated into a tyrant and forfeits all rights to his subjects' obedience."

William and Mary College specialized in training young men for the Anglican priesthood. At the time of Jefferson's arrival in 1761, in large measure due to the anticlerical backlash in Williamsburg against clerical featherbedding, Virginia's most prestigious educational institution was, as Noah Webster might have said, "demoralized." Its president, who doubled as the rector of Williamsburg's Bruton Church, was a sot; and the Board of Visitors, made up of prominent politicians, had recently axed two revered faculty members for lobbying too avidly for Maury's cause. Replacing one of the disgraced professors was Dr. William Small, the Scottish mathematician who became Jefferson's tutor. However inadvertently, Jefferson's first significant teacher thereby opened the door for his second, the man whom he would credit with fixing "the destinies of my life."

Among the "destinies" that Small helped fashion was his pupil's Enlightenment faith. When Jefferson left college at nineteen to take up the study of law in the offices of the finest classicist in Williamsburg, George Wythe, the young man's nimble intellect and progressive philosophy were well on their way to being honed.

Wythe's brilliant protégé soon became a familiar at the Governor's Mansion, where the select "Attic society" of Wythe, Small, and Governor Francis Fauquier, who spearheaded the crusade against clerical privilege, convened an Enlightenment salon with Jefferson as its fourth member. "At these dinners," Jefferson recalled having "heard more good sense, more rational and philosophical conversations than in all my life besides." By then, his apostasy from Maury's cause, if not from the man himself, about whom he always spoke fondly, was complete. The picture he had formed of the Anglican church establishment (lurid with avarice, drunkenness, and luxury) turned his sympathies from the teachers of his youth, whose liberal, dispassionate Christian faith he once seemingly found unobjectionable, to their opponents, not only his enlightened elders in Williamsburg but also the Bible-thumping dissenting Presbyterians and Baptists who were leading the charge in Virginia for freedom of conscience.

Jefferson's participation in organized religion before he became president can be sketched in a few brief lines. In Bristol Parish, his grandfather and namesake, Captain Thomas Jefferson, had built an Anglican meetinghouse known for half a century as "Jefferson's Church." His grandson's church existed for the most part in the mansions of his mind. Although he was elected to the vestry of St. Anne's Parish in Albemarle County, no record exists of Jefferson's having served in that capacity. He did support St. Anne's financially. Jefferson's charitable largess advanced his conviction that the church could get by nicely without government aid. But he was famous for not attending church and did so semiregularly only during his presidency and near the end of his life. To friends, he referred to himself variously as a "Theist," "Deist," "Unitarian," "Rational Christian," and "Epicurean." Anyone too eager to pigeonhole him should heed Jefferson's self-description: "I am of a sect unto myself, as far as I know."

If Jefferson put no stock in Christian theology, he does appear to have been intrigued by certain forms of Christian polity. Dolley Madison, who, as Abigail Adams did before her, quietly broke all his rules about women abstaining from politics, testifies to his fascination with Baptist democratic governance. In Baptist polity, each congregation managed its own affairs, free from any superintending ecclesial authority. The Baptist system of church governance "struck him with great force and interested him much," Mrs. Madison relates. He commended it, in her hearing, as "the best plan of government for the American colonies." If her report is accurate, Jefferson's fond notion of ward government (with local units gathered in 10-square-mile wards or "hundreds") may have evolved from Baptist congregational polity as well as being modeled after the New England town meeting, which Jefferson on another occasion deemed "the wisest invention ever devised by the wit of man for the perfect exercise of self-government." By the Baptist model, "Every man in the state would thus become an acting member of the common government, transacting in person a great portion of its rights and duties," he dreamed aloud to Mrs. Madison. "The wit of man cannot devise a more solid basis for a free, durable, and well-administered republic."

However inspired he may have been by Baptist polity, when Jefferson started out in politics his shyness of organized religion distinguished him from his fellow Virginia legislators. "Sure I am of one thing," averred one member of the Virginia House, "no *gentleman* would choose any road to heaven but the Episcopal." This primrose path was already becoming quite dusty. Early in the nineteenth century, a foreign visitor noted that no nation he ever visited was "less addicted to religious practice than the Virginians." Another traveler observed that in Virginia "between the mountains and the sea, the people have scarcely any sense of religion, and in the country parts the churches are all falling into decay." Of his fellow Virginians Jefferson would say, "We are an industrious, plain, hospitable and honest, altho' not a psalm-singing people."

Sacred Liberty's Two Holy Texts

Jefferson is best remembered for seven words, the unalienable rights he enumerated as "life, liberty, and the pursuit of happiness" in the Preamble to the Declaration of Independence. He grounded these rights in an Enlightenment metaphysic, guaranteeing them as a universal bequest from nature and nature's God.

In 1775, the thirty-two-year-old Virginia planter arrived in Philadelphia in his sleek phaeton, four fine horses high stepping before him and three slaves by his side. The following summer, he would pen his immortal hymn to human rights, the beating heart of the Democratic-Republican revival and centerpiece of Democratic Party platforms for decades to come. As he freely admitted, none of the propositions his Declaration contained was original to Jefferson but, when placed in the context of previous government charters, his "self-evident" truths were hardly self-evident. In fact, they were unique in the history of statecraft. Never before had government established itself on so egalitarian a footing. His contemporary, the philosopher Immanuel Kant, touted the "lordly ideal of a universal kingdom of reasonable individuals...to which we can only belong if we relate solicitously to one another according to the maxims of freedom as if they were laws of nature." To Jefferson, the maxims of freedom *were* laws of nature. Positing a benign Creator, a universal foundation for morality, and the ideal of civic virtue, he viewed the creation as a self-regulating whole, its full dispensations available to all, not to a chosen few. His ringing proclamation of liberty closed with a vow: "And for the support of this Declaration, we mutually pledge to each other our lives, our fortunes, and our sacred honor." Into this solemn oath, Congress interpolated the phrase "with a firm reliance on the protection of divine Providence." For Jefferson, the people's "sacred honor" was pledge enough.

To Jefferson, "life, liberty, and the pursuit of happiness" were interdependent ideals. "The God who gave us life gave us liberty at the same time," he said. "The hand of force may destroy, but cannot disjoin them." True happiness, in turn, could arise only in a life free from the shackles of tyranny. Jefferson spoke effusively of "the holy cause of freedom" and God's bequest of equality as a human birthright. "The will of the majority, the natural law of every society, is the only sure guardian of the rights of man," he declared. The Declaration of Independence elevated people's sights by placing human law on a higher moral pediment. The result was a civil ethic, in which the individual conscience received unprecedented priority. In his draft of the Preamble, the truths that we know as "inalienable"

Jefferson described as "sacred and undeniable." The transcendent point of reference was no longer the monarch but the people themselves, whose rights he endowed with sovereign, even divine, authority. Individuals thus became ends in themselves, not means by which to advance some other agent's ends. In his estimation, far from compromising faith, this emphasis on liberty perfected faith by ceding it full range.

By the fall of 1776, Jefferson was back in Virginia preparing the keynote for his lifelong campaign to separate church and state. Revising the Virginia Code, he began by rescinding the centuries-old "benefit of clergy," which hailed back to medieval times when anyone who could read scripture (in other words, literate clerics) received pardon for first offenses when convicted of all but the most heinous crimes. He also attacked the barbarity of legal statutes punishing blasphemy, profanity, and heterodoxy. "Millions of innocent men, women, and children, since the introduction of Christianity, have been burnt, tortured, fined, and imprisoned, yet we have not advanced one inch toward uniformity," he later said. "What has been the effect of coercion? To make one half the world fools and the other half hypocrites."

To update "tyrannical laws" that cast innocents into prison "for not comprehending the mysteries of the Trinity" required more than mere tinkering. Jefferson's sweeping answer to such laws, the Statute Establishing Religious Freedom in Virginia, would set the standard soon adapted tacitly by the framers of the U.S. Constitution, made explicit in the First Amendment, and echoed in constitutions around the globe. Its central resolution reads,

> Be it enacted by the General Assembly, That no man shall be compelled to frequent or support any religious worship, place, or ministry whatsoever, nor shall be enforced, restrained, molested, or burdened in his body or goods, nor shall otherwise suffer on account of his religious opinions or belief; but that all men shall be free to profess, and by argument to maintain, their opinion in mat-

ters of religion, and that the same shall in no wise diminish, enlarge, or affect their civil capacities.

Reversing almost two centuries of Anglican hegemony in Virginia proved an arduous task. Before final enactment, Jefferson's statute languished in and out of committee for years, subject to endless wrangling. After a lifetime spent fighting political wars, Jefferson would look back on the seven-year struggle to disestablish the church and establish religious freedom in Virginia as "the severest contest in which I have ever been engaged." He numbered the Statute for Establishing Religious Freedom in Virginia among three overridingly significant lifetime achievements. Together with his authorship of the Declaration of Independence and founding of the University of Virginia, he inscribed it on his tombstone (excluding, among other notable acts of service, his two terms as president of the United States). Yet without James Madison's brilliant political maneuvering, and certainly apart from the help of the Baptists, it might never have been enacted. More than Madison or even Jefferson, Virginia's Baptists had a spiritual stake in this struggle. They sought religious freedom in order to protect their own religious truth.

Throughout the seven-year struggle, if Jefferson's reforms were held in abeyance, so was the matter of state assessments, with a temporary stay reissued yearly. The legislation that inadvertently broke the logjam was not Jefferson's statute but Patrick Henry's call for a new, more "liberal" general assessment act. On the question of religious freedom, Henry was far from consistent. Although he made his name defending Baptist preachers and blasting the pretenses of the established clergy in the Two Penny case, he remained convinced that the church could not survive without state support. This placed him at loggerheads with Jefferson, Madison, and the Baptists, who would brook no compromise on freedom of conscience short of complete disestablishment. Henry drafted his assessment act as compromise legislation that would rally champions of the old order without offending moderate partisans of the new. His plan was to expand the playing field, by distributing tax dollars to non-Episcopal Christian bodies, even as he buttressed the status quo by maintaining the establishment of the Anglican state church. George Washington, among others, found it eminently reasonable. In the late fall of 1784, with a 60 percent majority, the House of Delegates ratified Henry's proposal in principle and sent it to a drafting committee.

Virginia's Baptists sounded the alarm. "The gospel wants not the feeble arm of man for its support," John Leland declared in trumpeting the Baptist General Committee's call for a petition campaign against Henry's assessment act. "Should the legislature assume the right of taxing the people for the support of the gospel, it will be destructive to religious liberty." When Jefferson, then in Paris, heard that Henry's gambit had prompted dissenting Protestants to take a stand, he professed his delight. "I am glad the Episcopalians have again shown their teeth and fangs," he told Madison. "The dissenters had almost forgotten them." Not that he underestimated his old foe's resourcefulness. "While Mr. Henry lives," his unparalleled influence in Virginia politics would continue to frustrate the proponents of reform. Henry's assessment proposal unleashed Jefferson's inquisitorial temper. "What we have to do," he confided to his lieutenant, "is devoutly pray for his death."

Henry argued that his bill was necessary to shore up the crumbling foundations of morality and piety, fallen into decay since war's end. Among its most passionate partisans were the Anglican clergy. Invoking "principles of public utility," they argued that Christianity presented the "best means of promoting virtue, peace, and prosperity." Madison, a tactical as well as analytical genius, turned these arguments on their head. Such a measure would instead undermine religion, he claimed, even as it abridged liberty.

Employing parliamentary sleight of hand to engineer a one-year postponement, Madison capitalized brilliantly on the delay. First, he collaborated with his allies to move Henry back into the Governor's Mansion, which, given the comparative weakness of the governor's power compared to that of the Assembly, lessened his influence. Second, he palliated critics by supporting a bill to incorporate (and thereby offer state protections for) the Episcopal Church. By demonstrating his willingness to facilitate the "partial gratification of its warmest votaries," Madison managed to stand close enough to the church to clip its wings. This gambit paid off. Madison won delay on the assessment act by a seven-vote margin, winning the votes of eight delegates who favored incorporation. Less ready to compromise, the Baptist General Committee commissioned John Leland to hound the Assembly into scrapping the incorporating act and with it most of the remaining privileges redounding to the Episcopal Church. Aided by his zealous importunity, Virginia's Baptists sealed their victory the following year by lobbying successfully for its repeal.

Third and finally, to defeat Henry's assessment act, Madison helped initiate a statewide mobilization against it. Of some eleven thousand signatures condemning the legislation, Madison's anonymous petition ("A Memorial and Remonstrance Against Religious Assessments") garnered 1,552 names, while 4,899 Virginians signed a dissenting Christian alternative likely sponsored by the Baptists, invoking "Christ" and "the Spirit of the Gospel" to make the case for liberty. In total, a remarkable 10,999 citizens petitioned to overturn Governor Henry's "liberal" assessment legislation.

Madison's "Memorial and Remonstrance" is an important document in its own right. Its language couched to rally Christian support for what Madison's opponents were branding an antireligious cause, it runs for several pages, but its main rubrics tell the story: Religion can only spring from reason and conviction, not force or violence; it must be exempt from government authority; ecclesiastical establishments corrupt the purity of religion and are unnecessary for its support; and, "The equal right of every citizen to the free exercise of his religion according to the dictates of conscience" is held by the same tenure as all other rights. To Henry's chagrin, the support Madison whipped up with his "Remonstrance," multiplied many times over by the more populist (and popular) efforts of the Baptists, not only doomed Henry's assessment act but also created a backlash of sympathy for Jefferson's Statute for Establishing Religious Freedom. Seven years after Jefferson first presented it to the Assembly, when Madison reintroduced this landmark bill in January 1786 it won swift and relatively easy passage.

First in Europe and then throughout the world, religious liberty would come to be viewed by progressive lawmakers as an American triumph. Shortly after receiving word of Madison's success, which spread like wildfire through the salons of Paris, Jefferson crowed from afar,

> The Virginia act for religious freedom has been received with infinite approbation in Europe and propagated with enthusiasm. I do not mean by the governments, but by the individuals which compose them. It has been translated into French and Italian, has been sent to most of the courts of Europe and has been the best evidence of the falsehood of those reports which stated us to be in anarchy. It is inserted in the new Encyclopedie and is appearing in most of the publications respecting America. In fact, it is comfortable to see the standard of reason at length erected, after so many ages during which the human mind has been held in vassalage by kings, priests and nobles, and honorable for us to have produced the first legislature who has had the courage to declare that the reason of man may be trusted with the formation of his own opinions.

Jefferson's original draft of the statute did not survive unscathed by amendment. He lamented "some mutilations in the preamble," small omissions that muted the expression of his Enlightenment faith. On all important points, however, Madison defended the act's integrity. Where Jefferson's text reads, "the holy author of our religion," by whom he meant "God," some delegates thought it vital to qualify this by adding "Jesus Christ." As Jefferson recalled in his *Autobiography*, "the insertion was rejected by a great majority, in proof that they meant to comprehend, within the mantle of its protection, the Jew and the Gentile, the Christian and Mahometan, the Hindoo, and infidel of every denomination."

"The Eden of the United States"

Jefferson was the most private of the founders. He found true happiness, his heart's desire, only at Monticello and in the bosom of his family. At twenty-nine, with little fuss or ceremony, he married the young widow Martha Wayles Skelton. Together they settled into a cherished domesticity at Monticello, the fantasy home he would spend a lifetime perfecting, nested atop a lofty hillock overlooking the valley below. Jefferson described the countryside surrounding Monticello as "the Eden of the United States." From his hilltop aerie, he looked out over a rolling sea of purple pines, the gentle Blue Ridge Mountains welling in the distance. It was here that he anchored his soul.

On New Year's Day 1772, Thomas and Martha were wed by two Anglican clergymen in a small family ceremony at Martha's home. Jefferson paid the fiddler twice what he offered the clergymen for their services. Martha's brother raised his glass and proposed a lovely toast to the bride and groom: "May business and play, music and the merriment of your family lighten your hearts."

Petite, frail, and by all accounts beautiful, the auburn-haired Martha offered her cultivated husband musical accompaniment as well as connubial companionship. Reputed "mild and amiable," she was admired by one contemporary for her "large expressive eyes of the richest shade of hazel." "Too wise to wrinkle their foreheads with politics," Jefferson's idealized females, among whom Martha occupied his highest pedestal, were beckoned to "soothe and calm the minds of their husbands returning ruffled from political debate." The two, literally, made beautiful music together, she on the pianoforte or harpsichord and he on a fine, imported violin.

Martha's father, John Wayles, died two years after her marriage to Thomas, doubling the value of her husband's estate. Included in Wayles's bequest was Popular Forest in Bedford County, a picturesque property that Jefferson developed as a second home. Another inheritance, historically more momentous, was the Hemings slave family. Several members strong, it included Martha's mulatto (and much younger) half sister, Sally.

Jefferson's domestic reverie was shattered by Martha's death in 1783, her delicate health sacrificed on the altar of childbirth. Giving birth to six children over the course of a decade—only two, Martha (Patsy) and Mary (Polly) survived to maturity—she died in her early thirties, eliciting from her husband the promise that he would never remarry. Jefferson was 39 when Martha died, all his "plans of comfort and happiness reversed by a single event."

Shortly before her death, on a scrap of paper that Jefferson squirreled away in his desk drawer where it remained until his own death forty-three years later, Martha had written (quoting Laurence Sterne's *Tristram Shandy*): "Time wastes too fast! every letter I trace tells me with what rapidity life follows my pen. The days and hours of it are flying over our heads like clouds of wind never to return more! everything presses on—." Before inscribing the entire passage as a final entry in his commonplace book, Thomas completed Martha's memorial reflections in his own hand—"and every time I kiss thy hand to bid adieu, every absence which follows it are preludes to that eternal separation which we are shortly to make!" Jefferson bundled this *memento mori* with a lock of Martha's hair, a singular keepsake of the marriage he otherwise honored in silence throughout the remainder of his days.

One aspect of God's dispensation for which Jefferson could find no imaginable utility was grief. In the weeks after Martha's death, Monticello became unbearable, haunted by her shade and a thousand reminders of his shattered domestic dream. He attempted to elude the shadow his wife's death cast by accepting Congress's appointment to join Benjamin Franklin and John Adams in the young nation's diplomatic corps in France. From that point forward, alternating between federal service and his beloved Monticello, Jefferson progressed through the upper echelons of government toward the presidency. As reluctant a president as George Washington was, he assumed the office not for personal gain but to redeem the nation, sacrificing his personal happiness to advance the cause of sacred liberty.

"FOR JEFFERSON AND LIBERTY"

Tell me what the preacher said,...
Why,—he talk'd of ruined states,
Demagogues and democrates,
Falling stars, and satan's baits....
To English notes his psalm was sung,
With politics the pulpit rung,
And thrice was bellow'd from his tongue,
"The President is always wrong."

—PHILIP FRENEAU,
"ON POLITICAL SERMONS"

A republican's picture is easy to draw,
He can't bear to obey, but will govern the law;
His manners unsocial, his temper unkind
He's a rebel in conduct, a tyrant in mind.

—ANONYMOUS

THOMAS JEFFERSON never missed a sunrise. On inauguration day, March 4, 1801, he was among the first to stir at Conrad and McMunn's boarding house at the corner of C Street and New Jersey Avenue in Washington. He dressed for his day of days with studied indifference, affecting the unadorned style of Swift's Gulliver. Jefferson's Federalist detractors made his egalitarian fetishes the object of great sport, lampooning the "corduroy small-clothes, red-plush waistcoat, and sharp-toed boots with which he expressed his contempt for fashion." Believing that liberty and equity need not exclude a nod to propriety, Republican admirers as well expressed discomfit at his comportment. Among them was the wife of Senator John Brown of Kentucky. When Jefferson arrived for breakfast on inauguration day and assumed his preferred seat at the darkened foot of the table, farthest from the warmth of the hearth, Mrs. Brown knew that she was supposed to applaud the president-elect's self-abnegation but instead impulsively offered him her seat nearer the fire, which he politely declined. "She felt indignant and for a moment almost hated the leveling principle of democracy," Margaret Smith reported, adding in her editorial voice, "Certainly this was carrying equality rather too far. There is no incompatibility between politeness and republicanism; grace cannot weaken and rudeness cannot strengthen a good cause."

In his official memorandum on proper republican etiquette, the new president spelled out the doctrine of "equality or pell-mell"—"when brought together in society, all are perfectly equal, whether foreign or domestic, titled or untitled, in or out of office." He anonymously upbraided one editor who spoke of the "Etiquette of the Court of the United States" by posting the following correction: "There is no 'court of the U.S.' since the 4th of [March] 1801. That day buried levees, birthdays, royal parades, and the arrogation of precedence in society by certain self-styled friends of order, but truly styled friends of privileged orders."

After breakfast, his hair unpowdered and without benefit of sword, the president-elect, disdaining the employment of an aristocratic carriage, joined a hodgepodge of partisans, housemates, U.S. marshals, and good soldiers from the outgoing administration outside Conrad's and walked with them freestyle to the unfinished Capitol Building. Peppered with a few black faces, more than half of Washington's tiny white population—Margaret Smith estimated the crowd at close to a thousand—was present. Jefferson delivered his inaugural address and took the oath of office. If Jefferson honored the same protocol that he followed four years later, an eyewitness to his second inauguration sheds light on the particulars of his first: Jefferson "kissed the book & swore before the Chief Justice to be faithful to the Constitution, then bowed & retired."

Reading between the lines, it would appear that in 1805 and, by extension, presumably in 1801 as well, Jefferson may have chosen to show his respect for the Bible without actually swearing on it. Correspondence he exchanged with Chief Justice John Marshall reinforces this impression. In February 1801, he asked the chief justice whether any oath must be sworn beyond that contained in the body of the Constitution. Marshall responded, "That prescribed in the constitution seems to me to be the only one which is to be administered." The only imaginable call for such an inquiry would be to determine whether the chief justice expected the president-elect to add to the prescribed constitutional language the additional vow "So help me God." Their exchange of letters suggests that Jefferson may have dropped Washington's religious codicil to the secular presidential oath. Such an omission would be in character, even as kissing first but not swearing on the Bible would symbolically suit Jefferson's dual purpose of maintaining a strict separation of church and state while honoring religion as an essential component of the public faith he hoped to foster.

"We Are All Republicans, All Federalists"

When Jefferson raised his voice, it would sink in his throat. Hopeless as an orator, he unveiled his inaugural address one quiet sentence at a time. In a country dangerously divided, where passions still were running high, one of these sentences fairly leapt from the page. The new president pronounced, "We are all republicans, all federalists."

This affirmation was not pious rhetoric. The vision of one sovereign people united in their liberty unfolded naturally from Jefferson's idealism. "The body of our people, tho' divided for a short time by an artificial panic, and called by different names, have ever had the same object in view, to wit, the maintenance of a federal, republican government, and have never ceased to be all federalists, all republicans," he assured a friend in a private letter, pointedly excepting "the noisy band of royalists inhabiting cities chiefly, and priests both of city and country." In Jefferson's mind, all that stood between a united American people and the fulfillment of their happiness was the New England clergy and their minions, "who had got a smell of union between Church and State, and began to indulge reveries which can never be realized in the present state of science." As the sun of knowledge rose higher, all America, he believed, would be enlightened and political divisions would vanish. "I shall hope to be able to obliterate, or rather to unite, the names of federalists & republicans," he revealingly told another correspondent. Years later, with the battle for America's soul effectively won, Jefferson could fairly state: "The republicans are the nation. Their opponents are but a faction."

The conceptual nub of Jefferson's "Revolution of 1800" lies here. What he really meant when he appeared to be reaching out to all Americans is that good people everywhere, *all* good people, shared a single vision—his own. The apostle of pluribus ironically deemed it the "duty of the chief magistrate to unite in himself the confidence of the whole people…produce a union of the powers of the whole, and point them in a single direction, as if all constituted but one body and one mind." John Adams could impishly have pointed out that this prescription for populist governance was precisely how democracy mutates into tyranny. The one acts with the proxy of the many, and the many disappear into the one.

Jefferson's inaugural address took up where the Preamble of the Declaration of Independence left off, with lasting rhetorical consequence to the American civic agenda. In it, Jefferson codified his Republican creed into the American creed. For the "sacred preservation of the public faith," he affirmed the sovereignty of the people through majority rule, while protecting as equally "sacred" the balancing principle of minority rights. He underscored the constitutional guarantee of "equal and exact justice to all men, of whatever state or persuasion, religious or political"; celebrated the diffusion of knowledge and settlement of differences "at the bar of the public reason"; and twice emphasized the first American liberty, "freedom of religion" ("having banished from our land that religious intolerance under which mankind so long bled and suffered"). Alongside liberty and equality, Jefferson called for fraternity—"the harmony and affection without which liberty and even life itself are but dreary things." Drawing on the spirit of '76 as a source of abiding renewal, the nation's new president closed by heralding his confidence in the founders' star map for America's quest:

> These principles form the bright constellation which has gone before us and guided our steps through an age of revolution and reformation. The wisdom of our sages and the blood of our heroes have been devoted to their attainment. They should be the creed of our political faith, the text of civic instruction, the touchstone by which to try the services of those we trust; and should we wander from them in moments of error or of alarm, let us hasten to retrace our steps and to regain the road which alone leads to peace, liberty, and safety.

In reprinting his inaugural address, the Federalist Boston *Centinel* was careful to edit out the president's principal reference to religion. Its surprised readers would have heard their reputedly faithless leader saying that America is "enlightened by a benign religion, professed, indeed, and practiced in various forms, yet all of them inculcating honesty, truth, temperance, gratitude, and the love of man; acknowledging and adoring an overruling Providence, which by all its dispensations proves that it delights in the happiness of man here and his greater happiness hereafter."

Jefferson's employment of religious diction to score secular points, here and throughout his address, was not accidental. Abraham Lincoln would do the same, if in a humbler, spiritually more haunting manner and from a darker and deeper religious place. Jefferson subscribed to the French *philosophes'* utilitarian notion of civil religion.

Following Rousseau's template, by affirming Providence and the afterlife he was advancing the vision of a "public faith" designed to reinforce moral behavior. Apart from these two broad tenets, his civil religious code transcended all doctrinal particulars. In his America, all citizens, drawing their revelation from knowledge and experience, would join their hearts in a universal moral compact. Jefferson's foes mistook the nature of their enemy when they branded him irreligious. His civil religious ambitions were at least as encompassing as those of the Christian commonwealthmen.

Apocalypse or Millennium?

In Federalist ranks, any suggestion that Jefferson might have harbored a religious vision for the nation would have been met by scorn. Four months into Jefferson's tenure, Theodore Dwight was waxing positively apocalyptic. "We have now reached the consummation of democratic blessedness," the prominent editor sarcastically exclaimed. "We have a country governed by blockheads and knaves; the ties of marriage with all its felicities are severed and destroyed; our wives and daughters are thrown into the stews; our children are cast into the world from the breast and forgotten; filial piety is extinguished, and our surnames, the only mark of distinction among families, are abolished. Can the imagination paint anything more dreadful on this side of hell?"

Emote as they might, Theodore Dwight and his brother Timothy were beginning to lose the attention of their audience. When Jefferson assumed office, the Republicans took center stage in the nation's sacred political drama. Their cast converged from opposite wings of the theater: philosophical idealists, who envisioned an Age of Reason with the Rights of Man (liberty, equality, and fraternity) enshrined by the state; and democratic evangelists, who foresaw the coming realm of perfect Christian freedom. Both welcomed Jefferson's "Revolution of 1800" as heralding the promise of a new age.

The inauguration of Jefferson's Empire of Liberty was feted on March 11, 1801, in a Democratic jubilee in Wallingford, Connecticut. In an Enlightenment festival inspired by Methodist camp meetings, leading citizens recited the Declaration of Independence and Jefferson's inaugural address, and Abraham Bishop delivered an oration, "Our Statesmen to the Constitution and our Clergy to the Bible." If any doubt remained, Bishop made it clear that a new era of American politics had indeed commenced. In a bit of "turn about is fair play," the self-styled "blazing meteor of Republicanism" charged his Federalist neighbors with "sedition, treason and rebellion," pronouncing it "criminal for a preacher to do these things, which are manifestly inexpedient and inconsistent with his profession." In the banquet that followed the festival, toasts were raised to the president, true religion, church-state separation in Connecticut, and an end to pulpit politics.

To wrest Connecticut from Federalist hands, Bishop knew that he first had to break the Standing Order's hammerlock. His express goal was to "detach politics, offices, applause and honors from New-England religion!" This goal could not have been more ambitious. The year before, Bishop had been invited by the Yale chapter of Phi Beta Kappa to deliver their annual address. When word filtered out that he intended to use the occasion to scold the establishment, "the 'friends of order' in the society," he reports, "held a conclave, which they called a regular meeting, and without any notice to me (though I was a member and a party concerned in the object of their convention) proceeded to pass *a rescinding act.*" Provoked rather than daunted by this slap, Bishop hired his own hall (a larger one), packed the place with fifteen hundred souls, and let rip with the Republican jeremiad he had intended to drop on Yale. Whether they attended as spies or as interested parties, he counted eight clergymen in his audience.

Adding a new weapon to the arsenal of liberty, Bishop reinforced his defense of secular government with what might appear to be an incongruous argument. Doubtless inspired by the turning

of the century as well as by Jefferson's victory at the polls, he declared the advent of the Millennium. Jefferson's election had cosmic portent, he proclaimed. Instead of triggering the Apocalypse,
as New England clerics had direly prophesied, the promised coming of the Kingdom was at hand. Pronouncing "this redeemed
continent...the grand theater of the millennial reign," he went so
far as to compare "the illustrious chief, who, once insulted, now
presides over the union, with him who, once insulted, now presides over the universe."

In a subsequent address, which carried the subtitle "A Discourse
on the Government of Christ, as King and President," Bishop identified Christian government with perfect liberty. Since "liberty is
possessed by all who believe in Christ," he said, so liberty is one
"branch or part of Christ's righteous government." Noting that Jefferson's enemies had prophesied that, if he were elected, the church
would die, Bishop pointed out that instead religion was thriving in
America. "Is religion banished?" Bishop asked. "It is not. Never was
there such a day as this. God is pouring out his spirit in a remarkable manner from north to south." Republican pulpits throughout
the land hymned a similar tune. "Moral light has darted its rays
upon the world," one exultant Jeffersonian preached, uplifting "the
human character to a state of splendid greatness and perfectibility
that no former age has ever yet recognized or experienced."

From the other wing of Jefferson's political theater entered the
Enlightenment chorus. Joel Barlow speculated that "such a state of
peace and happiness as if foretold in scripture and commonly called
the Millennial period, may be rationally expected to be introduced
without a miracle." Bishop James Madison envisioned just such a
second Eden arising, with America's Everyman the new Adam. Anticipating "those sentiments of equality, benevolence and fraternity,
which reason and religion and nature enjoin, to reassume their sovereignty over the human soul," he foresaw Providence "raising a
new race of men in [our] remote...blessed clime." Bishop Madison
perceptively heard through a cacophony of Republican voices the

commonality of a shared goal. The "divines looked for a millennium," he observed, "and the modern philanthropist for the epoch of infinite perfectibility."

While welcoming support wherever he could find it, Jefferson led the Enlightenment chorus. One by one, the old votaries of superstition would realize, he said, that

> since the mountain will not come to them, they had better go to the mountain: that they will find their interest in acquiescing in the liberty and science of their country, and that the Christian religion, when divested of the rags in which they have enveloped it and brought to the original purity and simplicity of its benevolent institutor, is a religion of all others most friendly to liberty, science, and the freest expansions of the human mind.

Bishop's championship of the Jeffersonian cause did not escape the president's notice. Exercising his patronage while tweaking the nose of the Connecticut establishment, Jefferson appointed Bishop's octogenarian father commissioner of the Port of New Haven, a post Abraham inherited on James Bishop's death shortly thereafter. In Connecticut, the president's favor to the radical Bishop family refocused the guns of the Christian Federalist opposition. Invigorated by the attention, Abraham Bishop decided to sponsor a second fourth of March "Republican Festival" (which actually took place on March 9, 1803), this time, with consummate cheek, in New Haven itself. One thousand revelers gathered in the heart of Federalist New England for a recitation of Jefferson's inaugural address, fireworks, and cannonades, all topped off by a pageant scripted by the entertaining, unpredictable, and quite possibly mad millenarian preacher, David Austin. One scene from Austin's play features a "Republican Diocese" (described as "a counterpart to the Republican administration of Thomas Jefferson"), first besieged by "the federal priesthood" and then redeemed by "the strength of popular suffrage and the unfailing support of Almighty God."

With a slightly disturbing lack of exactness, Austin had earlier predicted that Christ would return on either May 15 or 16, 1796. When the trump failed to sound on either day, the seer lost his Presbyterian congregation but not his faith. Austin's certitude in his divine appointment as "Joshua of the American Temple" only grew stronger. Consulting his Bible, he put his finger on the problem. Christ's reign would commence only once the Jews had returned to the Promised Land. Dubbing New Haven the New Jerusalem, he beseeched the world's Hebrew population to join him there for the last trump. In the meantime the picaresque Austin went broke, was thrown into prison, and escaped. When the New Haven sheriff put a $50 bounty on his head, he turned himself in to collect it. With abundant cause, friends worried that his near fatal bout of scarlet fever in 1796, during which he "beheld Jesus as our elder brother," had unhinged Austin's senses.

It certainly did nothing to dampen his enthusiasm. Austin was a born-again democrat. His gospel had both ancient roots and modern wings. It also enshrined long-standing prejudice. He believed that the "friends of order," who hated Jefferson, were aping the Jews' refusal to embrace Christ. Fixated on Jefferson as the herald of the Kingdom, Austin moved to Washington, established his mission church in a boarding house, and found himself on the Fourth of July, 1801, preaching to the Congress and passing his hat through the House chamber.

Austin was not so busy rustling doves from the millennial underbrush that he couldn't find time to beg for a job. With God as his most glittering reference, during Jefferson's first year in office he sent him thirteen applications, offering his services as private secretary, peace commissioner to France, and revenue collector for New Haven (the post that Jefferson would award to Bishop's father). Later, when the president was having trouble convincing anyone in America to be secretary of a then almost nonexistent navy, Austin applied for that post, too, noting that having a clergyman in the

Cabinet would quiet public murmurings about Jefferson's infidelity. He also hinted at his availability for the office of executive astrologer to assist the president in reading the "chart" of Providence's designs for the nation. When such offers failed to raise a reply, Austin threatened his champion with divine retribution: "I therefore, Sir, without the least hesitation state to you, in the name and by the authority of the most High God, that you are a dead man, in case you refuse obedience to the voice of Heaven." His stalking love twisting into hatred, Austin demanded "that you shut not the door of this American sanctuary against the legitimate knockings of the voice of the Almighty."

It is easy for us to dismiss Austin, but official Washington treated him with courtesy. On the lookout for politically correct preachers, the newly Republican Congress gave Mr. Austin the plum of the year when they invited him to preach on the Fourth of July. One hundred seventy citizens signed his petition to Congress to appropriate funds for a National Cathedral dedicated to the memory of George Washington. And untold numbers of senators and congressmen dipped into their pockets when he passed his hat importuning support for Lady Washington's Chapel, the shingle he had hung out as a temporary headquarters for the coming millennial army.

In his July 4th sermon, which he delivered to a packed house in the Hall of Representatives, Austin foresaw "the different denominations of professing Christians in the city [arriving at] a more united concurrence in the general principles of Christian unity." The nation's two most prominent Republicans responded to irenic fantasies like this one quite differently. Secretary of State James Madison never mistook the dream of Christian unity as anything less than a civil nightmare, with the separation of church and state its first casualty. But Jefferson had a sweet spot for such visions. When Austin wrote, "I have a mind to clothe the pacific operations of your administration with a glade of prophetic lights, such as I perceive the nation is entitled to receive, from the medium of providential atmosphere in which it moves," Jefferson may have regretted the messenger but surely approved the message. More taken by his religious politics than daunted by his death threats, he donated $25 to the God-intoxicated Mr. Austin's heavenly cause.

If Austin held a surprisingly prominent place in the Christian Republican choir, it contained a multitude of voices, high and low. "Father of the nations, our emperor, the man we love," a woman from Kentucky crooned to the president, "kerrect heaven if I said more; twere scarce a sin. You are all that's good and godlike." When the charismatic Christian clergyman the Reverend Elias Smith joined Bishop in placing Jefferson on the right hand of Christ in the millennial court—he called Jefferson the sixth angel of the Apocalypse—a stronger sense of irony than he possessed would have served the president well. "Thomas Jefferson was raised up the King of Kings," Smith confidently exclaimed. "The government of this country is the kingly government of Christ."

One spectator recalled looking out as a child over the Republican Millennium as it dawned. He remembered the elders of his congregation upbraiding their newfangled pastor for his political credulity. "Mr. Page," they chided, "we employ you to preach Jesus Christ and him crucified, but you preach Thomas Jefferson and him justified."

"Courting Popularity Is His Darling Project"

As devoted as Jefferson was to church-state separation, religion and politics mixed freely in Washington throughout his administration. On Sundays, the government played host to the church. The chapel in the Hall of Representatives, an elliptical temporary wing slapped onto the side of the incomplete Capitol Building and called, descriptively, "the Oven," arose out of necessity. At the time, there were but two churches in the city, one Catholic (a tiny frame building on F Street), the other Episcopalian (with makeshift quarters in a tobacco tanning house at the foot of Capitol Hill). Before long, various denominational bodies were taking up temporary residence in the War, Treasury, and Supreme Court office buildings as well. Prompting images of Max Weber's *Protestant Ethic and the Spirit of Capitalism,* a congregation of Presbyterians celebrated communion in the Treasury Department. To whatever extent Sundays in Washington may fairly be called the government at prayer, at the very least the Hall of Representatives served as a quasi-national chapel. Placed in charge of the holy offices on Sunday morning, Congress created a circuslike simulacrum to divine worship that must have given any serious Christian pause. It certainly offered an irresistible target to the gentle but ironic Mrs. Smith.

> The gay company who thronged the H. R. [Hall of Representatives] looked very little like a religious assembly. The occasion presented for display was not only a novel, but a favorable one for the youth, beauty and fashion of the city.... The members of Congress gladly gave up their seats for such fair auditors, and either lounged in the lobbies, or round the fire places, or stood beside the ladies of their acquaintance. This Sabbath-day-resort became so fashionable, that the floor of the house offered insufficient space, the platform behind the Speaker's chair, and every spot where a chair could be wedged in was crowded with ladies in their gayest costume and their attendant beaux...who led them to their seats with the same gallantry as is exhibited in a ball room. Smiles, nods, whispers, nay sometimes tittering marked their recognition of each other and beguiled the tedium of the service.

Halfway through the liturgy, a postman might shuffle in and drop a large mailbag at the foot of the "pulpit." Music came courtesy of the Marine Corps Band, whose shining instruments and scarlet uniforms "made quite a dazzling appearance in the gallery." Mrs. Smith merrily conceded, "The marches they played were good and inspiring, but in their attempts to accompany the psalm-singing of the congregation they completely failed." Her summation: "It was *too* ridiculous."

Congress hosted an ecumenical pulpit in the Hall of Representatives until after the Civil War. Unaccompanied by the Marines, whose services were politely dropped, and forgoing Christian sacraments, the congressional chaplains and noted national preachers held forth weekly, occasionally to notable effect. This nod to the church offered incomplete solace to advocates for a Christian commonwealth. To give but one indication of how far the equal opportunity national pulpit might stray from the established religious pasture, in 1805 the *laissez faire* Baptist speaker of the house, North Carolina's Nathaniel Macon, invited a woman to preach in the Hall of Representatives. Methodist evangelist Dorothy Ripley reported praying beforehand, "the Lord direct my tongue, and open my mouth powerfully, that His Name [by a woman] may be extolled to the great astonishment of the hearers, who no doubt will be watching every word to criticize thereon."

In the years before he became president, public sightings of Jefferson in a pew were as rare as those of a good New England Calvinist in a tavern on the Sabbath day. When he and James Madison toured New England together in 1791, they were quoted in the *Vermont Gazette* as having told Governor Moses Robinson, their host one Sunday, that they hadn't attended church in years. During the 1800 campaign Jefferson's absence from church became a political cause celeb. "How does he spend the Lord's day?" former House chaplain William Linn wondered aloud for all to hear. "Is he known to worship with any denomination of Christians? Where? When? How often?" David Daggett supplied the answer: "Mr. Jefferson never attended public worship during a residence of several years in New York and Philadelphia." So imagine their surprise when this "howling Atheist" (Connecticut Reverend Thomas Robbins's epithet for Jefferson) appeared one Sunday in the House for church.

One week before Congress opened session in the fall of 1801 Jefferson, his daughter Martha, a grandson, and Meriwether Lewis appeared out of the blue in the House chamber for Sunday worship. Two weeks later, as a Federalist congressman sarcastically records, "it was very rainy, but his ardent zeal brought him through the rain and on horseback to the Hall" once again. And, on January 1, 1802, the very day that the president unveiled to the nation his "wall of separation between church and state," Jefferson, for at least the third time in as many months, was conspicuously present in the national chapel.

Margaret Smith remembered her hero as a regular churchgoer from the day he arrived in Washington. By her account, he even deigned to worship with the tiny Christ Church congregation in the tobacco house chapel before establishing a permanent pew in the House of Representatives (held vacant for him and his secretary Meriwether Lewis every Sunday). He may well have dropped by the Episcopal chapel; he did support the Reverend Andrew McCormick's valiant efforts with a charitable donation. Yet such support didn't carry the force of assent. Jefferson would support as many as ten Washington churches over the course of his presidency, including, in addition to local Baptist, Episcopal, Methodist, and Presbyterian congregations, the independent church that alone followed Congress's liberal precedent by offering its pulpit to Dorothy Ripley. Whether or not he worshiped with the local Episcopalians—it would have been the first time in years—he certainly began attending worship on at least a semiregular basis at the Hall of Representatives. From halfway through his first year as president until near the end of his second term, Jefferson was a churchgoing animal.

Among those scandalized by the president's apparent posturing was the Reverend Manasseh Cutler, who represented Massachusetts's rock-ribbed Federalist Essex constituency in Congress. With Jefferson's longstanding clerical ally John Leland in the pulpit ("a poor, ignorant, illiterate, clownish creature," according to the reverend representative), "the President, contrary to all practice, made one of his audience." Cutler was sufficiently taken aback by the president's newfound piety to dedicate two letters in as many days to the subject. He took solace in reflecting that "Although this is no kind of evidence of any regard to religion, it goes far to prove that the idea of bearing down and overturning our religious institutions...has been given up." Jefferson had not given up anything. Destroying religion was never his goal. All he set out to destroy was the political power of the Federalist priesthood. If attending church, especially with a Republican in the pulpit, could pluck a few pins out of their voodoo dolls, so much the better. Apparently, Jefferson was succeeding. "The political necessity of paying some respect to the religion of the country is felt," Cutler acknowledged.

Margaret Smith marveled on his first Fourth of July in office at how "Mr. Jefferson mingled promiscuously with the citizens." To sway the unconverted, she gushed to her Federalist sister-in-law, "Thus you see that we are here at least all Republicans and all Federalists." Representative Cutler was less impressed by Jefferson's gifts as a peacemaker. Viciously but insightfully, he summed up the president's character: "Courting popularity is his darling project."

"The Mammoth Cheese"

Among those who took special note of the president's attendance at worship the first Sunday of 1802 was the preacher for the morning. In the ongoing battle over church-state separation in the early Republic, John Leland is like Zelig. With lank shoulder-length hair and mangy side whiskers framing a long, homely face, he pops up in every picture, from the campaign to disestablish religion in Virginia and religious debates over the Constitution to almost every other major sacred-political contest that was waged during the almost half century he served as pastor of the Second Baptist Church in Cheshire, Massachusetts, until his death at eighty-seven in 1841. During his peripatetic career, Leland baptized more than 1,500 adults and brought his democratic gospel to a multitude more. Leland began his career fighting for the rights of slaves to attend evening meetings. He also put Virginia's Baptists on record that

"slavery is a violent deprivation of the rights of nature, and inconsistent with a republican government." More impactfully, he helped
topple three state church establishments (Virginia in 1787, Connecticut in 1818, and Massachusetts in 1833). Leland even tried his
hand at electoral politics; in 1811, Cheshire sent him to Boston to
serve for a term in the Massachusetts Assembly. The Quixote of the
early American pulpit, Leland summed up his picaresque, uncompromising American pilgrimage in a single sentence: "Here lies
JOHN LELAND, who labored 87 years to promote piety, and vin-
dicated the civil and religious rights of all men."

In an ironically titled "Fashionable Fast Day Sermon," delivered
before his Cheshire congregation in April 1801, Elder Leland imagined God addressing America. "My children," the Almighty says,

> I raised up a JEFFERSON to state your abuses and tell the world,
> in the *Declaration of Independence,* your burden, your wishes, and
> your rights....As you are not all instructed in your inalienable
> rights and the nature of a republican government, I have preserved
> Jefferson to be a guide and father unto you. I have raised him up
> in righteousness and will strengthen his hands....I have taught
> him...that the religious opinions of men are not objects of civil
> government, nor anyways under its control.

In response to the charge that he was pledging his Baptist troth to
a notorious Deist, Leland boldly upbraided those who scorned him
for acting "in concert with infidels" by casting doubt on their own
Christian fidelity. "Why should we not [join them], so far as infidels make use of right reasons?" he asked. After all, he added with
consummate cheek, when it came to the (for him) all-important
struggle for freedom of conscience, "They are nearer to revelation
than any kind of a state church."

Among his many talents, Leland was a public relations genius.
In the summer of 1801, he hit on the perfect gimmick—to present
Jefferson with a giant cheese contributed to by the livestock of hun-

dreds of humble yet sovereign Berkshire yeomen, whose mighty effort would be an emblem of "the passion of republicanism in a state where it has been under heavy persecution." Taking up a subscription, Leland commissioned a specially built cheese vat, cider press, and winch to turn the cheese. He embossed the final product (a 1400-pound cheese wheel, six feet in diameter and almost two feet thick, trumpeted as THE GREATEST CHEESE IN AMERICA, FOR THE GREATEST MAN IN AMERICA) with Jefferson's motto, "Rebellion to tyrants is obedience to God."

In the making of the cheese—the project demanded 900 cows at a single milking—no Federalist cows were permitted to participate. This was not a problem, since Federalist cows were as scarce in Cheshire as Republican professors were at Harvard.

Leland's wasn't the first gargantuan cheese to grace a presidential board. A 110-pound Federalist cheese ("as big as a chariot wheel") from Rhode Island greeted John and Abigail Adams's arrival at the Presidential Mansion. Adams muttered, given the cost of running the household and his insufficient salary, that the family might be reduced to living off it for the remainder of his term. The precedent for such gifts appears to have been set by the grateful citizens of Nantucket, who presented a 500-pound cheese to Lafayette, when he brokered a deal protecting the duty-free status of their precious whale oil.

Leland's "mammoth" cheese was so named for more than the obvious reason. Early exponents of America's persistent anti-intellectualism, fomented by the New England clergy and participated in by Federalist academics from Harvard to Yale, could not resist making sport of their president's fascination with scientific learning. A sharp-eyed amateur vertebrate paleontologist, Jefferson spearheaded a spirited campaign to refute the European pop scientist Comte de Buffon's claim that Old World animals were larger (read "superior") than those found in the New World. The discovery of an enormous quadruped (mammoth) skeleton, which Charles

Willson Peale mounted in his Philadelphia museum, offered dramatic reproof to Buffon's assumptions. It also provided the otherwise elitist Federalists with populist ammunition. Jefferson and his minions "can talk by the hour about the rights of man, and about mammoth bones and oyster shells," one detractor sneered, and that "all mankind are equal as a set of nine pins."

In 1797, the week he was sworn in as vice president, Jefferson had received the, for him, higher honor of being installed as president of the American Philosophical Society, flanked by Joseph Priestley and Count Volney, an international popularizer of Enlightenment thought. Federalist editor William Cobbett lampooned the vice president, Volney, and Priestly as a "triumvirate of *atheism, deism, and nothingism.*" A more measured but no less dogged Federalist critic wrote, "Science and government are two different paths. He that walks in one, becomes, at every step, less qualified to walk with steadfastness or vigor in the other."

Jefferson's scientific forays to advance theories about everything from the earth's antiquity to the impossibility of Noah's flood lent themselves to religious ridicule as readily as would Charles Darwin's later suggestion that human beings were descended from apes. Dr. Dwight epitomized this divide. Even as Jefferson's research was advancing the science of vaccination, the president of Yale scolded those who were advocating inoculations, accusing them of tampering with the Divine will. "Of all the charges brought against me by my political adversaries," Jefferson fairly said, "that of possessing some science has probably done them the least credit."

In the religious establishment's defensive holding action against science's assault on the minds of the faithful, by far the juiciest target was Jefferson's fascination with mastadons. Anticipating his inauguration, one Federalist wisecracked, "I think it will be truly laughable to see the swinish multitude feasting on a Quadruped and swilling whiskey to seditious toasts." When the Lewis and Clark expedition failed to turn up further evidence of Jefferson's precious creature, none less than future president John Quincy Adams chortled,

> He never with a Mammoth met,
> However you may wonder;
> Nor even with a Mammoth's bone,
> Above the ground or under.

As a populist attraction, however, Federalist anti-intellectualism was no match for Leland's cheese. With the famous "mammoth priest" preaching to tremendous crowds at every stop, during its five-week journey south by sleigh, wagon, and boat, the cheese "universally excited" local inhabitants from Albany to Baltimore. A moveable centerpiece for festive civic happenings, when the cheese arrived, "The taverns were deserted; the heavy soup cooled on the table, and the cats unrebuked swelled on the custards and cream." Baltimore Republicans provided four "richly caparisoned" horses to lead the cheese on the last leg of its journey, and the president stood in his doorway personally to receive the much-heralded favor on December 29.

There, in a far-from-impromptu ceremony, Leland read a proclamation from his congregants. Presenting the cheese as a "sacrifice to republicanism" (not a royal tribute, but a mere "peppercorn...a mite cast into the scale of democracy"), he and his Baptist parishioners anointed the president with divine unction. "We believe the supreme Ruler of the Universe, who raises up men to achieve great events, has raised up a JEFFERSON at this critical day, to defend *Republicanism* and to baffle the arts of *Aristocracy*." In reply, Jefferson concurred "that the constitution of the United States is a charter of authorities and duties, not a charter of rights to its officers; and that among its most precious provisions are the right of suffrage, the prohibition of religious tests, and its means of peaceable amendment."

Courtesy of Leland's puckish inspiration, Jefferson's supporters capitalized on the Cheshire cheese from the moment it first captured the people's fancy. Leland's cheese "and the appointment of Abraham Bishop's father Collector of New-Haven...have probably drawn forth more *federal* objections against the new administration than any other two measures," one sympathetic editor chuckled. "The Cheshire Cheese has not yet been seriously represented to be in itself a violation of the Constitution," the Republican Pittsfield *Sun* deadpanned, but, "It is shrewdly suspect that [Treasury Secretary] Albert Gallatin, the Geneva instigator of Whiskey Insurrections, instigated the good women of Cheshire to enter into the *Cheese-plot,* the particulars of which may be expected in the *Appendix* of Dr. Morse's next *Thanksgiving Sermon.*"

As for Mr. Leland, he left Washington $200 the richer, pocketing a munificent gift from the president not for the cheese—even with shipping and handling charges thrown in, it was worth but a fraction of that—but for successfully advancing two of Jefferson's most cherished political ambitions: the building of a lasting ("eternal") wall of separation between church and state; and being perceived by the American electorate the way he viewed himself, as infinitely more faithful to Jesus than were the establishment clergy, whose theological retrenchment and reactionary politics proved them to be "mere usurpers of the Christian name, teaching a counter-religion made up of the deliria of crazy imaginations as foreign from Christianity as is that of Mohomet."

"A Wall of Separation Between Church and State"

In one of the first public rollouts of executive policy in American history, Jefferson orchestrated the New Year's launch of his program for church-state separation by conspicuously attending worship in the national chapel and welcoming Reverend Leland and his famous cheese to the White House. On the very afternoon that Leland preached in the Hall of Representatives, Jefferson posted a carefully crafted letter to the Danbury Baptist Association, who were protesting the persistence of established religion in Connecticut. Their appeal on behalf of the rights of conscience (not "as favors granted" but "as unalienable rights") provided him with the occasion he had "long wished to find" to spell out his views on church and state.

Before launching it, Jefferson edited his reply to the Danbury Baptists by deleting any reference to his intended proscription of state-appointed fast days and thanksgivings, representing a dramatic break in presidential policy. Attorney General Levi Lincoln, a native of Massachusetts, commiserated with Jefferson that, even under the aegis of his enlightened presidency, Federalist hegemony extended in New England "from the governor through all the grades of office, down to the Tithingman of the parish, with the clergy as an appendage." But, noting that many of the president's supporters revered the local customs as well, his attorney general convinced Jefferson that flaunting his blanket opposition to national prayer days might cause unnecessary offense. Though Jefferson followed Lincoln's lead and tempered the scope of his Danbury proclamation, he had long since written off converting his theological opponents. "I know it will give great offense to the New England clergy," he said, "but the advocate of religious freedom is to expect neither peace nor forgiveness from them." Neither should they expect such favors from him. To Lincoln, Jefferson unveiled his agenda for New England's Christian politicos—he would thrust them "into an abyss from which there shall be no resurrection."

Even in its tempered form, Jefferson's letter to the Danbury Baptists remains the single most influential presidential document in the history of American church-state relations, its central passage encapsulating a lifetime of thought and effort dedicated to liberating the individual from government interference in matters of religion.

Believing with you that religion is a matter which lies solely between man and his God, that he owes account to none other for his faith or his worship, that the legislative powers of government reach actions only, and not opinions, I contemplate with sovereign reverence that act of the whole American people which declared that their legislature should "make no law respecting an establishment of religion, or prohibiting the free exercise thereof," thus building a wall of separation between church and state. Adhering to this expression of the supreme will of the nation in behalf of the rights of conscience, I shall see with sincere satisfaction the progress of those sentiments which tend to restore to man all his natural rights, convinced he has no natural right in opposition to his social duties.

In his final edit, Jefferson removed the adjective "eternal" from the "eternal wall of separation" that he initially had fashioned. Yet the wall he built has proved both time worthy and abidingly controversial. Two full centuries after its drafting, it remains a metaphorical horror representing secular tyranny to those who seek to wed their Christian nation to a more explicitly Christian government. Scholars of varied opinion yet sympathetic to religious prerogatives have proposed other, less rigid metaphors to take its place, but to this day Jefferson's wall endures as a delineating symbol for American church-state separation.

No newspaper in Connecticut ran Jefferson's manifesto, but word of his express sympathy for the Baptist cause did percolate through the state with lasting political effect. It prompted leading Connecticut Republicans, whose rational religious views hitherto had held them aloof from the Bible-thumping Baptists, to expand their political circle. Awakening to the potential value of previously untapped resources, they blanketed the state with reprints of Jefferson's "Act for Establishing Religious Freedom" and Madison's "Remonstrance." By summer, the Connecticut *Gazette* was bewailing that "Among the various schemes which the enemies of our state government have adopted to promote their grand object...no one [scheme] has been so successful as their attempt to enroll under their banners the minor sectaries of Christians." Shortly thereafter, concerned Federalists challenged the local Baptists and Methodists to mind their faith when casting their ballots, lest their freethinking champion beguile them down the river to perdition. Yet Connecticut's dissenting Christians were anything but intimidated. "The greatest part of the revivals of religion which have been within the past year in…many towns of New England have been principally among republicans," a Baptist activist rejoined, noting the growing evidence of "religious flourishes amongst those who are called democrats in Connecticut."

Such observations were backed up by growing evidence. Throughout New England, sectarian Protestants were threatening to outpace the established orders in their evangelism. The Reverend William Bentley of Salem, Massachusetts, a rare Unitarian whose politics were as liberal as his theology, warned that Baptist Jeffersonians were plucking sympathetic Christians out of old New England pews. "The Baptists," he observed, "by attaching themselves to the present administration have gained great success in the United States and greater in New England than any sect since the settlement even beyond comparison. This seems to be a warning to the churches of other denominations." Bentley made little headway in converting his colleagues in the Standing Order to his political faith. "I am informed," he said, "that my friendship for Mr. Jefferson will subject me to great evils." The Republican preacher took considerable pride in this fact. "The abuse which I receive, when called by name in the Federal papers," he acknowledged, "obliges me to take great satisfaction in the able vindication of the man I esteem as the greatest national benefactor."

Bentley wasn't the only Republican clergyman to challenge the political orthodoxy of his colleagues. In New Hampshire, the Reverend Samuel McClintock openly celebrated the nation's liberation from the "junto of little tyrants" who had been lording over the country, acclaiming Jefferson as an outstanding citizen and great friend "of the natural rights of man." Another democratic activist, the Reverend Thomas Allen, who served a Congregational church in Pittsfield, Massachusetts, led the Berkshire Republican movement together with John Leland. Allen explained his embrace of Jefferson, whom his Congregational colleagues scorned as a Deist, ingeniously. All state religion smacks of Deism, he said—ergo those who argue for the separation of church and state are, in fact, anti-Deist. The Pittsfield maverick shared this same insight with the president. "The Deistical idea among Federalists, that there is no religion among the people but what springs from the coercion of civil government and that all religion is a mere engine of state, is demonstrably false." Jefferson must have chuckled at the curious montage of believers he was attracting to his holy crusade to quash Federalist apostasy and complete the unfinished work of American salvation history. He sent Allen a flattering word of encouragement. The Republican clergy in Massachusetts were engaged in a sacred struggle, the president told his clerical supporter. "Their character must be offered on the altar of the public good."

Shaken by Jefferson's growing strength in New England, the Federalist clerical watchdogs cranked up their propaganda machine, warning the credulous against a religious bait and switch. Don't be fooled or flattered when the president shows up in the pews, they cautioned, echoing the logic of New York Presbyterian pastor John Mason. Struggling to maintain his Christian composure, Mason had likened Jefferson to "the vile, the blasphemous Voltaire, [who] was building churches, and assisting at the mass, while he was writing to his *philosophical* confidants concerning our divine savior, 'Crush the wretch.'" Jedidiah Morse and Timothy Dwight, with an assist from Ashbel Green, founded a new periodical to counter the political spread of democratic infidelity. *The New England Palladium,* which appeared on the scene right before Jefferson's inauguration, had a clear-cut charge—to gird up "the government, morals, religion, and state of society in New England," while exposing "Jacobinism in every form, both of principle and practice." Paraphrasing this mission in terms that tellingly expose the cultural fault line dividing New England's Federal and Republican Christians, Federalist politico Fisher Ames said that "The *Palladium* should be fastidiously polite and well-bred. It should whip Jacobins as a gentleman would a chimney-sweep, at arm's length, and keeping aloof of his soot." The stakes, its founders sincerely believed, could not be higher. "If this project fails of success," Morse avowed, "we are destined by divine Providence, as a punishment for our sins, to experience the awful calamities necessarily consequent on a prevalence of Jacobinism."

The project enjoyed a vigorous launch, with lavish Federalist financial backing. Free copies were sent to every clergyman in New England, leading Attorney General Levi Lincoln to cry foul. Warning against the dangers of a politicized clergy, he suggested that patriotic citizens would soon rebel against having their state tax dollars go to the support of ministers who were employing their pulpits to preach against the president. Lincoln's warning was prescient. At tricolor Fourth of July banquets across New England, wits rose to strafe the establishment clergy. "Federal Religion—May it soon become Christian," went one published toast. Other Jeffersonians were more earnest: "The Clergy—May they preach the gospel of Jesus Christ—Not their own political gospel"; and "Religion—We love it in its purity, but not as an engine of political delusion."

Fearing that the last holy ground in America might soon fall to the enemy, a year after Jefferson took office Morse began contemplating secession. "Ought we suffer ourselves to be forced into the vortex of certain destruction & to sacrifice all that is dearest to our hearts at the shrine of the A[theists] and D[emocrats]?" he asked. Two years later, he was discussing the notion openly with New Hampshire senator William Plumer. If New England did not secede, he asked, would it not "be by degrees drawn into a vortex, in which our religious, political & literary institutions and all the principles & habits which are their fruits, and which are our glory & happiness, will be engulfed and lost?"

"What Is the Mark of a Christian If This Is Not?"

By issuing his most important proclamation on church-state separation before the pious backdrop of him sitting in a pew at the Capitol and ceremoniously receiving a clergyman at the White House, Jefferson furthered two related goals: 1) to signal his avowed intent to reform the church-state policy of his predecessor by keeping government out of the religion business; and 2) to reassure the more religious elements of the electorate that, all rumor to the contrary, he would honor the religious traditions of the land.

Jefferson held faithful to his intention never to declare a national prayer day. The increasingly pragmatic president would let a minuscule gesture of government support for Christian missions to the Indians slip past his censor, but as a whole his church-state policy, notwithstanding the sacred aura cast over his presidency by democratic preachers, is well represented by the memorable "wall of separation" that he employed to express his solidarity with the Danbury Baptists.

After separating church and state, Jefferson's second agenda was to separate his most intractable opponents from their base by infiltrating it. Republicans in Congress picked up on this strategy, milking the president's appearances in church for all they were worth in their constituent newsletters. Addressing the Freeholders of the Northwestern Congressional District of Virginia in early 1803, Congressman George Jackson addressed the hot question of religious politics in three ways: He forswore mixing religion and politics ("I trust...that religion will never be blended with politics"); he tried a little holy politicking of his own ("The federalists...are the children of the Devil, their father"); and he defended Jefferson's faith:

> I shall not pretend to say our President, Thomas Jefferson, is a religious man; I do not know to the contrary, though I believe him honest, virtuous, and sober. He is spoken of by some religious people as a very attentive man to the worship of God, as a chari-

table man to the poor and all religious institutions. What is the mark of a Christian if this is not?

Jackson was spouting what was clearly the Democratic-Republican Party line: *Who knows what Jefferson believes, but he is a virtuous man, goes to church, and contributes generously to religious causes.* The following week, adding an encomium to church-state separation, Congressman Robert Williams of North Carolina stayed on message to calm his district's fears about Jefferson's storied impiety:

> I know there is a considerable bickering against our present chief magistrate with regard to his religious opinions. What they are I know not; I know him to be moral, that he attends divine service regularly, is friendly to every denomination, without being an enthusiast for any, and regards the Constitution of his country too much to attempt to influence, or give a preference to any; that he is charitable to the poor, and is concerned for the happiness of mankind in general. Why then need you and I care what are his opinions, as to the course which he may think most proper to secure his future happiness. We want his services as a politician, and not as a pastor, and God forbid we ever should have a President who would attempt to unite Church and State.

Without recognizing it as a disguise, Jefferson had fashioned a Christian garment perfectly suited to his loose-limbed religious frame. This ruse didn't fool his closest Christian friends, such as Benjamin Rush (who was souring on the president), or his political enemies. But American Protestants, even those high-pulpit doomsayers who after the war had cursed the falloff in religious observance throughout the East, had few legitimate beefs. Far from being breached by an invasion of *philosophes,* Deists, and atheists (the specter that Timothy Dwight, Jedidiah Morse, and their fellow agitators prophesied would follow hard on an infidel victory), from the moment Jefferson entered office Christianity was on a roll. Deism in American actually appears to have declined during the early years of Jefferson's presidency. The market for Deist clubs and papers, sponsored by liberal religious evangelists such as the Reverend Elihu Palmer, peaked under the impetus of repression, only to wane once the infidel in chief was safely ensconced in office. Compared to Dwight and Morse, Bishop and Leland proved the better prophets. Liberty had served the church, not crippled it. One Republican paper crowed, "God is taking care of his own cause, for never since the settlement of this country has there been such glorious revivals of religion as since President Jefferson presided."

Trimmed of causal pretense, the same view echoed from across the great religious divide. The 1803 General Assembly of the Presbyterian Church, meeting in Philadelphia, acknowledged that during the first two years of Jefferson's administration, the "preached gospel" had prospered. Despite the president's questionable beliefs, throughout the land God once again was doing very well indeed.

UTOPIA MEETS REALITY

HAPPY the man, who's country seat
Affords a pleasing, calm retreat
Beneath its shady bow'rs:
No heavy cares of public life
No noisy partie' clam'rous strife
Disturb his peaceful hours.

—ANONYMOUS,
"THE PLEASURES OF RETIREMENT"
(FROM JEFFERSON'S SCRAPBOOKS)

LATE IN his first term, President Thomas Jefferson took out his scissors and pruned the Gospels. His account begins with Jesus's birth and ends with the rolling of the stone to close his tomb. In addition to snipping out the Virgin birth and the Resurrection, Jefferson excised Jesus's miracles and the Last Supper, leaving only his ethical teachings.

On the cover page of "The Philosophy of Jesus of Nazareth" (the first draft of what would come to be known as "Jefferson's Bible"), he describes its contents as "an abridgment of the New Testament for the use of the Indians, unembarrassed with matters of fact or faith beyond the level of their comprehension." Jefferson never excluded the Bible as a possible tool for civilizing the Indians, suggesting only it be employed at the end of the process. Arguing against taking him at his word, however, President Jefferson loved ciphers and would veil his critique a year later in his second inaugural address by pretending to speak of Indians when he was actually referring to the wayward behavior of his New England opponents. Since the New England clergy was never far from his mind when Jesus entered it, his title page may record a rare stab of irony. Clerical attacks inspired Jefferson to revisit the scriptures—mining for "diamonds" in the "dunghill," he called it—to prove, if only to his own satisfaction, that he was a more faithful disciple than those benighted rogues on the Christian payroll.

Jefferson's Bible and his "Syllabus on the Teachings of Jesus" fulfilled a promise Jefferson had made to Dr. Benjamin Rush that one day he would put his thoughts about Jesus into writing. Ever the optimist, he assured Rush that his views "ought to displease neither the rational Christian nor Deist, and would reconcile many to a character they have too hastily rejected."

Dr. Rush's principal contribution to American thought was made in medicine, but religion was his first love. He lobbied universalists of all denominations to welcome persons of every Christian society into their fellowships, dreaming of the establishment of an ecumenical body that might serve the interests of many in a shared and single cause. "All truths are related, or rather there is but one truth," Rush told the Reverend Jeremy Belknap in 1791. "Republicanism is a part of the truth of Christianity. It derives power from its true source. It teaches us to view our rulers in their true light. It abolishes the false glare which surrounds kingly government, and tends to promote the true happiness of all its members as well as of the whole world, for peace with everybody is the true interest of all republics."

The likeness his friend struck between Christianity and republican government must have fascinated Jefferson. Perhaps he thought he was following in its spirit when he set out to rescue Jesus from the church. In sending Rush his finished "Syllabus" of Jesus's teachings, Jefferson described it as "the result of a life of inquiry and reflection, and very different from that anti-Christian system imputed to me by those who know nothing of my opinions. To the corruptions of Christianity, I am indeed opposed; but not to the genuine precepts of Jesus himself." Rush, who looked to Jesus as his Lord and Savior, was underwhelmed by the Christian minimalism of Jefferson's "Syllabus" and told the president so.

A decade later, in 1814, rousting Jefferson into a furious bit of damage control, Jedidiah Morse would mischievously unveil Jefferson's secret, picked up from reading the biography of a British Unitarian minister that contained two private letters, in which Jefferson had alluded to his biblical handiwork. John Adams, for one, was intrigued by Morse's news and asked his new old friend for a copy. Jefferson primly told him, "I have performed this operation for my own use." By no means shocked by Jefferson's critical approach to the Gospels, Adams nursed his own doubts concerning biblical authority. "What suspicions of interpolation, and indeed of fabrication, might not be confuted if we had the originals!" he scribbled in the margin of one theological tome. "In an age or in ages when fraud, forgery, and perjury were considered as lawful means of propagating truth by philosophers, legislators, and theologians, what may not be suspected?" With astounding prescience, both amateurs anticipated the course academic biblical criticism would take over the following two centuries.

If Adams found Jefferson's surgery on the Gospels more intriguing than blasphemous, he stood with Rush on quainter ground. Adams, too, believed the Bible to be "the most republican book in the world," but for moralistic, not theological reasons. "The curses against fornication and adultery and the prohibition of every wanton glance or libidinous ogle at a woman I believe to be the only system that ever did or will preserve a republic in the world," he primly professed. "National morality never was and never can be preserved without the utmost purity and chastity in women: and without national morality a republican government cannot be maintained." Thinking no less idiosyncratically, Adams would point to the lax morals practiced by "women of rank, fashion and reputation" as a contributing factor to the collapse of French republicanism.

Female lasciviousness "can never support a republican government nor be reconciled with it," he pontificated. "We must therefore take great care not to import them into America."

Rush deemed women critical to American virtue, too, but for a different reason entirely: A vibrant republic demanded an educated citizenry. Any nation that neglected the education of half its population could never, in Rush's estimation, qualify as an enlightened republic. Men who opposed educating women were thwarting "the general diffusion of knowledge," he told the Visiting Committee of the Young Ladies' Academy of Philadelphia. When Rush and Adams squabbled over the Philadelphian's campaign to drop classical languages from the American curriculum (for promoting elitism), Abigail pounced on his argument and made it her own. "Mrs. Adams says she is willing you should discredit Greek and Latin because it will destroy the foundation of all the pretensions of the gentlemen to superiority over the ladies and restore liberty, equality and fraternity between the sexes," John laughingly said. Yet to her husband's fixation on republican morals, Abigail offered a dutiful echo: "The manners of women are the surest criterion by which to determine whether a republican government is practicable in a nation or not," she avowed. "The Jews, the Greeks, the Romans, the Swiss, the Dutch, all lost their public spirit, their republican principles and habits, and their republican forms of government, when they lost the modesty and domestic virtues of their women."

If Rush's identification of republicanism and Christianity was vastly more encompassing than anything suggested by Adams's moralistic reverie, it remained too crimped for Jefferson. Inspired by a religious vision more inclusive than the evangelical universalist would have deemed scripturally acceptable, he sifted through the Gospels, and would do so a second time as an old man, looking less for the historical than the intelligible Jesus. He sought to adduce testimony for universal moral principles, not to isolate a truth unique to either Jesus or Christianity. "It is not to be understood that I am with him in all his doctrines," Jefferson freely admitted in describing his view of Jesus. "I am a materialist; he takes the side of spiritualism. He preaches the efficacy of repentance towards forgiveness of sin; I require a counterpoise of good works to redeem it, etc. etc." Such differences notwithstanding, after he purged it of doctrinal impurities what remained of Jesus's gospel—love to God and neighbor—met the requisites for Jefferson's "national faith."

Hamilton's Last Hurrah

Among those cut adrift when the Federalist tide went out was Jefferson's old nemesis Alexander Hamilton. During the 1800 election he played Cassandra, warning that a Jefferson victory would be tantamount to the "overthrow" of the government. Jefferson's "Revolution of 1800" was in truth a "REVOLUTION after the manner of BONAPARTE," Hamilton warned on the eve of the election. But then he lost his lust for politics. The returns, compounded by the tragic death of his son Philip in a duel fought in defense of his father's honor, broke Hamilton's tenacious spirit. "What can I do better than withdraw from the scene?" he pined to his old ally Gouverneur Morris early in 1802. "Every day proves to me more and more that this American world is not for me." But soon melancholy yielded to bile, and Hamilton was back badgering his fellow Federalists to play the religion card.

Until the end of his life, Hamilton avoided the most casual appearance of religious devotion, leaving his evangelical wife to attend church alone and making no mention of Christ in his correspondence. He did turn to the scriptures for solace after Philip's death, but his last-gasp effort to save the government from Jefferson, ironically through the agency of a "self-created" society, was uninstructed by reverence. Returning to his political street-fighting ways, he alit on the perfect symbolic weapon: "The Christian Constitutional Society." He and his cohorts needed only wrap themselves "in the holy garments of Constitution and Christianity" to rally patriotic churchmen to the sacred Federalist cause. Hamilton's fidelity to the

Constitution, which he called a "frail and worthless fabric," was no greater than his reverence for the Bible, but the master of symbolism recognized the political advantages accruing to those who wrapped themselves in both.

Hamilton envisioned a coalition of religious patriots, who would revisit Article VI and Christianize the Constitution to ensure that the likes of Jefferson be forever barred from higher office. During the 1800 election, he told John Jay that "In times like these in which we live, it will not do to be over-scrupulous." In short, "Delicacy and propriety" must not "hinder the taking of a *legal* and *constitutional* step to prevent an *atheist* in religion and a *fanatic* in politics from getting possession of the helm of state." The Christian Constitutional Society would promote just such a goal. In founding a sacred action committee of sorts, governed by a president (himself?) and council of twelve (apostles?) with a mandate to employ "all lawful means in concert to promote the election of *fit* men," Hamilton's design, for purely political reasons, was to reverse the tables on Jefferson's blasphemous policy of church-state separation.

In a sign of the changing times, Hamilton failed to muster a minyan of disciples for his society, and his final bid to redeem the nation ended before it began. Federalist diehards Charles Pinckney and Theodore Sedgwick appear to have shown interest, but Senator James Bayard of Delaware argued vigorously against Hamilton's new scheme. Founding a network of Christian Federalist clubs "would revive a thousand jealousies and suspicions which now begin to slumber," he warned. That such jealousies were nodding off was precisely Hamilton's fear. To the Federalist senator Bayard, as for his Republican cousin Margaret Bayard Smith, the dream of "we are all republicans, all federalists" was sweet; to Hamilton, it was a nightmare, proof positive that the serpent plotting America's fall had delivered the apple.

Two years later Hamilton was dead at the hand of Vice President Aaron Burr. In their tragic appointment on the cliffs above the Hudson, with two pistol shots—one taking Hamilton's life, the other mortally wounding Burr's reputation—Jefferson's most nettlesome adversaries removed each other from the body politic. Morris, whose interest in religion, too, was purely rhetorical, eulogized Hamilton as Heaven's anointed messenger sent to redeem a fallen society. "God," he declared, "called him suddenly into existence, that he might assist to save a world!" Despite Morris's and Hamilton's best efforts, the world he was sent to save was changing.

If muffled by events, the Federalist drums rolled on. "From that fanatical spirit of liberty and equality which among democrats is the order of the day, we have everything to fear," intoned Theodore Dwight's unreconstructed *Connecticut Gazette.* "It attacks every institution of wisdom and antiquity and alike dooms to destruction our learning, our laws, and religion." These were strong, familiar words, but defaming liberty in the land of liberty was becoming an increasingly difficult sell. To the shrill-voiced Jeremiahs, most Americans had long since tuned out. The wolf of chaos, whose name they cried was Jefferson, had failed to bare his teeth.

Equal but Separate: Jefferson's Slavery Problem

In marked contrast to the political religious free-for-all during the election of 1800, the religious darts thrown during Jefferson's race for reelection proved little more than dull-pointed irritants. One moral issue, however, with all its attendant rumors, wouldn't go away—the continuing ambiguity surrounding Jefferson's attitude toward race.

The gap between President Jefferson's ideals and practice on race relations found dramatic expression in his terrified response to the slave rebellion in Haiti. He rushed to assure Napoleon that "nothing would be easier than to furnish your army and fleet with everything and to reduce Toussaint-Louverture to starvation." As the president was privately endeavoring to subvert the valiant ex-slave's struggle to establish a Dominican Republic, his disciple Abraham Bishop was quoting the Jeffersonian gospel chapter and verse on behalf of the Haitian rebels, invoking the Declaration of Independence to shame his fellow citizens into supporting the insurrection. "We have firmly asserted *that all men are free*," Bishop preached. "Yet as soon as the poor blacks...cried out, *It is enough*...we have been the first to assist in riveting their chains!"

What little ardor Jefferson displayed for blacks appeared to come from a different quarter entirely, his slave quarters, leaving tongues around the country wagging with rumors that he kept a Negro mistress. Scabrous wits could not resist the temptation to exploit these delicious whisperings, and rumors of his maintaining a sexual relationship with one of his slaves would dog Jefferson throughout his days. Two centuries later, with the plausible but slim possibility that his brother Randolph may in fact have been the culprit, DNA tests appear to have eliminated most doubt that these rumors were, in fact, true.

For someone who condemned slavery with theological flourish, the gratitude Jefferson expressed to Providence for the economic advantages of slave breeding is chilling. "I consider the labor of a breeding woman as no object, and that a child raised every two years is of more profit than the crop of the best laboring man," Jefferson advised his overseer. "In this, as in all other cases, Providence has made our interests and our duties coincide perfectly." He had not always been so callous. Years before, Jefferson summed up the moral peril attendant on slaveholders as well as anyone. "The whole commerce between master and slave," he said in *Notes on Virginia*, "is a perpetual exercise of the most boisterous passions, the most unremitting despotism on the one part, and degrading submissions on the other....The man must be a prodigy who can retain his manners and morals undepraved by such circumstances." In this respect, Jefferson was apparently no prodigy.

Jefferson possessed upward of 150 slaves when he authored the Declaration of Independence, and bought and sold at least that many over the course of his lifetime, including, always discreetly, during the years of his presidency. Less hypocritical than convoluted, his position on slavery rested on eight unshakeable principles. In isolation, these principles may appear to contradict each other but, following their internal logic, they cohere into a working (if unworkable) philosophy for defusing the nation's ticking time bomb without setting it off. Drawing from all Jefferson's reflections on the subject of slavery, one can condense his views as follows:

1. Slavery is evil, a gross violation of nature's laws of liberty and equality and God's law of justice. It must be abolished or God's mighty arm will come crashing down, shattering the institution of human bondage and leading to war between the races that will continue until one race or the other is exterminated. In this war, God will favor the cause of the slaves.

2. All Americans are victimized by slavery, master and bondsmen alike. Its depredations sully the moral character of everyone it touches.

3. Slavery is not America's fault. British profiteers persisted in foisting it on our country with the full, conspiratorial sanction of the king.

4. Emancipation must be gradual. Millions of freed blacks would certainly avenge themselves on their masters.

5. Deep-seated prejudice and bitter memory will never permit white and unshackled black to exist peaceably in the same society. Deportation to a sanctuary in Africa or the Caribbean must therefore be part of any scheme for emancipation.

6. Until the time is ripe to initiate gradual emancipation and exportation, the status quo must be maintained, lest the promise of liberty inspire bloody rebellion and the destruction of southern culture.

7. Northerners who call for abolition care nothing about the welfare of blacks. Instead they are evil apostates from republican principle, motivated by their heretical leaders and abetted by the New England clerical establishment to subvert Constitutional liberty (reinforced by states' rights) in an unholy crusade to restore monarchy,

aristocracy, theocracy, and with them all the privileges of caste that the founders fought to abolish forever.

8. He himself, whether as a statesman or as a master, could do nothing to end slavery that would not instead make matters worse. The resolution of this tragedy must be left to future generations.

In a brilliant satire, Jonathan Swift commended infanticide as the perfect solution for overpopulation. Late in life Jefferson entertained a chillingly similar notion. He would export all the children born into slavery, to be bundled off as soon as they were weaned, leaving their parents and grandparents to winnow America of their own presence actuarially through death. "I am aware that the subject involves some constitutional scruples," the sage of Monticello conceded with surpassing understatement. "The separation of infants from their mothers, too, would produce some scruples of humanity," he allowed. "But this would be straining at a gnat, and swallowing a camel." Jefferson never gave up on his scheme for ethnic cleansing by baby purchase and foreign distribution. "Newborn infants," he reckoned (in a letter to a clergyman written late in life) could be purchased by the government for "say twelve dollars and fifty cents" apiece and maintained in camps "until a proper age for deportation."

Jefferson said that freeing slaves was like "abandoning children." His fear was less for the abandoned children than for their masters. Immediate abolition, he believed, would lead to immediate bloodshed. Slavery "will probably never end but in the extermination of one or the other race," he direly prophesied, a sentiment that sums up Jefferson's lifelong dual conviction that 1) the evil of slavery must be terminated, and 2) America could only survive and flourish as a lily-white nation. "Nothing is more certainly written in the book of fate, than that these people are to be free," he declared in his *Autobiography,* "nor is it less certain that the two races, equally free, cannot live in the same government. Nature, habit, opinion have drawn indelible lines of distinction between them." The conflicting absolutes of justice and segregation painted Jefferson into a corner from which he couldn't escape without closing his eyes.

As slavery entrenched itself more deeply in American soil and soul alike, the southern inheritors of Jefferson's libertarian gospel swore that, being himself a slave holder, Jefferson was thinking only of whites when he proclaimed that all men were created equal. In *Notes on Virginia,* he did entertain some doubts. But in the same book, in a passage on slavery ennobled by the very theology he prided himself for outgrowing, Jefferson expressed his heart's ruling on the matter in no uncertain terms. "Can the liberties of a nation be thought secure when we have removed their only firm basis, a conviction in the minds of the people that these liberties are of the gift of God?" he asked, freely conceding that "they are not to be violated but with his wrath." Jefferson's fear, when he dared to face slavery's moral burden squarely, could not have been more palpable. "I tremble for my country when I reflect that God is just," and that "his justice cannot sleep forever." One day, "the wheel of fortune" would turn, leading to "an exchange of situation," with blacks lording over whites, quite probably brought about "by supernatural interference!" His conclusion: "The Almighty has no attribute which can take side with us in such a contest."

When provoked by the blasphemy of slavery, Jefferson's Deist God morphed into the biblical Jehovah, able to suspend nature's laws and interpose judgment. "We are not in a world ungoverned by the laws and power of a superior agent," Jefferson declared. He assured a French correspondent that the slaves' "tears and groans will awaken a God of justice to their distress," either "by diffusing light among their oppressors or by His exterminating thunder."

The inheritance of slavery that Jefferson bequeathed to future generations gives a perverse twist to his ideological conviction that the "earth belongs in usufruct to the living" and that each new generation must therefore be free to thrive unencumbered by past indebtedness. "Can one generation bind another?" he challenged Madison early in their partnership. "Every constitution then, and every law, naturally expires at the end of 19 years. If it be enforced longer, it is an act of force and not of right." Madison gingerly pointed out that, in effect, Jefferson's fantasy could only be realized if all property deeds were torched every nineteen years and the roads and bridges built by the previous generation ripped out. As fate would have it, events proved both men right. To remove slavery's curse from succeeding generations, its bonds would have to be broken and the land bathed in blood.

Freedom from the Press

In 1806, the Baptist Convention of North Carolina sent President Jefferson a letter of tribute, celebrating that, at long last, Micah's prophecy had been fulfilled: "there is none that shall make us afraid." New England Congregationalists had yet to receive this irenic message. Framing the ongoing struggle as one between "religion and infidelity, morality and debauchery, legal government and total disorganization," Federalists were still enlisting the state courts to prosecute ministers who employed their pulpits to advance the cause of infidelity, debauchery, and total disorganization. In response, one Connecticut Republican quipped, "it is more honorable to be called a republican felon than a Connecticut saint, but it is not comfortable to be dragged from your families and business and to be shut up in a jail." The Republican paper in Litchfield defined the rules of engagement as follows:

SLANDER—Whatever is said, truly or falsely, against Federalists.

TRUTH—Whatever is said against democrats.

GOSPEL PREACHING—calling Mr. Jefferson, in the pulpit, an *infidel,* a *debauccher* [sic] and a *liar.*

IMPARTIAL JUDGE—One who extols the men of one party, and denounces those of the other as "a stench in the nostrils of a holy God."

CHARITY—(obsolete).

Astonished by a Federalist newspaper that he picked up and read on a visit to the Presidential Mansion, Baron Alexander von Humboldt (accustomed to the civilities of a controlled press), asked his host, "Why are these libels allowed?" to which the president handsomely replied, "Put that paper in your pocket, Baron, and should you hear the reality of our liberty, the freedom of our press questioned, show this paper and tell where you found it." These proud words notwithstanding, Jefferson entertained private doubts about the prudence of his own first principle. Suggesting that papers should come conveniently divided into four sections (truths, probabilities, possibilities, and lies), he called it "a melancholy truth that a suppression of the press could not more completely deprive the nation of its benefits, than is done by its abandoned prostitution to falsehood."

Jefferson's pique received ample provocation. Joseph Dennie, for one, tried the president's patience on a weekly basis. A New Englander by birth, Dennie trained for the law at Harvard but entered the Republic of Letters instead. As editor of the *Port Folio,* he became Jefferson's most brilliant journalistic nuisance. Blending neoclassical literary style with antidemocratic, religiously charged politics, Dennie—he signed his early essays "Lay Preacher"—cottoned to the Episcopal religion, charting a middle course between Puritan sanctimony and modern insouciance. If too merry minded to suffer the world-denying imprecations of the Calvinists he grew up amidst, Dennie remained a devout establishmentarian. He firmly believed that the state had a Christian duty to give moral instruction to the otherwise self-interested rabble who, left free to wander wild, would unman the government.

Dennie saved his sharpest barbs for the *philosophes,* Jefferson foremost among them. "In the shape of Satan thou dids't crawl among the flowers of Eden, in the shape of freedom thou didst banish order and comfort from mankind," he intoned from his censorious editorial pulpit. A *Port Folio* writer warned, "Democrats suppose themselves, and our nation to be in a sinless state, from which they cannot fall." Jefferson's goal was in fact very nearly that, a sinless state, in which the people would be free to abound without federal interference. Dennie took a cartoonish view of the egalitarian president. "Ordered my horse," Jefferson notes in an imagined diary entry, "never ride with a servant—looks proud—mob doesn't like it—must gull the boobies."

Sally Hemings was a *Port Folio* fixture. A scurrilous ditty by the editor himself neatly captures Dennie's arty, moralistic bias:

> Resume thy shells and butterflies,
> Thy beetle's heads, and lizard's thighs,
>   The state no more control;
> Thy tricks, with sooty Sal, give o'er;
> Indulge thy body, Tom, no more;
> But try to save thy soul.

When Hemings began lasciviously popping up in sermons, the Republicans lost all patience and their cherished principles flew out the window. With Jefferson appointee Pierpont Edwards conveniently presiding over the federal district court in Connecticut, heretofore immune Federalist preachers began to get a bite of their own brimstone. Ministerial candidate Thaddeus Osgood defamed the president from the pulpit as "a base, traitorous infidel, debaucher and liar," and landed in federal prison. The Reverend Azel Backus (no relation to John) preached a sermon in staunch Congregationalist Litchfield County, pronouncing Jefferson "a liar, whoremaster, debaucher, drunkard, gambler....who keeps a wench as his whore and brings up in his family black females for that purpose." He added that the president qualified his federal appointments by elevating only fellow infidels to office. Arraigned for sedition in 1806, Backus, too, was locked up for his impudence.

The new federal sedition trials—Jefferson euphemistically called them "countervailing prosecutions"—placed the president in a quandary. Should he see his enemies punished or defend the republican principles of free speech and states' rights? Instinct told him that turnabout was fair play. Republican clergymen and editors had been harassed by judicial persecution for years. In Jefferson's eyes, these new cases simply countered the "interested aristocracy of priests and lawyers" who long had visited their vicious "falsehoods and artifices" on the courts. Cooling his vindictive temper, however, was the threat by defense counsel to subpoena his Virginia neighbors to validate the charges leveled against him from the pulpit. This gambit would, in effect, put the president himself on trial, presenting the Hemings rumors for public review and revisiting the ancient charge, the truth of which he privately conceded, of sexual harassment against a married neighbor before his marriage. Faced with the prospect of a spectacular show trial, Jefferson privately ensured that the cases would be dropped before he was made subject to further embarrassment. Supreme Court Justice William Johnson subsequently ruled that the federal bench stood without jurisdiction over libel cases against officers of the government. With this final stroke of the gavel, America's leading libertarian's awkward experiment in prosecuting libel came to a close.

The Empire of Liberty and the Second Great Awakening

Despite the Hemings sideshow, Jefferson won his race for reelection against Federalist governor Charles Pinckney of South Carolina in a walk, carrying all but the twelve electoral votes of Connecticut and Delaware and two from Maryland. He even broke the Federalist stranglehold on Massachusetts, which must have given both him and John Leland surpassing joy.

In his 1804 landslide victory, the electorate's approbation was for itself as much as for their president. Jefferson flattered the people in the finest way possible, sincerely believing every word of his flattery. His outspoken faith in popular sovereignty instilled in American hearts an inner nobility not unlike that inspired by camp evangelists. This new breed of Methodist and Baptist preachers were democratizing salvation, setting souls free to soar by preaching the liberating gospel of a one-to-one, unmediated relationship with Christ. Backwoods evangelist Joseph Thomas spoke for many itinerant preachers when he described his political sentiments as "republican throughout. For in the government of Christ, given to his people, I consider there is a perfect *equality* as it relates to power." Jefferson's Enlightenment faith and the populist Christianity of the democratic preachers melded perfectly. That two leveling movements, one secular, the other religious, were flourishing simultaneously helped to advance the "Revolution of 1800."

In his book *The Two Sources of Morality and Religion,* the twentieth-century French philosopher Henri Bergson speaks of alternating currents of spiritual energy that pulsate through the course of history. Dynamic periods, as he terms them, follow static ones. Then, after a burst of creative spiritual ferment, order is restored and another static period follows in turn. Jesus and Martin Luther, for instance, blew the tight lid off the religious establishments of their day by exhorting the people to liberate themselves from the sway of corrupt, encrusted religious hierarchies in favor of a direct relationship with God. When the revolutionary flame of their dynamic passion flickered out, as such flames always do, a static hierarchy stood at the ready to erect temples and churches in their holy names. To adopt Bergson's model, America's first two great awakenings were dynamic cycles in the alternating current of religious history. They were anti-establishmentarian, personal in their appeal, and radical in their message, which was *Don't let some self-interested ecclesiastical or government authority tell you what to believe, but read the Bible with your own eyes and open your heart directly to Jesus, who will take you into his sweet embrace and save your troubled soul.*

The First Great Awakening burst forth during the middle of the eighteenth century. Its liberating gospel shook the establishment rafters so vigorously that the roof was poised to collapse during the Revolutionary War. The Reverend George Whitefield, principal impresario of the First Great Awakening, introduced, in place of God the judge, a benevolent, loving Father, ready to save anyone who turned her eyes heavenward.

The Second Great Awakening, spanning the early decades of the nineteenth century, was a two-winged Christian revival. A spiritual breeze—call it the Holy Spirit—whistled through America, promising redemption at the hands of a saving God and transfiguring old-fashioned, establishment-dominated religious politics. The principal differences between the established and democratic wings of the so-called Second Great Awakening were cultural not theological, for Arminianism (the belief that any individual could be saved if she opened her heart to Christ) held an increasing purchase on both camps, with redemption hinging on individual moral choice, not on God's predetermined script.

On the establishment side, in the late 1790s and again in 1802, Timothy Dwight sponsored a revival at Yale. Halfway through Jefferson's first term, a full third of the student body pledged themselves to Christ. Soon, in new, more attractive packaging, Puritanism was following the waterways and trade routes from upstate New York into Ohio and then beyond toward the opening Western frontier.

Whether orchestrated by ecclesiastical authorities or more or less spontaneous, the Second Great Awakening was a democratic movement. Even the revivals in small-town New England took on a life of their own, leading many Standing Order pastors to resist their suasion until competition from the Baptists and Methodists demanded an answer in kind. Later, following the War of 1812, when Dwight's successors would shift their organizational prowess to the establishment of voluntary associations, they, too, became unwitting practitioners of the very democracy that Dwight had so disdained.

One social revolution triggered by the Second Great Awakening was that women began emerging in positions of spiritual power. Extreme pietistic sects, such as the Shakers, were founded and led by women. In the West, not only did women preach in camp revivals but they also received the greatest social benefit from the moral reforms that followed on their husbands being saved. And in the East, women were the engine that ran the charitable associations that emerged from the establishment wing of the Second Great Awakening. Moral movements do have a conservative impact on social behavior, but when those same movements liberate individuals who before operated only under the thumbs of their husbands and pastors, liberty is served.

Initially the breeze of spiritual renewal blew most steadily at the back of democratic Christians, who squandered none of their energy trying to convert the president of the United States, as long as he granted them full freedom to worship God as they pleased. With their anti-establishmentarian bias, flexible entry requirements for the clergy, and the premium they placed on a direct rather than mediated relationship with Jesus and the Bible, a solid majority of American Methodists and Baptists naturally embraced the Jeffersonian civic gospel. The Christian pioneer spirit and scrappy agrarian egalitarianism were joined at the hip. Commonsense religion—think of it as Bible- rather than church-centered Christianity—took flight like a transfigured phoenix out of old Tom Paine's disgraced ashes, investing American faith with many of the same radical attributes that Paine long before had contributed to American politics. Jeffersonian politics and Christian democracy advanced together. However bewildered Jefferson must have been by their religious enthusiasm, his noble yeomen remained noble yeomen when they came to Jesus. His Revolution of 1800 wasn't won in Washington alone but in camp revivals, too, and in log churches throughout the American West.

On the frontier, signs of a new ecstatic awakening first appeared in 1800 with the onset of camp revivals. Converts by the hundreds, from leading citizens to slaves, waved their arms to heaven, jerked, shouted, and rolled on the ground like hoops. Some religious enthusiasts fell stupefied into days-long comas, others barked for hours like dogs, causing wonderment or evoking derision, but in either case capturing the imagination of thousands at week-long camp meetings that vitalized American religion on the sin-riddled frontier. The famous revival in Cane Ridge, Kentucky, during the second week of August 1801 spawned tent festivals in the Cumberland Valley and elsewhere throughout the American West in the years to follow. Initially organized by Presbyterians but participated in by Methodist itinerant ministers and Baptist log cabin pastors as well, the Cane Ridge revival featured scheduled and spontaneous preaching, mass conversions, and a great communion (a revival fixture that Presbyterian immigrants carried to America from Scotland). Black Christians participated alongside whites; women and children testified.

As to the size of the Cane Ridge revival, estimates range to upward of twenty thousand souls. Entire families traveled great distances to attend as if on summer vacation, their tents dotting the valley floor, many of them gawkers but as many others sincerely moved by the call to be saved. The Reverend James Campbell offers vivid eyewitness testimony:

> Sinners dropping down on every hand, shrieking, groaning, crying for mercy, convoluted; professors [of religion] praying, agonizing, fainting, falling down in distress, for sinners, or in raptures of joy! Some singing, some shouting, clapping their hands, hugging and even kissing, laughing; others talking to the distressed, to one another, or to opposers of the work, and all this at once—no spectacle can excite a stronger sensation.

One anecdote featuring a child preacher sums up the leveling yet elevating spirit of Pentecostal revivalism. After testifying eloquently, dazzling bystanders by her Christian fluency, a little seven-year-old girl lay her head down on the shoulder of the man who had been holding her up to preach. When she closed her eyes, exhausted by her stirring efforts, one sympathetic observer suggested that the poor thing be put to bed. She opened and flashed her eyes in anger. "Don't call me poor," she cried out with absolute conviction, "for Christ is my brother, God is my father, and I have a kingdom to inherit, and therefore do not call me poor, for I am rich in the blood of the lamb."

These were by no means prim affairs, spiritually or otherwise. To supplement the Holy Spirit, intoxicating spirits were available in abundance. Less respectful commentators speculated that more souls were conceived than converted in the ecstasy of the moment. But converts there were aplenty, and a surge of Christian enthusiasm uplifted the American West. Competing merchants of heavenly elixirs multiplied, with little real need for denominational turf protection, given that the turf was burgeoning, replenishing hundreds of untutored evangelists with an eager abundance of souls ready to be saved. "We could not, many of us, conjugate a verb or parse a sentence and murdered the king's English almost every lick," cheerfully confessed the famed itinerant Methodist evangelist Peter Cartwright (the clergyman whom Abraham Lincoln defeated to win a seat in Congress), "but there was a Divine unction attended the word preached."

The Pursuit of Painlessness

Despite the spirited acclaim of an increasingly democratic-minded electorate, the sun of his presidency could not set fast enough for Jefferson's liking. "Never did a prisoner released from his chains feel such relief as I shall on shaking off the shackles of power," he sighed. "Nature intended me for the tranquil pursuits of science, by rendering them my supreme delight. But the enormities of the times in which I have lived have forced me to take part in resisting them, and to commit myself on the boisterous ocean of political passions." Jefferson went into government service, giving up "everything I love, in exchange for everything I hate," for one simple reason: to protect the future from the past. Luring him repeatedly back into the fray was the horror he felt when contemplating the ravages his benighted adversaries might wreak on his precious dream, if he were not on hand to hold the gate to the future open. With Republicanism triumphant and the Revolution of 1800 secured, now, eight years later, Jefferson could at last lay down his arms. Requisitioning his private ark of happiness with box loads of books and crates of the finest French wine, he put aside all further thought of sacrifice and embarked for Monticello.

Jefferson's dreams were better suited to ideal than to real conditions. They proved especially unsuited to economic exigency. As he prepared to depart Washington, a lifetime of lofty self-indulgence was finally taking its toll. Unable to deny himself a single cultivated pleasure or his guests the finest food and wine, after eight years of running "a general tavern" for the Washington elite, he was swimming in debt. As his financial situation disintegrated, Jefferson applied his philosophy to the problem, practicing avoidance to lessen his pain. "Not being apt to deject myself with evils before they happen," he explained to his daughter Martha, "I nourish the hope of getting along."

Whatever might befall him, Jefferson, born sunny side up, never failed to recover his resilience. His disposition was a wonder. "My temperament is sanguine," he told John Adams, one old man to another. "I steer my bark with hope in the head, leaving fear astern." Margaret Smith's parting panegyric as he left Washington for good at the end of his presidency placed Jefferson right where he wished to be, above the clouds: "The storms roll harmless beneath his feet, clouds which darken those below, obstruct not his view of the sun, and while the inhabitants of the valley are distressed and terrified by the strife of the elements, he enjoys perpetual sunshine." Even his sea of debt—"an approaching wave in a storm," he called it—would somehow lift his boat, not swamp it. "I think we shall live as long, eat as much, and drink as much, as if the wave had already glided under the ship," he assured his daughter. "Somehow or other these things find their way out as they come in, and so I suppose they will now." A master of better living through rationalization, Jefferson would let nothing, at least not for long, disturb the felicity he sought and found at Monticello, where he would dream through his days and rest his head at night throughout his valedictory years.

Thomas Jefferson Randolph remembered his grandfather's favorite passage from the Bible—the Fifteenth Psalm. In it, those blessed souls who win entitlement to dwell in God's "holy hill" speak the truth, eschew backbiting, fear the Lord, and avoid all usurious financial dealings. Taken broadly, in none of these four areas did the prodigiously talented Jefferson shine. Like a Puritan striving to rid the world of life's most beguiling lures, he fantasized about a faith tailor-made to save him from his self-indulgent ways. "Would a missionary appear who would make frugality the basis of his religious system and go through the land preaching it up as the only road to salvation," he mused, "I would join his school tho' not generally disposed to seek my religion out[side] of the dictates of my own reason and feelings of my own heart." Lacking such a missionary, when life's bills came due he paid the minimum and stuffed the balance deep into his drawer of forgetfulness.

Jefferson's abiding quest was the pursuit of painlessness, not the pursuit of happiness. "I am fond of quiet," he told Abigail Adams when the two were still close. In a rare self-revelatory moment, he confessed himself "willing to do my duty, but irritable by slander and apt to be forced by it to abandon my post. These are weaknesses from which reason and your counsels will preserve Mr. Adams." Mr. Adams required no such protection. He thrived on resentment. The fuel that powered his New England engines shut the gentle Virginian's down. Allergic to controversy and desperate for affection, easily wounded and no less quick to disown all responsibility for any wound he may have caused, Jefferson, far from being "eaten to a honeycomb with ambition," as Adams described him in 1797, had no stomach for politics and possessed as little desire for its rewards. Even his craving for affection could be satisfied more easily at a safe remove from the halls of power. Neither status nor station held the allure for him that they did for Adams. And he certainly didn't answer the trumpet of duty every time it sounded as George Washington did. Unlike his two distinguished predecessors, Jefferson was neither a Puritan nor a Stoic but an Epicurean, whose highest aspiration was to plant and keep his private garden uninter-rupted by the madding crowd.

Not that the world would leave him at peace. For one thing, his private religious opinions kept bubbling up in the press. When one vagrant letter offended his "dear and ancient friend," pious Charles Thompson (the messenger who brought Washington his presiden-tial call), Jefferson hastened to assure him, "I am a *real Christian,* that is to say a disciple of the doctrines of Jesus, very different from the Platonists, who call *me* infidel and *themselves* Christians and preachers of the gospel, while they draw all their characteristic dog-mas from what its author never said nor saw." When this letter, too, popped mischievously into print, Margaret Bayard Smith was quick to post her congratulations on Jefferson's conversion. In response, he gently disabused her of any shift in his religious opinions. "I have received, dear Madam, your very friendly letter," he graciously told his ever-faithful fan, "and assure you that I feel with deep sensibil-ity its kind expressions towards myself, and the more as from a per-son than whom no others could be more in sympathy with my own affections." He then seized the opportunity presented by Mrs. Smith's misunderstanding to reprise his long battle with the estab-lished clergy and offer his own definition of faith.

I recognize the same motives of goodness in the solicitude you ex-press on the rumor supposed to proceed from a letter of mine to Charles Thomson, on the subject of the Christian religion. It is true that, in writing to the translator of the Bible and Testament, that subject was mentioned; but equally so that no adherence to any particular mode of Christianity was there expressed; nor any change of opinions suggested, a change from what? The priests in-deed have heretofore thought proper to ascribe to me religious, or rather anti-religious, sentiments of their own fabric, but such as soothed their resentments against the Act of Virginia for establish-ing religious freedom. They wished him to be thought atheist, deist, or devil, who could advocate freedom from their religious dicta-tions, but I have ever thought religion a concern purely between our God and our consciences for which we were accountable to him, and not to the priests. I never told my own religion nor scrutinized that of another. I never attempted to make a convert, nor wished to change another's creed. I have ever judged of the religion of others by their lives; and by this test, my dear madam, I have been satisfied yours must be an excellent one, to have produced a life of such exemplary virtue and correctness, for it is in our lives and not from our words, that our religion must be read. By the same test, the world must judge me.

When Jefferson invited Smith to read his religion from his life and challenged the world to judge him accordingly, he was tempting fate in ways that he could scarcely have imagined. But this is our problem; it wasn't his. History may declare him guilty, but Jefferson appears to have remained blissfully unfraught by the dilemma historians ponder, finding solace from every hint of contradiction in the rocking cradle of his sweet ideals. "Mine, after all may be an Utopian dream, but being innocent, I have thought I might indulge in it until I go to the land of dreams, and sleep there with the dreamers of all past and future times," he wrote in a lyrical and sunny self-assessment. Even as he was carried through life on a pillow by slaves and refused "to plant thorns on the pillow of age," he cradled his thoughts on the "pillow of ignorance" that God had provided him—"made so soft for us knowing how much we should be forced to use it." On the same pillow (fashioned to ensure that his rest would be undisturbed by metaphysical quandaries) he cushioned his conscience as well, closing his eyes to slavery while daydreaming about the coming Age of Reason and the glorious Rights of Man. When the world's blaring contradictions became too much for him, he retreated to his library or placed a grandchild on his knee and gazed out on the sun setting over the woods and foothills surrounding Monticello, mistaking it for the dawn.

ACT IV

❧

JAMES MADISON

CONSTRUCTING
FREEDOM'S ALTAR

Tax all things; water, air, and light,
If need there be; yea, tax the night:
But let our brave heroic minds
Move freely as celestial winds,
Make vice and folly feel your rod,
But leave our consciences to God.

—BAPTIST ELDER DAVID THOMAS

M R. MADISON is to retire [from Congress]," John Adams
chuckled to Abigail in 1794. "It seems the mode of becoming great is to retire. Madison, I suppose, after a retirement of a few years, is to be president or vice-president. It is marvelous how political plants grow in the shade." James Madison did indeed grow, in the shade of Jefferson's long shadow, all the way to the White House. As brothers in a common cause, the two men were a classic odd couple, as different in their inner workings as they were in size. Jefferson's imagination was symphonic, bright and sweeping, romantic to its very core. Madison, in contrast, was classical in temperament—a chamber player. He balanced contrapuntal voices with disciplined reserve. Yet somehow this practical little man emerged as the lanky philosopher-statesman's indispensable confidant. Margaret Smith said admiringly, "I do believe that father never loved son more than [Jefferson] loves Mr. Madison." By John Quincy Adams's estimation, the son had much to teach to the father. He called Madison's partnership with Jefferson "the friendship

of a mind not inferior in capacity and tempered with a calmer sensibility and a cooler judgment than his own."

When Madison entered office, the Empire of Liberty seemed secure. The Puritan commonwealth was at once a distant memory and a broken dream. Jedidiah Morse had abandoned Washington to the Deists and Baptists, fretting more about the chaos his Unitarian political allies were wreaking in the theological parlors of Boston. Even the Federalist satirists retired their sharp pens. By 1808, William Dennie's *Port Folio* had deserted the Christian Republic to return to the Republic of Letters. No truce had been struck, but, like Jefferson himself, the forces of order were spent.

This ceasefire proved short-lived. Madison's presidential honeymoon was the political equivalent of a rainy weekend. Promise of a real war between the United States and Great Britain reawakened the clergy, who remounted their political pulpits, and before long the president found himself fighting to defend the Empire of Liberty on two fronts: against England in the War of 1812 and New England in the battle for the nation's soul. The nation split right down the middle, with New Englanders soon muttering about secession. Then, in a dramatic reversal of fortunes, the very war that threatened to be America's undoing brought her people together instead. Madison bequeathed to his successor a nation united, completing the lofty mission he had embarked on four decades before: imagining *E pluribus unum* into being; defining liberty's catechism; touting pluralism as essential to republican union; and etching the imperative of freedom into the First Amendment. The least prepossessing founding father was at once the architect of American union and sacred liberty's most faithful scribe.

After a Republican family spat between Madison and James Monroe was resolved in Madison's favor, as such quarrels always were, the 1808 election became a formality. He outpolled his Federalist opponent, again the hapless Governor Charles Pinckney of South Carolina, almost three to one.

Madison's inauguration was the most festive since 1789. After inviting Jefferson to accompany him to the ceremony in his carriage—Jefferson demurred, lest he detract from his successor's glory—Madison took the short ride from his F Street residence to the Capitol, there to be greeted by the host of celebrants overflowing the handsome new Hall of Representatives, where he took the oath of office and delivered his inaugural address. Jefferson would again decline the honor of sitting beside Madison, this time on the dais, justly provoking the familiar snipe that he took democracy to the point of silliness. Other eminences were displeased to find their assigned seats taken when they elbowed their way into the chambers. Manifesting a touch of hauteur, Margaret Smith chided, "There was an attempt made to appropriate particular seats for the ladies of public characters, but it was found impossible to carry it into effect, for the sovereign people would not resign their privileges and the high and low were promiscuously blended on the floor and in the galleries."

Madison cut a more vivid figure in the antechambers of government than on its stage. Ashen to begin with, he paled in the light. We know little of his swearing in, but, unlike the powerful address he scripted for Washington, his inaugural effort was instantly forgotten. "Mr. Madison was extremely pale and trembled excessively when he first began to speak, but soon gained confidence and spoke audibly," Margaret reported to her sister-in-law in a letter that captures the speech's flatness even as it evokes the day's other festivities with characteristic flair. His correct recitation of Republican orthodoxy did, however, enshrine liberty's most sacred canons:

- To avoid the slightest interference with the rights of conscience or the functions of religion, so wisely exempted from civil jurisdiction;
- To preserve in their full energy the other salutary provisions in behalf of private and personal rights, and of the freedom of the press.
- To favor in like manner the advancement of science and the diffusion of information, as the best aliment to true liberty.

Madison closed with a diffident acknowledgment of the Creator. On pledging his personal fidelity to the people and their representatives, with the mechanical "fervency" familiar to such occasions, he offered the Deity an oblique, impersonal ("which we have all been encouraged to feel" and "are bound to express") nod.

No sooner had the ceremonies ended than Dolley Madison was scurrying home to brace for the throng of self-invited visitors who would descend to honor her husband. For the first time in Washington history, F Street experienced gridlock, blocks on end packed horse to buggy with carriages. The Smiths had to wait a full hour before they could gain entry, only to discover every room, including the Madisons' bedroom, wall to wall with curiosity seekers. A tiny part of this movable feast then processed to the White House, where a serene Jefferson—Madison told him to take all the time he needed before vacating the premises—held court.

The inaugural ball took place at Long's Hotel on Capitol Hill. Jefferson was among the first to arrive. "Am I too early?" he asked Mrs. Madison, confiding to his hostess, "You must tell me how to behave, for it is more than forty years since I have been to a ball." However rusty Jefferson may have been, he knew more about dancing than Dolley did. Raised a Quaker, she had never learned how. This made for an awkward moment when the band struck up and all eyes fixed on the presidentess—John Adams's coinage had finally won currency—awaiting the ceremonial first number. So as not to play favorites, Mrs. Madison graciously bequeathed her ticket to the captain of the Marine Guard to allot as he would.

Soon the ballroom was jammed, the crush so smothering that hotel management was forced to break a number of windows for ventilation. The most decorous guests, Margaret Smith among them, abandoned all pretenses to decorum. "The room was so terribly crowded that we had to stand on the benches," she reports. "From this situation we had a view of the moving mass; for it was nothing else. It was scarcely possible to elbow your way from one side to another, and poor Mrs. Madison was almost pressed to death, for everyone crowded round her, those behind pressing on those before and peeping over their shoulders to have a peep of her."

Midway through the festivities, Mrs. Smith dined with the new president. She chose a place at the table where she "could see Mrs. M. to advantage." Smitten from the moment she had first laid eyes on Dolley eight years before, Margaret was reverent in her praise. "She really in manners and appearance, answered all my ideas of royalty," she exclaimed in the afterglow of the evening. "Mr. Madison, on the contrary, seemed spiritless and exhausted." Mrs. Smith did manage to steal a few moments of the president's flickering attention, sympathetically saying, "I wish with all my heart I had a little bit of seat to offer you." "I wish so too," Madison sighed, "but I would much rather be in bed."

Adams was dourly represented in absentia. Amid the press of humanity there glowered a severe young man who knew enough about human nature to mistrust stars, especially presidential ones. Senator John Quincy Adams of Massachusetts, who had ceded his vote to the Republicans but remained at heart a Federalist, tersely recounted in his diary, "the crowd was excessive, the heat oppressive, and the entertainment bad."

Undaunted by such trifles, Mrs. Smith worked the room, extracting from her evening two presidential keepsakes. The first, a conversation with the new president about her country home, displays Madison's wry wit and practical sensibility.

"The well-diggers are to go out very soon, and we shall try to get water," she told him.

"Truth is at the bottom of a well, is the old saying," the president smiled in reply, "and I expect when you get to the bottom of yours, you will discover most important truths. But I hope you will at least find *water.*"

Mrs. Smith and Thomas Jefferson then found each other, garnishing her day with a final grace note. "When he saw me, he advanced from the crowd, took my hand affectionately and held it five or six minutes."

"Remember the promise you have made me, to come to see us next summer, do not forget it," Jefferson insisted, pressing her hand.

She assured him that she wouldn't forget, adding, "I can now wish you joy with much more sincerity than this day eight years ago. You have now resigned a heavy burden."

"Yes indeed," he answered, "and am much happier at this moment than my friend."

"His Little Blue Eyes Sparkled Like Stars"

According to the books of ancient prognosticators, in addition to earthquakes, hurricanes, and floods, one sign said to mark the coming end times or advent of the Millennium was a freak of human nature: babies born old who grow up to die young. A soothsayer plying her trade in young America might have recognized just such a prodigy in the person of Madison. Although he was destined to survive every one of his fellow founders, death stalked him as a child and haunted him as an adolescent. He retired from the world almost on entering it, cursed with a (quite possibly psychosomatic) disease that, according to one relative, "suspended his powers of action." More pious in his youth than later in life, when he came of age at twenty-one Madison invested his hopes in eternity.

Rather than ending his life, the crisis of war revived it. A tiny stick of a man with parchment skin and a receding hairline, Madison appeared fully blown on the national scene at the age of twenty-five. From the moment he entered the halls of power, his elders recognized him as wise beyond his years, elevating their young colleague to the first bench in the councils of the Republic. His monumental contributions to U.S. history, at the Constitutional Convention and in the *Federalist Papers* and Bill of Rights, he made in his thirties at the apex of his public career. Throughout this period, he was sage, serious, and fixed in his ways. One contemporary, Martha Bland, described young Madison as "A gloomy, stiff creature, they say he is clever in Congress, but out of it he has nothing engaging or even bearable in his manners—the most unsociable creature in existence."

"A grave air hides many defects," little Jemmy Madison inscribed in his commonplace book as a boy. Apart from a bit of verbal roughhousing when at college, Madison was gravest when young. Even then, those who knew him better than Mrs. Bland apparently found him kind-tempered. At the Constitutional Convention, William Pierce of Georgia admiringly called Madison a "gentleman of great modesty—with a remarkably sweet temper." Attestations to his humility are legion. James Barbour, later governor of Virginia and a close family friend, deemed him "modest even unto bashfulness."

After a shy courtship, in his mid-forties Madison married Dolley Payne Todd. They had no children together but over the years Madison grew noticeably younger, his wife's life force animating his own. To the public eye, this transformation was for the most part hidden. In his fifties as a competent secretary of state under Jefferson and in his sixties, as the nation's most notable undistinguished president, he tiptoed through his appearances on the public stage, mumbled his speeches, and offered his counsel impassively, leaving a faint but venerable impression. Around intimates, however, this otherwise gray presence could be naughty, displaying an impish wit and delighting in off-color asides. Mischief danced in the corner of his eye only to vanish in a blink, giving "place to an expression ever solemn, when the conversation took a serious turn." Dolley's first cousin, Edward Coles, describes Madison as the world would have seen him during his Washington years:

> I never knew him to wear any other color than black; his coat being cut in what is termed dress-fashion; his breeches short, with buckles at the knees, black silk stockings, and shoes with strings or long fair boot tops when out in cold weather...He wore powder on his hair,

which was dressed full over the ears, tied behind, and brought to a point above the forehead, to cover in some degree his baldness....
His ordinary manner was simple, modest, bland, and unostentatious, retiring from the throng and cautiously refraining from doing or saying anything to make himself conspicuous.

On his retirement, Jemmy blossomed into a hearty adolescent. According to itinerant bookseller Samuel Whitcomb, who knew him in his seventies, he came across as "very sociable, rather jocose, quite sprightly, and active," sporting "a quizzical, careless, almost waggish bluntness of looks and expression which is not at all prepossessing." By all reports, he became livelier as he aged. Visitors marveled at "little Madison" as a spry seventy-five-year-old racing gleefully up and down his Montpelier portico with the irrepressible Dolley at his heels. "Mr. M.'s anecdotes were very droll and we often laughed very heartily," Margaret Smith reports of an 1828 visit to his Virginia estate. "He retains all the sportiveness of his character, which he used to reveal now and then to those whom he knew intimately, and Mrs. M. says he is as fond of a frolic and of romping with the girls as ever. His little blue eyes sparkled like stars from under his bushy grey eye-brows and amidst the deep wrinkles of his poor thin face."

In his eighties he was childlike in the purest sense, filled with delight, nonjudgmental, and kind. He died a baby, completely dependent and almost unbearably sweet, on the estate where he had been born eighty-five years before—gracious Montpelier ("Mount of the Pilgrim") overlooking the Rappahannock River in Orange County, Virginia, some 2,600 acres yielding crops of corn, wheat, and tobacco, cultivated as they had been in the year of his birth by slaves.

Anglican Town and Calvinist Gown

As did the bookends of Virginia's Republican presidential dynasty, Jefferson and Monroe, James Madison enjoyed a genteel upbringing. Born in 1751, the eldest of eight children, into what his father described as "the respectable though not the most opulent class" of Virginia planters, his family were pillars of the local Anglican establishment. James Madison Sr. served St. Thomas Parish as vestryman and warden and the family worshiped regularly at Brick Church, six miles from their estate. His paternal grandmother, Frances Madison, made a handsome gift of communion silver and later bequeathed to Brick Church her extensive, if antiquated, religious library filled with tomes from the old country. Mr. Madison oversaw an observant household, with daily prayers and Bible readings, in which all eight children participated.

In 1762, Madison's parents enrolled their eleven-year-old boy in the Donald Robertson School, which his cousin James (later bishop) Madison also attended. Robertson was a gifted Edinburgh-trained classicist. He introduced his young charge not only to the ancient texts and languages but also to the rudiments of modern scientific learning. Jemmy also received a solid grounding in Latin (in which he soon became proficient), Greek, mathematics, geography, literature, philosophy, and modern languages. The notebook he kept ("James Madison his Book of Logick") illustrates his careful manner and the generous scope of his early learning—from Locke and Descartes to Copernicus. His first official teacher expressed his own appreciation in his ledger: "Deo Gratia & Gloria. All paid."

In 1766, Madison returned to Montpelier to continue his studies under the direction of the Reverend James Martin, a graduate of Princeton, who was called to Brick Church as rector and later joined the Madison household to instruct James's younger siblings. Martin's influence factored into Madison's choosing Princeton over William and Mary, the college of choice for Virginia's elite. Another factor was the young man's health. Cholera morbus, a recurring gastrointestinal condition, plagued him and would continue to do so all his life. Destined to battle chronic fevers, seizures, and diarrhea, he also suffered from what appears to have been epileptoid hysteria, an ailment, caused by stress, that apes epilepsy. William and Mary, in Virginia's sultry Tidewater region, was, he feared, not the ideal place to park his fragile body. A third factor that weighed in his deliberations was the Madison family's growing dissatisfaction with Virginia's established church, not alone on account of corruption but also due to its callous treatment of religious minorities.

Legend has it that young James witnessed an indomitable Baptist parson preaching through the bars of his cell, a specter that fixed his sympathies forever. The persecution of Baptist preachers and the indolence of self-serving Anglican divines seemingly affected James Sr. no less than they did his son. Acting in his capacity as warden of St. Thomas Parish, he went out of his way to acknowledge his Baptist neighbor John Leland's plight, noting sympathetically that dissenting Christians had "long groaned under" oppressive laws. Madison's passion for freedom of conscience and church-state separation were groomed at Princeton but likely developed before that across the dinner table from his opinionated, civic-minded father.

Destined to become the finest second fiddle in the founders' orchestra, the shy young Virginian responded beautifully to the baton of Princeton's Calvinist president. Among John Witherspoon's pupils, and testifying to the scope of his influence, were fifty future members of Congress, three Supreme Court justices, and, of them all perhaps least likely to succeed, one president. Dr. Witherspoon was an untempered devotee of religious freedom. "The magistrate ought to defend the rights of conscience and tolerate all in their religious sentiments that are not injurious to their neighbors," he taught. The College of New Jersey offered "free and equal liberty and advantage of education [to] any person of any religious denomination whatsoever."

The Princeton spiritual regimen was strict, including prayers and scripture reading each morning at dawn and prayers and Psalm singing every evening. In between, Jemmy was steeped in American patriotism, Lockean liberalism, and Scottish moral-sense philosophy. His first biographer reports that Madison "explored the whole history and evidences of Christianity on every side through clouds of witnesses and champions for and against from the Fathers and schoolmen down to the infidel philosophers of the eighteenth century." He does appear to have risked censure by peeking into Voltaire on the sly, but Madison initially retained reservations about the *philosophes*, whose writings, through the good offices of Jefferson, his bookshelves would later host in such abundance. "I find them," he told his closest college friend, Billy Bradford, "loose in their principles, encouragers of free enquiry even such as destroys the most essential truths, enemies to serious religion, and extremely partial in their citations, seeking them rather to justify their censures and commendations than to give the reader a just specimen of the author's genius."

Apart from his anticlerical bias, born of his experience of Virginia's corrupt Anglican establishment, Madison's religious views remained conventional during his eighteen months at Princeton. "I have sometimes thought there could not be a stronger testimony in favor of religion," he said shortly thereafter, "than for men who occupy the most honorable and gainful departments and are rising in reputation and wealth publicly to declare their [humble inadequacy] by becoming fervent advocates in the cause of Christ." He would not grow up to follow his own counsel. In the most honorable departments of state, Madison became instead a fervent advocate of liberty.

Dr. Witherspoon's relentless critique of British oppression won the support of Princeton's undergraduate Whig Society. Under the leadership of future journalistic hellcat and Madison aficionado Philip Freneau, the waggish Whigs squared off against the members of a more deferential, if equally witty group, who called themselves the Clios (after the muse of history). A Christian revival swept Princeton when Madison was enrolled there, and the Clios imbibed its enthusiasm to the hilt. Six of the seven students Madison panned in his raucous poem "Clio's Proclamation" would enter the ministry. One of these divines in training—"sons of screech owls," he called them—Madison skewered with the mercilessness typical of the "paper wars'" literate ripostes:

> The lecherous rascal there will find
> A place just suited to his mind,
> May whore and pimp and drink and swear,
> Nor more the garb of Christian wear.

When he later heard from Billy that a Clio rival and now Presbyterian minister had been forced into wedlock when his paramour got pregnant, Jemmy acidly replied, "Who could have thought the old monk had been so lecherous." The Reverend Ashbel Green, a future participant in the Princeton Whig-Clio paper wars, conceded that they fostered "lasting alienations, if not resentments." Yet, in the 1770 commencement ceremony, immediately preceding Madison's arrival on campus, all twenty-two graduates united to make a political statement, donning robes of American homespun, a patriotic gesture that won them kudos in the Republican press.

Following an intense, health-shattering regimen, Jemmy graduated in 1771 after a year's study and then stayed on at Princeton, in part to convalesce. His health, he said, left him too weak to journey home. This accident made Madison one of America's first graduate students. Working with Dr. Witherspoon, he studied a little Hebrew and theology but, according to the autobiography he dictated to his stepson, in the main he pursued miscellaneous legal studies. Madison toyed with becoming a lawyer, but quickly convinced himself that his fragile health ill suited him for so boisterous a profession.

Presenting him with an honorary degree in 1787, President Witherspoon exclaimed that no one could take more satisfaction from his famed pupil's civic accomplishments than his old Princeton instructor did. That he should one day receive this handsome accolade would have astonished young Madison. After a semester of postgraduate study, seeking the refuge of solitude and contemplation he returned home in 1772 to die. With little confidence that he would last long enough to choose a vocation much less embark on one, Madison piously declared his almost empty cup to be instead a few heavenly drops full, having "little spirit and alacrity to set about anything that is difficult in acquiring and useless in possessing after one has exchanged time for eternity." About one matter the twenty-two-year-old retiree was firm. "I do not meddle with politics," he told his one and almost only friend. "A watchful eye must be kept on ourselves lest, while we are building ideal monuments of renown and bliss here, we neglect to have our names enrolled in the annals of heaven." Whatever ambitious Billy, who went on to serve briefly as Washington's attorney general, may secretly have thought of his friend's malaise, it must have concerned him when Jemmy sadly, self-importantly announced, "My sensations for many months past have intimated to me not to expect a long or healthy life."

And then he was saved by the war. Too weak to fight but strong enough to enlist the full attention of his dazzling mind, Madison went to work carving out a less pious, more worldly epitaph. As he recalled in his autobiography, he entered "with the prevailing zeal into the American cause, being under very early and strong impressions in favor of liberty both civil and religious."

For Witherspoon's gospel of church-state separation, Madison was the perfect disciple. His prose was routinely dry, but he basted the established church with spice and vinegar. To Bradford, he railed, "That diabolical Hell-conceived principle of persecution rages among some, and to their eternal infamy the clergy can furnish their quota of imps for such business." Disdainful of "pride, ignorance and knavery among the priesthood and vice and wickedness among the laity," Madison charged that the established church conspired to subvert the people's liberty. "If the Church of England had been the established and general religion in all the northern colonies as it has been among us here, and uninterrupted tranquility had prevailed throughout the continent," he speculated, "it is clear to me that slavery and subjection might and would have been gradually insinuated among us. Union of religious sentiments begets a surprising confidence and ecclesiastical establishments tend to great ignorance and corruption all of which facilitate the execution of mischievous projects."

Madison's anticlerical bias was so pronounced that it temporarily unsettled his young libertarian mind. In 1775, the Reverend Francis Moore Jr., who had replaced James Martin as rector of Brick Church, began disseminating Tory tracts hostile to the Continental cause. James Madison Sr. and the Orange County Committee of Correspondence, which he chaired, resolved (in a resolution quite possibly penned by his son) that the tracts Moore was disseminating be "publicly burnt as a testimony of the Committee's detestation and abhorrence of the writers and their principles." Whether James Jr. drafted this resolution or not, together with the other members of the committee the future champion of religious freedom exercised its limits by torching the pamphlets in a public burning. He reported that this primitive bonfire, reminiscent of barbaric scenes from the annals of the Inquisition, drew a crowd of "respectable" citizens, who "joined in expressing a noble indignation against such execrable publications and their ardent wishes for an opportunity of inflicting on their authors, publishers and their abettors the punishment due to their insufferable arrogance and atrocious crimes."

When Jefferson cooked up his fast day scheme to separate Virginia's saved Whigs from its damned Tories, the diminutive Orange County patriot stood tall among the enthusiasts. Whatever role Madison may have played in the book-burning incident, his letter to Bradford following Jefferson's fast day indicates not only how completely politics overrode religion at this juncture in his life but also how great a chill sacred politics can cast on freedom of expression. In an adjoining county, a local Scotch parson had refused to observe the fast. At once, the local vestry shut down his church and suspended the independent-minded preacher's pay. "If he does not get decked in a coat of tar and surplice of feathers," Madison sarcastically told Bradford, the good reverend could, for all he cared, retreat across British lines and fill his beggar's cup there. "We have one of the same kidney in the parish I live in," Madison chortled. "He was sometime ago published in the *Gazette* for his insolence and had like to have met with sore treatment; but finding his protection to be not so much in the law as the favor of the people, he is grown very supple and obsequious."

Over the years, Madison became more careful of individual liberty. But he never lost his animus toward the clergy. He wouldn't leave the church; neither would he join it; instead, Madison politely lost interest in the church, with one recurring exception. When reactionary clerics had the gall to interfere with his Jeffersonian crusade for national redemption, it was the severe young man who torched Moore's pamphlets, and not the frail reed who earlier cast his eyes heavenward, who jumped vividly back to life.

"The Free Exercise of Religion"

Madison's debut on the political stage set the scene for his career. It took place during the 1776 debate in the House of Burgesses over Virginia's Declaration of Rights. The youngest of those present, he privately objected to the original wording of Article XVI: "all men should enjoy *the fullest toleration in the exercise of religion* according to the dictates of conscience [my emphasis]." Madison considered tolerance a condescending virtue. As substitute wording, he proposed instead, "*the free exercise of religion.*" Too bashful to do so himself, he sought out an assemblyman of acknowledged stature to present his amendment on the floor, a favor that his future foe Patrick Henry graciously performed.

Like Jefferson, Madison imported the vocabulary of faith to the cause of freedom: "devoutly" defending "sacred liberty"; lifting up the nation's most precious "political scriptures"; and depicting his opponents' arguments as "heretical," while promoting "Constitutional orthodoxy" "with a holy zeal." In later years, he condemned his Federalist opponents with purblind partisanship, damning "the overbearing and vindictive spirit, the apocryphal doctrines, and rash projects which stamped on Federalism its distinctive character, and which are so much in contrast with the unassuming and un-avenging spirit which has marked the Republican ascendancy." When the Quakers invoked a higher law in challenging George Washington on slavery, their authority was the Bible. Madison's higher law was the law of nature and nature's God, enshrined at the outset of the American experiment. To Madison, Jefferson's Decla-ration of Independence was holy writ. In advancing the cause of sa-cred liberty, no individual, Jefferson included, would play a more decisive role.

Throughout the struggle for religious freedom, the two men shared similar goals but acted from contrasting motives. Jefferson supported freedom of religion to protect the state from the church but also to free the mind from the state. His dream was that one day, instructed by science, a free people, following the light of Reason, would all reach the same religious destination. Madison supported freedom of religion for a different reason. Rather than liberating the people to find a single truth, he sought to protect the state from the church by encouraging sectarian competition. In his most famous published essay, *Federalist No. 10*, he posited that "zeal for different opinions concerning religion" cancel each other out and thereby neutralize the danger of religious tyranny. In an early draft of the same argument, Madison bluntly expressed to Jefferson his wariness of religion as a social hazard. After raising the specter of spiritual "en-thusiasm," which kindles passions and unbalances legislative judg-ment, he went on to express doubts about organized religion in general, especially with respect to its influence on politics. "Even in its coolest state," he said, religion "has been much oftener a motive to oppression than a restraint from it." When he drafted the proto-type of a Republican Party platform in 1792, Madison declared, "Mysteries belong to religion, not to government."

In 1788, having helped frame and defend the Constitution, Madison found himself in the, for him, awkward position of running for election to secure its ratification. He was too timid to make a forceful candidate. And he couldn't take the electorate for granted, even in his home county. He had learned this lesson the hard way a decade before. When running for the Virginia Assembly in 1777 against a local tavern keeper, Madison disdained employing "the corrupting influence of spirituous liquors…as inconsistent with the purity of moral and of republican principles." This high-minded posture presented the tavern keeper with a decided advantage. By refusing to belly the electorate up to the bar, Madison was soundly thrashed at the polls.

Standing as a candidate for the Virginia ratifying convention, Madison had a new problem: winning over the one group he had always been able to count on, the Baptists of Orange County. He and his Baptist allies had collaborated brilliantly in the campaign to end assessments. But the issue that united them then threatened to divide them now. Liquor wouldn't twist a good Baptist's arm, but Madison's principled reluctance to include a Bill of Rights in the Constitution (as unnecessary, redundant, and potentially self-defeating) was proving a sticking point for many influential Baptists, including his old ally, John Leland.

Nearing the close of a thirteen-year itinerant ministry in Virginia, Elder Leland played a key role in Virginia's ratification of the Constitution. Initially he opposed ratification, because the Constitution lacked any explicit protection of religious freedom. Some Christians criticized the document for omitting all reference to God; Leland was chagrined by the absence of a clear declaration of the rights of conscience, and his defection was no trivial matter. He commanded several hundred votes in Orange County, a voting bloc that loomed large in the prospects for ratification nationally. Since a Madison defeat would remove from the floor the new Constitution's most knowledgeable advocate, ratification in closely divided

Virginia hinged on his election, even as national ratification hinged on the state of Virginia. Sensing trouble at home, James Sr. urged his son to return from New York immediately. "The Baptists are now generally opposed to [the Constitution]," he warned Jemmy, who received the same message from his friend James Gordon Jr. With Madison, Gordon made up the "pro" slate bidding to fill Orange County's two available seats at the convention. "The sentiments of the people of Orange are much divided," Gordon cautioned his running mate. "The best men, in my judgment, are for the constitution, but several of those who have much weight with the people are opposed—Parson Bledsoe and Leland, with Col. Z. Burnley. Upon the whole, sir, I think it is incumbent on you without delay to repair to this state, as the loss of the constitution in this state may involve consequences the most alarming to every citizen in America."

Their mutual neighbor, Captain Joseph Spencer, fingered Leland in particular as crucial to the outcome. He forwarded Madison a list of Leland's objections (notably the absence of a Bill of Rights to ensure complete religious liberty) and urged him to pay Elder Leland a personal visit, for in Baptist circles, rumor had begun to swirl that Madison was no longer a "friend of the rights of conscience." The moment Madison arrived in Orange County, just two days before the election, he spread out a peace blanket and the two men purportedly dined together. Virginia memorializes their meeting with a historic landmark (in Orange County's Leland-Madison Monumental Park), surely the only state memorial erected to commemorate a picnic. Whether this repast took place as advertised is uncertain, but the two men did sit down together and their meeting of minds deserves a historical salute. The following day, election eve, to confront his neighbors' "absurd and groundless prejudices against the federal constitution" head on, the mortally shy Madison delivered his first political stump speech. Leland ended up supporting ratification; Madison and Gordon won their seats handily; and Virginia, in a close division, ratified the Constitution. Near his life's close, Elder Leland recalled the issues then at stake: "When the Constitution first made its appearance in the autumn of 1787, I read it with close attention and finally gave my vote for its adoption; and after the amendments took place, I esteemed it as good a skeleton as could well be formed."

To translate Leland's support for ratification into a political endorsement when he ran for Congress, Madison had to convince Leland he was sincere in his willingness to propose a Bill of Rights. Madison's opposition to amendments on the floor of the Virginia Ratifying Convention was a practical necessity. He had one object in mind: achieving ratification. To this goal, any amendments, including a Bill of Rights, presented an impediment to swift passage of the Constitution, because individual states would then be ratifying unique documents rather than each voting on the authorized text submitted by the drafters.

In Virginia's convention, knowing that amendments of any kind would derail the ratification process, Constitution opponent Patrick Henry (crossing the aisle from where he had made his stand in favor of assessments two years before) theatrically trembled at the specter of resurgent religious tyranny if the Constitution should pass minus a Bill of Rights. "There is not a shadow of right in the general government to intermeddle with religion," an astonished Madison replied.

Madison prevailed over Henry on the convention floor and the Constitution won narrow passage in Virginia, giving it the nine states needed for ratification. Immediately thereafter, his opposition to including a Bill of Rights in the Constitution cast a shadow over his prospects for election to Congress. Unless Madison could again win over the local Baptists, who avidly favored federal protections for freedom of conscience, he stood to lose the race.

Madison found himself in this uncomfortable position because, with Henry's sponsorship, Richard Henry Lee had edged him out for a Senate seat. Governor Henry did everything in his considerable power to orchestrate Madison's second defeat as well. He began by drawing Madison's district in such a manner that the more radical candidate would be advantaged. Massachusetts's Elbridge Gerry, after whom the term "gerrymandering" was coined, would one day serve as Madison's vice president. For the moment, however, the election-averse Virginian stood in danger of being "Henried." To win his race, Madison had to convince his Baptist neighbors that, despite his earlier demurrers, he would lobby in Congress as strenuously for a Bill of Rights as his opponent, James Monroe, who had opposed ratification and supported amendments, surely would. On this single question the election turned. "I hope you will consider the necessity of uniting in favor of a gentleman who has been uniformly in favor of amendments," one broadside urged. "I mean James Monroe."

Madison had been arguing against amendments for so long that, even though they no longer posed a threat to the Constitution's passage, he had trouble convincing himself of their necessity. He understood their political importance, however, and promised his constituents that their grievances would be addressed. To Leland he avowed himself bound by the strongest motivations (presumably, his election and his word) to champion a Bill of Rights in Congress. To the Reverend George Eve, Baptist pastor of Orange County's Blue Run Church, Madison swallowed even harder and wrote, "It is my sincere opinion that the Constitution ought to be revised, and that the first Congress meeting under it ought to prepare and recommend to the states for ratification the most satisfactory provisions for all essential rights, particularly the rights of conscience in the fullest latitude, the freedom of the press, trials by jury, security against general warrants, etc." To this pledge, he ingenuously added, "I freely own that I have never seen in the Constitution as it now stands those serious charges which have alarmed many respectable citizens."

Taking Madison at his word, Reverend Eve boosted his hopes with "a very spirited and decided" endorsement at a Baptist political meeting. His supporters further arranged for the Fredericksburg *Virginia Herald* to reprint a letter in which Madison issued an "unequivocal pledge" to amend the Constitution if elected. The *Herald* also helpfully reminded its readers of Madison's pitched battle with the two-faced Henry against the Assessment Act. "Let me awaken both your recollection and your gratitude to the merits of Mr. Madison, for his able memorial on your behalf to the assembly against this law and his unwearied exertions in the House," pleaded one supporter. "You would at this moment have been groaning under the intolerable miseries produced by this law."

The contest was a civil affair. Madison and Monroe were old friends. They trudged together from town to town to present their views in a series of debates. Essential to Madison's success were the voters in expansive Culpeper County, a libertarian stronghold that Henry had added to Virginia's Fifth Congressional District for precisely that reason. In Culpeper, the Constitution was unpopular and Henry a folk hero. In addition to reaching out to dissenting clergy and speaking to several Baptist gatherings, Madison debated with Monroe following worship at Culpeper's Hebron Lutheran Church. His touching account of this encounter suggests that, if he kept church and state separate in his mind, religion and politics, as long as they were conducted on the church steps and not in the sanctuary, were another matter entirely.

> Service was performed and then they had music with two fiddles. They are remarkably fond of music. When it was all over we addressed these people and kept them standing in the snow listening to the discussion of constitutional subjects. They stood it out very patiently—seemed to consider it a sort of fight of which they were required to be spectators. I then had to ride in the night twelve miles to quarters and got my nose frostbitten, of which I bear the mark now.

Surprising Monroe by racking up a nearly two-to-one margin in Culpeper, Madison won the election with Baptists to spare, outpolling his opponent by 336 votes (out of 2,480 cast). Governor Henry rewarded Monroe for his efforts by appointing him to

Virginia's second Senate seat, when a vacancy opened a few months later.

On arriving in Congress, Madison fulfilled his promise to Elder Leland, Reverend Eve, and Parson Bledsoe. He became the driving force behind the Bill of Rights and handmaiden to the First Amendment. People say that without Madison there might be no Bill of Rights. That statement is true; yet, it is also incomplete and misleading. More accurately, without the principled obduracy of several hundred Virginia Baptists there might be no Bill of Rights. Monroe would certainly have supported such legislation, but it took the legislative genius of Madison to crowbar it through Congress. He persevered, against great odds, not because he believed a Bill of Rights was necessary but because he gave his word to the Baptists back home that he would deliver one.

The First Amendment

Apart from the nest of Baptists in Orange County, few clergymen weighed in publicly during the debate over amendments. Bishop James Madison gingerly told his cousin that they should at least be considered. Outside Virginia, those preachers who did express their opinions tended to be suspect of adding Constitutional protections for freedom of conscience. "Religion has much to do with government," argued Congregational minister John Lathrop. "The foundation of all social virtue is a belief of the existence and government of a Deity. A regard to the Deity cannot be maintained without some public exercises of religion. Social worship is therefore necessary to the happiness of society and to the easy administration of government, and, in this view, worthy of attention of every legislature."

Having battled the same establishmentarian logic for years, Baptist leaders were sensitive to the importance of explicitly spelling out laws defending religious freedom. For the moment, their cause was entrusted to the able, if heretofore reluctant, hands of Madison. On

June 8, 1789, little more than a month after Washington's inauguration, to fulfill his pledge Representative Madison presented on the
floor of the House a Bill of Rights to supplement the U.S. Constitution. With scant initial backing from Federalist or anti-Federalist
alike, he had to beg that his amendments receive congressional
consideration. What he grimly styled the "nauseous project of
amendments" took as great a toll on his nerves now that he was
championing them as it had before when he was arguing that they
were unnecessary. Deftly playing on his colleagues' multiple self-
interests, Madison finally triumphed, but not without a few significant setbacks. The amendment he promised Leland guaranteeing
freedom of conscience initially encompassed state as well as federal
jurisdictions: "No State shall violate the equal rights of conscience,
or the freedom of the press, or the trial by jury in criminal cases,"
he proposed. This sweeping power was abridged in committee to
exclude the states from its purview.

A second Madison proposal could have changed the tone of
American history. If he had prevailed, in addition to the ten amendments that made up the original Bill of Rights the Constitution
would have opened with a précis of Jefferson's American Creed,
straight from the Preamble of the Declaration of Independence—
affirming:

> That all power is originally vested in, and consequently derived
> from the people.
>
> That government is instituted, and ought to be exercised for the
> benefit of the people; which consists in the enjoyment of life and
> liberty, with the right of acquiring and using property, and gener-
> ally of pursuing and obtaining happiness and safety.
>
> That the people have an indubitable, unalienable, and indefeasible
> right to reform or change their government, whenever it be found
> adverse or inadequate to the purposes of its institution.

The House struck this language from the final bill, but all such dis-
appointments paled in face of Madison's monumental achievement.

His authorship of the First Amendment constitutes perhaps his most abiding legacy. Acting on the crucial impetus provided by his Baptist constituents, he etched church-state separation and freedom of conscience into the American code. Condensed into its present, familiar language, the final wording in the First Amendment balances what in history will go down as competing clauses banning "establishment" and protecting "free exercise": "Congress shall make no law establishing religion, or prohibiting the free exercise thereof."

"It Is Impossible to Be with Her and Not Be Pleased"

Madison's wife, the irrepressible Dolley Payne Todd, added luster to his existence, even as her flamboyant presence turned the White House into a target for moralizing critics, who fanned fears that she was importing Paris to Washington and placing the nation's soul in jeopardy. Dolley was in mourning for her young husband, John Todd, when she and Madison met. "Thou must come to me," she commandeered her niece. "Aaron Burr says that the great little Madison has asked him to bring him to see me this evening." The match was made swiftly, too swiftly for the doyens of propriety, who assigned a necessary year for mourning. She knew she would be "read out" of Friends Meeting for marrying a "stranger" and that the slaveholding her Quaker parents had banished from her past would become a part of her future.

Dolley Payne was raised in the Society of Friends by devout parents. But when church authorities ousted her beloved sister Lucy for marrying George Washington's Anglican nephew, George Steptoe Washington, and later jettisoned her brother Isaac for "resorting to houses of ill fame and gaming," her religious loyalties weakened. The censorious gossip that followed her from her first husband's death from yellow fever in 1793 to her marriage to Congressman Madison in 1794 dampened her religious affections further. In all, Dolley was the sixth member of her family to be cast from the Quaker fold. Philadelphia's Pine Street Meeting voted her out on the day after Christmas, charging her with the sin of having "disregarded the wholesome order of our discipline in the accomplishment of her marriage to a person not in membership with us, before a hireling priest."

On balance, her expulsion from the church spelled liberation. Mrs. Madison had modern tastes and a gay disposition that ill fitted the austere Quaker profile. When two Quaker matrons upbraided her for the unseemliness of entertaining crowds of visitors in her bedroom when she was undergoing an otherwise withering six-month convalescence in Philadelphia to heal an angry ulcerated knee in 1805, their chastisement recalled her to "the times when our society used to control me entirely and debar me from so many advantages and pleasures." Her recollections were vivid. "Although so entirely from their clutches," she confessed, "I really felt my ancient terror revive in a great degree."

If relieved to escape the rigors of Quaker austerity, Dolley nonetheless modeled Quaker loving kindness, called herself a Quaker when referring to her faith, and muted any animosity she may have harbored toward the religion of her childhood. Flowing from her generous nature and helping to kindle her husband's inner light, *agape* (Christian love) was a social sacrament at the Madison White House, even as *philia* (loving friendship) reigned there during Jefferson's day.

The White House was not new to the Madisons when they took up residence in the spring of 1809. At Jefferson's behest, they had lived there for a short time eight years before, on their arrival in Washington, lingering long enough to give him a fine notion. The widower Jefferson lighted on Mrs. Madison as the perfect hostess to preside over a Republican White House on those rare occasions when women graced the company. His hostess's ebullience fanned the breeze of gossip that followed him to Washington. Adding to the endless public fascination with Jefferson's private life, Mrs. Madison's riveting charms inspired a minor political sex scandal. The secretary of state, people whispered, was pimping his wife not only to Jefferson but to the entire Washington diplomatic corps. At these rumors, Jefferson seemed more flattered than chagrined. He mused out loud that he thought "my age and ordinary demeanor would have prevented any suggestions in that form."

Due to her rectitude, the scandalmongers' best efforts gained no traction from reality. The Madisons' devotion to each other so effectively quieted the rumor mill that even her increasingly out-landish appearance was adjudged by Washington society, if idio-syncratic, nonetheless delightful. John Jacob Astor seized on her prominence to boost the stock of his American Fur Company, sending her animal skins of every description, which she mixed and matched so recklessly that at times she appeared to be shouldering an entire menagerie. By no means was Dolley Madison a loose woman, but she had no qualms about sacrificing modesty to the latest fashion, and her freedom of sartorial expression occasioned much of the running patter against Madison's "loose" presidency. On the eve of her husband's inauguration, one prim acquaintance sent her a handkerchief as a coverup—"Accept and wear for the sake of the donor the enclosed handkerchief. It claims no other merit than being thought worthy of my valuable friend Mrs. Madi-son, of shading her lovely bosom from the admiration and gaze of the vulgar." Dolley was undaunted. She delighted indiscriminately in the admiration and gaze of all, seemingly less out of narcissism than with an eye to their delight.

Predictably, American moralists were aghast. She was the public face of her husband's administration. That proper Bostonians should sniff at her manners was almost inevitable. Adding to the Puritan umbrage, Paris fashion was taking Washington by storm. The most demure Parisian fashions were enough to horrify American moral-ists, who professed shock that the First Lady invested thousands of dollars a year in high-waisted Empire gowns with plunging neck-lines and her beloved, ostentatious turbans, festooned with ostrich plumes or foot-long feathers from exotic birds of paradise.

That Mrs. Madison was breaking precedent did not pass unno-ticed, particularly by her sole surviving predecessor. Abigail Adams's standards were of biblical proportion: "With respect to Mrs. Madison's influence," she carped, "it ought to be such as Solomon describes his virtuous woman's to be—one who should do him good and not evil all the days of her life—so that the heart of her husband may safely trust in her." In grudging sympathy with her son John Quincy's defection to the Republicans, she joined her husband in voting for Madison, but her successor's behavior tested her Puritan and Francophobe patience to the hilt. In Paris, Abigail had grown accustomed to high-kicking dancers, but this was America, not France. She was particularly appalled that ladies, under her successor's watch, were inflicting themselves on the White House cinched and plumped to the point that they resembled "nursing mothers." Since Mrs. Madison had adopted the latest fashions and seemed in every way delighted with the French-influenced manner, "it might safely be assumed," Lady Adams censoriously concluded, that the president too must enjoy "luxuriant feminine displays." "I believe I may say with safety that her predecessors left her no evil example," she primly allowed.

Yet, for all the Puritan quills that Dolley ruffled, this other-centered center of attention transformed Washington. At the outset of Madison's administration, of the 164 senators and congressmen only a handful brought their wives to live with them during the five months Congress was in session. By its end, the nation's capital was home to dozens more congressional wives, due in no small measure to the social energy emanating from a feminized White House.

By supplying in abundance the public personality that her husband decidedly lacked, it was Dolley, while distancing herself from any appearance of meddling in the policy debates that so fascinated her, who set the tone for her husband's presidency. Like Franklin and Eleanor Roosevelt or John and Jacqueline Kennedy, people viewed them as a presidential team. "I was beaten by Mr. and Mrs. Madison," rued Federalist candidate Charles Pinckney in the aftermath of his thumping defeat. "I might have had a better chance had I faced Mr. Madison alone."

DEFENDING THE EMPIRE
OF LIBERTY

Ye ministers that wait on preaching,
Teachers and exhorters too,
Don't you see your harvest wasting,
Arise, there is no rest for you,...

To see the land lie in confusion,
Looks dreadful in our mortal eye
But O dear sinners, that is nothing,
To when the day of doom draws nigh.

—RICHARD ALLEN, "SEE! HOW THE
NATIONS RAGE TOGETHER"

FROM MONTICELLO, Jefferson foresaw President Madison's political sun rising on an unclouded horizon. In his estimation, for America to reign triumphant all that remained was "to include [Canada] in our confederacy, which would [happen as a matter] of course in the first war, and we should have such an empire for liberty as [the world] has never surveyed since the creation." America's first war since the Revolution sorely tested Jefferson's prophetic prowess. Far from swiftly incorporating Canada, the Empire of Liberty found itself instead under siege.

With the benefit of hindsight, it is difficult to decode from the available grievances a sufficient rationale for the War of 1812. Suffice it to say that land lust (Canada seemed there for the taking), blood lust (the Indians received British support for their depredations on the American frontier), free trade (England imposed unfair restrictions on American merchantmen), offended pride (the British navy was cherry-picking seamen, British defectors for the most part, from American ships), and lofty ideals (the ongoing battle to the death between modern republican principle and benighted monarchy) conspired to drive the nation to war. In attempting to place these provocations in perspective, the antiwar faction revealed its own principles and prejudices: 1) By no means evil, England was a Christian nation, more Christian, in fact, than the United States since it continued under a Christian government; 2) the federal policy against Native Americans was a national disgrace, which should inspire moral sympathy not vengeful outrage toward the Indians (a more rarely expressed moral opinion); 3) the tars impressed from American ships tended to be Irishmen (think "Catholic and, therefore, expendable"); and 4) less important than the political distinction between royal and republican governments was the sacred gulf between godly and godless ones.

When Senator George Logan of Pennsylvania petitioned for peace in early 1812, Madison gave him a sympathetic ear. Logan's Quaker pacifism, he said, was "honorable to your judgment as a patriot and to your feeling as a man." Madison told Logan that he wished to avoid "the vortex of war" no less than the senator did, but matters were out of his hands. He saw no options beyond "absolute disgrace & resistance by force." Confident of his sympathy, Logan wrote to Jefferson and bade him intervene with his successor to "come forward with just and honorable proposals for peace." Jefferson assured Logan that they shared the same goal, but, to his mind, peace with the English could only be secured by going to war with them. Disappointed by his Republican allies, Logan hopped the next boat for London to broker peace there. At this bit of rogue diplomacy (a reprise of Logan's peacemaking trip to Paris thirteen years earlier), the president looked the other way—in fact, he entrusted Logan with a letter for the American minister in London.

American Quakers were not alone in expressing their opposition to a possible war with Great Britain. During Madison's first year in office, the *New England Palladium*, a Federalist Christian mouthpiece under Timothy Dwight's general sponsorship, added pacifist fuel to its pious fire by publishing "An Appeal to Christians of All Parties, on Our Duty to Preserve a Peace with England." The author, who adopted the Puritan moniker "Mather," pronounced that waging war against England "would be a GROSS IMPIETY." By resisting Napoleon's European juggernaut, England was defending the world "from the more desolating taint and pestilence of French Principles." God, "Mather" sadly concluded, could not help but punish America for its mutiny "against Heaven." Early signal flares such as this one marked the beginnings of what would grow three years later into a full-scale moral rearmament campaign that threatened to undermine Madison's presidency.

Until impending war blew new life into it, the Federalist flame had been flickering out, even in Massachusetts. Overcoming the combined efforts of the religious and political establishments, Jeffersonian convert Elbridge Gerry won election to the governorship in 1810. The custom of annual thanksgiving proclamations was too entrenched for the new governor to abandon, but in his 1811 declaration Gerry cautioned the clergy against seizing the opportunity to preach "under the guidance of passion, prejudice, and worldly delusion."

Paying Gerry no mind, the Standing Orders of New England reentered the political fray with a vengeance. Following the *Palladium*'s cue, by 1811 Congregational preachers were openly speculating that France, under the aegis of Napoleon, was conniving to suck the United States into war with England. The Reverend Ethan Smith published *A Dissertation on the Prophecies Relative to Antichrist and the Last Times* with that very threat foremost in mind. The old, familiar invective against France and the horrors of democracy had returned with a vengeance to haunt American religious discourse. With war on the horizon, a colleague told Jedidiah Morse, "As long as we are a sinful people, it looks to me, a righteous God will scourge us. This *demon* of democracy will twist into every shape, come up in new dresses & corrupt our country till we are ruined."

The rush toward war quickened in 1812, a presidential election year. Madison's nomination for reelection hinged on only one imponderable—whether he was willing to buy into the program of Henry Clay, John C. Calhoun, and the other war hawks in Congress. This faction, a clear majority of Republicans, was convinced that a war with Great Britain would pay for itself by bringing Canada into the Union while restoring American honor, which was being tarnished by British insolence. When Madison asked Congress for a declaration of war, he secured the support of the war hawks, but at the expense of revitalizing the Federalists, who joined forces with renegade Republican De Witt Clinton of New York.

The whooping of the war hawks notwithstanding, their opponents' moral arsenal was so well stocked that the vote for war was more closely contested than is customary when a president calls the nation to arms. Federalists commanded only a quarter of the seats in the House and but five of thirty-two in the Senate, but enough Republican "scarecrows" lined up with the Federalists to make a contest of it. The War Act passed by less than 70 percent in the strongly Republican House and by six votes (19 to 13) in the Senate, the narrowest margin for such a resolution in U.S. history.

"War is declared," Gerry exulted, "God be praised." Not every American shared his religious enthusiasm. Christian Ellery, a Rhode Island Republican, reported to Madison that the same news provoked a threnody of chimes intoning mournfully from all the local meetinghouses. Throughout New England, flags hung at half-mast; church bells tolled; and shopkeepers, treating the somber day like a Sabbath, shuttered their doors. On a cheerier note, Ellery added that "The spirit of Independence lives yet in some breasts. Roused by the insolence of toryism, the recruiting drums were made to drown the dismal sounds from the steeples of the holy temples."

The day Congress declared war, President Madison uncharacteristically bestirred himself from the White House to visit the War

and Navy Departments. Declaring war also prompted the liturgically lax Madison to make a rare appearance at Sunday services. The
British minister, John Foster, made condescending note of this
presidential break in custom: "Met Mr. Madison, coming from
church in a coach and four, being but the second time he has been
out these seven months. He now went to show he is not afraid."

"My Country, Right or Wrong"

In the buildup to the 1812 election, which took place half a year
after war was declared, the revival of pulpit politics provoked anger
among Madison partisans. Describing a widely distributed sermon
delivered by Massachusetts clergyman Dr. Elijah Parish as a "plain
direct exhortation to rebellion," Governor William Plumer of New
Hampshire, a reformed Federalist who was familiar with the prejudices of those whom he was now attacking, shouted across the state
line, "It is high time these sedition priests were punished."

Not only the war, but also Madison's perceived infidelity heated
the campaign rhetoric. At the height of his reelection bid, one "sectarian" Republican, the Reverend Samuel Worcester of Salem, Massachusetts, delineated the national divide in stark religious terms.
"Sectarians [Baptists and Methodists], as the Standing Order call
them, are almost universally in favor of the government, and the
Standing Order [Congregationalists and Unitarians] are nearly as
universally against it." That being the case, he said, how much better it would be to reelect Madison and his Republican allies, "who
have been denounced as infidels and atheists, because they have advocated and established universal freedom of opinion in religion."

Conversely, the Reverend Pashal Strong beseeched his fellow
Federalists to "vote Christian" in 1812. "When we find Christian
men of high consideration and influence maintaining and publicly
abetting the election of an infidel in preference to a Christian," he
chided, "what, I ask, has become of the *authority of God* as the consciences of men, in the discharge of their political duties?" Such

rhetoric revealed how little some of his pious contemporaries thought of Madison's faith. Supreme Court Justice John Jay cast his vote on the matter in a letter to Reverend Morse. "Providence has given to our people the choice of their rulers," he declared. "And it is the duty as well as the privilege and interest of a Christian nation to select and prefer Christians for their rulers."

Shortly after the war commenced in the summer of 1812, the Federalist opposition, already successful in riding the antiwar sentiment in Massachusetts back into the governorship (with Caleb Strong unseating Gerry), ratcheted up its lobbying efforts for an immediate truce with England. The Massachusetts House petitioned Congress to do "duty to themselves, to posterity, and to God" by honoring "the invincible and growing opposition of the people." Republican Assemblyman William Austin of Charlestown, Massachusetts, introduced a measure in the House forbidding ministers to "profane the Holy Sabbath by introducing into their pulpits political discourses." To this proposal, Dr. Dwight's *Palladium* cried foul. What had raised the vindictive ire of Republican statesmen, it insightfully editorialized, was not "the clergy's *preaching politics*... [but] the *politics which they preach*."

The presidential contest turned out to be close. Madison secured 128 electoral votes to Clinton's 89, but a shift of the hotly contested state of Pennsylvania, with its twenty electoral votes, would have swung the election to Clinton. In his second inaugural address, on March 4, 1813, Madison pronounced the war just and unavoidable. As his clerical critics would never tire of pointing out, it was probably neither. The next twenty-two months would be the most trying of Madison's long public life.

More eager than prepared for war, the victorious Republicans were soon slapped in the face by reality. Marching north in the wildly miscalculated confidence that Canada would fall of its own weight, General William Hull lost Detroit instead without firing a shot. A shell exploded in his officer's mess, and he ran up the white flag.

Madison's military arsenal turned out to be less well stocked than the Federalists' moral one. With but 7,000 active militia, when the president called for 10,000 fit and able soldiers, the War Department struggled to muster half that number. As for the Navy, Jefferson had all but beached it. His fanciful vision of a fleet made up exclusively of gunboats offered the British little more than target practice. Madison called for twelve ships of the line, only to learn that the lumber earlier requisitioned for six such ships had been whittled down to toothpicks to build Jefferson's ridiculous "mosquito fleet." The Secretary of Navy suggested that the only way to protect his ships was to draw them into dry dock; General William Henry Harrison proposed that Madison let the navy wage the war and remove the army from the field instead.

At times the army removed itself from the field of battle. When General Winfield Scott ordered his troops over the border into Canada, half his army sat on its hands, arguing that he had no Constitutional authority to send the New York State Militia into a foreign land. If it were not for an improbable victory at sea, with Stephen Decatur gaining earthly immortality for saying, "My country, right or wrong," the first months of the contest would have proved an unmitigated embarrassment for the United States. Worst of all, a third of the nation was cheering for Great Britain. "The seditious opposition in Mass. and Connecticut with the intrigues elsewhere insidiously co-operating with it," Madison lamented to Jefferson, "have so clogged the wheels of the war, that I fear the campaign will not accomplish the object of it."

Prayers for Victory versus Prayers for Peace

Ruminating on the future from his Arcadian plantation looking out over the Blue Ridge Mountains, Jefferson surely numbered among those who would have cheered Assemblyman Austin on in his failed attempt to separate religion from politics. A window on his still developing views on church and state opened when Republican Representative Peter Hercules Wendover of New York forwarded Jefferson a book of political sermons by the Reverend Alexander McLeod, a Presbyterian clergyman from New York City. Wendover presumed that the former president would find McLeod's views, which sanctioned Madison's war on religious grounds, congenial. The problem lay in the details. "Ministers have the right of discussing from the pulpit those political questions which effect Christian morals," McLeod argued in rationalizing his foray into political discourse. "The spirit of true religion is friendly to civil liberty," he went on to claim, but with one significant caveat: "The separation [of church and state] cannot be complete [or] the undivided management of national affairs [will] be transferred into the hands of infidels."

Jefferson recoiled. He agreed with the minister on the war, but contested his right to bring politics into the pulpit. No clergyman is equipped to preach "from the pulpit in chemistry, in medicine, in law, in the science and principles of government, or on anything but religion exclusively," Jefferson said, adding that, unless every congregant should sign off on his or her minister's political sentiments, any clergyman so imprudent as to impose his political views from the pulpit would be guilty of a "breach of contract." Sermons must be delivered "with the consent of every individual" in the congregation, Jefferson fancifully argued, "because the association being voluntary, the mere majority has no right to apply the contributions of the minority to purposes unspecified in the agreement of the congregation." With this bold if wholly impracticable entry into ecclesiastical jurisprudence, Jefferson, having built a wall of separation between church and state, added to his estate a wall of separation between religion and politics.

As Jefferson's line between church and state hardened, Madison's was wavering, at least on the question of national prayer days. At the war's outset, pressure mounted for the nation's chief executive to reinstate the practice. Even without government sanction, the Presbyterian and Dutch Reformed churches joined forces to proclaim a national day of repentance. From Madison's perspective, public proclamations penned by ecclesiastical critics of the war were softening national resolve. To be sure, their calls to prayer were anything but neutral. "Under the dominion and dispensation of Jehovah, the peace and prosperity of our common country are threatened," the Dutch Reformed fast day declaration read. "The rod of His indignation is shaken over us,...we are a guilty people; a sinful nation....We are each one personally implicated in that mass of crimes, which rises up as a cloud to the heavens, crying out for the vengeance of the Almighty upon us."

New England's governors followed in lockstep. In his fast day proclamation, Massachusetts governor Caleb Strong (author of a book titled *Patriotism and Piety*) beseeched his people to pray for everything from justice for the Indians to peace with Great Britain, "the nation from which we are descended and which, for many generations has been the bulwark of the religion we profess."

Eager to regain the religious upper hand, the Republican Congress instructed the president to issue a patriotic summons to prayer, invoking God's aid and favor in prosecuting the war. To absolve himself from responsibility for this infraction against sacred liberty, Madison explained that he was simply doing Congress's bidding. In his first fast day proclamation, Madison invited the American people to offer "their common vows and adorations to Almighty God, on the solemn occasion produced by the war, in which He has been pleased to permit the injustice of a foreign Power to involve these United States."

Both Madison and the Massachusetts governor were using religion to play politics. One reason that early American religious purists deemed state or federal prayer proclamations pernicious is that, in formulating their language, politicians could attempt to shape the people's spiritual agenda. The Federalist governors, laying the burden of moral responsibility for the war on the infidels in Washington, charged the citizens of their respective states to pray for repentance, whereas Madison and his Republican Congress, positing the war as just, instructed the people to pray for divine aid in ensuring victory.

Madison's call to prayer—he issued four such proclamations during the course of the war—stood the American religious body politic on its head. Southern Christians who had balked at Adams's fast days as an infringement on their liberty welcomed the religious proclamation from their Republican standard bearer, whereas the Standing Orders of New England, which repeatedly had chastised Republican presidents for refusing to issue such declarations, scorched Madison for doing so. Adams described the reversal of roles elegantly: "Our two great parties have crossed over the valley and taken possession of each other's mountain."

To the inheritors of the Black Regiment's mantle, nothing about Madison's proclamations was pleasing. One preacher deplored that a "Bible Christian" would be sorely tested to find in them a single utterance "which could be offensive to the ear of a pagan, an infidel, a deist, and scarcely to that of an atheist." Another New England parson who ignored Madison's summons to prayer acknowledged to his congregation that "With my persuasion of the unrighteousness and tendency of the war, I cannot make the prayer which is recommended." And a Unitarian minister in Philadelphia greeted the president's invitations to prayer by preaching against them instead.

As many preachers spoke up for the war as opposed it. The nation was divided religiously, politically, and geographically along parallel fault lines. A majority of America's democratic Christians in the South and West deemed New England's antiwar moralists unconscionable for honoring their bonds with London (and the international missionary societies headquartered there) more highly than they did their own government in Washington. Baptists in particular, including those marooned in New England, were avid in their support of the war. Seventy-eight-year-old Baptist chaplain David Jones, who had also served in the Chaplain Corps during the Revolution, pledged to keep preaching through his dysentery to encourage the men to "stand fire." After damning New England's moralists, he told the president, "It would do your heart good to hear the Baptist clergy pray for you and the army. It would be well for us, if we were all Baptists."

A majority of American Catholics stood behind the president as well. In commending Madison's fast day "recommendations," Roman Catholic bishop John Carroll stated pointedly that every faithful American "ought to feel an equal interest in the welfare of these United States during the awful crisis now hanging over them." The war furnished Bishop Carroll a welcome opportunity to grandstand Catholic patriotism. In Boston the much-despised Irish were as likely to volunteer to defend their country as their Brahman neighbors were to pray for its defeat. One independent-minded Presbyterian pastor from Newbury, Massachusetts, extolled his Roman Catholic colleagues. They were "good citizens," he said. By the same logic, most ministers of the gospel in New England's Standing Orders were bad citizens, unwilling to stand by their president at a time of national trial. Popular toasts at Republican rallies roasted the religious establishment:

> To our clergy—May all those who preach sedition or treason from the pulpit, be branded with eternal infamy and left to earn their bread by the sweat of their brow.

> To the Tory-clergy—May they fight more against the devil and less against their country.

Napoleon the Antichrist

Massachusetts was ground zero for the Federalist opposition. In 1813, arguing against taking any other than a purely defensive military posture, Federalist stalwart Josiah Quincy introduced the following motion on the floor of the State Senate:

> *Resolved,* as the sense of the Senate of Massachusetts, that in a war like the present, waged without justifiable cause and prosecuted in a manner which indicates that conquest and ambition are its real

motives, it is not becoming a moral and religious people to express any approbation of military or naval exploits which are not immediately connected with the defense of our sea-coast and soil.

Senator Timothy Pickering of Massachusetts, who as Adams's Secretary of State stood ready to throw the federal book at the slightest peep of sedition, confessed that "the sound of union" had lost its former "magic." He told a fellow Federalist, "If the great objects of union are utterly abandoned—much more if they are wantonly, corruptly, and treacherously sacrificed by the Southern and Western States—let the Union be severed."

By 1814, a handful of Massachusetts townships were openly toying with the idea of secession. The town of Newburyport boasted that "The rights which we have received from God we will never yield to man," pledging in turn to support the Massachusetts legislature in any action it might deem appropriate to protect "the liberties of this free, sovereign, and independent state." Newburyport Reverend Elijah Parish struck a similitude between New England's bondage to the federal government and Israel's bondage in Egypt, whose oppressions offered "a powerful motive for them to dissolve their connection with the Ancient Dominion." Out of long-latched closets came specters of old—the infidel French and their American fifth column—for New England's sacred guardians to exorcise. John Lowell wrote a pamphlet titled *Mr. Madison's War,* in which he declared Madison responsible for leading the country into a conflict "undertaken for *French* interests and in conformity with repeated *French* orders."

As it had since the tumultuous advent of its revolution, France presented a challenge to Republican ideologues. Joel Barlow lost his Enlightenment faith and, tragically, his life on an 1812 American diplomatic mission. Assigned by Madison to negotiate a commercial treaty with France, Barlow followed Napoleon across Europe to Moscow on a pilgrimage that would destroy both men's dreams. Deathly ill, in a decrepit coach inching out of Russia in the train of

Napoleon's shattered army, Barlow composed a fierce valedictory poem, his farewell to the Age of Reason. In place of the utopia he devoutly had believed was dawning, Barlow's "Advice to a Raven in Russia" instead mourns the anarchy and social degradation that had followed in revolution's wake. The frozen eye of a dead French soldier "stares to God, as if to know/In what curst hands he leaves his world below." Jefferson and Madison deemed Barlow's demise a tragedy, but it was a friend of his lost youth, fellow Connecticut Wit Timothy Dwight, who would have understood the rage behind his parting curse against the God that failed. Before Barlow's dying eyes, the Enlightenment was laid to rest on the bloody Russian steppes.

Napoleon constituted a problem for his Protestant Christian despisers as well. When he placed the pope under house arrest in the Vatican and brought the Spanish Inquisition to an end (actions that heralded to delirious Protestants the death knell of the Catholic Church), Napoleon, the Lord's regent in overthrowing the then Antichrist, was demonstrably playing a significant role in Christian salvation history. Opportunistic memories are short, however. Soon the New England clergy had pushed the temporary fall of the papacy from mind. Anointing Napoleon with the title, they resurrected the Antichrist as a rhetorical godsend. Since France and America were both at war with Great Britain, any ally of God's enemy was a friend of the Devil, they said. New Hampshire Congressman George Sullivan painted the unholy alliance between the United States and France against England as "the wormwood...the gall, which the wrath of heaven has mingled for the nations." When Napoleon fell from power, lest anyone remain confused as to whose side God was on, Connecticut Senator David Daggett pronounced Napoleon's abdication "more glorious than any which have been proclaimed to the world, since the appearance of the angels to the shepherds of Bethlehem."

Their fondness for the mother country may have united New Englanders, but it divided New England from the rest of the Union. However poorly Madison's War was going, to credit

DEFENDING THE EMPIRE OF LIBERTY ∽ 339

the nation's humiliation to God, who was, by the severe logic of covenant theology, punishing the United States for abetting atheistic France in her struggle against Christian England, offended more Christians than it seduced. To call for Madison's resignation, as several New England Federalists did, was one thing, but to enlist God on England's side and then sit on their hands, while secretly (and sometimes openly) praying for America's downfall was tantamount to treason. Benjamin Rush surveyed the political landscape and issued a pox on both houses. "We are not 'all Federalists and all Republicans,'" he told John Adams, "but we are (with the exception of a few retired and growling neutrals) all Frenchmen or all Englishmen."

Unlike subsequent wartime presidents, Madison did nothing to restrict American freedoms, suffering near-treasonous calumnies with principled passivity. Yet, his leadership was passive in another sense as well. Madison had difficulty hoisting the American flag into battle. Apart from being temperamentally unsuited to the task, he couldn't raise taxes to bankroll the war. It violated Republican doctrine. So the government funded the war by printing and borrowing money with principled abandon. As late as 1814, the Republican Congress remained unwilling to offend its constituencies by raising taxes. Nor did they dare risk imposing an unpopular draft. It was one thing to bend Republican principle by calling for a national day of public humiliation and fasting to implore God's assistance, but to tax and draft a sovereign people was tantamount to Republican apostasy.

"And Now, Dear Sister, I Must Leave This House"

The most dramatic scene in Madison's presidency was the British burning of Washington in August 1814. Up to the eve of their city's destruction, Washington society maintained a gay, unwarranted nonchalance. One glittering ball followed another, all featuring a newly imported dance, the waltz.

As the nation's guardians waltzed, their capital was about to burn. On the day of reckoning, in a drama casting His Majesty's Regulars against American Keystone Cops, every military miscalculation imaginable cleared an open path for British Admiral George Cockburn's marines to march from the Chesapeake to the nation's capital, where, with a toast to "Jemmy's health," they torched the Capitol and White House, leaving official Washington a charred ruin.

At personal hazard, both President Madison and Secretary of State Monroe distinguished themselves during the American retreat. But it was Madison's hands-off leadership and Monroe's handicap of having to cede military tactics to a criminally incompetent secretary of war, John Armstrong, that had placed the city in jeopardy in the first place. The weakness of their leadership rendered their valor at best pyrrhic and at worst (the form it took in taverns and around the nation's supper tables) laughable. Satirists in the Federalist press had a field day, one ditty chortling,

> Fly, Monroe, fly!
> Run, Armstrong, run
> Were the last words of Madison!

With final victory but half a year away, both men would win swift absolution, but if ever Madison's temperamental ineptitude for firm executive leadership was revealed for all to see, it was here. Henry Clay declared, "It is vain to conceal the fact. Mr. Madison is wholly unfit for the storms of war. Nature has cast him in too benevolent a mold. Admirably adapted to the tranquil scenes of peace—blending all the mild and amicable virtues—he is not fit for the rough blasts which the conflict of nations generate." An equally flattering negative portrait came after the war courtesy of a Kentucky congressman: "Mr. Madison is perhaps 'too good' a man for the responsible office he holds."

Mrs. Madison was triumphant in adversity. "I would rather fight with my hands than my tongue," Quaker Dolley avowed, again proving herself, in all but their pert interest in politics, Abigail Adams's ideal opposite. She boasted keeping an "old Tunesian saber within reach" for that very purpose and later expressed her shame that the American army cut and ran, adding the wish that she could have stayed to defend the nation's property as well as her own. "I have always been an advocate for fighting when *assailed,* tho *a Quaker,*" she declared. Among the last to leave the capital, she recorded her final minutes in the White House in heart-stopping (if subsequently polished) detail. "I insisted on waiting until the large picture of Gen. Washington is secured, and it requires to be unscrewed from the wall," she told her sister, presumably while the rescue mission was still in progress. "This process was found too tedious for these perilous moments; I have ordered the frame to be broken, and the canvass taken out, it is done, and the precious portrait placed in the hands of two gentlemen of New York, for safekeeping. And now, dear sister, I must leave this house." Mrs. Madison salvaged the family silver and shoveled "as many cabinet papers into trunks as to fill one carriage." Within an hour the White House was in flames.

As the capital smoldered, one Federalist divine promenaded through the ruins with an air of righteous satisfaction. The Presbyterian minister John Breckenridge—Margaret Smith said that he "made up in zeal and fidelity what he lacked in natural talents or acquired knowledge"—had pronounced at the outset of the war that God would punish the government for permitting the American people to backslide on their observance of the Sabbath. God, he warned, was livid at the nation's executive and legislative leaders for dedicating God's day to pagan amusements. Anticipating the donnybrook that would rage over the same issue during Jackson's presidency, a pet peeve of "this pious and reverend preacher" was the Sunday mails. Congress, he said, had placed thousands of postal workers' souls in jeopardy by forcing them to work on the Sabbath. "It is not the people who will suffer for these enormities," Breckenridge prophesied in his Fourth Commandment jeremiad, but rather, "you, the law-givers, who are the cause of this crime, will in your public capacity suffer for it."

One morning, shortly after returning to Washington, Mrs. Madison was chatting with her sister on the stoop of her makeshift residence when Mr. Breckenridge happened to stroll by. "I little thought, Sir, when I heard that threatening sermon of yours, that its denunciation would so soon be realized," Dolley called out as he tipped his hat. Mr. Breckenridge sternly replied, "Oh, Madam, I trust this chastening of the Lord may not be in vain."

"I am afraid the good man's hopes were never realized," Mrs. Smith dryly observed when recounting this anecdote, for there was no discernible "change in the observance of the Sabbath." As matters turned out, with American victory in the offing and, in its train, the wholesale embarrassment of the orthodox religious establishment, whatever prayers "Mr. Madison's war" may have answered, Mr. Breckenridge's almost certainly were not among them.

"And Where Is Our New England Bound?"

By 1814, with no sign of an end yet in sight, the war had settled into, at best, a standoff, propelling New Englanders to consider taking matters into their own hands. With two Massachusetts counties under British occupation, the most extreme Federalist leaders were pleading for the government to cede them permanently to England to purchase peace. Governor Strong entered into secret negotiations with the British, offering part of Maine as a bargaining chip.

Jefferson had a wry remedy for the witches of sedition. The handful of Federalist rebels in the South could be subdued easily, with negligible impact on Naval stores, by sending a barrel of tar to each state. For the Federalists of New England, however, "rougher drastics" might be required, something on the order of "hemp and confiscation." Jefferson went so far as to fantasize the United States embarking on a real war against Massachusetts. He boasted, "we can get ten [soldiers] to go to Massachusetts, for [every] one who will go to Canada." True to form, Jefferson's New England's antiwar Anglophiles were "monarchists in principle, bearing deadly hatred to their republican fellow-citizens, impatient under the ascendancy of republican principles, devout in their attachment to England, and preferring to be placed under her despotism, if they cannot hold the helm of government here." Scorning the "crimes only of the parricide party, which would have basely sold what their fathers so bravely won from the same enemy," Jefferson keened, "Oh, Massachusetts! How have I lamented the degradation of your apostasy! Massachusetts, with whom I went with pride in 1776, whose vote was my vote on every public question, and whose principles were then the standard of whatever was free or fearless."

As Jefferson seethed, his archenemies plotted. In December 1814, a quasi-constitutional convention, scheduled to convene in Hartford, Connecticut, led to the irony of America's law and order faction employing all the gadgets in liberty's toolbox, including states' rights and nullification, to hammer out a common protocol of resistance to their own government. Jedidiah Morse told his father that the Hartford Convention "is, under Providence, the source of my hope of salvation to our country."

Belying the grim seriousness with which it was carried out, the Hartford Convention turned out to be a piece of low farce. Aging lions, once the young pride of New England, stretched their creaking haunches and set out for Connecticut, where God's truth remained in safe government hands. Henry Adams, whose grandfather and great grandfather knew them all, described the source of Morse's hope as "only twenty-three persons, mostly cautious and elderly men, who detested democracy, but disliked enthusiasm almost as much." On the thin shoulders of this "popular body" the New England resistance rested.

As the march toward Hartford commenced, one crotchety old Puritan would have no part in such folderol. John Adams affixed special blame on the local clergy. "There is an alliance between our Essex Junto and our New England theologians—Unitarians and

Athanasians, Hopkintonians and Freewillers and all," Adams disgustedly observed of New England's politicized clerics. "*Bos, fur, sus, atque sacerdos* [Ox, thief, pig, and priest]." In no mood for pacific rhetoric, Adams adapted a quote from the Gospels that served his purposes admirably. "The Christian religion was intended," Adams declaimed, "not to send civil or political peace upon earth but a sword, and a sword it has sent."

Adams pronounced the War of 1812 not only a just war but also a useful one. He knew full well what the God of history was up to. "I believe," he told Rush,

> that wars, at times, are as necessary for the preservation and perfection, the prosperity, liberty, happiness, virtue, and independence of nations as gales of wind to the salubrity of the atmosphere or the agitations of the ocean to prevent its stagnation and putrefaction. As I believe this to be the constitution of God Almighty and the constant order of his Providence, I must esteem all the speculations of divines and philosophers about universal and perpetual peace as shortsighted, frivolous romances.

Adams reserved his greatest odium for George Cabot, who presided over the Hartford Convention. The hatred he felt toward Cabot inspired a memorable anecdote. A young visitor, George Ticknor, reports,

> I was seated in Mrs. Adams's parlor—where was no one but himself and Mrs. Adams, who was knitting—he began to talk of the condition of the country with great earnestness. I said not a word; Mrs. Adams was equally silent; but Mr. Adams, who was a man of strong and prompt passions, went on more and more vehemently. He was dressed in a single-breasted dark-green coat, buttoned tightly by very large white metal buttons over his somewhat rotund person. As he grew more and more excited in his discourse, he impatiently endeavored to thrust his hand into the breast of his coat.

The buttons did not yield readily; at last he *forced* his hand in, saying, as he did so, in a very loud voice and most excited manner: "Thank God! Thank God! George Cabot's close-buttoned ambition has broke out at last: he wants to be President of New England, sir!

"And where is our New England bound?" Adams sarcastically asked. "To Hartford Convention? And how many Paines and Callenders, Robespierres and Napoleons are to be begotten by that assemblage?" For once, he and Jefferson simultaneously seized on the same preposterous analogy. In a letter to Lafayette, Jefferson would assert that "The Marats, the Dantons, and Robespierres of Massachusetts are in the same pay, under the same orders, and making the same efforts to anarchise us that their prototypes in France did."

In point of fact, New England's governing elite had been conservative for so long that even those leaders most committed to what John Quincy Adams called "this mad project of national suicide" had trouble remembering how to be radical. Their firecracker was a dud, in part because the state legislatures sent their most cautious members to Hartford and in part because the delegates who gathered there were fated to set it off under water. On the eve of the Hartford Convention, Josiah Quincy asked what this articulate band of stalwarts might accomplish. "A GREAT PAMPHLET," George Cabot darkly jested in reply. Although the convention produced a text that might better be scored for somber strings than impetuous brass, its very existence, given the seditious road its participants had traveled to get there, raised cries of Republican outrage. General Andrew Jackson quite plausibly pronounced that if his command had included New England, he would have rounded up the "monarchists and traitors" who gathered in Hartford and court-martialed the lot of them.

Mistiming their caucus to occur just as the winds of war were swiftly and permanently shifting in America's favor, the Hartford Convention men and their fellow travelers must have felt abandoned

346 ⓒ JAMES MADISON

by the God of history. Right before England cried uncle, on his way to the Hartford Convention John Lowell called for American surrender. He was not alone in begging Madison to throw in the towel. A month before peace fell out of the sky to stun New England into a wary silence, Jedidiah Morse dressed down the president in a personal letter. The war, he said, was "cruel, unnecessary, [and] unjust;...esteemed so by thousands of good people of the United States and the expenses of it, too heavy and grievous to be borne." With American victory, the New England elite, which Lowell and Morse so gallantly personified, had lost what little remained of their purchase on the nation's political soul.

"To Celebrate the Goodness of the Great Disposer of Events"

The three Hartford Convention emissaries commissioned to present their tiny assembly's solemn deliberations to the president entered Washington just as victory bells began to chime. A great naval triumph on Lake Champlain, British withdrawal from occupied American territory, and word that General Jackson had driven a stake through the enemy's heart were spiriting jubilant crowds into the streets. The news from New Orleans was as dramatic as any since 1803, when the Louisiana Purchase made this French bayou town a part of the United States. England suffered more than 2,000 casualties; Jackson's American forces, only twenty-one. One journalist trumpeted, "Glory be to God that the barbarians have been defeated and that at Orleans the intended plunderers have found their grave."

Now that they no longer had any business to transact, the wise men from the East were divided over whether to grace the president with their presence. Lacking a personal invitation to Madison's open house, Harrison Grey Otis, who led the Hartford visitors, declined to demean himself by attending, boasting to his wife that with a little luck, "I believe...we should have succeeded, and that the little pigmy [would have shaken] in his shoes at our approach."

American victory and Federalist humiliation added irony to Madison's final national fast day, designated for January 12, 1815. Declared before war's end to rally a weary people's flagging spirit, it heralded instead a feast day. The doomsayers who had scorned Madison's godless leadership by predicting American defeat at the hands of Christian England were served up crow for this national thanksgiving. God has spoken, exulted the Republican clergy. "We have abundant evidence to believe it was a holy war," an administration paper echoed, "for the Lord has fought for us the battles and given us the victories, which have been signal and marvelous on water and on land. In how much then ought we to have confidence in the political opposers, who have declared the war unholy and unjust?" Adopting similar logic, one Democratic pundit chastised his New England countrymen for denouncing "Madison's war" and spurning his fast days.

> Approach, ye Holy Evangelists, whose desks have been polluted with your maledictions against the [war] measure and the government who adopted it—yet who profanely cursed our armies, while God was blessing them. Approach and behold your confutation, in the victories and glories we have gained....Say ye, was not the Lord God of Hosts with our republican armies?...Dare you persist in your denunciations and refrain [from] rendering thanksgiving to God for the marvelous deliverances He has vouchsafed our Republic?

Timothy Dwight was visited with particular scorn. "Our Mother who art in England," one satirist had him mouth. "Thy kingdom come: Thy will be done in New England." At the outset of the war, Dr. Dwight had pulled out his trusty script denouncing America as a Godless republic. "We formed our Constitution without any acknowledgement of God," he warned, and we continue "under the present system without God." By this logic, God's punishment could not help but follow in the wake of the nation's sins. Punishment did indeed follow, but not on the government, whose bumbling leaders were suddenly heroes. When the war ended in what patriotic Americans fashioned a victory, the punishment fell instead on the yellow bellies of New England, deemed by their fellow citizens men of little faith, who abetted the enemy by refusing to embrace the divine American cause.

To ordain the final congressional fast, Madison overcame a debilitating illness to arise from his sickbed in mid-November and affix his signature to the law. Two months later, with victory in hand, its text intoned a litany of providential acts, featuring the saga of the United States as an extended chapter of salvation history.

> No people ought to feel greater obligations to celebrate the goodness of the Great Disposer of Events and of the Destiny of Nations than the people of the United States. His kind providence originally conducted them to one of the best portions...for the great family of the human race. He protected and cherished them under all of their difficulties and trials.... Under His fostering care, their habits, their sentiments, and their pursuits prepared them for a transition in due time to a state of independence and self government...distinguished by multiplied tokens of His benign interposition...He reared them into the strength and endowed them with the resources which have enabled them to assert their national right and to enhance their national character in another arduous conflict...now so happily terminated by a peace and reconciliation with those who have been our enemies. And to the same Divine Author of every good and perfect gift we are indebted for all those privileges and advantages, religious as well as civil, which are so richly enjoyed in this land.

Congressional Republicans seized the occasion to consolidate their gain. It was Republican practice, especially in the South and West, for members of Congress to send printed and franked annual letters to their constituents. Two such letters reflect the party line. Whether the two members were in cahoots or simply staying on message (cribbing from boilerplate provided by party leaders) is uncertain. But, as was earlier the case in the party line on Jefferson's religion, the similarities in these circulars are too pronounced to be accidental. In stepping down from Congress, Representative John Kerr of Virginia wrote on February 22, 1815,

> We have reason to adore the God of the universe for his paternal care, he has been 'our refuge in the day of trouble,' and crowned us with victory; virtue has triumphed, and peace and prosperity are restored to our beloved country. If we now unite like brethren of the same great family, and bury in oblivion all party bickering, and strive to excel only in patriotism and virtue, permanent tranquility and happiness are ours.

Scoring identical points in the same order and with similar rhetoric, Representative John Sevier of Tennessee told his constituents a week later,

> We are bound to adore Divine Providence, whose paternal care over us in the time of peril and trouble crowned us with victory. Justice has triumphed; peace and prosperity are restored to our happy country. Let us now unite as one great family and bury all our past bickerings in oblivion, and we shall soon become the most happy nation on the globe.

Even in victory, the president's animus toward the established clergy burned on. Speaking of New England, he said, "The greater part of the people in that quarter have been brought by their leaders, aided by their priests, under a delusion scarcely exceeded by that recorded in the period of witchcraft." He wasn't unremittingly grim. One evening at war's end, Boston's peripatetic George Ticknor dined with the president at the Octagon House, which, since the burning of the White House, had served as the Madisons' temporary abode. Over dinner, Madison indulged in a bit of jocular conversation about "religious sects and parties." "Mr. M. gave amusing stories of early religious persecutions in Virginia," Ticknor reported, "and Mrs. M. entered into a defense and panegyric of the

Quakers, to whose sect, you know, she once belonged." Ticknor left with the clear impression that Madison was a Unitarian. At this particular juncture, most Unitarians, having vigorously opposed the war and thus embarrassed by the peace, would surely have preferred not to claim him.

At least two old Unitarians were cheering on the sidelines. "I sincerely congratulate you on the peace," Jefferson wrote the president, "and more especially on the éclat with which the war was closed." True to form by being at once more extravagant in his praise and blunter in qualifying it, Adams told Jefferson that "notwithstanding a thousand faults and blunders, [Madison's] administration has acquired more glory and established more union than all three predecessors, Washington, Adams and Jefferson put together." As fulsome as these words may sound, Adams was not far from the mark. Henry Clay declared, "A great object of the war has been attained in the firm establishment of the national character." Treasury Secretary Albert Gallatin perhaps said it best: "The war has renewed and reinstated the national feelings and charters which the Revolution had given and which were daily lessened. The people have now more general objects of attachment... They are more American; they feel and act more as a nation; and I hope the permanency of the Union is thereby better secured." In one of history's endless ironies, out of a thirty-month national embarrassment arose a new sense of nationhood. Reprising his role in the Constitutional Convention, Madison was again the impresario of *E pluribus unum*. It is not completely unfitting that fifty-seven towns and counties across the land are named for Madison, more than for any other president.

Was James Madison a Christian?

In 1816, stately St. John's Episcopal Church opened for worship in Washington with the president and his lady in attendance. Offered his dibs of choice front center pews by Dr. William Willner, Madison opted for less prestigious seating near the back of the nave, but still among the white worshipers—blacks worshipped God in the balcony. Near the end of her days, when, after long deliberation, Mrs. Madison decided to join the Episcopal Church, she described it as the church she had attended throughout her life. How frequently, she does not say. But no one who knew James and Dolley Madison the least bit well would mention their attachment to organized religion.

Madison spoke openly about his religious silence. "The letters and communications addressed to me on religious subjects have been so numerous, and of characters so various, that it has been an established rule to decline all correspondence on them," he stated as a matter of policy. Not that he would always be mute in the face of religious badgering. When one minister had the presumption to claim that, as secretary of state, Madison had faithfully consulted the scriptures on a daily basis during Jefferson's first term only to abandon this practice during his second, Madison was livid. "The passage is a sad example of pulpit authenticity, justice and delicacy," he fumed to the correspondent who forwarded him the sermon in which this baseless claim was made. "In what relates to me there is scarcely any part wholly true in the sense intended. How such a string of misinformation could have been gathered it is not easy to imagine.... [The charge] of my studying the Bible on the Sabbath during the first term and abandoning during the second term of my service in the Department of State is, throughout, a sheer fabrication."

That Madison refused to reveal the particulars of his faith by no means conclusively argues against his retaining Christian beliefs, but his lifetime of silence on the subject, coupled with no evidence of a spiritual life, weighs against the claim that he was a secret believer. Episcopal bishop William Meade of Virginia, who gathered and published a mountain of hearsay to prove that George Washington was a devout Christian, made no such effort or claim on Madison's behalf. On the contrary, he sadly concluded that Madison's interest in religion "seems to have been short lived. His political association with those of infidel principles, of whom there were many in his day, if they did not actually change his creed, yet subjected him to the general suspicion of it." Meade admitted that Madison was not hostile to religion, but a conversation he had with the president "left the impression on my mind that his creed was not strictly regulated by the Bible." Further testimony to Madison's relaxed religious views comes courtesy of Dolley's pious Quaker cousin, Sarah Coles Stevenson. She confirmed his casual attitude toward Sabbath day observances in an embarrassed note. "I hope my beloved Mr. Madison was not displeased at my reference to his opinions on the Sabbath. They were to me new, & so adverse to my own, that I confess they startled me."

Chief among the infidels whom Bishop Meade doubtless held responsible for leading Madison astray, Jefferson did call on his friend to perform one religious service. In 1824 he deferred to Madison's early study in theology, asking him to recommend books on the subject for the University of Virginia Library. The antiquated list Madison apologetically forwarded—he declared the project beyond his depth and protested the "scanty materials" he had to draw on—is frozen in time like a bee in amber. Initially he balked at accepting "a task that I found extremely tedious," until Jefferson assured him that a primary syllabus would more than meet his needs. Drawing from "a hasty glance of a few catalogues & my recollection," Madison stitched together and dutifully dispatched a short list of books on theology and religion. It included Reformation standards from Luther, Calvin, and Wesley to the Unitarian Socinus and the Quaker William Penn, together with representative selections of Restoration Roman Catholic thought. He also ventured beyond the Christian fold to include the Koran. The list's only additional curiosity is the inclusion of the King's Chapel Liturgy. This venerable Boston institution combined Congregational polity, Episcopal rites, and Unitarian theology, a unique olio that may offer a speculative hint of Madison's mature religious tastes.

Lacking Adams's affection for the church and Jefferson's interest in philosophy, Madison appears to have been a reverent agnostic (in the gentlest sense of the word, i.e., "unknowing"), too modest to advance any claims of his own and respectful of the claims promoted by others. As he once quipped to Margaret Smith, there might be great truths at the bottom of the well, but the more reasonable and practical hope would be to seek water there.

Madison's Second Thoughts

A year or two after leaving the White House, Madison collected his thoughts on the role of religion in government. These "Detached Memoranda," apparently intended for posterity but unfinished and then lost until they were discovered in the late 1940s, reveal the extent to which he considered himself to have compromised his principles on strict church-state separation during the course of his presidency.

Madison entered the White House with an exacting eye for any possible trespass of religion across government lines. When Congress enacted separate pieces of legislation to incorporate the Episcopal Church of Alexandria in the District of Columbia and cede federal property to a Baptist church in Mississippi, he vetoed both bills. The Episcopalians proposed to serve the District through their charitable offices, offering alms to the needy and education for the poor. In Madison's mind, this bill raised the old specter of the established church in Virginia operating as the state's officially sanctioned welfare department. The Baptist case threatened to create an even clearer "precedent for the appropriation of funds of the United States for the use and support of religious societies." Citing First Amendment guarantees, Madison argued that the line between church and state must be drawn "as distinctly as words can admit, and the limits to this authority established with as much solemnity." Reaffirming in his first veto "the essential distinction between civil and religious function," he colorfully proclaimed in his second, "Every provision for [any law] short of this principle will be found to leave crevices at least through which bigotry may introduce persecution; a monster feeding and thriving on its own venom gradually swells to a size and strength overwhelming all laws human and divine." Madison congratulated the members of two other Baptist churches for standing by him. "Among the various religious societies in our country," he granted graciously and aptly, "none has been more vigilant or constant in maintaining that distinction [between religion and civil government] than the society of which you make a part, and it is an honorable proof of your sincerity and integrity, that you are as ready to do so in a case favoring the interest of your brethren as in other cases." Shortly thereafter, Madison issued his first national fast.

On his retirement, Madison examined his own record, including its inconsistencies, with an objectivity unsurpassed by any president before or since. Writing in 1819 (or thereabouts), in his "Detached Memoranda" he spoke with pride of his early victories against Patrick Henry and Virginia's religious establishment. Then he shifted his attention to the nation's unfinished church-state business.

His overriding concern was the danger posed by an exponential growth in church wealth. Not only should the government give no official sanction to religious establishments, he now argued, but it should also act aggressively to monitor and limit the independent growth of ecclesiastical bodies. Madison saw religious corporations as threatening the people's liberty in direct proportion to the amount of economic clout they wielded. Unregulated religious corporations amassing capital posed the stealth danger of an extragovernmental establishment, gobbling up land and dictating policy through the power of its collective purse: "Besides the danger of a direct mixture of religion & civil government," he said, "there is an evil which ought to be guarded against in the indefinite accumulation of property from the capacity of holding it in perpetuity by ecclesiastical corporations." Sounding not a little like the trustbusters of a century later, Madison added, "The power of all corporations ought to be limited in this respect. The growing wealth acquired by them never fails to be a source of abuses." His principal concern, however, was the potential abuse of ecclesiastical corporate power.

> Are the U.S. duly awake to the tendency of the precedents they are establishing in the multiplied incorporations of religious congregations with the faculty of acquiring & holding property real as well as personal? Do not many of these acts give this faculty, without limit either as to time or as to amount? And must not bodies, perpetual in their existence, and which may be always gaining without ever losing, speedily gain more than is useful, and in time more than is safe? Are there not already examples in U.S. of ecclesiastical wealth equally beyond its object and the foresight of those who laid the foundation of it? In the U.S. there is a double motive for fixing limits in this case, because wealth may increase not only from additional gifts, but from exorbitant advances in the value of the primitive one. In grants of vacant lands, and of lands in the vicinity of growing towns & cities, the increase of value is often such as if foreseen would essentially control the liberality confirming them. The people of the U.S. owe their independence & their liberty to the wisdom of descrying in the minute tax of 3 pence on tea the magnitude of the evil comprised in the precedent. Let them exert the same wisdom in watching against every evil lurking under plausible disguises and growing up from small beginnings.

Throughout the religious section of his "Detached Memoranda," Madison casts himself as an outside critic of the political establishment, not as a man who just stepped down after eight years as the nation's chief executive. There is a reason for this. Following in the light Republican steps of his mentor, Madison didn't believe in a strong presidency and certainly not in abusing his executive power by employing his office as a bully pulpit. If his postpresidential reflections criticize national policy during the course of his administration as if that policy were not of his own devising, in his view it actually wasn't. Although they adapted to changing social and economic demands that required a stronger government, all three Republican presidential dynasts were ideologically shy of wielding a big stick, holding presidential power to be strictly limited by the Constitution. Unlike Jefferson, however, a strong leader who made up his own rules as he went along, Madison and Monroe were each inclined to follow the nation rather than lead it.

In reference to national prayer days, Madison made no bones about their questionable constitutionality. "They seem to imply and certainly nourish the erroneous idea of a *national* religion," he concluded. He himself, he said, followed Washington's prudent example by invoking God in the most universal language possible and by doing so in such a way that the president never became party to religious faction. He was always careful not to demand but only to invite citizen participation, yet he couldn't help arguing against his own decision to declare national days of fasting, prayer, and humiliation. Since "an *advisory* Government is a contradiction in terms," he said, "even to recommend a national prayer day oversteps the bounds of propriety." Nonetheless, and despite Jefferson's principled example to the contrary, Madison couldn't find it in his presidential mandate to deflect Congress's will. When Congress passed a wartime resolution calling for just such a proclamation, "It was thought not proper to refuse a compliance altogether; but a form & language were employed, which were meant to deaden as much as possible any claim of political right to enjoin religious observances by resting these expressly on the voluntary compliance of individuals."

Madison tackled a third church-state infraction in these papers that he let slide during his presidency, the question of congressional and military chaplaincies. Raising like objections to both, about the former he asked, "Is the appointment of chaplains to the two Houses of Congress consistent with the Constitution and with the pure principle of religious freedom?" Answering his own question, Madison concluded, "In strictness the answer on both points must be in the negative. The Constitution of the U.S. forbids everything like an establishment of a national religion." Pointing out that chaplains feed from the public trough, he went on to argue, "Does not this involve the principle of a national establishment, applicable to a provision for a religious worship for the constituent as well as of the representative body, approved by the majority, and conducted by ministers of religion paid by the entire nation? The establishment of the chaplainship to Congress is a palpable violation of equal rights, as well as of Constitutional principles."

Madison justified abandoning his Constitutional scruples when in office by invoking the legal maxim that the law doesn't "bother with trifles." He employed the same rationale to explain looking the other way when Congress hired chaplains in the first place. "It was not with my approbation," he said on another occasion, "that the deviation took place in Congress, when they appointed chaplains, to be paid from the national treasury," adding that "It would have been a much better proof to their constituents of their pious feeling if the members had contributed for the purpose a pittance from their own pockets." However improperly, the issue had long since been decided. "As the precedent is not likely to be rescinded, the best that can now be done may be to apply to the Constitution the maxim of the law, *de minimis non curat* (['Laws] don't bother with trifles')."

In his "Detached Memoranda," Madison cited the same legal principle to explain his national fast days, not to extend to his successors equal latitude but to strip from his example the weight of precedent. "Rather than let this step beyond the landmarks of power have the effect of a legitimate precedent," he enjoined anyone who might be tempted to invoke his example that "it will be better to apply to it the legal aphorism *de minimis non curat lex.*" Conscious that his action might later be adduced by religious partisans and twisted against his own first principle, Madison belatedly reminded himself, "We are always to keep in mind that it is safer to trust the consequences of a right principle, than reasonings in support of a bad one."

Madison's conceptual consistency on church-state separation remained unbroken throughout four decades of public service. When defending the practical genius of this position, he was fond of quoting the Enlightenment heresiarch, Voltaire. In his entry on "Tolerance" in the *Dictionaire Philosophique,* a compendium of modern learning that Jefferson sent Madison from France, Voltaire observed about England something that held even truer of the United States: "If one religion only were allowed in England, the government would possibly become arbitrary; if there were but two, the people would cut each other's throats; but, as there are such a multitude, they all live happy and in peace."

Peace was on Madison's mind when he bade the American people adieu. With a rare nod to the scriptures, in his farewell message to Congress on December 3, 1816, the nation's fourth president commemorated the thirtieth anniversary of the Constitution, commending it for balancing "public strength with individual liberty." In honoring the framers' moral vision, he hailed the nation state he helped establish,

> A government pursuing the public good as its sole object, and regulating its means by the great principles consecrated in its charter, and by those moral principles to which they are so well allied; a government which watches over the purity of elections, the freedom of speech, and the press, trial by jury, and the equal interdict against encroachments and compacts between religion and state; which maintains inviolably the maxims of public faith, the security of persons and property, and encourages in every authorized mode that general diffusion of knowledge which guarantees to public liberty its permanency and to those who possess the blessing, the true enjoyment of it; a government which avoids intrusion on the internal repose of other nations and repels them from its own...a government, in a word, whose conduct within and without may bespeak the most noble of all ambitions—that of promoting peace on earth and good will to men.

With this stirring invocation of America's "public faith," Madison handed the presidential office over to his old friend James Monroe.

ACT V

∞∞

JAMES MONROE

13

∞∞

ALL FOR ONE AND
ONE FOR ALL

The moral beauties of the mind
  If man would to a blessing turn,
And the great powers to him assign'd
  Would cultivate, improve, adorn:
    The sun of happiness, and peace
    Would shine on earth and never cease

—PHILIP FRENEAU, "THE NEW AGE"

IN 1819, the Baltimore clergyman and American humorist Jonas
Clopper penned a political satire lampooning the state of American religious politics. The opposite of a salvation history, in revisiting thirty sorry years of diminishing presidential fidelity it recounts the nation's fall from grace and reprises, if from a partisan perspective, the major themes of our tale. Heaven was smiling when the "immortal" George Fredonius (Washington) triumphed on the field of battle to establish Bawlfredonian (American) independence; three decades later God punished a faithless people with an otherwise senseless war.

Modeled loosely on Jonathan Swift's satire, *Gulliver's Travels*, from a Tory, not Whig, perspective, Clopper's *Fragments of the History of Bawlfredonia* (think "Howlingfreedomland" or "Screaming-me-meville") damns democracy as an anarchistic scourge eating away at the nation's moral fiber. It stars Thomas Jefferson as Bawlfredonia's blackguard in chief, with Tom Paine and James Madison making cameo appearances as his impious henchmen. No one escapes Clopper's poison pen. He can't resist parodying the money-pinching inhabitants of New England (Asylum Harbor), but his devil's backyard is a similitude of old Virginia (Blackmoreland), whose proprietors underwrite their addiction to gambling and wenching by growing and selling Stinkum-puff. Clopper's antihero, King Thomas Bawlfredonious (Jefferson), hails from Blackmoreland. His guiding passions are pop science, Deism, and a favorite concubine, his "black Venus."

Flattering the gullible mob into submission while duping it into infidelity, Thomas, in a proto-Darwinian flourish of satanic imagination, teaches that human beings evolved from "tadpoles who, having cast their tails, are now making a rapid march to perfectibility." He further postulates that "the great continent of Bawlfredonia was not formed by the Almighty, but by a fortuitous conglomeration of sands pushed together by winds and tides." To discredit Christianity, Thomas counsels his acolytes to pose "sly insinuations against particular portions of the Bible; suggest doubts which may perplex and stagger the faith of the illiterate, but avoid an open avowal of hostility to the scriptures or religion." In his infamous book, *The History of Blackmoreland,* Thomas posits "that it made no difference to him whether a man worshipped one God or fifty gods," as long as he didn't "take away his black Venus by force." Harping forever on their "*imperscriptible,* imperishable, and natural rights," the Bacchesians (Republicans) are great champions of sacred liberty. "I invoke the genius of liberty," one partisan avows, "to preserve to the Blackmorelanders the right of doing as we please."

"The sober, plodding, industrious" Asylumonians of Puritansville will have none of this. At the nation's Constitutional Convention they argue that "In the fundamental articles of the government, the Almighty should be acknowledged as the supreme governor of nations and His revealed will taken as a standard of civil and political morals." Thomas's followers, raising banners proclaiming "LIBERTY OF CONSCIENCE" and "Beware of hypocrisy and priestcraft," counter that "To acknowledge the Almighty in our fundamental laws would be most unphilosophically 'mixing the affairs of church and state.'"

Like its historical counterpart, the story Clopper tells is filled with drama and intrigue. After King George Fredonius ("The chief earthly instrument" of Providence) laid down his scepter, "a most insufferable egotist," John of Onionville (Adams) was "elevated by the votes of the Christians" and became king. As king, John pretended for political purposes "to treat the name of the holy Redeemer with veneration, notwithstanding his secret denial of his divinity." The leading theological infidel of the time, Doctor Phlogiston (Joseph Priestley), a scientific madman who believed that Thomas Bawlfredonius would usher in the "beginning of a millennium of holiness and happiness" and his friend Potasia (Thomas Cooper) defamed John in an effort to depose him. Convicted for sedition under laws newly passed to protect the sanctity of the kingdom, Potasia was "shut up for thirty days in a cage, set opposite to a most restless, slavering and spitting lyon [Congressman Matthew Lyon]."

Challenging King John, Thomas, with the aid of his trusty Blackmoreland squire, Pigman Puff (James Madison), invoked the nation's founding principles, which he conveniently happened to write. When people dared to question Thomas's moral integrity and Christian fidelity, he was quick to remind his supporters that to avoid "the least shew of persecution or illiberality, no moral qualifications have been required as prerequisites in our legislators and kings." This posed no danger, Thomas said, because, "they are to be elected by the people, who in this enlightened kingdom cannot err, [so] you will choose the good only to rule you." The Democratic Party platform put it simply: "A public favorite can do no wrong."

Notwithstanding Thomas's diabolical cleverness, John of Onionville orchestrated his own doom. A closet heretic, he "could not be brought to believe that [his soul] would be saved according to the old and received doctrine taught by Saint Paul and the apostles."

For all his many failings, John was nonetheless a political martyr: "His most meritorious conduct was grossly vilified, his most upright intentions called in question, and every effort made by him to secure the rights and liberties of our country were represented as the most wicked machinations for enslaving and oppressing his subjects."

Following Thomas as king was his satellite, Pigman Puff, "a remarkable nice little fellow who wore ruffled shirts and nicely blacked shoes on his pretty little feet." Pigman had studied religion at the nation's finest seminary but, on being introduced to Tom Anguish (Paine) and Thomas Bawlfredonious, "he spurned the instructions of his Asylumonean counselors...and became the most decided and malignant enemy of the Asylumoneans."

Pigman's notorious wife, too, fell from grace. Exchanging the "plain drab colored dress" of her pious childhood for "a thin robe with naked arms and shoulders, surrounded by a numerous collection of animals, in wide boots and huge neck-pads, bearing a striking resemblance to newly caught monkeys and baboons," the queen dared her subjects to go and sin likewise: "Many chaste and modest women, both young and old, rather than be pointed at for singularity, threw aside their petticoats and exposed their delicate limbs to the chilling frosts and scorching sun." During Pigman's lamentable reign the consequences for such immorality were harrowing: "Heaven, in vengeance for our sins, permitted this little man to ascend the throne, and plunge our country, unprepared, into a most bloody war."

That, in a satiric nutshell, is one Federalist clergyman's take on the religious politics of the young republic. Washington is a saint; pompous Adams receives censure for his insufficient faith from a political ally; Jefferson is the devil incarnate; Madison, a religious changeling with a bawdy wife.

When *Bawlfredonia* was published in 1819, Monroe, as secular as any of his predecessors, had been president for two years. Tailor-made for Christian target practice, that he should escape both notice and blame from the Reverend Mr. Clopper reflects a new dawn in the nation's religious politics.

"The Reputation of a Brave, Active, and Sensible Officer"

During Monroe's eight years in the White House, America's secular government and religious populace coexisted in a relaxed détente. Marking the end of an era of bad feelings, precipitated to a significant degree by religious differences, Monroe's feel-good presidency succeeded in large measure because of a religious truce that served the church as much as it spared the state.

There is not much room in America's crowded history books for the nation's fifth president. Monroe labored under the disadvantage of sharing history's stage with a colorful company of compulsively articulate leading men. His intellect, more than competent but hardly luminous, seems dim when set next to the brilliance of Jefferson, Madison, and Adams. As for his most illustrious predecessor, even in his finest Continental Army uniform, replete with a bullet hole in the shoulder, Monroe disappears almost entirely when standing next to George Washington. Yet he possessed qualities as rare and morally more estimable than a shimmering intellect or towering physique, each an accident of birth, and he served the nation both faithfully and well.

In dress and manner—he wore old-fashioned buckled shoes, smallclothes (close fitting knee britches), and a Revolutionary era tricorner hat—Monroe was a throwback to an earlier time. Whenever he opened the door on a room of his contemporaries, he appeared to have come straight out of the Republic's opening chapter. His aspirations matched those of the nation's first president as well: to cultivate harmony and ensure liberty by maintaining order. Although the two men quarreled and eventually were estranged, Monroe's moral and religious character is closer in almost every respect to Washington's than to those of his senior partners in the Republican troika, Jefferson and Madison. He was a Stoic, a Mason, secular to the bone, conservative by nature, and not interested enough in religion to bother being disrespectful toward anyone's cherished beliefs. When he arrived at the pinnacle of American politics, Monroe sought to complete less the promise of Jefferson's Revolution of 1800 than that of Washington's inauguration of 1789, fulfilling Washington's dream of a united people served inconspicuously and well by a nonpartisan government whose leader they regarded with gratitude and respect.

Monroe was born in Fredericksburg, Westmoreland County, in the Northern Neck of Virginia in 1758 and baptized Anglican in Washington Parish. His every significant rite of passage (baptism, marriage, and death) took place within the Anglican preserve. During his White House years, when he chose to attend Sunday worship—about his attentiveness in this regard, history pays no notice—President Monroe traveled a short block to St. John's, which he looked out on from his bedroom window.

We know little of Monroe's religious convictions. In his compendious literary remains, he never cites the scriptures. Nor does he mention Jesus Christ. His library contains but a handful of religious volumes, mostly gifts. If a spiritual connection can be made at all, it is, like for Washington, with the Brotherhood of Freemasons, which he joined as a student in 1775. As an officer in the Continental Army and young lawyer, Monroe identified himself as a Mason. He participated in the Fredericksburg Lodge during his brief legal career. While serving as president, he was invested in Washington's Naval Lodge No. 4. In his *Autobiography,* Monroe raised the subject of religion only once: to chide the clergy for interfering in politics.

James received a sound classical education at well-regarded Campbelltown Academy, where he struck up a friendship with future Chief Justice John Marshall. Daily they would walk together several miles through the virgin forest on their commutes to and from school. In 1774, at the age of sixteen and on the death of his father, James arrived in Williamsburg to attend the upper form of William and Mary College. The Phi Beta Kappa Society was founded at William and Mary College in December 1776, with Marshall listed among the first class elected to membership. Monroe, unsurprisingly, didn't make the cut. By then, however, he and Marshall were engaged in a more significant, if less exclusive club: the Continental Army. Shortly after graduation, eighteen-year-old Second Lieutenant James Monroe of the Virginia Third was beating a hasty retreat through New Jersey toward the west bank of the Delaware River with the tattered remnants of General Washington's command. At their moment of greatest peril, an embedded reporter bolstered their spirits and lifted their sights. "These are the times that try men's souls," Thomas Paine wrote. "The summer soldier and the sunshine patriot will, in this crisis, shrink from the service of his country; but he that stands it now, deserves the love and thanks of man and woman. Tyranny, like hell, is not easily conquered. It would be strange indeed if so celestial an article as freedom should not be highly rated."

In the familiar painting "Washington Crossing the Delaware" by Emanuel Leutze, Second Lieutenant Monroe, flag in hand, stands directly behind the general. He nearly carved his historical niche as one of but a handful of American casualties at Trenton. After the icy early morning crossing, Monroe charged into the cannon's mouth to neutralize the nest of artillerymen who were putting up the most resistance, and a Hessian bullet cut him down. He would have died that day if a New Jersey doctor had not awakened before dawn spontaneously to join the march, suspecting that his services might be needed. They were; he saved the future president's life. Promoted for his bravery, Monroe enhanced his rank but lost his standing during a two-month convalescence.

Monroe's closest friend in the army was a Frenchman, Pierre DuPonceau, who accompanied the barely of-age Marquis de Lafayette on his American adventure and opened Monroe's mind to the world of the French *philosophes*. A letter Monroe penned to him contains an early indication of the stolid Virginian's intellectual humility. He apologized in advance to his French friend for the quality of his family library. "So towering are your thoughts, so great are your expectations that I fear sending you any of our books," James allowed, describing the modest pickings he was forwarding as "a plain and simple collection, only well adapted to a retir'd clergyman." By introducing him to such Deistical tracts as the sermons of James Watson, who provocatively said, "Where mystery begins, religion ends," DuPonceau made Monroe's mind spin. Whatever thought he may have given to religion before, evidence suggests that it ended here; Monroe appears to have lacked sufficient faith to overcome the arguments of philosophy or the intellectual rigor necessary to convert philosophy into faith. More tellingly, DuPonceau introduced his friend to the poet Mark Akenside, who touted the virtues of Stoicism. Jibing nicely with the Virginian ethos, Stoicism's duty-driven set of rules for proper comportment held the practical advantage of shoring up any doubts the young officer may have entertained about his natural abilities in a fortress of correct behavior sturdy enough to protect him from the world's censure.

After recovering from his wounds, Monroe never quite caught up with the war. Finding no place in the state command structure—the Continental Army was as overstocked with officers as it was begging for soldiers—the seasoned teenager returned to Virginia in 1778, armed with a stirring letter of recommendation from General Washington.

> I very sincerely lament that the situation of our service will not permit us to do justice to the merits of Major Monroe, who will deliver you this, by placing him in the army upon some satisfactory footing. But as he is on the point of leaving us and expressed an intention of going to the southward, where a new scene has opened, it is with pleasure I take occasion to express to you the high opinion of his worth.... He has, in every instance, maintained the reputation of a brave, active, and sensible officer.

Alexander Hamilton also put in a good word on Monroe's behalf to Lieutenant Colonel John Laurens, who was fighting against prejudice to create a Negro regiment in the South. "Monroe is just setting out from Headquarters," Hamilton wrote. "He will relish your black scheme if anything can be done for him in that line." By suggesting that Monroe might be suitable for command in a black regiment, the admirably unprejudiced Hamilton hints that his young Virginia acquaintance held more modern views on race than too many of his southern cohorts for Laurens's visionary plan to succeed.

Never far removed from a mentor, Monroe landed in Williamsburg, where Thomas Jefferson took him under wing, directing his study of the law with the aid of a new system that he'd just invented: the case method. We know what books Jefferson told his ward to purchase, but apart from hints that Monroe cottoned, in particular, to the Stoic Epictetus, we have no idea what, if anything, he thought of them.

Jefferson invested Monroe's life with purpose. "Believe me, I feel that whatever I am at present in the opinion of others, or whatever I may be in future, has greatly arisen from your friendship," Monroe told Jefferson. "My plan in life is now fixed, has a certain object for its view & does not depend on other chance or circumstance." Both chance and circumstance would intervene, but Jefferson's sponsorship would drive the narrative of this unremarkable man's extraordinary ascent up the political ladder. Jefferson summed up his protégé's character sweetly in a letter to Madison: "Turn his soul wrong side outwards and there is not a speck on it."

Monroe followed Jefferson to the state capital when the latter became governor of Virginia in 1778. From the moment he arrived in Richmond, Monroe's political career skyrocketed. At twenty-four he was seated in the Assembly, soon to be elevated to Virginia's Executive Council as its youngest member. In 1783, the twenty-five-year-old assemblyman won election to Congress, where he served for three years. He went on to a seat in the U.S. Senate and twice represented his nation overseas in the diplomatic corps. Subsequently, he served as governor of Virginia and Secretary of State under James Madison, before capping his political ascent as the fifth president of the United States.

Like Washington's, Monroe's straightforward life can be read on the cover sheet of his existence. Six feet tall and with a muscular frame, he was deferential, plainspoken, slightly bumbling, and unfailingly polite. Lacking Washington's magnetism, he presented the world a robust, frank countenance, with a deeply dimpled chin, watery gray eyes—they are variably described as "inviting confidence" and "more kind than penetrating"—and luminous smile, which people rarely saw. "Nature has given him a mind neither rapid nor rich," his attorney general, William Wirt, said, hastening to add that "he is embued with a spirit of generous and restless emulation, a judgment solid, strong and clear, and a habit of application, which no difficulties can shake, nor labors can tire." "Good old Col. Monroe," Dolley Madison's sister Sarah called him. His prescription for good government was equally unadorned: "Nothing is wanting but common sense & common honesty," he said. The first professional politician to assume the presidency, Monroe cultivated few if any other interests, never once straying for longer than a few months from the political path that guided him to the White House.

The Houseguest from Hell

New England's Black Regiment would have known (or thought they knew) only one thing about Monroe's religion: While serving President Washington as American minister to France, Monroe secured Thomas Paine's release from prison in 1794 and took him into his home to care for him during a lengthy convalescence.

On Paine's behalf, Monroe performed double service. He expressed gratitude to a major catalyst of American cohesiveness during the early days of the Revolution and did his duty on behalf of a fellow citizen. Having taken his idealism to France and parlayed it into a seat in the National Convention, Paine fell from favor when he opposed, for humanitarian reasons, the execution of King

Louis XVI. He himself escaped the guillotine by a fluke. On the night before his scheduled execution, a warden put the fateful chalk mark on the wrong side of his prison door, which had been mercifully propped open to permit a breeze entry to assuage a chronic fever. Shut later that evening, the door was bypassed the following morning by guards collecting prisoners slated for execution. Three days later Robespierre's head fell from his shoulders and with it the Terror, if not the chaos, ended. Four months passed before Monroe's pestering of the authorities finally secured Paine's release in November 1784. "I shall certainly pay the utmost attention to this gentleman," Monroe said, "as he is one of those whose merits in our revolution were most distinguished."

No longer a Monroe booster, Alexander Hamilton saw things differently. He imagined two heretics lounging together late into the evening, "fraterniz[ing] and philosophiz[ing] against the *Christian religion* and the absurdity of religious *worship*." Adams huffed that Monroe's Paris home was a "school for scandal." Whatever Paine and Monroe talked about during their extensive time together, Monroe's controversial houseguest remained for nearly two years completing part two of *The Age of Reason* while Elizabeth Monroe heroically nursed him back to health. At this point in his drinking career, Paine's alcoholism hadn't yet deformed him from a charming conversationalist into a garrulous sot. Yet, already on the way to drinking his way first into bankruptcy and then to death, he would never repay the money Monroe lent him. He also, without giving a thought to his host's reputation, employed his government ink, desk, paper, and pen to craft a noxious, self-destructive character assassination of President Washington. Monroe vainly begged his self-absorbed houseguest not to publish this letter, knowing full well how much dust it would raise and how close he stood to its source.

Paine believed, as Monroe explained to Madison, that Washington "winked at his imprisonment, and wished he might die in gaol." Paine's self-avenging broadside, a thirty-page rant, was easily the single most scurrilous verbal attack ever to be leveled at Washington. Calling "the whole of your administration...deceitful, if not perfidious," he lambasted the president for kowtowing to England, betraying France, "and, all the while, encouraging and swallowing the grossest adulation." Adding injury to insult, when not attacking Washington, Paine was lauding Monroe. He appended to his screed the encomium that Monroe had sent him in prison. "You are considered by [the American people] as not only having rendered important service in our own revolution," the big-hearted American minister had said, "but as being, on a more extensive scale, the friend of human rights and a distinguished and able advocate in favor of public liberty. To the welfare of Thomas Paine, the Americans are not, nor can they be, indifferent." This statement should have been true, but it wasn't. In 1794, when Monroe wrote these words, they told only half of a developing story that he could not possibly keep up with, given the ocean that lay between him and America's fast moving sacred-political parade.

When Paine finally returned to America some years later, his arrival to the country he helped liberate was met with scorn. John Adams summed up the collective outrage, born in large measure of Paine's outspoken disdain for Christianity and radical democratic political views: "For such a mongrel between pig and puppy, begotten by a wild boar on a bitch wolf, never before in any age of the world was suffered by the poltroonery of mankind to run through such a career of mischief." Even Jefferson tiptoed around his erstwhile soul mate, always correct in his behavior but maintaining a prudent distance. Paine accused Jefferson of shying away from him, "as if you stood in fear of federal observation."

That Monroe was out of step with the changing music of American politics is understandable. He was frozen in much the same time warp that earlier made it so difficult for Adams to find his sea legs on returning to shifting American ground after a decade in Europe. Monroe would recover his balance; Paine did not. All but

friendless, the most persuasive voice for American independence retired to a tiny village in upstate New York and disappeared into his
bottle.

Throughout his rocky diplomatic tenure, Monroe won little
confidence within Washington's administration. As the French revolution progressed from one outrage to another, his sympathy for
France and polite embrace of the French leadership offended the
president. The word in the street, promulgated by the Federalist
press, was that Monroe served France more faithfully than he did
the United States. In 1796, Washington recalled his ambassador.

On returning to America in 1796, Monroe wrote a 450-page
document-laden defense of his service in France and protest against
his recall by the president. Oliver Wolcott assured Washington that
his rogue diplomat would turn no heads beyond those of Paine
and his democratic cabal. Monroe's standing at the time among
Federalists, and liberty's standing as well, was well summed up by
Fisher Ames, a dismissive *let him go home to his friends:* "Monroe
will, if he likes, return to France to embrace liberty again."

The Era of Good Feelings

Two decades later, in 1817, fifty-eight-year-old Monroe rolled into
the presidency. His opponent, New York's Federalist senator Rufus
King, captured only the electors of Massachusetts, Rhode Island,
and Delaware. One New Englander who voted for Monroe took
care not to abandon his trademark truculence. John Adams, who
deemed his son John Quincy "the fittest man in all creation for the
Presidency," groused that he would have to wait his rightful turn
"till all Virginians shall be extinct."

After being sworn into office in the Senate Chamber by his boy-
hood friend Chief Justice John Marshall, the president delivered his
inaugural address. Of this earnest call to republican virtues, one reporter commented, "As to the style of the speech, it is, like the suit

of clothes which President Monroe wore on the occasion, very good home-spun, and quite fine enough. It forms no objection with us that there are no flowers of rhetoric scattered through it."

Monroe looked to the past for inspiration. During the course of his remarks, he tempered the Jeffersonian ideology of the Republican presidential dynasty that his election had extended to a third generation by echoing a refrain from Washington. After affirming popular sovereignty—"The Government has been in the hands of the people. To the people, therefore...is the credit due"—he qualified the privilege of freedom by cautioning against its misuse. "It is only when the people become ignorant and corrupt, when they degenerate into a populace, that they are incapable of exercising the sovereignty," he declared. "Usurpation is then an easy attainment and a usurper soon found. The people themselves become the willing instruments of their own debasement and ruin."

Monroe closed his inaugural address with a formal nod to the Almighty, its formulation and "fervency" cribbed from Washington's abiding script: "Relying on the aid to be derived from the other departments of the Government, I enter on the trust to which I have been called by the suffrages of my fellow-citizens with my fervent prayers to the Almighty that He will be graciously pleased to continue to us that protection which He has already so conspicuously displayed in our favor."

The Cabinet Monroe selected, crowded with dueling presidential aspirants, was fractious but exceptionally strong. Displaying iron confidence, he appointed Federalist convert John Quincy Adams, William Crawford, his opponent for the Republican presidential nomination, and leonine Senator John Calhoun of South Carolina to the Departments of State, Treasury, and War. Three of the brightest stars in government service, they performed their duties with a combined dedication and efficiency not witnessed since Washington's first term.

Shortly after inauguration day, Monroe set out on a journey through New England. Crawford, still smarting for being edged out by Monroe in the Republican caucus, wondered at the "general absolution of political sins" that graced the advent of his adversary's presidency. He sarcastically told Albert Gallatin, his predecessor in the Treasury Department, that "The President's tour through the East has produced something like a political jubilee. They were, in the land of steady habits, at least for the time, 'all Federalists, all Republicans.'" The similitude to a biblical jubilee, where old debts are forgiven and society begins anew on an even footing, was apt. In a part of the country where once he could almost have counted his partisans on one hand, Monroe's harshest critics were cheering. The New Haven *Herald* exulted, "The demon of party for a time departed and gave place for a general burst of national feeling." Boston's *Columbian Centinel* coined a tag line for Monroe's tenure that would find its way into history:

ERA OF GOOD FEELINGS

During the late Presidential Jubilee many persons have met at festive boards, in pleasant converse, whom party politics had long severed. We recur with pleasure to all the circumstances which attended the demonstration of good feelings.

Changes in the way New Englanders commemorated the Fourth of July offer one gauge of the shifting and softening political winds. In 1815, after years of dividing into two celebrations, one Federalist (black cockade) and one Republican (tricolor), the Federalists of Worcester, Massachusetts, whether out of bitterness, embarrassment, or both, didn't even bother to celebrate Independence Day. Two years later, concurrent with Monroe's visit, for the first time since before Jefferson took office Worcester's competing political factions collaborated to plan and participate in joint Fourth of July festivities. One symbol of the changing climate was the surprise Fourth of July emergence from his burrow of a stubborn old groundhog, whose lack of a shadow forecast pleasant national weather. John Adams, who had boycotted the Boston Independence Day celebrations for almost a decade, returned in 1816 to grace his neighbors with his venerable presence, an act of conciliation so conspicuous that it was consecrated in the local press. Celebrating the new national mood, one editor would marvel, more or less accurately, that "eight millions of people united in one festive celebration of the National Birthday."

Monroe built his presidency not on the spoils of war but on the reformation of American nationhood and character that arose from its ashes. He perceived the value of the War of 1812 as fourfold: "to unite our people, to draw out our resources, to invigorate our means, and to make us more truly an independent nation." This is the message he brought with him to New England. It was a message that resonated.

> The visit of the president seems wholly to have allayed the storms of party. People now meet in the same room who would before scarcely pass [in] the same street, and move in concert, where before the most jarring discord was the consequence of an accidental encounter...It is found that citizens in opposite parties are not so unworthy of reciprocal respect as before they were thought to be, and that each have qualifications which entitle them to the esteem of the others. The spirit of exclusive self-love wears away, and the intercourse with each other shows even to prejudiced minds that the virulence of party spirit...is not so strong or immovable as has been suspected. This harmony is a harbinger of a better order of things, and we trust it will continue beyond the cause which produced it.

In the public accolades Monroe received during the course of his journey, a sigh of relief is palpable. The president's visit made us "one people," the once truculent *Columbian Centinel* editorialized, "for we have the sweet consolation...to rest assured that the President will be president, not of a party, but of a great and powerful nation." This "plain and substantial, but well informed, farmer" went one unlikely step further. Having charmed the journalists, he proceeded to win the hearts and minds of New England's flinty intelligentsia, who extended him the ultimate peace offering, an honorary degree from Harvard.

Connecticut at the Crossroads

During his New England tour, Monroe paused in Hartford, Connecticut, to receive a tribute the graciousness of which suggests as much as any other memento from his journey the dawn of a new morning in America's religious politics. To an avowed Republican from whom the residents of Hartford could expect no religious favors, these hoary partisans, without betraying their first principle, divine order, expressed their gratitude for the end of factional strife:

> The people of this state, while they cherish the high spirit of freedom, are, from the force of our institutions and habits, distinguished also for their love of order and submission to the laws. In pursuing a policy, which as we confidently expect, will give the best effect to the principles of our government…and secure to our country those high advantages, which seem destined for her by Providence, you may be assured of a hearty respect.

The Connecticut that hailed Monroe in 1817 had been as unsettled by the culture war between divine order and sacred liberty as any other state in the Union. Connecticut fashioned itself a Christian commonwealth. The power of the clergy was magnified by the lack of a state constitution. This absence left its citizens at the collective whim of an elite minority, whose disdain for democratic process was almost as great as their faith in God's divine governance. Given Connecticut's recent history, the Hartford town fathers' encomium to Monroe borders on the miraculous, because at that very instant the orthodox party of Connecticut was in the fight of its life, bracing for its own Waterloo, a desperate last battle to save Connecticut's Christian soul.

Not until 1811 had major cracks begin to show in Federalist Connecticut's hold. In that year, overcoming decades of Congregational hegemony, a combination of Episcopalians and Baptists secured the governor's chair, electing not a Republican, but a Federalist maverick who was not a pillar in good standing in the Congregational Church. Rocked by the first electoral insult to the established church, Congregational impresario Lyman Beecher, Timothy Dwight's most passionate disciple, was left all but speechless. His lament after the loss underscores how imperiously the Standing Order of Connecticut exercised its sway.

> All the infidels in the state had long been leading on [the Republican] side; the minor sects had swollen and complained of having to get a certificate to pay their tax where they liked; our efforts to enforce reformation of morals by law made us unpopular; they attacked the [established] clergy unceasingly and myself in particular, in season and out of season, with all sorts of misrepresentation, ridicule and abuse; and, finally the Episcopalians who had always been staunch Federalists were disappointed of an appropriation for the Bishop's fund, which they asked for, and went over to the Democrats. That overset us. They slung us like a stone from a sling.

For a time, order was reestablished, as popular opposition to "Madison's War" revitalized a tired Federalist Party, but the period of retrenchment was brief. After the debacle of the Hartford Convention in 1814, with the Christian establishment reeling under patriotic fire, Connecticut's Baptists and Episcopalians joined forces once again, this time to plot the demise of the Standing Order. Shortly before Monroe passed through the state, a witty, illuminating advertisement ran in the Danbury paper calling the dissidents to arms.

> Long have the Congregational Order held domination over the civil government of this state; long has every other denomination submitted to their domination. The Baptists have prayed and importuned; the Episcopalians have prayed and importuned and

prayed again; while the Methodists and other denominations, beholding the futility of importunities and prayers, have quietly submitted to their fate. An opportunity will present itself to the friends of equal rights on the 8th of April next to place all denominations of Christians on an equal footing.

From such meetings, the Republicans cobbled together a Toleration or Fusion Party ticket and contested the Federalists with unprecedented electoral strength. Even the Methodists perked up. With Methodists now joining the Baptists and Episcopalians, the Republicans rode the rising tide of sectarian partisanship deftly. "The ruling party insists that one particular denomination of Christians ought, by the aid of human laws, to be endowed with peculiar rights and privileges," one Toleration Party declaration read. "Republicans contend that such laws have a strong tendency to produce an unnatural and adulterous connection between church and state."

Oliver Wolcott (Jedidiah Morse's erstwhile confidant and John Ogden's nemesis in the long-forgotten Lyon controversy) emerged to play a starring role in the Republican triumph. Like an avenging angel, Wolcott, whose liberal religious views, support of the war, and revulsion toward the Hartford Convention conspired to transfigure his once sturdy Federalist politics, emerged at the head of the Toleration Party ticket and won election as governor in 1817.

In addition to seizing the governor's office, even as Monroe was passing through, Connecticut was about to change even more profoundly: The Toleration Party was advancing the novel notion of a written state constitution. "The Charter of King Charles II [under which the government was still operating forty years after independence] contains principles obnoxious to a Republican government," a widely circulated reform petition read. The religious establishment, from John Cotton Smith to John Edwards Jr., pledged their ringing Puritan names in eternal opposition to such a document, but, in early 1818, by the narrow vote of 13,918 to 12,361, a written constitution guaranteeing equal rights and privileges to all denominations was enacted into law, severing, in the words of one still faithful preacher, "the ancient spirit which had...linked [Connecticut]...to the throne of the Almighty for almost two hundred years." Beecher was crushed. "Why should this little church be sacrificed?" he beseeched Heaven as the lights went out over the Connecticut Standing Order.

On the other side of the great divide, in his Monticello aerie one long-interested student of Connecticut politics was uncorking his finest champagne. "What need we despair of after the resurrection of Connecticut to light and liberality?" Jefferson chortled to Adams, who by then had as little use for the Standing Order of Connecticut as his old opponent did. Celebrating "the last retreat of monkish darkness, bigotry, and abhorrence of those advances of the mind which had carried the other states a century ahead of them," Jefferson expressed his wonderment that

They seemed still to be exactly where their forefathers were when they schismatized from the covenant of works, and to consider as dangerous heresies all innovations, good or bad. I join you, therefore, in sincere congratulations that this den of the priesthood is at length broken up, and that a Protestant popedom is no longer to disgrace the American history and character.

A Voluntary Establishment of Religion

Monroe was able to enjoy the religious peace for one reason above all others: The New England Federalist clerics, so long dedicated to preserving the sanctity of state religion, lost their political franchise. Having abandoned their claim to the title of patriotism at the end of the War of 1812 and subsequently stripped of power in their Connecticut stronghold during Monroe's first year in office, their once vivid voices, dependably indicting any hint of presidential infidelity, were stilled.

Although no longer harassing the president, the New England clergy were anything but passive. With their establishment in ruins and the government in secular hands, the deposed lords of Connecticut wasted little time nursing their wounds. Having lost first the White House and then the State House, they set their sights higher: on the entire nation.

With the near-simultaneous deaths of "Pope" Timothy Dwight in 1817 and the Connecticut church establishment in 1818, New England's Standing Order had reached a fateful crossroads. By rededicating their smoldering moral ambition to educating ministers, disseminating Christian tracts, battling intemperance, combating the Masonic heresy, defending the Sabbath day, protesting Sunday mail delivery, and abolishing the curse of slavery, Beecher and a new generation of Congregational clergymen would arise to rekindle from old embers a "voluntary establishment" that, even more effectively than the old involuntary one, promised to transform American moral discourse.

Their new strategy for America's moral redemption would have lasting impact on American sacred politics. Voluntary associations had begun locally in pockets throughout the country years before, but emerged as a nationwide movement only after the War of 1812. Beginning in earnest in 1816, a bevy of national Christian associations leapt into action, their mission: to propagate the gospel and save the nation's soul, one Christian at a time. This radical change in mission, which would democratize the old religious establishment in keeping with a nationwide trend that before they had done everything in their power to buck, can be epitomized in the labors of a single preacher, Beecher himself. Rather than waste energy on Monroe's lack of faith, Beecher looked beyond Washington to redeem America.

Today Beecher is best remembered as a father. His daughter Harriet Beecher Stowe grew up to write *Uncle Tom's Cabin,* and his son Henry Ward Beecher became the nineteenth century's most charismatic liberal preacher. Yet in his own time, Beecher wielded great influence, becoming the principal Congregationalist broker for a new grassroots, morally driven national Christian movement. He took Dwight's dream of the Kingdom of Heaven on earth, hinted at in the gentle Millenarianism of "Greenfield Hill," and forged it into a practical Christian vision for establishing a "Benevolent Empire," first in America and then throughout the world. Beecher's Benevolent Empire was the Christian counterpart to Jefferson's Empire of Liberty, both visions contributing to the emergence of American Manifest Destiny. The two empires coalesce (although Jefferson would never concede this) in another sense as well. In his ideal of "Godly Government," Beecher transmuted Dwight's "Godly Federalism" into something akin to "Godly Democracy."

In the disestablishment of the Congregational Church in Connecticut, Beecher divined a hidden blessing. Disestablishment was "the best thing that ever happened to the State of Connecticut," he soon believed. "It cut the churches loose from dependence on state support. It threw them wholly on their own resources and on God." Far from losing influence, the clergy prospered. "The fact is, they have gained," Beecher allowed. "By voluntary efforts, societies, missions, and revivals, they exert a deeper influence than ever they could by queues and shoe buckles and cocked hats and gold-headed canes."

At the outset of Monroe's presidency, Beecher put a benchmark on his movement's success. "The prevalence of pious, intelligent, enterprising ministers through the nation at the ratio of one [to] a thousand," he calculated, "would establish schools, and academies, and colleges, and habits, and institutions of homogeneous influence." In addition to expanding the Christian commitment to ministerial education, the linchpin of this campaign was the voluntary association, which Beecher described as "a sort of disciplined moral militia." During the course of Monroe's presidency, with most of the major organizations founded between 1816 and 1824, charitable and tract societies sprang up like wildflowers to color the nation's discourse.

American voluntary associations—self-created societies, if you will—began as local Bible, social service, temperance, tract, abolition, and Sunday school societies, usually under the sponsorship of a ministerial association. As such, they dotted New England and most major American cities by the outset of the War of 1812. Even as the war united the nation, the spirit of union that followed America's victory, coupled with the collapse of Christian federalism and the channeling of Christian energy into constructive moral channels, nationalized Christian voluntarism, which took on a less provincial, more ecumenical flavor. All the old established churches pitched in. Bishop William White, for example, cofounded America's first Sunday school association with Dr. Benjamin Rush as early as 1790, but the movement only took off on the postwar wings of the Second Great Awakening's second phase, when national voluntary associations became the order of the day in religious missionary circles. White established the first Episcopal Sunday School in 1814, and the movement went national shortly thereafter.

It is no surprise that many of the nation's most influential religious voluntary organizations emerged in New England immediately following the War of 1812 and contemporaneous with the collapse of the Connecticut Standing Order. "A complete remedy to a political disease is seldom found until something like a crisis occurs," Monroe keenly observed. The crisis that brought down the orthodox party in Connecticut and clipped its wings elsewhere throughout New England gave new vigor to the wounded Christian establishment. The year 1816 saw the birth of the American Bible Society (with Elias Boudinot its first president and John Jay its second) and the American Education Society (to supply clergy sufficient to blanket the country in line with Beecher's plan). Soon the American Temperance Society, the American Tract Society, and dozens of other self-created national reform and evangelical groups arose to further Beecher's dream of a voluntary establishment to replace the governmentally sanctioned ones. On leaving Congress, the Reverend Manasseh Cutler, whom we last observed fulminating against Jefferson's religious posturing, served as president of the "Bible Society of Salem," an evangelical instrument established to distribute Bibles to the poor at home and to missions overseas.

American voluntarism also prompted a shift in the establishment's view of democracy. Most members of the Democratic-Republican Party were not literally "democrats," advocating direct participatory governance. But even representative democracy discomfited the authoritarian Christians who had long held sway in New England. "I consider Unitarianism as the democracy of Christianity," Jedidiah Morse said with explicit savagery. To most Unitarians, who were no less fiercely antidemocratic, anti-French, and anti-atheistic than he, his careful choice of epithets constituted the most unconscionable slur imaginable. Yet, lifted by the populist tide of the Second Great Awakening, by the time of his death even Morse was prepared to admit that democratic Christian was not an oxymoron.

However much it changed the complexion of national sacred politics, the end of the War of 1812 did not bring theological peace to New England. In fact, the breakdown of a united front to defend social order against Jacobin infestation freed theological adversaries to attend to their religious differences. The Standing Order of Massachusetts in particular was rent by internecine strife. Culturally compatible Congregationalists and Unitarians split asunder on the fine points of Christology, taking their battles into the courts, with the more conservative church bodies (made up of active communicants) splitting from the increasingly liberal parishes. Most judges in Massachusetts were Unitarian, so the parishes tended to win possession of the meeting houses and, more important, the church silver. Because of this division, you will find at least two white clapboard churches on most every small New England town green. Writing to a New Hampshire congressman who sent him pamphlets relating to the much-published debate, Jefferson lauded the Unitarians, if faintly, for continuing the "half-reformation" of Christianity.

Jefferson cheered the Unitarians on for a more pressing reason: If successful, they might put the brakes on Lyman Beecher's resurgent Puritanism, which Jefferson disdained no less than he did its establishmentarian predecessor. Pondering the shift in the Congregational Church's strategy, Jefferson found Beecher's formula for converting the nation at once threatening and presumptuous. "[New England] is now looking to the fleshpots of the South and aiming at foothold there by their missionary teachers," he sardonically groused. "They have lately come forward boldly with their plan to establish *a qualified religious instructor* over every thousand souls in the US and they seem to consider none as qualified but their own sect." Quoting Beecher, Jefferson attentively beamed in on the strategy underlying this new approach to religious politics: "'newspapers, tracts, magazines, must be employed; the press be made to groan, & every pulpit in the land to sound its trumpet long and loud—a more homogeneous (i.e. new England) character must be produced thro' the nation.' That section then of our union, having lost its political influence by disloyalty to its country, is now to recover it under the mask of religion."

Jefferson was not the only ex-president to scorn the new Congregational missionary efforts. Now squarely on the same religious page with his old political foe, John Adams mistrusted his Christian neighbors' motivations no less profoundly. "We have now, it seems a National Bible Society to propagate King James's Bible through all nations," he winked to Jefferson early in their renewed correspondence. "Would it not be better to apply these pious subscriptions to purify Christendom from the corruptions of Christianity, than to propagate these corruptions in Europe, Asia, Africa and America." When Jedidiah Morse attempted to enlist him to defend orthodoxy against the Unitarians, Adams bluntly expressed his preference for the distaff side of the faith. Not that he would enter the fray. Adams found the Protestant penchant for infighting odious.

Jefferson's unwillingness to applaud the democratization of organized Christendom arose from a different set of concerns. When it came right down to it, he didn't approve of organized religion in any save its most innocuous form. "I acknowledge the right of voluntary associations for laudable purposes and in moderate numbers," he said near the close of his life.

> I acknowledge too the expediency, for revolutionary purposes, of general associations coextensive with the nation. But where as in our case, no abuses call for revolution, voluntary associations so extensive as to grapple with and control the government, should such be or become their purpose, are dangerous machines, and should be frowned down in every regulated government.

In his old age, like Washington before him, Jefferson was ready to bring down the hammer on all self-created societies that did not advance his vision for America's future.

Whether driven by religious (Adams) or political (Jefferson) scruples, Adams's and Jefferson's distaste for Beecher's voluntary establishment would have been all but lost on Monroe. This fact accounts, in some measure, at least, for his remarkable success as a political healer. He didn't obsess about the clergy in the way that his predecessors had. As long as the church was not imposing its theological strictures on government, Monroe welcomed its activities as a stabilizing force in society. In return, not recognizing in him an enemy, Christians of all denominations embraced their president as a friend.

Of yet greater significance to the new tone marking the country's sacred discourse was the changed attitude on display among America's Christian activists. In closer synch with republican doctrine, New England's new voluntary establishment was gradually abandoning its fixation on aristocracy, deference, and a Christian federal authority. Instead, it actively engaged the people in a shared, participatory campaign for moral renewal. One offshoot of this redirection was that the most secular president to date was himself free to operate on behalf of all Americans, irrespective of faith, without engendering the animus of Christians manifestly more devout than he.

"The *Royal* Family"

After touring New England, President Monroe settled down in Washington, where the symbolism of his old-style leadership bolstered a growing confidence that the executive ship was steady as she goes. Monroe's conservative personal style tempered and refined the image of the White House, whose gilded fixtures and functions cast a formal, retro aura. The first lady played a central role in this makeover. In 1786, Congressman Monroe, then twenty-eight, had courted and won the hand of the astonishingly beautiful Elizabeth Kortwright, a seventeen-year-old New York social butterfly of refined tastes. When she announced her engagement, her friends expressed bewilderment that she had not done better by herself. With Mrs. Monroe's elite manner, desire for privacy, and nostalgia for European court pageantry setting the tone, public entertainments at the White House reverted from the pell-mell of the Dolley Madison days to formal levees reminiscent of Washington's time. The result was a combination of French trappings and British sobriety, each with a regal accent.

Yet, not all was quiet on the eastern front. Loose public manners in the nation's capital remained a target for moralistic clucking. "There is a great deal of gayety, splendor, and as I think, extravagance in the manners and habits of the city," Judge Joseph Story, a very proper Bostonian, sniffed disapprovingly. "The old notions of republican simplicity [of the black cockade variety] are fast wearing away, and the public taste becomes more and more gratified with public amusements and parades. Mr. Monroe, however," Story was careful to add, "still retains his plain and gentle manners; and is in every respect a very estimable man." As Story's observation suggests, the social whirl in the nation's capital may have remained under suspicion, but a modicum of order had been restored to the White House.

Although marred by the inevitable crush of voyeurs and favor seekers, Wednesday evenings at the White House again had an elevated air about them. The Monroes modeled their White House on the Presidential Mansion of Washington's day, sponsoring a symbolic break with the Republican past that could not help but further mollify Federalist skeptics. The president posted red-breasted, smartly decorated Marines at the White House gates, even as his first lady, Elizabeth, outfitted a small company of black retainers in evening formal wear to serve her husband's guests crystal chutes of French champagne off sterling silver platters. Unlike Adams, almost no one branded Monroe a "monocrat" for introducing such pomp to American state hospitality. For one thing, the clientele, from frontiersmen in deerskin and spurs to perfumed merchants, was decidedly more mixed than in Washington's day. For another, Monroe was perhaps the least regal politician in America. Yet, singling out a tiara-crowned Mrs. Monroe for special praise, one visiting baron perceived similarities between the American "court" and those he frequented in Europe. First lady in waiting, Louisa Adams, praised her predecessor for dressing always "in the highest style of fashion and [moving] not like a queen, for that is an unpardonable word in this country, but like a goddess."

Federalist senator David Daggett of Connecticut was enthralled by the magnificent face-lift the White House had received in rising from the ashes of war. Daggett is best remembered for his vicious bombardment of Monroe's Republican predecessors. In his 1799 Independence Day address, he dismissed the entire Enlightenment within the compass of a brilliant twelve-word title: "Sun Beams May Be Extracted from Cucumbers, but the Process Is Tedious." On dining with Monroe, however, he declared the table "splendid enough for any *Republic*. The plates are of beautiful French china, with the American coat of arms in the centre. The *plateau* (I believe they call it) is magnificent beyond anything I ever witnessed."

The company around the table was less scintillating. The unreconstructed Republican William Rives was so depressed after one memorably dull White House dinner that he included in the compass of his scorn every aspect of the evening, including the *plateau* (a long, mirrored centerpiece, replete with candles and flowers) that Daggett had found so "magnificent." "It is a mere ornamental expletive," Rives huffed, "intended to fill up vacant space, of which there is an abundance on the President's table."

One evening Senator Rives reported a rare public sighting of "the President with the *royal* family" at the Unitarian church for the "miserable" dedication of a new organ, featuring a choral ensemble about which "the best that can be said...is that it was a *fit accompaniment.*" Beyond its rare jab at royalty, this anecdote is precious to a religious historian, indeed almost unique, for catching Monroe in a pew.

Two years after his progress through New England, President Monroe took his pacific show on the road again. On his second tour of the nation—the United States had doubled in girth and number over the past twenty years—he turned southward, with the same admirable effect. During his tour of the southern states, among those the president honored for a lifetime of public service was Federalist presidential standard-bearer Charles C. Pinckney, who had tilted so haplessly against Jefferson and Madison. Monroe believed that the president "ought not to be the head of a party, but of the nation itself." Following in his footsteps without carrying the chip on his shoulder that gave a passive-aggressive edge to Jefferson's protestation that "We are all republicans, all federalists," Monroe's strategy for achieving national unity was to beguile the Federalist remnant "into the republican fold as quickly as possible." Lacking Jefferson's religious intolerance, he was well suited to this task.

Unlike his predecessors, Monroe had few clerical detractors. Yet, his presidential concourse with clergymen is almost nonexistent. One minister, the Reverend Horace Holley, spent a private evening with President and Mrs. Monroe, an event made memorable for being related in such lavish detail in a fifteen-page letter home.

When in Washington, Holley was the first Unitarian clergyman to preach in the Hall of Representatives. He paid visits to Secretary of State John Quincy Adams and Congressman Henry Clay, and then dropped by the White House in the company of Senator Harrison Gray Otis of Massachusetts. Monroe welcomed the two men with his characteristic kindness, courtesy, and simplicity, Holley reports. In a very different time not so long before, on completing his mournful journey from Hartford to an exultant nation's capital, Senator Otis had refused to demean himself by visiting "the pigmy" in the White House. Four years later, he doubtless was tickled pink to win a private interview for Mr. Holley and himself with Madison's successor. Senator Otis's change in mood marks a sea change in American sacred politics.

CONSIDERATIONS OF
HUMANITY

Still one great clime, in full and free defiance,
Yet rears her crest, unconquered and sublime,
Above the far Atlantic.

—LORD BYRON, "THE AMERICAN REPUBLIC"

UNLIKE HIS predecessors, President Monroe was neither
hated nor beloved. Instead he was almost uniformly respected, bringing honor to the presidency. As for the churches, that
the pulpit grew silent on the question of presidential infidelity and
Christian governance by no means lessened its role in shaping
the nation's moral discourse. Especially on the question of slavery,
among the most eloquent calls for abolition were issued by preachers. The church's moral voice in the great debates of the time would
grow to a crescendo by the eve of the Civil War.

Monroe's modest yet steadying contribution to the commonweal
is illustrated by the two major challenges of his tenure: the Missouri
controversy (whether Missouri would enter the Union slave or free);
and the international threat posed by the "Holy Alliance," leading to
the formulation of the Monroe Doctrine. His first moral challenge,
however, was the ongoing plight of America's Indians.

President Monroe was a pragmatist, not a purist. The one exception to his otherwise pristinely secular White House was his Indian
affairs policy, which was marked by a sharp (yet still paltry) increase
in federal aid to religious charitable missions. In his first annual

message to Congress, hinting at the notion of Manifest Destiny, the president pronounced the westward march of civilized progress (which "the rights of nature demand and nothing can prevent") inevitable. "It is our duty," he added as a point of conscience, "to make new efforts for the preservation, improvement, and civilization of the native inhabitants." This moral afterthought elicited a barbed note from Madison, who found critiquing his successor's Indian policy easier than articulating one of his own. Madison challenged "the latitude of the principle on which the right of a civilized people is asserted over the lands of a savage one." The Congress was more blunt and considerably less philosophical in their reply to the president's address. "The sons of the forest should be moralized or exterminated," read a committee report on the subject, together with the recommendation that the president explore the former option before exercising the latter.

A quick recap of American Indian policy reveals a continuous failure of moral imagination. Washington's initial view, before he became president, was rooted in heartless opportunism. Rather than "driving the wild beast of the forest which will return as soon as the pursuit is at an end and fall perhaps on those that are left there," he recommended proceeding with tact and patience, confident that "the gradual extension of our settlement will as certainly cause the Savage as the wolf to retire; both being beasts of prey tho' they differ in shape." By the time he became president, Washington's views were more tempered. He argued that treaty obligations must be upheld and vigilante violence curbed. Washington was hesitant about the value of Indian missionary activity, however, including missionary schools, which he perceived as dividing the population not redeeming it. Rather than convert the Indians, he proposed instead that we "convince them that we are just and to show them that a proper and friendly intercourse with us would be for our mutual advantage." The $1,500 per year appropriated during his tenure could not, under executive order, be employed for evangelical purposes, only to teach Indians who had already converted to Christianity. Washington was the first of several presidents to advance Jefferson's pet solution to the "Indian problem" (braves planting and reaping and squaws spinning), but this dream held little purchase on reality. Washington's Indian policy, predicated on the noble proposition that America's original residents could expect to "possess the lands to which they are entitled by some known and fixed principles," was an abject failure.

Adams viewed Indians as, at best, "troublesome allies," helpful in thwarting British encroachments on the American frontier. Although "they conduct their wars so entirely without faith and humanity," their "cruel, bloody disposition against any enemy whatsoever," he said, made them useful auxiliaries against the British. Adams's Secretary of State, Timothy Pickering, was more alert to Native American well-being. He found the efforts of Quaker missionaries particularly promising. "Their object is not to teach peculiar doctrines," Pickering noted admiringly, "but useful practices, to instruct the Indians in husbandry and the plain mechanical arts and manufacturers directly connected with it."

If Adams paid the Indians almost no constructive mind, Jefferson, by temporizing on Native American policy throughout his years in office, was almost as ineffectual. Jefferson's stated goal was to "gradually circumscribe" the tribes, limiting their territory to that which they could effectively manage and ultimately cultivate. It proved instead a gradual disaster. Most Indians had no interest in being domesticated. "Indian men regard labor as degrading, and fit only for women and slaves," John Jay observed, adding insightfully, "Prejudices associated with a sense of honor are not easily overcome." When braves did consent to cultivate the land and thereby approach the civilized state that Jefferson believed would guarantee their survival, the land they cultivated became more attractive to their pioneer neighbors, increasing the pressure for tighter circumscription and ultimate displacement. Typical of national policy during the Jefferson years, future president William Henry Harrison, military governor of Indiana, dedicated his territorial administration to snookering local chiefs out of their lands in exchange for government wampum and under-the-table booze.

Human greed powered Indian and settler alike. In an 1803 letter to Governor Harrison, Jefferson evinced few qualms about playing the Native Americans like fish to the lure. "To promote this disposition to exchange lands, which they have to spare and we want, we shall push our trading houses and be glad to see the good and influential individuals among them in debt, because we observe that when these debts get beyond what the individuals can pay, they become willing to lop them off by a cession of lands." At the same time, Jefferson's campaign to urge the tribal leaders to desist from internecine warfare irked Governor Harrison. "Tranquility between the neighboring tribes will always be a sure indication of war against us," Harrison said.

The upsurge in the displacement of Native Americans under Jefferson's watch mars the illusion that his personal fancy for Native Americans appreciably softened his hard-headed policy to maximize available arable land for the national march westward. Jefferson cared about the American Indian abstractly, not with the passion that missionaries carried with them into the frontier, both in their quest to save souls and also in their larger human sympathy. Disdaining the Indians' "sanctimonious reverence for the custom of their ancestors," he forgot his Saxon dream of natural liberty. Should they fail to accommodate themselves to the advance of civilization, he cautioned, they would simply disappear. "It is impossible not to look forward to distant times," Jefferson dreamed aloud to Monroe, "when our rapid multiplication will...cover the whole northern, if not the southern continent, with a people speaking the same language, governed in similar forms, and by similar laws; nor can we contemplate with satisfaction either blot or mixture on that surface." To this idyll of ethnic cleansing, the native population could impose no lasting impediment.

During Madison's presidency, an unprecedented opportunity for détente between the Indians and the government presented it-

self with the emergence of two remarkable Native American leaders. Tecumseh and his charismatic brother, best known simply as
the Prophet, weaned several tribes from the bottle and induced
them to stop killing each other, promising steps toward the establishment of peace on the frontier. On paper, Tecumseh was Jefferson's dream come true. He enforced a strict ban on alcohol, bought
into Jefferson's proposal to cultivate the land, and promised that his
braves would put down their tomahawks and live in peace as long
as their basic human rights were not violated and the government
kept its word.

Preferring to divide and conquer the more pliant tribal leaders,
Harrison proceeded to undermine Tecumseh's authority. When the
Indian leader traveled south in 1811 to consolidate his confederacy,
Indiana's opportunistic governor turned to Washington for arms
and aid to disband the coalition by seizing Prophet's Town, its capital, which was located in the center of contested Indian territory.
Ignoring his commander in chief's express order, Madison's Secretary of War, William Eustis, authorized the first preemptive military
strike in U.S. history. Decades later, Harrison would broker his "triumph" at Tippecanoe into a campaign slogan ("Tippecanoe and
Tyler Too") and one month's tenure in the White House.

In his seventh annual message to Congress in 1815, Madison euphemistically confessed that Indian cruelty "had compelled us to
chastise into peace." Henry Adams apportioned the responsibility
more evenhandedly, concluding that "no one could doubt that after
provoking the Indian war, Americans ought to be prepared to wage
it with effect, and without complaint of its horrors."

Federal executive policy toward Native Americans provoked remarkably little religious political friction. Rhetorically at least, the
nation's leading secular and sacred authorities shared a common,
humanitarian mission: to incorporate America's first residents,
rather than destroy them. With Elias Boudinot and Jedidiah Morse
standing beside Jefferson and Madison, the church participated ea-
gerly, with no complaint from the state, in what today would be

called "faith-based initiatives," administered by the churches and funded by the Indian Affairs office, which was lodged in the War Department. Under Jefferson's watch, the government sanctioned denominational efforts to pacify and educate the Indians, occasionally building schools for this purpose. Jefferson believed that civilization should precede conversion, but was not averse to evangelization to temper Indian savagery. Until Monroe's Civilization Fund was established in 1819, upping the government ante, religious bodies received modest federal aid to help underwrite missions created to "civilize" (Jefferson's hope) and "Christianize" (Morse's and Boudinot's aim) the natives. Just how modest this support was cannot be exaggerated. On one occasion during Madison's presidency, Secretary Eustis authorized the purchase of six hoes, six axes, and two plows for one Cherokee mission.

The Christian and government missions dovetailed. Indians "who come to Christ and join the church," Moravian evangelist David Zeisberger said, "turn to agriculture and raising stock, keeping cattle, hogs and fowls." But for reasons beyond the control of most missionaries' kind hearts, this joint mission tragically and perhaps inevitably failed. Inexorable economic and cultural forces pressed the tide of removal from one temporary interior beachhead to the next; violence continued unabated; and the native populations dwindled toward threatened extinction.

President Monroe articulated his Indian policy more carefully in his second annual message, proposing policies of national guardianship designed to reverse the momentum toward extinction through increased governmental intervention in supporting Native American agriculture, assisting in the establishment of stable communities, and investing more heavily in education. Although representing a magnum leap in direct government aid, the modest $10,000 Congress set aside for Native American welfare was fixed in the budget at that level for years to come. The act establishing the government's Civilization Fund stipulated that the monies be invested "to employ capable persons of good moral character to instruct the

Indians in the mode of agriculture suited to their situation; and for teaching their children in reading, writing, and arithmetic, and performing such other duties as may be enjoined, according to such instructions and rules as the President may give and prescribe for the regulation of their conduct, in the discharge of their duties."

Awakening to the horror of threatened genocide, several Christian denominations had long been pressing for a more humane national policy toward America's native populations. "Considerations of humanity and benevolence, which have now great weight," drove his policy, Monroe said, and would invest it with "an augmented force." Religious missions were quick to take advantage of the new program. John Calhoun reported at the end of its first full year in operation that Cherokee, Choctaw, Wyandots, Seneca, and Shawnee tribes had participated in twenty-one programs sponsored by Baptist, Moravian, Congregational, and Presbyterian missions. Far more extensively than the handshake and blessing that summed up the tiny appropriations authorized by earlier administrations, this act marked the beginning of a concerted church-state partnership dedicated primarily to Native American education. In 1824, the final year of Monroe's presidency, of some $200,000 dedicated to this object, donated in large part by individuals and private foundations, approximately 6 percent of the total (almost $13,000) was appropriated under the auspices of the Civilization Fund, supporting twenty-one schools run by the Presbyterians, Methodists, Episcopalians, Roman Catholics, Baptists, and Congregational-based American Mission Board. In this singular, if not insignificant, respect (the government subcontracting religious groups to help implement its limited welfare program), Monroe's secular administration blurred the line between church and state.

In his second inaugural address, the president called for a further revision in national policy—no longer to negotiate with the Indians as if they were independent nations but to treat them as individuals (in other words, as U.S. citizens). With admirable bluntness, he confessed, "The distinction [being treated as independent nations] flattered their pride, retarded their improvement, and in many instances paved the way to their destruction." Henceforth, Monroe idealistically urged,

> Their sovereignty over vast territories should cease, in lieu of which the right of soil should be secured to each individual and his posterity in competent portions; and for the territory thus ceded by each tribe some reasonable equivalent should be granted, to be vested in permanent funds for the support of civil government over them and for the education of their children, for their instruction in the arts of husbandry, and to provide sustenance for them until they could provide it for themselves.

This earnest proposal, beset with all the difficulties one might encounter in transferring tropical fish from an aquarium to a terrarium, was politely ignored by Congress, and the final solution, deportation and subsequent near annihilation, loomed one step closer.

"A Fire-bell in the Night"

The moral dilemma posed by the nation's treatment of its native populations would be resolved by gradual default through the force of a terrible inertia. Concurrently a second consideration of humanity, the slavery dilemma, was rising to the top of America's moral agenda. In 1820, the country was split right down the middle, eleven slave states and eleven free. As the national boundary opened west, this balance and with it the fate of the Union teetered in jeopardy. With Missouri's petition for statehood on the table, President Monroe's modest gifts would be tested by a controversy that threatened to bankrupt the store of amity he so ably had accumulated during his first three years in office.

One new player in the debate over slavery was the American Colonization Society, a big-hearted, small-minded ecumenical organization that dedicated its moral energies to deporting slaves (and with them the slave problem itself) to Africa. The Colonization Society was one of the many voluntary associations to arise from the ashes of the defunct sacred-political establishment. Most of its founders were old Federalists. New Jersey Presbyterian minister and Princeton graduate Dr. Robert Finley came up with the idea. "I know this scheme is from God," Finley averred. Elias Boudinot's foster son, Elias Boudinot Caldwell, co-organized the effort in 1816, and many Federalist Christian clergymen bought into the dream. Among its strongest early advocates were Episcopal Bishop William White and future Bishop William Meade of Virginia. George Washington's nephew, Supreme Court Justice Bushrod Washington, was drafted to lend his ringing name as the society's first president, and Timothy Dwight served on one of its many Committees of Correspondence.

Rarely have so many well-intentioned people worked so hard to accomplish so little as did the good souls at the helm of the Colonization Society. In 1821, the society bartered for a tract of land near Cape Montserado on the African coast, offering a shipload of gunpowder, mirrors, pipes and tobacco, muskets, cookware, beads, and cotton in exchange for an African sanctuary. By 1830, some 1,500 liberated slaves had arrived to homestead Liberia. At the time, more than a thousand times that many souls languished in slavery in the land of the free, waiting, by the almost incomprehensible calculus of the society's otherwise sensible leaders, to join them. Even when offered liberty in exchange for banishment, many slaves balked. Few among them were as eager to leave America as their liberal southern masters and good-hearted northern pastors were to have them gone.

Madison had been boosting the idea of colonization since 1789, when he first suggested that such an asylum "might prove a great encouragement to manumission in the southern parts of the U.S. and even afford the best hope yet presented of an end to slavery." Just before leaving office, Madison met with Reverend Finley and signed on to his plan. Madison would spend the final years of his life as president of the Colonization Society and provided for its ongoing work with a $2,000 bequest in his will. Six years before his death, he swore his fidelity to any practicable scheme "for removing from our country the calamity of its black population." His successor in the White House embraced the same fantasy. Colonization was the silver bullet that would end slavery without bloodshed. President Monroe won plaudits from Colonization Society members for his efforts on their behalf, in recognition of which they christened the capital of Liberia Monrovia.

As the Colonization Society plodded earnestly along, the debate over slavery erupted west of the Mississippi, drawing an entire nation into its grip. In 1820, with Missouri and Maine banging on the statehood door, if both states should enter the Union as free states the perfect balance of a nation half slave, half free would be lost, placing southern political power and, with it, an otherwise serviceable national equilibrium, in jeopardy. Because it would tilt the political table to its advantage, the vigorous northern campaign to restrict slavery in Missouri struck President Monroe as a political ploy, which in part it surely was.

When the issue of Missouri statehood was first raised, the president turned to his predecessors for advice. Madison nodded in agreement that the northern representatives were seeking political gain under the cover of morality. Following the same train of thought around the bend, Jefferson foisted blame for the Missouri controversy on the disgraced Hartford Convention men, who, in his conspiratorial view, had risen from the dead to launch a new crusade to divide the union, fueling the northern animus toward slavery in order to revive their flagging political fortunes. Agonizing that New Englanders would somehow leverage slavery to "regain the ascendancy from which their sins had hurled them," he dismissed the entire debate over slavery in Missouri as "a mere party trick."

The Bible played an active if ambivalent role in adjudicating the moral questions slavery raised. In the years leading up to the Civil

War, North and South alike quoted the Bible to anoint their cause with Heavenly sanction. This phenomenon first emerged in force during the Missouri controversy. In *The Book and Slavery Irreconcilable*, George Bourne declared that "Every man who holds slaves and who pretends to be a Christian or a Republican is either an incurable idiot who cannot distinguish good from evil, or an obdurate sinner who resolutely defies every social, moral, and divine requisition." When preachers began denouncing slavery as unholy in Missouri camp meetings, the slaveholders answered, "God had made Negroes for slaves and white men for masters, or he would not suffer it to be so."

Once plantation owners began convincing themselves that slavery was not a sad fact of southern life, but instead a moral ornament, the Bible became their primary proof text. This newfound reliance on scripture received a cogent, if chilling, summation by William Smith of South Carolina on the Senate floor. "Christ came to fulfill the law not to destroy it," Senator Smith preached to his colleagues. "Mr. President, the Scriptures teach us that slavery was universally practiced among the holy fathers.... Christ himself gave a sanction to slavery. He admonished them to be obedient to the masters; and there is not a word in the whole of his life which forbids it."

Several protagonists in our tale played prominent roles in the Missouri debate. Sounding the opening bell in the crusade to keep the new state of Missouri free was old Presbyterian Elias Boudinot, as prominent in America's emergent voluntary association movement as he had been in Congress. Joining a group of local Quakers, Boudinot convened an antislavery caucus in Burlington, New Jersey, on August 30, 1819, the first such meeting in the United States. Out of this caucus arose a statewide convention held in Trenton that fall, which Boudinot also chaired. The gathering declared that it "would view with unspeakable pain and mortification any measure adopted by the *federal legislature* tending to extend and perpetuate slavery among us." Boudinot expressed confidence that God would back up these stirring words with heavenly deeds, bringing slavery to a swift and certain end. "For my own part," he averred, "I devoutly trust that He, who has carried us thro' six & seven troubles, will yet carry us thro' to the glory of His holy Name."

Among the last Connecticut Wits to wield a pen, Theodore Dwight, cried out that "The judgments of Heaven brood over a land cultivated by slaves." Describing any slave state or territory as "soil that is watered with tears and enriched by blood," he began editorializing against "the sin of slavery" in the *Connecticut Current* in early 1819, well before the Missouri question divided the nation. That November, he attended a meeting in New York that issued a proclamation stating its abhorrence of slavery in the very words he and his brother had once anathematized. The question, this moral caucus declared, was "whether, in this enlightened and philanthropic age, a mighty empire of slaves shall be permitted to be formed on the soil and under the sanction of Republican America, and admitted into her Union; or, whether that new empire is to be composed of men who shall have a *constitutional,* as well as natural, right, '*to life, liberty, and the pursuit of happiness.*'" From the outset of the national debate over slavery, Jefferson's gospel of Liberty sang out from the heart of New England with new moral force and conviction, touted, astonishingly enough, by his old political foes.

Whether Jefferson knew that an abolitionist memorial had been received at the Connecticut statehouse in Hartford quoting the Declaration of Independence and proclaiming that "the illustrious authors of that document never contemplated the farther extension of slavery in these United States" is an intriguing but unanswerable question. It certainly could not have escaped his notice that northern antislavery crusaders were invoking his "national covenant" that "all men are created equal" with nettlesome regularity in their campaign to frustrate slavery's westward march. Boudinot, too, in a letter "read in the North with a feeling akin to veneration," reminded his fellow citizens that the United States of America was founded

on the proposition that "all men are created equal." The employment of sacred liberty as a moral touchstone was a novelty for the
old Federalists, many of whom, until recently, had cited the Declaration of Independence, even on the Fourth of July, only to contest
its assumptions. The battle against slavery inspired divine order's
defenders to seize the flag of Jefferson's Empire, make it their own,
and plant it on higher moral ground.

As the apostles of order were rediscovering liberty's moral allure,
liberty's protectors were contriving by every means possible to ex-
tricate themselves from the letter of their creed. When the freedom
of slaves was at issue, the principle of sacred liberty supplied its
most devout champions with a flexible standard. Adapting quickly
to the southern climate as president of the University of South Carolina, longtime slavery opponent Thomas Cooper reversed course
and defended the practice as an expedient that should not be tam-
pered with by legislation that could limit states' rights. Invoking
the law of nature to argue that Negro protestation of their own
bondage was fatuous, he penned an embarrassing series of articles
for a Philadelphia gazette, claiming, among other things, that history, in its every chapter, confirmed that slavery was, self-evidently,
as natural as sunlight.

President Monroe didn't solicit John Adams's counsel, but
Adams's angst over the future of the Union was no less profound
than his successor's panic. Recognizing how easily biblical sanction
could be adduced to defend slavery, he snorted dismissively, "The
Bible itself has not authority sufficient in these days to reconcile
Negro slavery to reason, justice & humanity." Where Adams differed from his Virginia successors is that they believed violence
would follow upon abolition, whereas he, in his heart of hearts,
foresaw bloodshed if slavery were *not* abolished. "I shudder when I
think of the calamities which slavery is likely to produce in this
country," Adams told his daughter-in-law, Louisa. "You would
think me mad if I were to describe my anticipations. If the gangrene

is not stopped, I can see nothing but insurrections of the blacks against the whites and massacres by the whites in their turn of the blacks."

Ignoring the yelps of his southern allies, Monroe refused to veto the legislation that ended the Missouri controversy, Henry Clay's eventual compromise. Clay's package deal admitted Missouri as a slave state, Maine as a free one, and then drew a line from Missouri's southern border westward, above which slavery would be banned. Although the Missouri Compromise postponed the horrors of civil war for four tortured decades, one visionary gazed into the nation's future. "This momentous question, like a fire-bell in the night, awakened and filled me with terror," the irrepressibly lyrical Jefferson exclaimed. "I considered it at once as the knell of the Union. It is hushed, indeed, for the moment. But this is a reprieve only, not a final sentence." And then he, too, drifted back to sleep.

"A Hemisphere of Freedom"

Summing up Monroe's presidency, John Quincy Adams called tranquility "the pole-star of his policy." This star exercised a magnetic pull on the electorate. In his campaign for reelection, Monroe carried both Massachusetts and Connecticut by comfortable margins. Out of 232 electors only 13 were Federalists, all of whom voted for Monroe. Old John Adams, serving as a Massachusetts elector, sat among them. If his son had not received a protest ballot from the increasingly erratic William Plumer of New Hampshire, Monroe would have repeated George Washington's unique feat by sweeping the entire Electoral College. His electoral landslide was all the more amazing in that it wasn't buoyed by national prosperity. A year before election day, the cotton and land booms had gone bust and the nation was plunged into a depression. Yet the president won reelection by virtual acclamation. Clearly, the American citizenry felt kindly toward "good, old Col. Monroe." As election day approached,

John Adams insightfully sensed "an effervescence among mankind at present, which is portentous of changes in religion and government—I hope for the better in both."

Unlike most two-term presidents, Monroe's second term didn't constitute a slap in the face of his first. It witnessed, in fact, his one historic triumph, the Monroe Doctrine of 1823, by which America's secular government answered the threat of Christian imperialism.

The Holy Alliance first surfaced in 1815 on the Plain of Vertus near Chalon, France, where Tsar Alexander of Russia staged a magnificent religious festival. Dozens of chanting priests lifted the host over seven altars, stirring the victorious troops into a patriotic religious frenzy and so impressing the king of Prussia and emperor of Austria that soon thereafter they joined forces with the tsar in a modern-day crusade. Its stated object was "to manifest before the whole universe their unshakable determination to take as their sole guide, both in the administration of their respecting states and in their political relations with other governments, the precepts of religion, namely the rules of justice, Christian charity, and peace." In forging the Holy Alliance, Tsar Alexander vowed to bind their united people in spirit as "members of the same Christian nation." Pledging their kingdoms to fulfill "the duties which the Divine Savior has taught to mankind," and to guide their concerted policies by "the sublime truths which the Holy Religion of our Savior teaches," the three kings set out to build an international Christian Coalition. Within months, the king of the Netherlands had joined his scepter to theirs. Christian enthusiasts in New England were all aglow about the sacred mission. At its founding meeting in 1816, the Massachusetts Peace Society sent Tsar Alexander official greetings, recalling "to the attention of His Imperial Majesty that the Society was founded in the very week in which the Holy League of the three sovereigns was announced...to disseminate the very principles avowed in the wonderful Alliance."

Jefferson and the Sultan of Turkey were decidedly less beguiled, the latter pronouncing the Holy Alliance a "jihad" against Islam, the former recognizing that its divine lance was pointed straight at the heart of liberty. Jefferson saw the alliance for what it was, a cabal of "reactionary sovereigns who sought to enforce an anti-republican, counterrevolutionary settlement in Europe."

With republican movements fermenting in Greece, Italy, Portugal, and Spain, the Holy Alliance pledged its Christian troth to defend the divine right of kings. By 1823, France was in league. Lafayette bemoaned "the bed of lies which the *Sainte Alliance* are holding over the European world." Through France's agency, the Alliance restored Spain's King Ferdinand to the throne in 1823. Chateaubriand, the French foreign minister, then floated the notion of a restorationist movement in the Western Hemisphere, extending the mission field of the Holy Alliance to America's backyard.

For contrasting reasons, the specter of a Christian royalist crusade set off alarm bells both in the Monroe White House and in England, which viewed the alliance as a threat to its sovereignty over the seas. A British bid to join forces with America in protecting the South American states from its designs was the presenting cause for Monroe's greatest triumph. As was his wont, the deferential, often legitimately puzzled president turned to his predecessors for advice. Noting that "the state of Europe & our relation to it is pretty much the same as it was in the commencement of the French revolution," to Jefferson he wondered aloud, "Can we, in any form, take a bolder attitude in regard to it, in favor of liberty, than we then did? Can we afford greater aid to that cause, by assuming any such attitude, than we now do, by the form of our example? These are subjects on which I should be glad to have your sentiments."

In Monticello, Monroe's question elicited a eureka. Hidden at the heart of Monroe's dilemma Jefferson recognized "the most momentous [opportunity] which has been ever offered to my contemplations since that of Independence. That made us a nation," he lectured his old pupil. "This sets our compass and points the course which we are to steer thro' the ocean of time." Jefferson proceeded to spell out what, in essence, would become known as the

Monroe Doctrine. "Our first and fundamental maxim should be never to entangle ourselves in the broils of Europe," he said, "our second never to suffer Europe to intermeddle with Cis-Atlantic [Western Hemisphere] affairs." More than two decades earlier, in his first inaugural address, Jefferson had memorably warned against "entangling alliances," while at the same time calling for coming generations to ignite liberty's sacred fire. What a monumental opportunity this new alignment of diplomatic stars represented—the chance to draw a striking geopolitical contrast between the Christian monarchies of Europe ("a domicile of despotism") and the free republics of America ("a hemisphere of freedom"). Ultimately the West could have a system of her own, charting the map of the future, while Europe would remain fatefully mired in the past.

This foreign policy breakthrough appeared at an opportune moment in American domestic politics. None other than Jedidiah Morse, in the 1819 revision of his *American Universal Geography,* found something good to say about republican revolutions in the hemisphere, welcoming them as a Protestant mission opportunity. Morse retained his suspicions about democracy, carping that it placed a premium on "mere numbers" over "intelligence and worth," but he had long since removed it from Satan's presumed sponsorship. By the time of his death in 1826, courtesy of his spirited involvement in Christian voluntary associations, Morse's antidemocratic animus had all but disappeared.

After weeks of consultation and fine-tuning, Monroe's final statement of policy, spelled out in an address to Congress, followed the blueprint of Jefferson's original exultant letter—noninterference in Europe and defense of liberty in the Americas. Most historians credit neither Jefferson nor Monroe but John Quincy Adams for the Monroe Doctrine. Certainly it was a collaborative effort. Yet Adams's own father, never shy to toot his son's horn, gave full honors to the president. "Mr. Monroe has got the universal character among all our common people of 'a very smart man,'" John Adams told Jefferson. "And verily I am of the same mind. I know not another who could have executed so great a plan so cleverly."

John Quincy Adams predicted that the Monroe administration would go down in history as "the golden age of this republic." Both men would have to settle for "the silver age," eight years of peace ushering in a period of unprecedented economic expansion. That, however, is not what the Monroe Doctrine was about. However complex its motivations, it was above all a statement of national moral principle, founded on the dual doctrine of nonintervention overseas and a firm commitment to the revolutionary ideals of independence and liberty in the Americas. Far from being the United States's first gesture toward imperialism, by honoring the nation's republican legacy the Monroe Doctrine put the United States publicly on record *against* imperialism and in favor of self-determination.

The American Republic had come into being in rebellion against the sway of Christian Empire. In reprise, the Monroe Doctrine arose to protect self-determination in the Western Hemisphere against Christian imperialist encroachment. It demonstrated to the people of the Americas as well as to the enemies of the United States that the U.S. government, without invoking Christ or God, could take a vigorous moral stand against overt Christian imperialism by invoking and defending the nation's founding principle of liberty for all.

The leaders of the Holy Alliance understood Monroe's intentions and had a private fit of pique. Metternich muttered that the Monroe Doctrine constituted nothing less than "a new act of revolt, more unprovoked, fully audacious, and no less dangerous" than the American Revolution itself. At home the president received not extravagant but certainly polite kudos all around. Typical of the reaction in Congress, Kentucky senator John Crittenden said of his message, "It has given us a more dignified and heroic attitude. It has made us the protector of the free governments of South America and arrayed us boldly against any attempts on the part of the Holy

Alliance to extend to this hemisphere that despotism and slavery which it has fastened on Europe."

In the face of Monroe's frontal assault, the Holy Alliance quickly lost its allure for nostalgic New England theocrats, who initially had welcomed its promise of Christian governance. When it refused to assist Greece in her crusade against the Turkish infidel in the early 1820s, whatever role the Holy Alliance might imaginably have played in salvation history—some true believers deemed the fall of Islamic Turkey essential to God's master plan—went up in smoke.

"For a Term of Eight Years, Strengthening His Country"

One student of his presidency describes Monroe as being almost unique among presidents, public men, or rulers of any kind for having an "easy conscience." In this regard, Monroe emulated his illustrious predecessor, George Washington. Both men conformed the art of appearances to the dictates of moral behavior and demands of public virtue so exactly that they had little difficulty sleeping well. In John Quincy Adams's elegant summation, Monroe's was "a mind anxious and unwearied in the pursuit of truth and right, patient of inquiry, patient of contradiction, courteous even in the collision of sentiment, sound in its ultimate judgments, and firm in its final conclusions."

In 1825, the Monroes retired to Oak Hill in Albemarle County, Virginia, to the home Jefferson had designed for them during Monroe's second term. The major project of his final years was his unfinished book, *The People, the Sovereigns*. Infused with republican principle, yet respectful of the mediating role to be played by government, in it he defines two competing forms of sovereignty: "the people and them only" and "an individual or the few." As anchor for the Republican dynasty, not surprisingly Monroe endorsed government by the people, but he did so in classic republican, not newfangled democratic fashion. In Monroe's book, the people's sovereign power is brokered by governing representatives, whose tempering influence mitigates against tyrannical dangers implicit in the popular will. Insisting that populism would invite first anarchy and then tyranny, Monroe formulated a commonsense argument for republican democracy. Celebrating democracy while cautioning against its intrinsic impulse to degenerate, he argued (given the force of human passions) that without the benign direction of governmental authority "there can be no order in society." The balance Monroe struck between a sovereign people (endowed with liberty and equality) and a directing governmental authority (charged with maintaining order) perfectly captured the American ideal of *E pluribus unum*.

Like the man himself, Monroe's unpublished book is nothing if not prosaic. "What then is man?" he asked. "Naturalists give him the highest grade among created beings, and our religion makes his soul immortal. Still he is in a great measure the creature of circumstances. His natural endowments, his passions and principles, are always the same, but these are essentially controlled by moral causes; by the state in which he is, and in consequence in which the society is, of which he is a member." With these lumbering words, Monroe dismissed every *a priori* philosophical and theological assumption that might impose itself as an ideal for society. Those who contrive governments either "by reference to sacred history" or on "visionary and fanciful speculations" are both wrong, Monroe argued. They do violence to humankind's unfolding potential to create a better world by adopting and then adapting a system of governance through trial and error that would at once enhance human rights and temper human wrongs.

Sounding more like Adams than Jefferson, Monroe concluded that "To commit to the unlettered, ignorant, and vicious, trust whose duties require the highest talents and greatest virtue, would be to sacrifice the interests of the community, to abandon all respect for principle or character." Yet unlike Adams, Monroe never forgot the abiding reason why order must be established in the first place:

to secure and foster the people's liberty. Grown suspicious of the rhetorical drumbeat driving the march toward either a Commonwealth of God or an Empire for Liberty, he emerges in his final, instantly forgotten work as a pure American pragmatist. In his unadorned yet studied opinion, the nation would advance precisely to the extent that neither order nor liberty was permitted to vanquish the other.

As a political tract, Monroe's *The People, the Sovereigns* more closely anticipates emergent Whig Party doctrine than it does the popular enthusiasm of Jacksonian democracy. Certainly he harbored a deeper suspicion of the people's untutored civic genius than Jefferson did. His eyewitness experience of the tragic transmutation of democratic idealism into tyranny during the latter days of the French Revolution immunized him against sentimentalizing the people's innate liberty and equality into a mandate for unmediated power. Yet unlike Adams (and Washington near the close of his presidency), Monroe's dedication to popular sovereignty never wavered. His predicate was republican to the core: "All men are by nature equally free," he wrote. "Their Creator made them so, and the inequalities which have grown up among them, and the governments which have been established over them, founded on other principles, have proceeded from other causes, by which their natural rights have been subverted."

After both men's presidencies were fading from popular memory, John Quincy Adams, who couldn't help but respect this man whose intellect paled into insignificance when placed beside his own, honored Monroe's years in the White House with seemingly extravagant yet due praise:

> There behold him for a term of eight years, strengthening his country for defense by a system of combined fortifications, military and naval, sustaining her rights, her dignity and honor abroad; soothing her dissension, and conciliating her acerbities at home; controlling by a firm though peaceful policy the hostile spirit of the

European Alliance against Republican south [America] from the stipulated acknowledgement of Spain....thus strengthening and consolidating the federative edifice of his country's union, till he was entitled to say, like Augustus Caesar of his imperial city, that he had found her built of brick and left her constructed of marble.

If Monroe taught his contemporaries anything, it was *never un-derestimate an overachiever.* With his good-hearted nature, he comforted a Republic in need of healing. His oblique gift to American Christianity was no less significant. Monroe's Era of Good Feelings rode out a depression and national schism over slavery, leading to as complete a mandate as any president since has received at the outset of his second term. He succeeded, in part, because the executive branch of government and the nation's religious constituencies made a peace they both honored. During his tenure, religious politics, so recently whirling at a demonic pitch, took a refreshingly Christian turn.

On reflection, given the ferocity of the combatants in the decades-long contest to redeem the government and save the nation's soul during the early years of the Republic, the pulpit silence concerning presidential faith and Christian government during Monroe's presidential tenure is breathtaking to behold. This same silence echoes even more tellingly, given Monroe's notable indifference to Christianity and the negligible ceremonial role the church played in his administration. In the three and a half decades we have traversed, the American people, together with their Christian guides, had at long last come to accept George Washington's maxim on church-state separation. "I am persuaded, you will permit me to observe, that the path of true piety is so plain as to require but little political direction," the first president told a group of disconsolate Presbyterians in 1789, adding with abiding moment for succeeding generations, "To this consideration we ought to ascribe the absence of any regulation respecting religion from the Magna Charta of our country."

Monroe's balancing act—keeping God out of the White House without offending the churches—would be passed along to his presidential successors. They would adapt his model of a religiously neutral and disengaged White House, more or less successfully and regardless of faith or party, throughout ten succeeding administrations. Religion and politics would continue to mix, sometimes combustively, in the country at large, but for decades to come no president would have to suffer anything close to the religious calumnies that spiritual partisans had lavished on John Adams, Thomas Jefferson, and James Madison during the height of America's first great culture war. With the collapse of the Standing Orders of New England and their reemergence at the vanguard of a voluntary establishment of religion, the battle to save the American government, either from French infidelity or Puritan theocracy, had finally ended. Only with the coming of the Civil War and the emergence of Abraham Lincoln as national theologian did God reenter the White House. But that is another story.

PROMINENT FIGURES who die of natural causes tend to die well. They sense the world watching—indeed, they sense it judging, gossiping, and weeping—and show their best profile one last time. Dying memorably is an art. Inspired by the heroes of their youth, whose stories they learned by heart and strove to emulate, public figures see their lives the way the world does—as morality tales, not ones that end in the middle like most people's stories do, but at the end, where any stirring biography should, with a lesson for the ages. "'Tis well," George Washington affirmed, summing up his magnificent life in two tiny words. "This is the Fourth of July?" Thomas Jefferson asked, leaving little doubt about his final goal. Competitive to the end, a mistaken John Adams uttered what posterity unkindly would record as his best-remembered words, "Thomas Jefferson still survives." Famous last words aside, all three capped their storied lives with a death befitting fame's rigorous demands.

To punctuate his life with a final exclamation point, James Monroe could not have timed his exit any better. Like a mother who summons breath to survive until her children arrive to kiss her goodbye, he held on to his tenuous lifeline long enough to die poetically, on July 4, 1831, fifty-five years to the day that the nation was born. It was just the sort of thing a man seeking to add a final feather to his fame might muster up his last available ounce of adrenaline to do. There was only one problem. The chorus necessary to hymn his feat was otherwise occupied. Typical of Monroe's entire career, this memorable gesture was instantly forgotten (as were his final words). It was an act for the ages, to be sure, but imitative, redundant, already old. The fifth president's return to dust was obscured almost entirely by the dust raised on the simultaneous demise of his illustrious predecessors five years before. On July 4, 1826, John Adams and Thomas Jefferson had the mutual foresight or brilliant good luck to take their leave together, entering the democracy of death with unforgettable flourish, augmenting the celebration of the nation's first half century with a paroxysm of self-congratulatory grief, and providing patriotic preachers with a convincing proof text of America's divine anointment. Monroe dutifully added his dying gesture to theirs, but by then it was old hat, like the antique tricorn he respectfully wore long after Revolutionary toppers had passed out of fashion.

As for James Madison, whose humility was spontaneous not constructed, despite the destiny manifest in his colleagues' precedent, rather than expiring on the sixtieth anniversary of the Republic he made his quiet exit six days early, more secure in his name and person than any of them. On June 28, 1836, he closed his twinkling blue eyes for the last time, and with him the Revolutionary generation passed into history.

"The True Religion of Statesmanship"

The final chapter of Monroe's life was almost unremittingly sad. Throughout his waning years, his delicate physical condition and disintegrating finances preoccupied his full attentions. One letter after another finds him pining over his empty bank account and broken health. On losing long-suffering Elizabeth to death in 1830, Monroe was forced to put Oak Hill on the market, but it failed to find a buyer. To cut costs, he moved to New York, where he lived as a semirecluse and died destitute the following year. Most New Yorkers were surprised to learn that he had been their neighbor. His memorial service took place at City Hall, where he laid in state, with Columbia University's president delivering the eulogy. Monroe was buried out of Trinity Parish's St. Paul's Chapel, the funeral liturgy conducted by its rector and the local Episcopal bishop. Thousands of curious New Yorkers escorted his cortege to Manhattan's Marble Cemetery, where Monroe's body was laid to rest to the accompaniment of minute guns on the Battery, whose seventy-three reports commemorated the illustrious years of a modest American hero.

Characteristically, his predecessors' years in retirement were more deeply contemplated, both by themselves and by the world. Jefferson, his old gray head emerging on crooked neck like a turtle's from its shell, aged well. His body was his temple. At seventy-six, he boasted that he rarely contracted colds, had never lost a tooth by age, possessed a fully serviceable digestive system, and, over an entire lifetime had suffered only two or three times from fevers of more than a day in duration. Time was less kind to Madison, but so had it always been. He walked through life gingerly, holding death's hand. Yet in spirit he grew younger as he aged, and spirit will shine through.

Jefferson leaned on Madison to the end. "You have been a pillar of support through life," he told his political little brother, assuring him "that I shall leave with you my last affections." To this bequest he attached one final favor: "Take care of me when dead." Promising that he would, Madison honored his lifelong hero with a touching elegy. "You cannot look back to the long period of our private friendship & political harmony with more affecting recollections than I do," he said. "If they are a source of pleasure to you, what ought they not to be to me?" Having learned the language of republican faith at Jefferson's knee, Madison oversaw his legacy at the University of Virginia, serving as second rector of the "temple thro' which alone lies the road to that of liberty." Jefferson once said that he could not replace, only succeed Benjamin Franklin as American minister to France; Madison adjudged himself unworthy even to "succeed" Jefferson as sachem of his college. "It would," he said devotedly, "be the pretension of a mere worshipper 'remplacer' of the tutelary genius of the sanctuary."

When historian Charles J. Ingersoll visited Montpelier, he found himself entering a mansion "decayed and in need of considerable repairs," but "glittering with interest and filled with the warmth of hospitality within." In this respect, the mansion reflected its republican lord.

Among the many pilgrims who wended their way to "Pilgrim's Mount" during Madison's long farewell was a strikingly beautiful thirty-two-year-old English author and liberal religious activist, Harriet Martineau. Her deafness obliged Martineau to attend to Madison's wee voice with an ear trumpet, evoking the fascinating picture of two engaging conversationalists rapt in mutual admiration, the great little Madison disappearing into his chair, Martineau leaning over him with a large horn attached to her ear. Martineau was struck by Madison's "inexhaustible faith" in the immortality of the American Republic. Capturing his civic faith as well as anyone, she extolled him for embodying "the true religion of statesmanship, faith in men, and in the principles on which they combine in an agreement to do as they would be done by." They would talk for a time; he would drift off and then awaken to continue his thought. "The principles of justice in which such a commonwealth originates never die out of the people's heart and mind," Madison told his beguiling houseguest. Perceptively, she adjudged his "political religion" sufficiently devout to sustain "the spirit through difficulty and change, and leaving no cause for repentance, or even solicitude, when, at the close of life, all things reveal themselves to the meditative sage."

However much she admired the sage of Montpelier, who "reposed cheerfully, gaily, to the last, on his faith in the people's power of wise self-government," Martineau couldn't forbear confronting him on slavery. Madison's concern, she discovered to her dismay, was as much for the white plantation owners' wives and daughters as for their poor black slaves. He expressed "deep feelings for the sufferings of ladies under the system, declaring that he pitied them even more than the Negroes, and that the saddest slavery of all was that of conscientious Southern women." Madison went on to detail his earnest efforts on behalf of the American Colonization Society. "It was as painful as it was strange," she would recall, "to listen to the cheerful old man, as he proved that there was no chance for his country, except from a scheme which he, as its president, found unmanageable."

Shortly before Jedidiah Morse died, he sent Madison a questionnaire on the nature and condition of free blacks. "Generally idle and depraved" was Madison's curt reply—"appearing to retain the bad qualities of the slaves with whom they continue to associate, without acquiring any of the good ones of the whites, from whom [they] continue separated by prejudices against their color and other peculiarities." These prejudices and peculiarities would be resolved by deportation, he claimed, but Madison was too smart to fall for his own scheme. In his conversations with Martineau, when he beamed in on slavery's stark reality he was anything but sanguine. Confessing himself close to despair, he pronounced the barbarous institution guilty of "all the evils with which it has ever been charged." For its stranglehold on the southern soul, Madison characteristically blamed the clergy. "The whole Bible is against Negro slavery," he assured Martineau, but, unfortunately, "the clergy do not preach this, and the people do not see it."

Years before, after a flash flood, Madison had told one of his bondsmen, "Why, this is bad business, Tony." "Yes masser ver bad—ver bad indeed," Tony answered. "I tell you what, masser. I think Gor Almighty by and large, he do most as much harm as good." Madison may sincerely have believed that the scriptures threw the book at slavery, but proslavery biblical literalists had little difficulty opening their Bibles to one passage after another pronouncing the barbarous institution that powered their economy the very Word of God.

"Nothing, My Dear, but a Change of Mind"

If they walked side by side through the wilderness of early American politics, Madison and Jefferson parted company on one signal proposition. Like many southerners, Jefferson was a *pluribus* man to the end. If he posited in the Declaration of Independence the ideal of equality that finally freed America's slaves, he was also the libertarian father of what one scholar insightfully calls "the genealogy of secession," beginning in 1776 and running on through the Virginia and Kentucky Resolutions of 1798 to its fateful culmination in 1861. In sharp contrast, Madison, architect of union and philosopher of pluralism, remained true to the difficult symmetry of *E pluribus unum,* his lineage tracing back instead to the Constitutional Convention of 1787.

Right before he died, Madison etched out a paragraph of "Advice to My Country," a secular prayer of sorts on behalf of American union. His entire career, he stated there, was dedicated to "the cause of its liberty," yet in bidding his countrymen adieu, Madison's modestly scaled farewell address honors union no less reverently. "The advice nearest to my heart and deepest in my convictions is that the Union of the States be cherished and perpetuated," he prayed. "Let the open enemy to it be regarded as a Pandora with her box opened; and the disguised one, as the serpent creeping with his deadly wiles into Paradise." When he wrote these "famous last words" (taking no unnecessary chances on the muse abandoning him on his deathbed), the serpent had long since wormed its way into the American Eden. To expel the curse of slavery, events would exact the payment Madison most dreaded. Yet even as the United States emerged from "Madison's War" united as never before, the shattered Union, too, would reemerge from the horrors of the Civil War—Abraham Lincoln called it "a new birth of freedom"—transformed into something potentially greater, one nation, rededicated to Jefferson's founding proposition that "All men are created equal."

Very like his old age, Madison's death had something sweet about it. His mother's namesake, Nelly, watched her uncle take a bite of food and pause. He couldn't swallow, his manservant Paul Jennings reported. "His head...dropped, and he ceased breathing as quietly as the snuff of a candle goes out." "What's the matter, Uncle James," Nelly asked the moment before his spirit flickered into memory. Leaving this world on a grace note, Madison smiled and said, "Nothing, my dear, but a change of mind."

He was buried on the grounds of Montpelier, where he was born. Faithful Paul Jennings joined the other slaves and Mrs. Madison in a solemn procession from the manor house to the family cemetery. Paul sobbed throughout the interment, later reporting that, when Madison was lowered into the ground, not only he and those around him, who were closest to their master, "but the hundred slaves gave vent to their lamentations in one violent burst that rent the air." A month later, Dolley sold Jennings to Daniel Webster for $120. He worked off his indenture at $8 a month and was free within two years.

Financial exigency continued to cast a shadow over Mrs. Madison's widowhood. Her husband's debts forced her to sell Montpelier and with it Madison's remaining slaves. This final act of obeisance to the economics of slavery ripped the veil off the Madison family idyll. "Every day or two, a Negro trader would make his appearance & was permitted to examine the Negroes," Dolley's Quaker brother-in-law, Edward Coles, censoriously reported. "It was like the hawk among the pigeons." Mrs. Madison was well aware of the blot slavery placed on her memory. In offering the bare bones of a personal memoir to her biographer, Margaret Bayard Smith, she made a special point of mentioning that her parents had freed their slaves for religious reasons and reared her according to the antislavery strictures of the Quaker faith.

Supported by the sale of her husband's papers and aided by charitable bequests from the likes of John Jacob Astor (who had once
supplied her so lavishly with furs), Mrs. Madison returned to Washington in 1844 to live out her final years. Congress passed an unprecedented resolution that "whenever it shall be her pleasure to
visit the House that she be requested to take a seat within the Hall."
How often she chose to roam the floor of the House is uncertain,
but she did find a pew to her liking at St. John's Church. Dolley officially joined the Episcopal fold three years before her death. To become "a worthy member of the church" was a matter about which
she confessed devoting a great deal of thought. On the day of her
confirmation, "We had an excellent sermon from the Bishop of
New Jersey," she writes, "a fine preacher and beautiful champion for
charity which 'suspects not, thinks no evil.'"

Mrs. Madison took one final bow before her public. The woman
who more than three decades before had rescued Washington's portrait from the White House sat on the dais in 1847, when the grand
master of the local Masonic Temple, following the order's "ancient"
rite, laid the cornerstone for the Washington Monument, a word-
less obelisk evocative of Egypt's towering cenotaphs. Washington's
monument required no hieroglyphs. His name alone was enough.

Two years later, at eighty-one years of age and surrounded by
"devoted relatives & hosts of untiring friends," Dolley Madison
"expired without a struggle or apparent pain, at peace with her
maker, & with all the world & it with her." Her state funeral was
the largest in Washington's fifty-year history.

The Fall and Resurrection of Christianity in Virginia

Sweetening Madison's contemplations as he reviewed his long,
eventful career was a profound sense of satisfaction that his lifelong
campaign to secure religious freedom had benefited church and
state alike. In 1832, when the Reverend Jasper Adams circulated to
every prominent individual in the land a fervent call for Christ's re-

turn to his rightful seat in government, most of the dignitaries who bothered to respond congratulated him politely for his piety. Madison was polite as well, but he firmly insisted that "The tendency to a usurpation on one side or the other, or to a corrupting coalition or alliance between [church and state] will be best guarded against by an entire abstinence of the government from interference in any way whatever, beyond the necessity of preserving public order and protecting each sect against trespasses on its legal rights by others." He then offered Reverend Adams a brief American history lesson. "The prevailing opinion in Europe, England not excepted," Madison said, was "that religion could not be preserved without the support of government nor government be supported without an established religion." Not so, Madison vigorously argued. In America, this "great and interesting subject" had been brought, he stated with full confidence, "to a fair, and finally to a decisive test."

In proof of his claim, Madison could point to the fall and rise of religion in Virginia. In 1821, looking back on the Act for Religious Freedom some four decades after its enactment, he drew a picture of religion in Virginia before and after Jefferson's signature legislation passed into law.

> That there has been an increase of religious instruction since the revolution can admit of no question. The English church was originally the established religion. Of other sects there were but few adherents, except the Presbyterians who predominated on the West side of the Blue Mountains....At present the population is divided, with small exceptions, among the Protestant Episcopalians, the Presbyterians, the Baptists, and the Methodists....Religious instruction is now diffused throughout the community by preachers of every sect with almost equal zeal, tho' with very unequal acquirements, and at private houses and open stations....On a general comparison of the present and former times, the balance is certainly and vastly on the side of the present, as to the number of religious teachers, the zeal which actuates them, the purity of their lives, and the attendance of the people on their instructions. It was

the universal opinion of the century preceding the last, that civil government could not stand without the prop of a religious establishment, and the Christian religion itself would perish if not supported by a legal provision for its clergy. The experience of Virginia conspicuously corroborates the disproof of both opinions. The civil government tho' bereft of everything like an associated hierarchy possesses the requisite stability and performs its functions with complete success, whilst the number, the industry, and the morality of the priesthood, and the devotion of the people have been manifestly increased by the total separation of the church from the state.

Illustrating Madison's morality tale, the fall and resurrection of the Episcopal Church in Virginia succinctly reprises our story. Propped up by state assessments until the Revolution, unincorporated in 1787, with all ties severed by 1799, the Church of Virginia was under moral and political attack as the founders came into their maturity, its waning secular power matched only by its advancing spiritual decay. The Virginia founding presidents' coolness toward organized Christianity was prompted in no small measure by the corruption steaming at the core of their ancestral faith.

By 1811, when Bishop James Madison ordained future Bishop William Meade, the Church of Virginia was staggering on its last legs. At Williamsburg's Burton Parish the pews were empty, the bishop left early, and Meade had to deliver his own ordination sermon. He was one of only three new ministers to receive Episcopal ordination over more than a decade. By the time Madison was elected president, fewer than 2,000 Episcopal communicants remained in Virginia, and 60 percent of their churches were in mothballs. Those who argue that, as good Virginians, the founders' abiding Episcopal faith must be accepted as a given, overlook how few of their contemporaries remained true to the Church of Virginia. Cut from the umbilical cord of state support, the corrupt Episcopal establishment languished. At the end of "Madison's War," only seventeen Episcopal priests, a handful of them active, appeared on the Episcopal Church rolls. When Meade persuaded the affable and devout Reverend William Channing Moore of New York to move to Virginia as bishop, Moore confessed himself more than a little daunted by the task.

> The undertaking in which we had engaged formed an object of such magnitude as to excite my fears; the difficulties with which we had to struggle were sufficient to appall the stoutest heart, and to excite tremblings in the firmest mind. To have beheld our dilapidated churches without alarm was impossible; to have reflected upon the scattered flocks which one filled their courts, without laboring under an apprehension that they might never again be collected, would have evinced a temper arrogant and presumptuous. Sensible of the prejudices which existed against the church and frequently wounded by the observations which were made in my presence...I trembled for the Ark of God.

In 1816, when Bishop Moore performed the rite of confirmation for old Nelly Madison and her neighbors, the state of Anglicanism in Orange County was showing a hint of life for the first time in years. After the Revolution, Brick Church, the Madison family congregation, had been shuttered and remained so for the better part of three decades. With Meade's valiant assistance, Bishop Moore reanimated Virginia's Episcopal Church one household at a time. Instilling the discipline of family worship and daily prayers, the bishop "repudiated the sacerdotal theory of the ministry." In its place, Moore encouraged Virginia Episcopalians to join ecumenical tract, temperance, and Bible societies and regirded the lax theology of the old established communion with evangelical discipline. By an 1818 decree, the Virginia Episcopal Convention required that church members no longer "visit the post office, transact any secular business, or make or receive social visits on the Sabbath." Bishop Moore unseated a vestryman he surprised playing whist; communion was denied to members who attended dances; and no church activities

were permitted in any building employed by Masons for social purposes. Moore "believed that the Christian Church, like Gideon's
army, is often greater in power for being less in number." But by
aiming to do good, the bishop also did well. Compared to the three
paltry ordinations that took place from 1801 to 1811, there were 55
ordinations from 1819 to 1829, and the Episcopal Church in Virginia increased five-fold.

William Meade succeeded Moore as bishop and continued his
vigorous spiritual leadership. "Perhaps he was lacking in a certain
breadth of mind," one chronicler allowed, "but his convictions were
very deep." The same might be said of the church as a whole. Distinguished during its glory days for "breadth of mind," the revived
Church of Virginia, independent of the state and forced to stand on
its own, found sounder spiritual footing. In this regard, members
of the Virginia chapter of the Second Great Awakening followed
much the same path through the secular wilderness that its Connecticut chapter was blazing: Cast from state favor, they rediscov-
ered God.

By 1835, when the Second Great Awakening had run its course,
twice as many Americans numbered themselves as church members. Although the figures were still small (moving from 7 to 14 percent of the population since 1800), like an iceberg most of the active
Christian populace was hidden beneath the surface of church rolls.
No matter how one reckons the actual percentage of active American Christians, the number doubled over the first third of the century, all during a time when direct government support of religion
fell under attack and then finally disappeared.

The Red Queen and the Cheshire Cat

John Adams and Thomas Jefferson reconciled in 1812, with their
mutual friend, Benjamin Rush, playing yenta. At once the storm
clouds parted, dazzling their mutual memory with the sunshine of
reminiscence. "You and I ought not to die before we have explained

ourselves to each other," Adams proposed at the outset of their correspondence. Uneager to open closed wounds, Jefferson politely excused himself from venturing too far into "the forest of opinions, discussion and contentions" on Adams's eager arm. "The *summum bonum* with me is now truly Epicurean," he pristinely explained, "ease of body and tranquility of mind; and to these I wish to consign my remaining days." Jefferson had no interest in Adams, or anyone else for that matter, planting "thorns on the pillow of age, worth, and wisdom."

Adams would have none of that. Avoiding the thickets was impossible for him. By introducing a series of tacitly agreeable topics, religion foremost among them, he gradually cajoled Jefferson into indulging the pleasures of armed intellectual combat, not (for the most part) against each other—Adams was too delighted by the renewal of Jefferson's affections to risk alienating them—but as allies in a noble struggle against the callow new generation of Americans who insulted them both by neglecting their legacy.

Adams boasted to Jefferson that he never "corrected or revised anything" he wrote. He was exaggerating, of course, but not by much. Adams took a "ready, fire, aim" approach to life. He presented his thoughts to the world rudely cut, so unvarnished, in fact, that one's eye cannot help but be drawn to their blemishes. Jefferson, in contrast, was fastidious about protecting his image from unwanted depredation and his person from unwelcome intimacy. Theirs was a friendship between the Red Queen and the Cheshire Cat. At the slightest provocation, Adams shouted, "Off with their heads"; at the first hint of conflict, Jefferson disappeared until nothing remained but his smile. The two men's letters mirror their respective natures: the uninhibited, pugilistic, skeptical, self-revealing Adams, hot and stormy; the tempered, gracious, doctrinaire, elusive Jefferson, sunny and cool.

Adams did manage to win a concession on one matter that had separated the two men for decades—Jefferson finally acknowledged that Adams had been right about France. How a people "so great, so dignified, so distinguished by science and the arts…threw off suddenly and openly all the restraints of morality, all sensation to character, and unblushingly avowed and acted on the principle that power was right" defied the canons of rationality, which he held sacred. Looking at history as it passed him by, the old Virginia optimist plaintively asked his skeptical New England friend (who knew the cruel answer by heart), "Are we to surrender the pleasing hopes of seeing improvement in the moral and intellectual condition of man?" Jefferson's philosophy of reason hadn't prepared him for history's blemishes as adequately as Puritanism and a lifelong study of unruly passion had fitted John Adams, who called Jefferson's rare admission of error "one of the most consolatory" he had ever been privileged to receive. In return, Adams was gentle about slavery, and Jefferson's pillow remained free of thorns.

More than any other subject, religion lay at the heart of their fourteen-year valedictory dialogue. Long since relieved from the pressures of placating and marshaling their respective religious-political allies, the two old savants were free to course back and forth along the arc of religion's vivid rainbow, sharing like beliefs across its visible spectrum and differing only near its edges where perceptive observation must yield to speculation and knowledge to faith.

Adams opened their discussion on religion characteristically, with a boast. "For more than sixty years I have been attentive to this great subject," he said. "Controversies between Calvinists and Arminians, Trinitarians and Unitarians, Deists and Christians, Atheists and both, have attracted my attention, whenever the singular life I have led would admit, to all these questions." Adams delighted in theology, wringing pleasure even from "lunatics" like Wesley and Swedenborg. In this singular respect, he knew full well that Jefferson was not in his league. "I have been a diligent student for many years of books whose titles you have never seen," he justly claimed. Yet Adams's enthusiasms—"I have read away bigotry if not enthusiasm," he avowed—were merely that, innocent playthings affording endless amusement, not a theological code by which others must order their metaphysical priorities in order to be saved. "These things are to me, at present, the marbles and ninepins of old age," he told Jefferson. "I will not say the beads and prayer-books." Freed from the controlling influence of politics, Adams's theological speculations resemble nothing so much as creative play.

In his radical old age, Adams drank from the fountain of his youth, reanimating the young man's wariness toward the collusion of miter and crown. "The question before the human race," he told Jefferson (sounding very much like him), "is whether the God of nature shall govern the world by his own laws or whether priests and kings shall rule it by fictitious miracles? Or, in other words, whether authority is originally in the people, or whether it has descended for 1800 years in a succession of popes and bishops or brought down from Heaven by the Holy Ghost in the form of a dove, in a phial of holy oil?" He predicted a dark future for American religious politics. "Oh, Lord!" he asked Jefferson, poised to launch into a conspiracy theory worthy of his correspondent.

> Do you think that a Protestant popedom is annihilated in America? Do you know that the General of the Jesuits and consequently all his host have their eyes on this country? Do you know that the Church of England is employing more means and more art to propagate their demipopery among us than ever? Quakers, Anabaptists, Moravians, Swedenborgian, Methodists, Unitarians, Nothingarians in all Europe are employing [underhanded] means to propagate their sectarian systems in these states.

Painting a hydra-headed religious conspiracy bearing all the marks of Jedidiah Morse's dread Bavarian Illuminati, he continued,

> The multitude and diversity of them, you will say, is our security against them all. God grant it. But if we consider that the Presbyterians and Methodists are far the most numerous and the most likely to unite, let a George Whitefield arise with a military cast, like Mahomet or Loyola, and what will become of all the other sects who can never unite?

When they mount their anticlerical hobbyhorses, it is difficult sometimes to identify with any degree of confidence which of the two men is speaking. As one might readily guess, it was Jefferson who claimed that creeds "made of Christendom a slaughter house," but Adams, too, vaunted, "I set at defiance all ecclesiastical authority—all their creeds, confessions & excommunications." Issuing his theological declaration of independence, Adams proclaimed, "I assert the divine right and sacred duty of private individual judgment and deny all human authority in matters of faith." The advice Adams sent to his granddaughter Caroline De Windt in the early 1820s could have been lifted word for word from Jefferson's counsel half a century before to his nephew Peter Carr, whom he told to submit every tenet of received theology to the test of open inquiry. Suggesting that she think freely and question boldly, Adams exhorted his granddaughter to join him in never fearing to embrace "the truth when we see evidence for it, although it may contradict our earlier opinions." His definition of religion in the same letter evokes Jefferson's claim to Margaret Smith that "It is in our lives and not from our words that our religion must be read." In Adams's version, "I believe that his cannot be wrong whose life is in the right." The doctrinal voice of Adams's Puritan childhood was muted, as it had been for decades, by cosmic wonder and theological humility. "The longer I live, the more I read, the more patiently I think, and the more anxiously I inquire, the less I seem to know," he readily allowed. "Worm!"—Adams addresses his granddaughter as if he were speaking to himself—"Ask no such question! Do justly; love mercy; walk humbly: This is enough for you to know and to do. The world is a better one than you deserve; strive to make yourself more worthy of it." His trans-Christian dream was that the world's scriptures might be translated into all the world's tongues: "Then our grandchildren and my great-grandchildren may compare notes and hold fast all that is good."

Adams's religious erudition made him more, not less, skeptical minded than Jefferson, whose brief against organized Christianity was not matched by an equal wariness toward the dogmas of modern thought. Tweaking his old friend's enlightened credulity, Adams provocatively declared, "I would trust these liberal Christians in London and in Boston with power, just as soon as I would Calvin or Cardinal Lorrain." Jefferson devoted his life to comprehending the universe; Adams threw up his hands at such presumption, while ever seeking to secure his cosmic hope with faith's foothold. Of the two, unable to believe with the same degree of abandon that Jefferson enjoyed, Adams faced the more daunting challenge. When depressed by his close examination of passion-swept human nature's futile quest for balance, he sighed, "If believing too little or too much is so fatal to mankind, what will become of us all?"

Jedidiah Morse's Last Great Dream

Ushering out the first long chapter of American religious-political history, the redoubtable Reverend Jedidiah Morse died a month before Jefferson and Adams did, on June 9, 1826. Morse's son, Samuel F. B. Morse, would go on to invent the telegraph, linking the nation with its future. Connecting him to his father and the country's past, Samuel Morse would also figure prominently as an anti-Catholic agitator.

In his final years, Jedidiah Morse was an avid participant in Lyman Beecher's voluntary establishment. Among his final contributions to American sacred politics was an ambitious scheme for a national ecumenical organization, the American Society for Promoting the Civilization and General Improvement of the Indian Tribes of the United States, to be hosted by the living presidents and composed of every federal legislator, college professor, and clergyman in the country. Madison automatically signed on to Morse's ambitious project, as did President Monroe. Jefferson, as was his wont, did the math. Estimating the prospective clergy membership at 8,000 and the assemblage of secular participants at 400, "the clergy will constitute nineteen twentieths of this association," he answered his old adversary, "and, by the law of the majority, may command the twentieth part." Unwilling to add his card to so stacked a deck, Jefferson rhetorically asked Morse, "Can this formidable array be reviewed without dismay?"

> It will comprehend, indeed, all the functionaries of the government; but seceded from their constitutional stations as guardians of the nation and acting not by the laws of their station, but by those of a voluntary society.... Under its authority, as a precedent, future associations will arise with objects at which we should shudder at this time.... The present is a case where, if ever, we are to guard against ourselves; not against ourselves as we are, but as we may be; for who can now imagine what we may become under circumstances not now imaginable?

The very thought of a future government being submerged, even voluntarily, in a sea of clerics was Jefferson's worst nightmare. Madison politely suggested that Jefferson lay down his ancient cudgel. Declaring Morse's "laudable" scheme "rather ostentatious than dangerous," he fell back on his old belief that strength in numbers would overwhelm the design of faction, describing the proposed membership of this projected voluntary association as "too numerous, too heterogeneous, and too much dispersed, to concentrate their views in any covert or illicit object." Having thus explained himself, Madison then respectfully bowed to Jefferson. If he had paid the matter closer attention, Madison conceded, he, too, would have withheld his name.

In the early 1820s, commissioned by a group of Indian mission societies, Morse toured the country to study the Native American plight firsthand. One of his proposals to help solve the "Indian problem" was intermarriage. Until then, Benjamin Rush had been the leading American advocate of intermarriage between races. Rush went so far as to commend miscegenation as a tonic for the gene pool. "The mulatto has been remarked, in all countries, to exceed, in sagacity, his white and black parent," Rush noted. "The same remark has been made of the offspring of the European and North American Indian." In his old age, Jedidiah Morse, too, became a staunch advocate of intermarriage as a solution to the crisis facing America's Indians. "Let intermarriage with them become general, and the end which the Government has in view will be completely attained. They would then be literally of one blood with us, be merged in the nation, and saved from extinction," he advised in his 400-page *Report to the Secretary of War of the United States, on Indian Affairs.* Little changed as a result of his prodigious efforts, but a congressional movement to halt all funding for Christian educational missions failed in face of Morse's relentless lobbying.

Morse was a hard man to love. Over the years, support for him in his own congregation waned, until finally he lost the critical favor of his deacons. His parishioners were "longing for opportunities for Christian conversation with their minister, not on disputes and controversies or politics, but on *real, internal, experimental religion.*" When stripped of his pulpit in 1819, Morse took practiced umbrage. Citing three decades of "arduous and constant warfare," throughout which he had sacrificed his "slender constitution," he speculated, "in what manner this event is to affect the interests of this church and parish and the cause of religion in this region cannot be foreseen." As recently as a decade before, Morse's dismissal might well have impacted the course of religion in his extensive neighborhood, but in the midst of the Era of Good Feelings, skilled sacred-political controversialists were neither needed nor welcome, even in New England. Shared moral concern was taking precedence over the finer points of political theology.

The Reverend Lyman Beecher hailed the bevy of new Christian moral associations as "providential substitutes" for the old Standing Orders. By 1827, the logic of populist Christianity had convinced the apostle of "voluntary establishment" to abandon Godly Federalism entirely. Not only must "political power rest in the hands of the people," he now said, but "the rights of conscience" must also "be restored to man," with church and government alike no longer dictating "what men shall believe and in what manner they shall worship God." About the old established church, he issued a relieved and telling post mortem: "[Christianity] has survived the deadly embrace of establishments nominally Christian." The secret to the church's escape and subsequent triumph was simple. When people began freely supporting religion on their own volition, the church and the people's faith alike grew stronger. From his populist pulpit, Beecher sounded very much like Jefferson. "The progress of truth will be without resistance," he said, as long as the nation's leaders remain "impartial" and exempt themselves from "sectarian zeal." Statesmen needn't "profess religion or afford evidence of piety." To ban good people from government simply because they were not Christian was the error, he said, "of our pious fathers," who blurred the categories of "communion and civil trust," thereby mistaking the state for the church and compromising religion's independent moral authority.

Beecher's new gospel came naturally to America's Baptists. Joseph Joslin was a Connecticut farmer and self-described "Republican of the old stamp," one of the few residents of Thompson, Connecticut, to cast his ballot for Jefferson in 1800. By July 4, 1806, the Republican Party was rising in his part of the state, lifted on the wings of Baptist evangels. "Met a number of Republicans to celebrate independence," he notes. "There was a good entertainment—a good oration delivered by Elder Amos Wells of Woodstock, [Baptist Elder] John Nichols made a prayer and read the Declaration of Independence." Two years later, Joslin helped erect a 60-foot liberty pole and attended part of a five-day Methodist camp revival. He celebrated Madison's victory in 1808 and sent his son to war in 1812. By 1818, his hometown finally rejected the Federalists, voting two to one to disestablish the Congregational Church. Alike punctuating the reform of America's most Puritan state and the fiftieth anniversary of Jefferson's Declaration of Independence, in 1826 Joslin was elected on the Republican ticket to a seat in the State Assembly in Hartford.

Encapsulating the resurrection of the Episcopal establishment in Virginia, the transformation of New England's Standing Orders, and the triumph of the Baptists in Connecticut, two items from the closing pages of Morse's contentious life sum up the paradigm shift in American religious politics. John Adams, standing his practice as president on its head, refused to attach his name to Morse's Indian Society—religious associations, he now said, had no place interfering in the affairs of government. And, in the 1824 race for president between New England favorite son John Quincy Adams and Tennessee's fierce-eyed Democrat, Andrew Jackson, Morse supported the Democrat.

"Is It the Fourth?"

Adams and Jefferson alike fretted about how history would remember them. Adams fought doggedly to set the record straight for years, dedicating reams of turgid prose to the cause with a zeal that can charitably be described as embarrassing. In familiar contrast, being by nature nothing if not surreptitious about such matters, in his memoirs Jefferson doctored the historical record as nimbly as he could, employing the functional equivalent of yellowing papers in an oven to make them look authentically old.

Adams knew that he had more cause to fret than Jefferson did. Practiced in the bittersweet pleasures of political martyrdom, he acknowledged to Jefferson with characteristic bluntness, "Your administration will be quoted by philosophers as a model of profound wisdom; by politicians as weak, superficial, and shortsighted," adding with a whine, "Mine, like Pope's woman, will have no character at all."

Jefferson's optimism needed bolstering to convince him that the pessimistic Adams was right about how gloriously he himself would be remembered. As time distanced him from the stage he once dominated, insecurity found him grasping at the straws of affection. Expressions of concern about the state of his health were gratifying, he acknowledged, since they "manifested a sentiment that I had not been a useless cipher of society." Writing to solicitous Charles Thompson, Jefferson posited the hope that "Notwithstanding the slanders of the Saints, my fellow citizens have thought me worthy of trust."

Giving Jefferson a permanent advantage, popular memory was focused on their services to the nation only once a year. Every Fourth of July, Adams watched his place on the American stage being eclipsed by what he called "the theatrical show" that elevated Jefferson's importance while proportionally diminishing his own. With uncanny prescience, he had predicted Independence Day's future importance to the national identity. But over the intervening years, Jefferson "ran away with all the stage effect," Adams pouted, "and all the glory of it." The Declaration of Independence, Mercy Warren had proclaimed in her history of the Revolution, "ought to be frequently read by the rising youth of the American states, as a palladium of which they should never lose sight, so long as they wish to continue a free and independent people." And so it was. Even as his fickle friend awarded Jefferson the palm, of the Declaration itself Adams harbored nothing but scorn. "There is not an idea in it," he sniveled, "but what had been hackneyed in Congress for two years." Yet because of how elegantly its author had framed the American gospel of sacred liberty—Jefferson never claimed originality for it—Adams rightly feared that future philosophers would cite Jefferson "as a model of profound wisdom," while he would fade from memory entirely. "Mausoleums...statues, monuments will never be erected to me," he half-boasted. "Panegyrical romances will never be written, nor flattering orations spoken, to transmit me to posterity in brilliant colors." Not the last president to observe that life is unfair, Adams could do little but count the floats as Jefferson's parade marched by.

If the Fourth of July had a prophet, however, it was Adams, not Jefferson. When every other mind in Congress was fixed on the tumultuous present, Adams was imagining the American future with startling exactitude. On July 3, 1776, the day after Congress for-

mally declared the colonies independent from British parliamentary
or royal governmental authority, he predicted to Abigail in speaking of the nation's birthday,

> I am apt to believe that it will be celebrated by succeeding genera-
> tions as the great anniversary festival. It ought to be commemo-
> rated, as the day of deliverance, by solemn acts of devotion to God
> almighty. It ought to be solemnized with pomp and parade, with
> shows, games, sports, guns, bells, bonfires, and illuminations, from
> one end of this continent to the other, from this time forward,
> forevermore.

If Adams's Federalist partisans had triumphed, these words and not
Jefferson's Declaration of Independence might well be lifted up in
memory every Fourth of July. Not that they didn't try to do just
that. Boston's Federalist press exerted its increasingly limited influence to imprint Adams's words instead of Jefferson's on the popular
memory. For years, the local gazetteers faithfully published his Independence Day letter to Abigail each Fourth of July, hoping that,
by dint of sheer repetition, it might gradually displace Jefferson's insolent creed in people's affections.

Foremost in Jefferson's mind as the nation's Jubilee drew near
was the same document that gave Adams fits. He gazed down from
his mountaintop to admire the monumental contribution he had
made to the American ethos being hypostasized for the ages into a
sacred American icon. Marquis de Lafayette performed the offices
of consecration. Traveling in the company of his son, George Washington Lafayette, he barnstormed the country on a triumphant tour
of American shrines in celebration of the nation's Jubilee. After
being honored at a great Masonic festival in Richmond, he traveled
north to Monticello. From the "portico" of this "temple erected on
the hills of liberty"—Lafayette was as given to civil religious rhetoric as Jefferson and Madison were—he descended into the valley,
where in Charlottesville, under "the hollow vault of heaven" at a
great banquet in the rotunda of Jefferson's "Pantheon," liberty's

three votaries were feted at a great banquet. Jefferson was too ill to speak, but Madison rose to offer a poetic toast to "Liberty, which has virtue for its guest and gratitude for its feast." The celebrated French pilgrim journeyed on to the "hallowed" Philadelphia Court House, henceforth to be known as Independence Hall. "Here within these sacred walls," Lafayette exclaimed, "was boldly declared the independence of these United States."

Jefferson celebrated the anniversary of his fame the way he knew best. His final letter, a hymn to freedom meticulously written and scrupulously revised, rings with the convictions of a lifetime. Intoning, with doctrinal rectitude, "the inherent and unalienable rights of man," and anathematizing the "chains" of "ignorance and superstition," Jefferson hailed the anniversary of sacred liberty's immortal triumph, looking forward to its consummation.

> All eyes are opened or opening to the rights of man. The general spread of the light of science has already laid open to every view the palpable truth, that the mass of mankind has not been born with saddles on their backs, nor a favored few booted and spurred, ready to ride them legitimately by the grace of God. These are grounds of hope for others. For ourselves, let the annual return of this day forever refresh our recollections of these rights, and an undiminished devotion to them.

On the London gallows in 1685, Colonel Richard Rumbold had dedicated his dying breath to the holy poor, with "saddles on their backs," ridden mercilessly by "a favored few booted and spurred." His well of inspiration almost dry, Jefferson borrowed the famous last words of a Puritan soldier, whose antiroyal sacred politics he could not help but admire, to pronounce his final benediction on sacred liberty.

"This is the Fourth of July?" Jefferson wondered aloud the night before he died. No one dared contradict him. "Ah," he said, with a sigh. "Just as I wished." Refusing a sedative, he lingered through a final night of vivid dreams. "Warn the Committee to be on the alert!" he bolted upright to blurt out. Then he scribbled an invisible note on the bedcovers with an imaginary pen. One last meeting to conduct. One final letter to write. According to his daughter Martha, he even tossed up a Hail Mary of sorts, the *Nunc Dimmitis*—"Lord, now lettest thou thy servant depart in peace"—but that was earlier in the week. The last books he thumbed were Seneca, Aristotle, and a couple of French pamphlets. Years before, Jefferson mused that if he could close his presidency with the people's affection undiminished and the nation prosperous and at peace, he could pronounce "the *nunc dimmitis Domine* with a satisfaction leaving nothing to desire but the last great audit." The great audit had arrived.

Jefferson died midday on the Fourth, fifty years to the hour—according to instant legend—that the Declaration of Independence was ratified in Congress. One unreconstructed old Federalist accused him of committing suicide by an overdose of laudanum in order to secure an unforgettable death. Margaret Smith, in her adoration, was closer to the truth. "Never," she confidently exclaimed, "was a death more serene and happy than Mr. J.'s."

"Thomas Jefferson Still Survives"

John Adams outlived Jefferson by some five hours. He, too, died at peace. "I am answerable for my own sins," he said, confessing to himself as much as to God. "I know they were my own faults; and that is enough for me to know." He also knew they were trivial faults, not mortal ones—venial, not venal sins.

Adams spent his intellectually rambunctious dotage entertaining guests and grandchildren as the amiable sage of Braintree, his angular nature softened by time, his wit undiminished. Surrounded, as he often was, by a company of young visitors, one day, interrupting a lively debate over the respective advantages of one Christian sect over another, Adams dismissed the bigotry inherent in them all. What he longed for, he puckishly interjected, was "the old Roman system of permitting every man to worship how and what he pleased." A shocked young man declared Adams guilty of paganism. Indeed I am, the lifelong churchgoing animal chuckled in reply. "In dogmatizing, laughing, and scolding, I find delight," he conceded happily to the Reverend Francis van der Kemp, a favorite correspondent of his final years, "and why should not I enjoy it, since no one is the worse for it and I am the better." It was all in good fun. "I damn nobody," Adams boasted, not quite accurately, before launching into his trademark cosmic reverie. "I am an atom of intellect with millions of solar systems over my head, under my feet, on my right hand, on my left, before me, and my adoration of the intelligence that contrived and the power that rules the stupendous fabric is too profound to believe them capable of anything unjust or cruel."

Unlike Jefferson, Adams didn't draft a brilliant letter to commemorate the upcoming Jubilee festivities—Boston mayor Josiah Quincy undertook them locally as "a solemn, and somewhat a religious, duty"—but he did provide a toast for the occasion ("Independence forever") and a cautionary note: "[The United States] is destined in future history to form the brightest or the blackest page, according to the use or the abuse of those political institutions by which they shall in time to come be shaped by the *human mind*." When asked if he had anything to add to his two-word toast, "Not a word," he replied. What remained of his Puritanism, as reflected in his warning, was a healthy skepticism concerning human nature. In Adams's estimation, God would not direct America's future. The American people, for better or worse, would shape their own destiny, guided perhaps but not determined by the legacy that he so passionately had dedicated his long, eventful life to shaping. Mayor Quincy harbored a more specific fear: that forthcoming generations would desecrate the "temple of liberty" by neglecting its "moral architecture." In good New England fashion, to save the "temple of liberty" from the excesses of liberty, he prayed that a new generation of citizens would rise up to supplement its "glorious arching of celestial wisdom" with the "purest faith."

"Do you know what day it is?" a servant inquired, after cannonades and church bells had awakened Adams on the final day of his life. "Oh yes," he replied. "It is the glorious Fourth of July—God bless it—God bless you all." That afternoon, his health took a fatal turn. Within two hours of his collapse, Adams was dead. His final words appear to have been "Thomas Jefferson still survives"—the verb was slurred, but there is no doubt that Jefferson was the last thing on Adams's restless mind.

Among the hundreds of eulogies pronounced from America's doubly blessed pulpits and lecterns, Senator Daniel Webster of Massachusetts commemorated the nation's two ancient icons' simultaneous deaths with characteristic grandiloquence: "On our fiftieth anniversary, the great day of national jubilee, in the very hour of public rejoicing, in the midst of echoing and reechoing voices of thanksgiving, while their own names were on all tongues, they took their flight together to the world of spirits." Webster was far from alone in divining the intervention of Providence on the young nation's most momentous anniversary. Looking back on the act that gave birth to the Republic, Jefferson, too, perceived a "holy purpose" at work. Congress's facsimile publication of the Declaration of Independence, issued to commemorate the nation's Jubilee, inspired him to muse on the nation's "reverence for that instrument," viewing the congressional action as "a pledge of adhesion to its principles and of a sacred determination to maintain and perpetuate them."

Most Americans celebrated the portentous deaths of their storied founders with awe, but one mourner, crushed with a sense of loss, carried a lingering torch. Following her heart, Margaret Bayard Smith went on a pilgrimage to Monticello. Words were insufficient "to describe all the feelings which swelled my bosom while standing by the side of that lonely and lowly grave in the solitude of the mountains, or the reflections on human life and human greatness, which rushed on my mind," she sighed.

> No kind friend with his gracious countenance stood in the portico to welcome us, no train of domestics hastened with smiling alacrity to show us forward. All was silent. Ruin has already commenced its ravages—the enclosures, the terraces, the outer houses. But we drove to the door, ascended the steps, knocked, and after a while a little negro girl poorly dressed open'd those once wide portals. We entered the hall once filled with busts and statues and natural curiosities to crowding, now empty! Bare walls and defaced floor, from thence into the drawing room, once so gay and splendid, where walls were literally covered with pictures like the hall—bare and comfortless.... The animating spirit was gone. And yet it was not gone, but seemed to be invisibly hovering near.

Across space and time, her hero's animating spirit has hovered near ever since. Adams may have outlived his old rival by a matter of hours, but he was right when he declared, "Thomas Jefferson survives."

Jefferson's arcadian vision would survive in triumphant dress in Andrew Jackson's Democracy. In Jackson's sentimental and pure America, honest laborers (yeomen of city and country) jealous of their liberty and eager to contest the combinations of corporate and aristocratic power would extend and by so doing reanimate Jefferson's Empire of Liberty. Jefferson's invocation of nature's god, who by universal birthright imposed lofty moral standards on future generations of Americans, would endure as well, and more lastingly. Not only America's slaves but also American women, laborers, racial minorities, homosexuals, indeed every class of citizen who rightly demand a fair share of the liberty, equality, and happiness that he wrote into the nation's promise, owe America's most multifaceted president some part of their liberation. In 1831, Nat Turner arranged for his slave revolt to begin on July 4; on July 4, 1854, ex-slave Frederick Douglass cited Jefferson's preamble to the Declaration of Independence in Rochester, New York, to prove his contention that the nation was undermining the founders' ideals; civil libertarian Henry David Thoreau elected the same day to move into his Walden Pond cabin; in 1848, the women gathering at Seneca Falls, New York, opened their groundbreaking Declaration of Rights with the ringing words "We hold these truths to be self-evident, that all men and women are created equal."

More than a century later, Martin Luther King Jr. would preach from the steps of the Lincoln Memorial, "I look forward to the day when this nation will rise up and live out the true meaning of its creed." King then recited the words of a beloved American anthem. "This will be the day when all God's children will be able to sing with new meaning, 'My country 'tis of thee, sweet land of liberty, of thee I sing. Land where my fathers died, land of the pilgrims' pride, from every mountainside let freedom ring.'"

> When we let freedom ring, when we let it ring from every village and every hamlet, from every state and every city, we will be able to speed up that day when all God's children, black men and white men, Jews and Gentiles, Protestants and Catholics, will be able to join hands and sing in the words of that old Negro spiritual, "Free at last! Free at last! Thank God almighty, we are free at last."

Nine score and seven years after it was written, King was proclaiming Jefferson's American Creed. Visitors by the millions admire it every year on the marble walls of the Jefferson Memorial in Washington. Franklin Delano Roosevelt chose the passages engraved there. Four of the five honor God and celebrate sacred liberty. Among them, in addition to two passages from the Declaration of Independence, are the immortal words that best express Jefferson's sacred-political faith: "I have sworn on the altar of liberty eternal hostility against every form of tyranny over the mind of man."

Jefferson failed to live up to his idealistic rhetoric but, in a way, his failure is unimportant. His dream proved so lasting that it would never cease to trouble the conscience of a nation. On the eve of the Civil War, Abraham Lincoln raised his proverbial glass: "All honor to Jefferson," he justly said, "to the man who, in the concrete pressure of a struggle for national independence by a single people, had the coolness, forecast, and capacity to introduce into a merely revolutionary document an abstract truth, applicable to all men and all times, and so to embalm it there, that today, and in all coming days, it shall be a rebuke and stumbling-block to the very harbingers of reappearing tyranny and oppression."

For himself, in his scrapbook, Jefferson was content to paste, how wistfully we will never know, an anticipatory epitaph, William Ray's "Patriotic Song":

> When words cannot save—
> Green garlands shall wave,
> And Liberty blossom o'er Jefferson's grave,
> To prove nature's equal, eternal decree—
> Heav'n ne'er form'd us slaves—man was born to live free.

Did George Washington Say "So Help Me God"?

∞⌒∞

T HE LONG-STANDING tradition that George Washington capped his oath of office on April 30, 1789, with the words "So help me God" has recently fallen into question. Critics argue that these words, together with the image of Washington bending down to kiss the Bible after swearing his oath, belong in the historical dustbin together with the story of young George cutting down the cherry tree.

It is true that the first report of Washington avowing "So help me God" dates from sixty-seven years after the event. In *George Washington: A Biography*, Washington Irving writes:

> The chancellor [Robert R. Livingston] advanced to administer the oath prescribed by the Constitution, and Mr. [Samuel A.] Otis, the secretary of the Senate, held up the Bible on its crimson cushion. The oath was read slowly and distinctly, Washington at the same time laying his hand on the open Bible. When it was concluded, he replied solemnly, "I swear—so help me God!" Mr. Otis would have raised the Bible to his lips but he bowed down reverently and kissed it.

Irving's most recent biographer considers his book on Washington, which Irving deemed the capstone of his literary career, "well-researched, highly energetic, and still-accessible." The question remains: Was Irving's imagination a bit too energetic in drawing this

reverent portrait? A contemporary account of the inaugural ceremonies, coupled with other secondary evidence, suggests that it
was not.

One vivid portrait of Washington taking the presidential oath
comes from an eyewitness to the ceremony, courtesy of a letter written three days after the inauguration, which Philadelphia's *Federal
Gazette* published on May 8.

> The scene was solemn and awful, beyond description. It would
> seem extraordinary that the administration of an oath, a ceremony
> so very common and familiar, should, in so great a degree, excite
> the public curiosity. But the circumstances of his election—the
> impression of his past services—the concourse of spectators—the
> devout fervency with which he repeated the oath—and the rever-
> ential manner in which he bowed down and kissed the sacred vol-
> ume—all these conspired to render it one of the most august and
> interesting spectacles ever exhibited on the globe. It seemed, from
> the number of witnesses, to be a somber appeal to heaven and earth
> at once. Upon the subject of this great and good man, I may, per-
> haps, be an enthusiast, but, I confess, I was under an awful and
> religious persuasion that the Gracious Ruler of the Universe was
> looking down at that moment with peculiar complacency on an
> act, which, to a part of his creatures was so very important. Under
> this impression, when the Chancellor pronounced, in a very feel-
> ing manner, "Long live George Washington," my sensibility was
> wound up to such a pitch, that I could do no more than wave with
> the rest, without the power of joining in the repeated acclamations
> which rent the air.

Clearly Irving was not mistaken about Washington bending down
to kiss the Bible. Whether the spectator's account of "the devout
fervency with which he repeated the oath" arose from Washington
avowing God's name in his pledge we cannot know. But it certainly

accords with the spirit of this testimony, which, in turn, confirms other details in Irving's description of the event.

Less tellingly, but reinforcing the same impression, Washington's principal aide, David Humphreys, who accompanied the president-elect to Federal Hall on Inauguration Day, rejoiced at Washington's civil piety as if it were a matter of public record. On May 9, nine days after the inauguration, he gave thanks in an article written for the *Pennsylvania Mercury* that the new nation had been consecrated on a Christian footing. Crediting him with more faith than Washington would presume to claim for himself, Humphreys wrote in the afterglow of the president's swearing-in and subsequent worship ceremony:

> I rejoice in the exaltation of a person to the head of the Union, who professes himself to be a Christian, who is not ashamed to confess Christ, glory in his cross, and publicly honor his institutions; and hope and pray, that all our rulers may follow his illustrious example, and be politically as well as religiously wise to promote, both by law and practice, the best interests of their country, by promoting the Christian religion.

Although only six years old at the time, Irving, too, was present in person at the inauguration of his famous namesake. In doing research for his biography or sharing reminiscences over the years, he likely tested his memories against those of other eyewitnesses. Irving's biography is free of the pious cant that compromises certain other early treatments of Washington's life, and he certainly had no religious ax to grind, being himself a thorough secularist. Taken together, these considerations, coupled with the above evidence, add strength to the verisimilitude of Irving's testimony.

Despite the secular language prescribed by the Constitution, that Washington should invoke God at the end of his oath of office would by no means have seemed exceptional at the time. Earlier that month, on April 6, the House drafted language for its own members' swearing-in ceremonies that included the same sacred codicil: "I,_____, a Representative of the United States in the Congress thereof, do solemnly swear (or affirm, as the case may be) in the presence of Almighty GOD, that I will support the Constitution of the United States. So help me GOD." Two months later they reversed themselves, voting into law language stripped of all religious reference, requiring members of Congress only "to support the Constitution of the United States." These competing oaths frame the vigorous debate being waged at the outset of the first Congress between those legislators who wished to guide government practice strictly by the Constitution and others who believed that a nod to the deity was essential to reverent statecraft. The leader of the latter faction, Senator Richard Henry Lee of Virginia, chaired the joint committee responsible for planning the inaugural festivities. It was Lee who proposed adding inaugural worship to the ceremony, which he appears to have fashioned on British precedent. That Lee, a pious Anglican, was responsible for fashioning the inaugural script further suggests that Washington might logically have capped his oath with the sacred vow familiar to British coronations.

One final piece of evidence endorses the credibility of Irving's account. On March 2, 1801, two days before his own inauguration and referring to the act of Congress from June 1789 that removed God language from the oath for federal officeholders, Thomas Jefferson posed a curious question to Chief Justice John Marshall, who would be administering the presidential oath: "I would pray you in the meantime to consider whether the oath prescribed in the Constitution be not the only necessary to take. It seems to comprehend the substance of that prescribed by the act of Congress to all officers, and it may be questionable whether the legislature can require any new oath from the President." Marshall replied, "That [oath] prescribed in the constitution seems to me to be the only one which is to be administered." I can conceive of no other reason for this exchange apart from Jefferson wishing assurance from Marshall that he would not be required to add the words "So help me God" to the oath spelled out in the Constitution. Given his firm commitment to church-state separation, Jefferson would have taken this scruple very seriously indeed.

Although every other piece of Irving's account of the swearing-in ceremony is confirmed by contemporaneous testimony, we may never know for sure that Washington pledged "So help me God" when he was inaugurated. In either case, the nation's first great state occasion, from the "reverential manner" in which Washington bent down to kiss the Bible to the *Te Deum* that closed inaugural worship, was laden with religious portent.

ACKNOWLEDGMENTS

PUNCTUATION, CAPITALIZATION, and spelling in the late eighteenth and early nineteenth century were anything but standardized. Without otherwise changing the passages I cite, I have conformed all three to modern practice. Those who wish to consult the original quotations can follow the footnotes to their sources.

The block of open time needed to write this book came via the generous gift of a yearlong sabbatical from the congregation of All Souls Unitarian Church in New York City. Over three decades, the people of All Souls have nurtured me with their faith and love. To them I gratefully dedicate this book.

My thanks go out as well to the dedicated folks at Harcourt: to Tim Bent, my longtime editor, for bringing me with him to this splendid publishing house; to Andrea Schulz, editor in chief, for her capable editorial guidance and steadfast support; to brilliant Katie Hall, who joined forces with me at a critical juncture to help sculpt a rough manuscript into the book you have before you; to managing editor David Hough, and copy editor Debbie Hardin, who trimmed my margin of error significantly; and to Pat Tierney, president and CEO of Harcourt, who gave his heart to this project from its very inception and buoyed my spirits along the way.

Two dedicated young scholars, Marc Loustau and Helena Shanahan, assisted me with my research—Marc at the outset of the project and Nell over the course of my first draft. Gary Dorrien, Niebuhr Professor at Union Theological Seminary; Edwin Gaustad, dean of

American church historians; and my dear friend Robert Oxnam were kind enough to read early drafts, offering encouragement and wisdom.

Finally, and with all my heart, I thank my wife, Carolyn, who bolstered body and soul during my bout with cancer in the fall of 2006. I can say without exaggeration that I would never have been able to complete this project without her by my side.

ENDNOTES

∞∞∞

ABBREVIATIONS

INDIVIDUALS

AH	Alexander Hamilton
JA	John Adams
AA	Abigail Adams
DM	Dolley Madison
GW	George Washington
TJ	Thomas Jefferson
BR	Benjamin Rush
JM	James Madison

COLLECTIONS

AFC *Adams Family Correspondence,* ed. L. H. Butterfield et al. (Cambridge, MA, 1963–)

AFPEA *Adams Family Papers: An Electronic Archive,* Massachusetts Historical Society (www.masshist.org/digitaladams)

AJL *The Adams-Jefferson Letters: The Complete Correspondence Between Thomas Jefferson and Abigail and John Adams,* ed. Lester J. Capon (New York, 1971)

DAJA *Diary and Autobiography of John Adams,* ed. L. H. Butterfield et al., 4 vols. (Cambridge, MA, 1961)

DGW *The Diaries of George Washington,* ed. Donald Jackson and Dorothy Twohig (Charlottesville, VA, 1976–1979)

JEG *Jefferson's Extracts from the Gospels,* ed. Dickenson W. Adams (Princeton, NJ, 1983)

PAH *The Papers of Alexander Hamilton,* ed. Harold C. Syrett and Jacob E. Cooke (New York, 1961–1979)

PJM *The Papers of James Madison,* ed. William T. Hutchinson et al. (Chicago and Charlottesville, VA, 1962–)

PJMP   *The Papers of James Madison: Presidential Series,* ed. Robert A. Rutland et
        al. (Charlottesville, VA, 1962–)

PTJ   *The Papers of Thomas Jefferson,* ed. Julian P. Boyd et al. (Princeton, 1950–)

PWC   *The Papers of George Washington: Colonial Series,* ed. W. W. Abbot,
        Dorothy Twohig, and Philander D. Chase (Charlottesville, VA,
        1983–1995).

PWCF   *The Papers of George Washington, Confederation Series,* ed. W. W. Abbot
        and Dorothy Twohig (Charlottesville, VA, 1992–1997).

PWJA   *The Political Writings of John Adams,* ed. George W. Carey (Washington,
        D.C., 2000)

PWJM   *The Political Writings of James Monroe,* ed. James P. Lucier (Washington,
        D.C., 2001)

PWP   *The Papers of George Washington: Presidential Series,* ed. W. W. Abbot and
        Dorothy Twohig (Charlottesville, VA, 1987–).

PWR   *The Papers of George Washington: Revolutionary War Series,* ed. W. W.
        Abbot, Dorothy Twohig, and Philander D. Chase (Charlottesville, VA,
        1985–)

PWRT   *The Papers of George Washington: Retirement Series,* ed. W. W. Abbot
        (Charlottesville, VA, 1985–)

ROL   *The Republic of Letters: The Correspondence Between Thomas Jefferson and
        James Madison, 1776–1826,* ed. Richard Morton Smith (New York, 1995)

SOF   *The Spur of Fame: Dialogues of John Adams and Benjamin Rush,* John A.
        Schultz and Douglas Adair, eds. (Indianapolis, IN, 2001)

TJW   *The Writings of Thomas Jefferson,* ed. Andrew A. Lipscomb and Albert E.
        Bergh (Washington, D.C., 1903)

WJA   *The Works of John Adams,* ed. Charles F. Adams (Boston, 1850–1856)

WJM   *The Writings of James Madison,* ed. Gaillard Hunt (New York, 1900–1910)

WTJ   *The Works of Thomas Jefferson,* ed. Paul Leicester Ford (New York,
        1900–1910)

WW   *Writings of George Washington,* ed. John C. Fitzpatrick (Washington,
        D.C., 1931–1939)

INTRODUCTION

PAGE
1 "Our statesmen"   "Reverses Needed" Winthrop S. Hudson, ed., *Nationalism and
    Religion in America,* 75–84.
10 "It is in our lives"   To Margaret Bayard Smith, August 6, 1816, *The First Forty
    Years of Washington Society,* Gaillard Hunt, ed., 126–27.
12 "Jefferson's Bible"   *Jefferson's Bible* (Boston, 2000); *The American Creed: A
    Biography of the Declaration of Independence* (New York, 2002); *The Separation
    of Church and State: Writings on a Fundamental Freedom by America's Founders*
    (Boston, 2004).

14 "America might"   Martin Luther King Jr., "I Have a Dream," Taylor Branch, *Parting the Waters* (New York, 1988), 880.

CHAPTER ONE

PAGE

17 "Fame stretched her wings"   Werner Hartmann and Piers A. Vaughan, "The George Washington Inaugural Bible," www.stjohns1.org.

18 "His entrance on"   Washington Irving, *George Washington*, 651.

19 "bear a vacancy"   JM to TJ, *PTJ* 7: 592; James Thomas Flexner, *George Washington and the New Nation*, 82.

19 "gloomy apprehensions"   TJ to JM, 29 March 1798, *ROL* 2: 1030.

19 "I feel very much"   David Humphreys, *Life of General Washington*, 50–51.

19 "You ought sometimes"   Rosemarie Lagarri, ed., *Life of General Washington by David Humphreys*, xlviii.

20 "My only ambition"   David Humphreys, *Life of General Washington*, 47.

20 "frugality, simplicity"   Carl J. Richard, *The Founders and the Classics*, 185.

20 "We are afraid"   Jay Fliegelman, *Jefferson, Natural Language, and the Culture of Performance*, 109.

20 "To forsake the"   James Thomas Flexner, *George Washington and the New Nation*, 111.

21 "The citizens of America"   Farewell Circular, 8 June 1783, *WW* 26: 485.

21 "some advisory hints"   GW to George S. Washington, 23 March 1789, *PWP* 1: 438–39.

23 *Annuit coeptis*   Malcolm Kelsall, *Jefferson and the Iconography of Romanticism*, 45–68.

23 "The defender of the mothers"   K. Silverman, *A Cultural History of the American Revolution*, 605.

24 "fit young gentlemen"   Fred J. Hood, *Reformed America*, 12.

24 "The very water"   Page Smith, *John Adams* 2: 746.

25 "mounted on an ass"   John Armstrong to Horatio Gates, 7 April 1789, *PGWP* 2: 114–15.

25 "We are a young nation"   GW to John Augustine Washington, 15 June 1783, *WW* 27: 13; cf. Edmund S. Morgan, *The Genius of George Washington*, 20.

25 "We are in a wilderness"   James Roger Sharp, *American Politics in the Early Republic*, 18, n.6.

25 "As the first of everything"   GW to JM, 5 May 1789, *PWP* 2: 216–17.

25–26 "Many things which appear"   GW to JA, 10 May 1789, *PWP* 2: 246–47.

26 "him on a level with"   David McCullough, *John Adams*, 405.

26 "Religion and government"   Page Smith, *John Adams* 2: 754.

26–27 *"Fear God and honor the King"*   William Maclay, *The Journal of William Maclay*, 22–23.

27 "despise him to all eternity"   William Maclay, *The Journal of William Maclay*, 26.

27 "No title of nobility"   U.S. Constitution, Article VI.

27 "contraband language"   William Maclay, *The Journal of William Maclay*, 27.

27 "His Highness"   JM to TJ, 23 May 1789, *ROL* 1: 612.

27 "the most superlatively"   TJ to JM, 29 July 1789, *ROL* 1: 626.

27 "Chamberlain...proportioned to them"   JA to GW, 17 May 1789, *PGWP* 2: 312–13.

28 "other name can"   "Three Letters to Roger Sherman," *PWJA,* 448.

28 "When the President"   Page Smith, *John Adams* 2: 747.

28 "His superfluous Excellency"   Joel Achenbach, *The Grand Idea,* 162.

28 "His rotundity...monarchy in America"   William Maclay, *The Journal of William Maclay,* 31, 36, 49, 53, 63.

29 "His Highness"   Lance Banning, *The Sacred Fire of Liberty,* 34; Peter Shaw, *The Character of John Adams,* 213–14.

29 "Formalities and ceremonies"   30 June 1770, *DAJA* 1: 355.

30 "all the fooleries"   William Maclay, *The Journals of William Maclay,* 24.

31 "wise and free republic...unbalancing the Constitution"   Edmund S. Morgan, "The Puritan Ethic and the American Revolution," 28; Page Smith, *John Adams* 1: 440; Gordon Wood, *Creation of the American Republic,* 521.

32 "Refiners may weave...civilized and strange"   Oliver Perry Chitwood, *Richard Henry Lee,* 202; Forrest McDonald, *Novus Ordo Seclorum,* 44.

32 "to take under"   Stanley Elkins and Eric McKitrick, *The Age of Federalism,* 47.

33 "he possessed the gift"   JA to BR, 11 November 1807, *SOF,* 106–7.

33 "divine services"   William Maclay, *The Journal of William Maclay,* 4; *PGWP* 2: 154.

33–34 "liberal regard for"   James Grant, *John Adams,* 318–19.

34 "no Bishop no King"   Walter Herbert Stowe, ed., *The Life and Letters of Bishop William White,* 71.

34 "We have neither departed"   Walter Stahr, *John Jay,* 234–35.

34 "when people are more"   Stacy Schiff, *A Great Improvisation,* 376.

35 "There was no part"   Walter Herbert Stowe, ed., *The Life and Letters of Bishop William White,* 97.

35 "Lee offered"   William Maclay, *The Journal of William Maclay,* 4; Martin J. Medhurst, "From Duché to Medhurst: The Birth of Inaugural Prayer," 582–86.

35 "The things which"   "Coronation of the British Monarch: 3) Recognition and Oath," wikipedia.com.

36 "I declare we forgot it!"   Arthur M. Schlesinger Jr., *War and the American Presidency,* 147–48.

36 "a new phenomenon"   GW to John Lathrop, 22 June 1788, *PWCF* 6: 349.

37 "In the name of"   Jay Fliegelman, *Prodigals and Pilgrims,* 178.

37 "we should not have"   Morton Border, *Jews, Turks, and Infidels,* 22.

37 "I am persuaded"   GW to Presbytery of Massachusetts and New Hampshire, 23 October 1789, *WW* 30: 453.

37 "I am a being"   JA to AA, 9 March 1797; Lynne Withey, *Dearest Friend,* 247.

37 "Gentlemen, I wish for"   William Maclay, *The Journal of William Maclay,* 7–8.

38 "Sir, the Senate"   Flexner, *George Washington and the New Nation,* 187.

38–39 "bound by the oath"   Thomas C. Thompson, "Perceptions of a 'Deist Church' in Early National Virginia," 47.

39 "It is done"   George Dangerfield, *Chancellor Robert R. Livingston of New York,* 242.

39 "The president, I suppose"   William Maclay, *The Journal of William Maclay,* 7; Stanley Elkins and Eric McKitrick, *The Age of Federalism,* 47.

39 "I shall take my"   GW to the Senate and the House of Representatives, First Inaugural Address, 30 April 1789, *PWP* 2: 176–77.

40 "if the blessings...by human depravity"   GW, Undelivered First Inaugural Address: fragment 33–34, April–June 1789, *PWP* 2: 166.

40–41 "The foundations of...the United States"   GW to the Senate and the House of Representatives, First Inaugural Address, 30 April 1789, *WW* 30: 291–96.

41 "the invisible hand"   Adam Smith, *The Wealth of Nations,* IV, 2; Forrest Church, *The American Creed,* 138.

42 "Long live the President"   New York Historical Society Collections.

43 "Remember in these cloisters"   John P. Riley, "'Go and Make a Grateful People Happy,'" 4304.

43 "scandalous, malignant priests"   Martin H. Quitt, "The English Cleric and the Virginia Adventurer," 15–24.

44 "When you speak"   "Rules for Behavior," *George Washington Writings,* ed. John Rhodehamel, 10.

44 *The Royal English Grammar*   Paul K. Longmore, *The Invention of George Washington,* 8–9; Willard Sterne Randall, *George Washington* 53: 120–21; John E. Ferling, *The First of Men,* 10–11.

45 "swilling the planters"   Dumas Malone, *Jefferson the Virginian,* 129.

45 all three clergymen   Paul K. Longmore, *The Invention of George Washington,* 59–60.

46 "He is a modest man"   Don Higginbotham, "George Washington and Revolutionary Asceticism," 150.

46 "As vestryman for"   Joseph F. Freeman III, "The Church of Virginia Before Independence," 13.

46 "truly remarkable"   Paul F. Boller, *George Washington and Religion,* 74–75.

47 "I believe in one God"   Thomas Paine, *The Age of Reason,* 50; David L. Holmes, "The Faiths of the Founding Fathers," 46.

47 "warm Deist"   Edwin Gaustad, *Sworn Upon the Altar of God,* 143.

47 "Providence...Author of all Good"   Frank E. Grizzard Jr., *The Ways of Providence,* 4–5.

47 "Being no bigot myself"   GW to Marquis de Lafayette, 15 August 1787, *PWCF* 5: 295.

47 "Could you"   GW to Burwell Bassett, 28 August 1762, *WW* 37: 484–85; Thomas Flexner, *George Washington: The Forge of Experience,* 237.

48 "I presume it is"   James Thomas Flexner, *George Washington: The Forge of Experience,* 244.

48 "sending the bottle"   Joel Achenbach, *The Grand Idea,* 129.

48 110-gallon kegs   Thomas J. Fleming, *First in Their Hearts,* 47; Samuel Eliot Morison, *The Young Man Washington,* 9.

48 "By God, I"   James Thomas Flexner, *George Washington: Anguish and Farewell*, 67.

48 "He was always in"   James Thomas Flexner, *George Washington and the New Nation*, 28.

49 $2000–$2500 today   Henry Wiencek, *An Imperfect God*, 126–31.

49 "Let no one go hungry"   GW to Lund Washington, 26 November 1775, *PWR* 2: 432; Don Higginbotham, "George Washington and Revolutionary Asceticism," 149.

49 "Nothing but harmony…public felicity"   GW to Marquis de Lafayette, 29 January 1789, *WW* 30: 186.

49–50 "most gracious speech…drawn my sword"   William Maclay, *The Journal of William Maclay*, 9–11, 84.

50 "If our new government"   William Maclay, *The Journal of William Maclay*, 52, 172.

50 "coronation"   Gordon S. Wood, *Revolutionary Characters*, 51.

50 "Tomorrow is the day"   *The Gazette of the United States*; cf. *A Great and Good Man*, eds. John P. Kaminski and Jill Adair McCaughan, 127.

50–51 "The impression of"   *Federal Gazette*, 8 May 1798; cf. Jedidiah Morse, *American Geography* (London, 1794), 271–72.

51 "O Washington"   Gordon Wood, "The Greatness of George Washington," 311.

51 "the odor of incense"   Garry Wills, *Cincinnatus*, 13; GW to Oliver Wolcott Jr., 9 December 1789; K. Silverman, *A Cultural History of the American Revolution*, 599.

51 "Visits of Compliment"   JA to GW, 17 May 1789, *PGWP* 2: 312.

52 "Gentlemen, THE PRESIDENT"   *PTJ* 1: 216.

52 "too free an intercourse"   GW to JM, 12 May 1789, *PWP* 2: 282.

52 "To draw such a line"   GW to JM, 12 May 1789, *PWP* 2: 282; cf. GW to David Stuart, 15 June 1790, *PGWP* 2: 248.

52 "eastern lama…with great attention"   William Maclay, *The Journal of William Maclay*, 21, 172.

52 "Your Majesty"   Gore Vidal, *Inventing a Nation*, 72.

52 "a dignity that"   William M. S. Rasmussen and Robert S. Tilton, *George Washington*, 112.

52 "Her Presidentess"   Carl Sferrazza Anthony, *First Ladies*, 46.

53 "To the chorus of"   *New York Times*, 29 April 1989, A, 1; 30 April 1989, A, 1.

CHAPTER TWO

PAGE

54 "Proceed, great chief"   Steven Goul Axelrod, Camille Roman, and Thomas Travisano, eds., *The New Anthology of American Poetry, Volume One: Traditions and Revolutions, Beginnings to 1900* (Rutgers, NJ, 2003), 115.

54 "might soon expect"   GW to Marquis de Lafayette, 8 December 1784, *PWCF* 2: 175.

54–55 "sleep with my fathers…the shades below"   Peter R. Henriques, "The Final Struggle Between George Washington and the Grim King," 250–71.

55 "respecting [Cicero's] belief"   GW to Annis Boudinot Stockton, 31 August 1788, *PWCF* 6: 497; cf. Willard Sterne Randall, *George Washington,* 445.

55 "A fine healthy girl"   Willard Sterne Randall, *George Washington,* 175.

55 "He seemed less concerned"   Patricia Brady, *Martha Washington,* xv, 165–67, 188, 201; Carl Sferrazza Anthony, *First Ladies,* 43–44.

56 "too illiterate"   Paul Johnson, *George Washington,* 9, 96.

56 "the central stone"   JA to BR, 19 March 1812, *SOF,* 230; Page Smith, *John Adams* 2: 794.

56 "A kind destiny"   GW to Martha Washington, 18 June 1775, *PWR* 1: 3–4.

57 "a flock of ducks"   Stacy Schiff, *A Great Improvisation,* 169.

57 "the favor of divine"   GW, General Order, 27 February 1776, *PWR* 3: 380.

57 "making a disturbance"   James Thomas Flexner, *George Washington in the American Revolution,* 28; David McCullough, *1776,* 32.

58 "incessantly, Sundays not"   GW to Samuel Washington, 20 July 1775, *PWR* 1: 135.

58 "No fatigue parties"   GW, General Orders, 2 May 1778, *PWR* 15: 13.

58 "season of general joy"   GW, General Orders, 7 May 1778, *PWR* 15: 69; John E. Ferling, *The First of Men,* 241–42.

58 "Gaming of every kind"   GW, General Instructions for the Colonels and Commanding Officers of Regiments in the Continental Service, 1777, *WW* 10: 242.

58 "the Sabbath was"   Jon Butler, *Awash in a Sea of Faith,* 210–11.

58–59 "no furloughs will be granted"   GW, General Orders, 15 February 1783, *WW* 26: 136.

59 "has a tendency to"   GW to the President of Congress, 8 June 1777, *PWR* 9: 231.

59 Pope's Day   James Sharpe, *Remember, Remember,* 141–45.

59 "As the Commander"   GW, General Orders, 5 November 1775, *PWR* 2: 300.

60 "While we are contending"   GW to Colonel Benedict Arnold, 14 September 1775, *PWR* 1: 456.

60 "I need not explain"   GW to the Reverend John Ettwein, 28 March 1778, *PWR* 14: 335; Bruce Chadwick, *George Washington's War,* 233.

61 "affording them an opportunity"   Paul Johnson, *George Washington,* 103.

61 "a business with which"   Paul F. Boller Jr., *George Washington & Religion,* 63.

61 "mimicking…European customs"   Peter Kross, "Elias Boudinot, America's First President," 1.

62 "cooked up"   Garry Wills, *Under God,* 359–60; Dumas Malone, *Jefferson the Virginian,* 172–73.

62 "Day of Fasting"   Willard Sterne Randall, *George Washington,* 260.

62 "God Save the King"   Willard Sterne Randall, *George Washington,* 260–61.

62 "like a shock"   *WTJ* 1: 12; Dumas Malone, *Jefferson the Virginian,* 173.

63 "making such a solemn"   Catherine Albanese, *Sons of the Fathers,* 197–98.

63 "devoutly acknowledging"   James Thomas Flexner, *George Washington and the New Nation,* 184n.

63–64 "a decidedly Christian"   Fred J. Hood, *Reformed America,* 104.

64 "that great and glorious"   GW, The Thanksgiving Proclamation, 3 October 1789, PWP 4: 131–32.

64 "that to admit Jews"   James A. Monroe, Hellfire Nation, 71.

64 1,243 Jewish citizens   David L. Holmes, The Faiths of the Founding Fathers, 1.

65 "All possess alike"   GW to the Hebrew Congregation in Newport, Rhode Island, 18 August 1790, PWP 6: 285; John P. Kaminski and Jill Adair McCaughan, eds., A Great and Good Man, 181.

65 "May the children"   GW to the Hebrew Congregation in Newport, Rhode Island, 18 August 1790, PWP 6: 285; Paul F. Boller, George Washington and Religion, 153, 187–88.

65 "With me, it has"   GW to James Anderson, 21 December 1797, PWRT 1: 525–26; Malcolm L. Cross, "Washington, Hamilton, and the Establishment of the Dignified and Efficient Presidency," 102.

65 "Exitus Acta"   William M. S. Rasmussen and Robert S. Tilton, George Washington: The Man Behind the Myths, 18–19.

66 "In politics, as in religion"   GW to James Anderson, 24 December 1795, WW 34: 407.

66 "Restraints on conscience"   James Thomas Flexner, George Washington: The Forge of Experience, 48; Willard Sterne Randall, George Washington, 235.

67 "As mankind become"   GW to a committee of Roman Catholics, 15 March 1790; Paul F. Boller, George Washington and Religion, 182.

68 "a wall of separation"   Edwin A. Gaustad, Sworn on the Altar of God, 72; Forrest Church, The American Creed: A Biography of the Declaration of Independence, 10–18.

68 "We as a society…time of peace"   Virginia Baptist General Committee to GW, 8 August 1789; Reuben E. Alley, A History of Baptists in Virginia, 370.

68–69 "If I could have"   GW to the General Committee of the United Baptist Churches in Virginia, May 1789, PWP 2: 424; Paul F. Boller, George Washington and Religion, 169–70.

69 "quiet to the state"   GW to George Mason, 3 October 1785, PWCF 3: 292–93.

69 "firm friends to civil"   GW to the General Committee of the United Baptist Churches in Virginia, May 1789, PWP 2: 424.

70 "Conscience has nothing"   Richard D. Birdsall, "The Second Great Awakening and the New England Social Order," 352.

70 "The unfortunate condition"   "George Washington's Remarks," David Humphreys, Life of General Washington, ed. Rosemarie Lagarri, 78; Henry Wiencek, An Imperfect God, 272.

71 "There is not a man living"   GW to Robert Morris, 12 April 1786, PWCF 4: 16.

71 "Blacks are capable of much good labor"   GW to Arthur Young, 18–21 June 71, PWP 10: 461.

71 "Religion produced a"   John Chester Miller, The Wolf by the Ears, 75.

71 "very troublesome species"   GW to Alexander Spotswood, 23 November 1794, WW 34: 48.

72 "a late publication"   G. Adolf Koch, *Republican Religion,* 11–12.

72 "his opinion against"   Dorothy Twohig, "The Controversy over Slavery," 134, n.21.

72 "He informed us"   James Thomas Flexner, *George Washington: Anguish and Farewell,* 119.

72 "treated with all"   JM to TJ, 22 January 1786, *ROL* 1: 405.

72 "by slow, sure"   GW to John Francis Mercer, 9 September 1786, *Washington: Writings,* 697.

73 "Unfeigned righteousness"   Sydney V. James, *A People Among Peoples,* 283.

73 "wish and desire"   GW to the Society of Quakers, in response to their letter to GW sent on 28 September 1789; Paul F. Boller Jr., *George Washington & Religion,* 179.

73 "vice, infidelity and irreligion"   Sydney V. James, *A People Among Peoples,* 283.

73 "At two o'clock"   GW, 13 October 1789, *Diaries* 5: 460.

74 "promoting the abolition"   Joseph J. Ellis, *Founding Brothers,* 81–87.

74 "an atrocious debasement"   Edmund S. Morgan, *The Genuine Article,* 227.

74 "promote mercy and"   Gordon S. Wood, *The Americanization of Benjamin Franklin,* 227.

74 "base invective"   William Maclay, *The Journal of William Maclay,* 216.

74 "If we forbear"   Gordon S. Wood, *The Americanization of Benjamin Franklin,* 228; Joseph Ellis, *Founding Brothers,* 111.

75 "exercise [its power]...shamefully indecent"   Stanley Elkins and Eric McKitrick, *The Age of Federalism,* 151–52.

75 "might come before me"   GW, 16 March 1790, *DGW* 6: 47.

75 "very *mal-apropos*"   GW to David Stuart, 28 March 1790, *PWP* 5: 288.

75 "The introductions of"   GW to David Stuart, 15 July 1790, *WW* 31: 52.

75–76 "The Senate have met"   Robert Allen Rutland, *James Madison: The Founding Father,* 240.

76 "rather with a sneer...along with them"   William Maclay, *The Journal of William Maclay,* 191, 226.

76 "This Society is"   GW to Robert Morris, 12 April 1786, *PWCF* 4: 15.

77 "There is no avoiding"   GW to Robert Morris, 12 April 1786, *PWCF* 4:16.

78 One Boston paper   *The Massachusetts Centinal,* 16 December 1789.

78 "against the law to travel"   8 November 1789, *DGW* 4: 50.

78 "immorality, impiety"   Vernon Stauffer, *New England and the Bavarian Illuminati,* 15–16.

78 "to enliven morality"   Ralph Ketcham, *Presidents Above Party,* 47–52.

78 "'Tis not in mortals"   Fredric M. Litto, "Addison's *Cato* in the Colonies," 433.

79 "Being in the language"   *DGW,* 3 July 1791; Paul F. Boller Jr., *George Washington and Religion,* 31.

80 "those in elevated"   Paul F. Boller Jr., *George Washington and Religion,* 34.

80 "I do not believe"   Paul F. Boller Jr., *George Washington and Religion,* 89.

81 "I am by no means"   Walter Herbert Stowe, ed., *The Life and Letters of Bishop William White,* 11.

81 "for the comfort of the needy"   GW to Reverend William White, 1 January 1794, *WW* 33: 230; Bird Wilson, *Memoir of the Life of Bishop White*, 198–99.

81 "His behavior in church"   Bird Wilson, *Memoir of the Life of Bishop White*, 189; Paul F. Boller Jr., *George Washington and Religion*, 34.

CHAPTER THREE

PAGE

83 "Oh, God, the source"   Colonel David Humphreys, "MOUNT VERNON: AN ODE, inscribed to GENERAL WASHINGTON, Written at Mount Vernon, August 1787" (in response to Shays's Rebellion), *The Miscellaneous Works of David Humphreys* (Gainesville, FL, 1968), 224–25.

84 "wardens with truncheons"   James Thomas Flexner, *George Washington: Anguish and Farewell*, 88–90.

84 "in the year of Masonry"   John L. Brooks, "Ancient Lodges and Self-Created Societies: Voluntary Association and the Public Sphere in the Early Republic," 273–74; Steven C. Bullock, *Revolutionary Brotherhood*, 137.

84–85 "founded in benevolence"   GW to the Maryland Masons, 8 November 1798, *WW* 37: 13.

85 25,000 members   Catherine L. Albanese, *Sons of the Fathers*, 130; Stacy Schiff, *A Great Improvisation*, 159, 220.

85 "leave their particular"   Mark A. Tabbert, *American Freemasons*, 12.

85–86 "I receive your kind"   GW to the Grand Lodge in Pennsylvania, 3 January 1792, *PWP* 9: 371.

86 "a just application"   GW to King David's Lodge, Newport, RI, 18 August 1790, *PWP* 6: 287.

86 "for the benefit of the whole"   GW to James McHenry, 22 August 1785, *PWCF* 3: 198.

86 "the public good"   GW to Comte de Moustier, 1 November 1790, *PWP* 6: 608.

87 "rulers run without"   S. Hugh Brockunier, in Richard J. Purcell, *Connecticut in Transition*, xi–xii.

87 "Le Marseilles"   Walt Brown, *John Adams and the American Press*, 17.

88 "a womanish attachment"   AH to Edward Carrington, 26 May 1792, *PAH* 11: 439.

88 "a fatal stroke"   James Thomas Flexner, *George Washington: Anguish and Farewell*, 67.

88–89 "It has aptly been observed"   AH to GW, 18 August 1792 (Objection 14), *PAH* 12: 252.

89 "Far from being matters"   Simon P. Newman, *Parades and the Politics of the Street*, 55.

89 "Liberty's hair with a bow"   Simon P. Newman, *Parades and the Politics of the Street*, 57; Jay Fliegelman, *Jefferson, Natural Language, and the Culture of Performance*, 107.

90 "health and morals"   Darren Staloff, *Hamilton, Adams, Jefferson*, 121.

90–91 "the pernicious effects...without the benefit of clergy"   Thomas P. Slaughter, *The Whiskey Rebellion*, 63–64, 136–37, 194.

91 "Doctor Davidson preach…pitied nor spared" GW, 5 October 1794, *DGW* 6: 182.

91 "The Whiskey boys" Thomas P. Slaughter, *The Whiskey Rebellion*, 205–8.

91 "An insurrection was announced" TJ to James Monroe, 26 May 1795, *PTJ* 28: 359.

91 "the army of the Constitution" GW to AH, *WGW* 34: 7–8.

92 watermelon army Forrest McDonald, *The Presidency of George Washington*, 144–46.

92 "there is no law" James Thomas Flexner, *George Washington: Anguish and Farewell*, 175; Thomas P. Slaughter, *The Whiskey Rebellion*, 206–21.

92 "The essential principles" GW to Governor Henry Lee, 20 October 1794, *WW* 34: 6.

92 "enemies of order" GW to Governor Henry Lee, 20 October 1794, *WW* 34: 5–7.

93 "the most diabolical" GW to Governor Henry Lee, 26 August 1794, *WW* 33: 476.

93 "hostile to the liberties" Thomas P. Slaughter, *The Whiskey Rebellion*, 161.

93 "Fostered and embittered" GW, Sixth Annual Address to Congress, 19 November 1794, *WW* 34: 28–29.

94 "cause of liberty…God of liberty" John F. Berens, *Providence & Patriotism in Early America*, 51, 75–85, 123.

95 "as a check" Joseph W. Phillips, *Jedidiah Morse and New England Congregationalism*, 21, 28–33, 53.

96 "Opinions…human happiness" Alexander Hamilton, "Views on the French Revolution," 1794, *PAH* 26: 738–41.

97 "I consider politics…nine out of ten" Joseph W. Phillips, *Jedidiah Morse and New England Congregationalism*, 62, 71.

97 "I love your plain" Eugene Perry Link, *Democratic-Republican Societies, 1790–1800*, 197–99.

98 "May the God of order" David Osgood, "A Sermon Delivered on the Day of Annual Thanksgiving, November 20, 1794," Ellis Sandoz, ed., *Political Sermons of the American Founding Era*, 1218, 1221–36.

98 "put into the hand" Vernon Stauffer, *New England and the Bavarian Illuminati*, 114.

98 "Ambition and tyranny" Eugene Perry Link, *Democratic-Republican Societies, 1790–1800*, 119–20.

98 "I hate treason" Joel Achenbach, *The Grand Idea*, 202.

98 "It is wonderful" TJ to JM, 28 December 1794, *ROL* 2: 867.

98 "double delicacies" TJ to JM, 28 December 1794, *ROL* 2: 868.

99 "For God's sake" TJ to JM, 7 July 1793, *ROL* 2: 792.

99 "high treason" TJ to JM, 1 October 1792, *ROL* 2: 740.

99 "the foreigners and degenerate" JM, "Letters of Helvidius, No. 1," *WJM* 6: 138.

99 "an American Psalm" Richard V. Pierard and Robert D. Linder, *Civil Religion & the Presidency*, 77.

99 "Let us unite"   GW, Sixth Annual Address to Congress, November 1794, *WW*
   34: 29.
100 "the kind Author"   GW, Thanksgiving Day Proclamation, 3 October 1789,
   PGW 4: 129–30.
100 "Samuel, Bishop of"   Richard J. Purcell, *Connecticut in Transition,* 39.
100 "afford an opening"   Gary B. Nash, "The American Clergy and the French
   Revolution," 408.
100 "grumbletonians"   Joseph W. Phillips, *Jedidiah Morse and New England
   Congregationalism,* 46–50.
100–101 "reciprocal influence of"   Gary B. Nash, "The American Clergy and the
   French Revolution," 398.
101 "We have too many…them have done"   Joseph W. Phillips, *Jedidiah Morse
   and New England Congregationalism,* 55–56, 68.
102 "In vain had"   Bishop James Madison, "National Fast Day Sermon, 19th of
   February, 1795" (Richmond, VA, 1795); *Presidential Sermons of the American
   Founding Era, 1730–1805,* Ellis Sandoz, ed., 2: 1310–11.
102 "The clergy are"   William White, "A Sermon on the Reciprocal Influence of
   Civil Policy and Religious Duty" (Philadelphia, 1795); Gary B. Nash, "The
   American Clergy and the French Revolution," 411.
103 "As this address"   *PGW* 35: 31–51; James Thomas Flexner, *George Washington:
   Anguish and Farewell,* 293.
103–4 "Of all the dispositions"   GW, Farewell Address, 19 September 1796, *WW*
   35: 229.
104 "I have regretted"   GW to AH, 1 September 1796, *WW* 35: 199.
105 "the future guardians"   GW, First Annual Address to Congress, 8 January 1790,
   WW 30: 493.
105 "Promote then"   GW, Farewell Address, 19 September 1796, *WW* 35: 229.
106 "In his answer"   Bird Wilson, *The Memoirs of the Life of Bishop White,* 190.
106 "It affords edifying…own religious society"   Paul F. Boller Jr., *George
   Washington and Religion,* 171–72, 176.
106 "many professed Deists"   Reverend Stephen Peabody, Election Day Sermon
   (Concord, NH, 1797), *Presidential Sermons of the American Founding Era,
   1730–1805,* Ellis Sandoz, ed., 2: 1332.
107 "just and pious…of universal harmony"   GW to the Clergy of Different
   Denominations Residing in and near the City of Philadelphia, 3 March 1797,
   WW 35: 416; Paul F. Boller Jr., *George Washington and Religion,* 80–82.
107–8 "[Rush] had it"   *WTJ* 1: 284; Jefferson's *Anas.*
108 "the old fox"   Paul Boller Jr., *George Washington and Religion,* 83.
108 "I shall quit"   GW to Reverend William Gordon, 23 January 1778, *WW* 10: 338.
109 "I am become"   GW to Marquis de Lafayette, 1 February 1784, *WW*
   27: 317–18.
109 "in the calm"   GW to Charles Cotesworth Pinckney, 24 June 1797, *WW*
   35: 471.
110 "Doomsday Book…for the epaulettes"   James Thomas Flexner, *George
   Washington: Anguish and Farewell,* 341, 419.

110 "I possess a good"   GW to Tobias Lear, 6 May 1794, *WW* 33: 358.

110–11 "Upon the decease"   GW, Last Will and Testament, *WW* 37: 276.

111 special watermark   James Thomas Flexner, *George Washington: Anguish and Farewell*, 453 (image).

111 "I was the *first*"   GW to Burges Ball, 22 September 1799, *PWRT* 4: 318.

111 "'Tis well"   Peter R. Henriques, *Realistic Visionary*, 187–204.

112 "playing a solemn dirge"   Patricia Brady, *Martha Washington*, 187; Douglass Southall Freeman, *Washington*, 754.

112 "It is my express"   GW, Last Will and Testament, *WW* 37: 270.

112 "first in war"   David McCullough, *John Adams*, 533.

112–13 "Bind it in your Bible"   Francois Furstenberg, *In the Name of the Father*, 52.

113 "national honor and"   Mark D. Kaplanoff, "Religion and Righteousness: A Study of Federalist Rhetoric in the New Hampshire Election of 1800," 3, 7.

113 "He has left"   Reverend Jedidiah Morse, "Funeral Sermon for Washington" (Boston, 1800), 30, 36, 43.

113 "secret devotion"   John R. Fitzmier, *New England's Moral Legislator*, 172.

113 "And indeed, my"   David Humphreys to GW, 17 July 1785, *PWCF* 3: 131.

113–14 "who broke the"   Francois Furstenberg, *In the Name of the Father*, 86–87.

114 "He had much…He was more moral"   Franklin Steiner, *The Religious Beliefs of Our Presidents*, 40.

114 "Life is not so"   David Hackett Fischer, *Albion's Seed*, 416.

114 "not the greatest"   JA to BR, 21 June 1811, *SOF*, 196–97.

CHAPTER FOUR

PAGE

117 "Mark his majestic"   AA to JA, 16 July 1775, *The Letters of John and Abigail Adams*, ed. Frank Shuffelton, 77.

117 "moved with a grace"   Henry Wiencek, *Imperfect God*, 36; Forrest McDonald, *The Intellectual Origins of the Constitution*, 192.

117 "Those who deify"   New Letters, 28 January 1800; Phyllis Lee Levin, *Abigail Adams*, 378.

118 "wise, virtuous and good"   JA to AA, 26 October 1777, *AFPEA*.

118 "We ought not"   Levin, *Abigail Adams*, 377.

118–19 "One great advantage"   14 August 1796, *DAJA* 3: 240–41.

119–20 "a social compact…religion, and morality"   "The Report of a Constitution, or Form of Government, for the Commonwealth of Massachusetts," *PWJA*, 499–500, 501 n.10.

120 "as good a performance"   Morton Borden, *Jew, Turks, and Infidels*, 12.

121 "When a man is hurt"   Page Smith, *John Adams* 2: 622.

121 "a self-examination"   Edmund Fuller and David E. Green, *God in the White House*, 20.

121 "All spent in"   27–30 October 1758, *DAJA* 1: 57.

121 "all meat and spirits"   JA to AA, 26 September 1775, *AFC* 1: 285; *DAJA* 3: 269, 272.

121 "What am I doing?"   January 1759, *DAJA* 1: 73.

121 "sober, industrious, frugal"   JA to BR, 21 August 1811; BR to JA, 4 June 1812, *SOF,* 208, 241.

121–22 "I should think"   Louise Durbin, *Inaugural Cavalcade,* 11.

122 "What has preserved"   JA to BR, 14 March 1809, *SOF,* 239.

122 "In Adam's fall"   Page Smith, *John Adams* 1: 11.

122 "Frigid John Calvin"   *DAJA* 1: 1.

122–23 "good riddle solvers"   18 February 1756, *DAJA* 1: 8.

123 "great readers of"   *DAJA* 3: 265–66.

123 "original sin"   25 October 1758, *DAJA* 1: 55.

123 "Mystery is made"   *DAJA* 1: 8.

124 "To damn the whole"   *DAJA* 1: 42.

124 "a strange religious dogma"   C. Bradley Thompson, *John Adams and the Spirit of Liberty,* 10.

124 "an awful blasphemy"   John Butler, *Awash in a Sea of Faith,* 215.

124 "may not this question"   19 October 1758, *DAJA* 1: 52.

124 "was an impious"   Marginalia in Winthorp's "Lecture on Earthquakes," *DAJA* 1: 61–62.

125 "I should make a"   *DAJA* 3: 263.

125 "Steady, manly"   *DAJA* 3: 262.

125 "degenerated from the virtues"   John Ferling, *John Adams,* 21.

125 "The study and practice"   *DAJA* 1: 43.

125 "*Glory* attends the"   "The Discourses on Davila," *PWJA,* 320.

125–26 "The love of…sublimest kind"   Peter Shaw, *The Character of John Adams,* 20–21, 35, 79.

126 "The desire of"   "Discourses on Davila," *PWJA,* 313.

126 "Christmas. At home."   25 December 1765, *DAJA* 1: 273.

126 "to hold himself"   *DAJA* 3: 291–94.

127 "a popularity very general"   *DAJA* 3: 293–94.

127 "Reputation ought to be"   14 March 1759, *DAJA* 1: 78.

128 "I have constantly lived"   8 January 1812, *Old Family Letters;* Zoltan Haraszti, *John Adams & The Prophets of Progress,* 2.

128 "The times alone"   26 April 1779, *DAJA* 2: 362–63.

128–29 "thinking women"   January 1759, *DAJA* 1: 68.

129 "Remember the ladies…of his wife"   Carl Sferrazza Anthony, *First Ladies,* 68; David McCullough, *John Adams,* 468.

129 "totally obliterated"   JA to AA, 2 February 1797, *AFPEA.*

129 "so long slackened"   AA to JA, 27 November 1775, *AFC* 1: 329.

129 "I have no confidence"   JA to AA, 18 November 1775, *AFC* 1: 327.

129 "a perfect viper"   16 January 1766, *DAJA* 1: 295.

129 "poor wretches"   JA to AA, 9 October 1774, *AFC* 1: 167.

129 " A native of America"   "A Dissertation on the Canon and Feudal Law," *PWJA,* 12.

129 "dull as beetles"   JA to AA, 7 March 1777, *AFC* 2: 170.

130 "Deliver me from"   AA to JA, 5 August 1776, *AFC* 2: 79.

130 "whose noise and vehemence"   AA to JA, 4 July 1790; Page Smith, *John Adams* I: 772.

130 "harmoniously upon the"   20 December 1772, *DAJA* 2: 71.

131 "we were so divided"   Walter Stahr, *John Jay*, 37.

131 "accident...providential"   7 September 1774, *DAJA* 2: 126.

131 "Plead my cause"   Psalm 35: 1–3 (King James).

131 "Go on, ye chosen"   James H. Hutson, *Religion and the Founding of the American Republic*, 51.

131–32 "Dr. Cooper himself"   JA to AA, 16 September 1774, *AFC* 1: 156.

132 "zealous friend...and a traitor"   JA to AA, 16 September 1774, *AFC* 1: 156; JA to AA, 25 October 1777, *AFC* 2: 359.

132 "Our people call...July, 1776"   Walter Herbert Stowe, ed., *The Life and Letters of Bishop William White*, 41–52.

133 "the first gentleman"   JA to AA, 17 September 1775, *AFC* 1: 281.

133 "circuit rider"   *Political Sermons of the American Founding Era, 1730–1805*, Ellis Sandoz, ed., 1: 328.

133 "the new Reformation"   William G. McLoughlin, *Isaac Backus and the American Pietistic Tradition*, 8–9, 11–16.

134–35 "some Anabaptists...permitted to go on"   22 August 1774, *DAJA* 2: 107

135 "the late elections"   *DAJA* 3: 313.

135 "Is not all America"   William G. McLoughlin, *Isaac Backus and the American Pietistic Tradition*, 24–25; *DAJA* 3: 311–13; Franklin Hamlin Littell, *From State Church to Pluralism*, 37.

136 "habituated to higher"   JA to AA, 25 November 1775, *AFC* 1: 326.

136 "This inequality of property"   JA to AA, March 31 1776, *AFC* 1: 381.

136 "often so powerful"   JA to AA, 29 October 1775, *AFC* 1: 318.

137 "sorry to hear"   BR to JA, 4 June 1812, *SOF*, 241.

137 "'carried out in spirit'"   David McCullough, *John Adams*, 127.

137 "Even the chimes"   Page Smith, *John Adams* 1: 274.

137 "Le Washington"   29 November 1782, *DAJA* 3: 85.

138 "The falsest...of continual dissipation"   *DAJA* 2: 367; 4: 118.

138 "[His] very statue"   Stacy Shiff, *A Great Improvisation*, 410.

138 "For God's sake"   JA to AA, 20 February 1779, *The Letters of John and Abigail Adams*, Frank Shuffelton, ed., 355.

138 "I believe I am grown"   JA to AA, 28 February 1779, *AFC* 3: 181.

139 "He hates Franklin"   TJ to JM, *PTJ* 6: 241.

139 The departure of"   Merrill Peterson, *Thomas Jefferson and the New Nation*, 346.

139 "He is vain"   TJ to JM, 30 January 1787, *ROL* 3: 462.

140 "wicked unprincipled debauched"   AA to JA, 21 October 1781; Stacy Schiff, *A Great Improvisation*, n.271.

140 "To be out of fashion...a parent's breast"   Page Smith, *John Adams* 2: 605–9.

140 "the delightful enjoyments"   *DAJA* 4: 47.

140–41 "with some compensation"   *DAJA* 4: 96.

141 "These ecclesiastics"   *DAJA* 4: 58.

141 "Price and Priestley" JA to BR, 11 November 1806, *SOF,* 74.

142 "They do not believe" JA, "Discourses on Davila," *PWJA,* 362.

142 "produces a love" *WJA* 5: 289; cf. C. Bradley Thompson, *John Adams & the Spirit of Liberty,* 198–201.

142 "the restoration of" John McWilliams, *New England's Crises and Cultural Memory,* 194.

142–43 "These ceremonies" 7 June 1778, *DAJA* 4: 133.

143 "Order is heaven's" JA, "Discourses on Davila," *PWJA,* 344.

143 "This world was not" 14 August 1756, *DAJA* 1: 41.

143–44 "The world grows" JA, "Discourses on Davila," *PWJA,* 355.

144 "limited monarchy" C. Bradley Thompson, *John Adams & the Spirit of Liberty,* 91–228.

144 "Beds of roses" David McCullough, *John Adams,* 496.

144 "There is something more" JA to AA, 27 October 1799, *AFPEA.* www .masshist.org/digitaladams.

144 "I am not made" Edith B. Gelles, *Portia,* 173.

144–45 "liberal good sense" Edmund Fuller and David E. Green, *God in the White House,* 24.

CHAPTER FIVE

PAGE

146 "In vain thro'" Kenneth Silverman, ed., *The Connecticut Wits,* 261.

146 "TRIUMPHAL ENTRY OF" Simon P. Newman, *Parades and the Politics of the Street,* 74.

146 "I am heir" JA to AA, 20 January 1796, *AFPEA.*

146–47 "I have a pious…and the Devil" JA to AA, 20 January 1796; JA to AA, 15 April 1794, *AFPEA.*

147 "The wise and the good" Walter Stahr, *John Jay,* 237.

147 "If the majority" Zoltan Haraszti, *John Adams and the Prophets of Progress,* 93–94.

147 "the uniform advocate" Page Smith, "Election of 1796," 1: 71.

147 "Thou shalt provide" Reverend Stephen Peabody, "Election Day Sermon, 1797," *Presidential Sermons of the American Founding Era, 1730–1805,* Ellis Sandoz, ed., 2: 1325.

147 "The sight of the sun" JA to AA, 5 March 1797, *AFPEA.*

147–48 "And now, O Lord" AA to JA, March 1797; John Quincy Adams and Charles Francis Adams, *John Adams* 2: 210.

148–49 "the spirit of party" JA, Inaugural Speech to Both Houses of Congress, *PWJA,* 640.

149 "must be armed" Page Smith, *John Adams* 2: 897–98.

149 "It is a happiness" Joseph Lathrop, "A Sermon on the Dangers of the Times: Infidelity, Immorality, and Conspiracy Against Religion and the Government" (Springfield, MA, 1798), 23.

149 "O Lord!" Susan Jacoby, *Freethinkers,* 44.

149 "Since our late" Joseph Lathrop, "A Sermon on the Dangers of the Times" (Springfield, MA, 1798), 12.

149–50 "The late contest" Emory Elliot, *Revolutionary Writers*, 38–39.

150 "perfect aristocracy" Richard D. Brown, *The Diffusion of Information in Early America, 1700–1865*, 80.

150 "Universal tolerance" James King Morse, *Jedidiah Morse*, 37.

150 "We look only to" Stacy Shiff, *A Great Improvisation*, 7.

150 "Dragons' teeth" JA to AA, 14 January 1793, *AFPEA*.

151 "be sent to" Jay Fliegelman, *Jefferson, Natural Language, and the Culture of Performance*, 25.

152 "poured the soul" Philip F. Detweiler, "The Changing Reputation of the Declaration of Independence: The First 50 Years," 560.

152 "the anniversary of" Lee Travers, *Celebrating the Fourth*, 90.

152 "Our greatest danger" Dumas Malone, *Jefferson and the Ordeal of Liberty*, 44–45.

153 "the voice of" John F. Berens, *Providence & Patriotism in Early America*, 123.

153 "a badge of despotism" Noah Webster, "The Revolution in France," *Presidential Sermons of the American Founding Era, 1730–1805*, Ellis Sandoz, ed., 2: 1270.

153 "demoralized" Cynthia Crossen, "After U.S. Revolution, Country Was Split over France's War," *Wall Street Journal*, 31 July 2006, B1.

153 "the seductive doctrines" Philip F. Detweiler, "The Changing Reputation of the Declaration of Independence: The First 50 Years," 569.

153 "There is so much" Sidney Earl Meade, *Nathanial William Taylor*, 22–23.

154 "The same principles" Stephen E. Berk, *Calvinism Versus Democracy*, 31.

154 "Godly Federalism" John R. Fitzmier, *New England's Moral Legislator*, ix.

154 "the grand pabulum" Stephen E. Berk, *Calvinism Versus Democracy*, 154; Emory Elliot, *Revolutionary Writers*, 58.

154 "Connecticut is almost" Sidney Earl Meade, *Nathanial William Taylor*, 76.

154 "complete disorganization" Stephen E. Berk, *Calvinism Versus Democracy*, 36.

154 "Religion has nothing" John R. Fitzmier, *New England's Moral Legislator*, 178.

155 "right and duty" Daniel Walker Howe, *The Unitarian Conscience*, 12.

155 "infidel and irreligious" Gary B. Nash, "The American Clergy and the French Revolution," 403.

155 "an equality which" Conrad Wright, *The Beginnings of Unitarianism in America*, 244–45, 250.

155 "sided with the" Daniel Walker Howe, *The Unitarian Conscience*, 9.

155 "Statesmen may plan" Edwin Gaustad, *Faith of our Fathers*, 92.

156 "I know not what…Age of Reason" Conor Cruise O'Brien, *The Long Affair*, 9, 86.

156 "God forbid that" TJ to W. S. Smith, 13 November 1787, *WTJ* 4: 466–67.

156 "ignorant, restless" AA to TJ, 29 January 1787, *AJC*, 168.

156–57 "The spirit of resistance" TJ to AA, 22 February 1787, *AJC*, 173.

157 "The tree of liberty" TJ to William Smith, *PTJ* 12: 356.

157 "Latitude ought" JM to N. P. Trist, May 1832; Dumas Malone, *Jefferson and the Ordeal of Liberty*, 268.

157 "May heaven favor" TJ to Lafayette, 16 June 1792; Conor Cruise O'Brien, *The Long Affair*, 135.

157 "all my friends there" TJ to Tobias Lear, 5 November 1793; Dumas Malone, *Jefferson and the Ordeal of Liberty*, 185.

157 "some infernal...jawbone of Jefferson" Lee Travers, *Celebrating the Fourth*, 100, 175.

157–58 "nonsensical...government and liberty" Zoltan Haraszti, *John Adams and the Prophets of Progress*, 45, 92, 96, 226, 245.

158 "We shall very soon" Lance Banning, *The Jeffersonian Persuasion*, 120.

158 "anglo-monarchico" Eugene Perry Link, *Democratic-Republican Societies*, 47.

159 "theologians who" Darren Staloff, *Hamilton, Adams, Jefferson*, 30.

159–60 "For what end...of the Illuminati" David Hackett Fischer, *The Revolution of American Conservatives*, 286, 472 n.9.

160 "The pious and" JA to BR, 4 September 1812, *SOF,* 267.

160 "an atheist" Noble E. Cunningham Jr., "Election of 1800," 1: 109.

160 "(and morality *must*" *The Stand* 3 (April 7, 1798); James H. Hutson, *The Founders on Religion*, 192.

160 "Our constitution" James H. Hutson, *The Founders on Religion*, 76.

161 "We want no" Noble E. Cunningham Jr., "Election of 1800," 1: 122.

161 "formidable innovations" Stephen E. Berk, *Calvinism Versus Democracy*, 124.

162 "to prevent" Page Smith, *John Adams* 2: 1029.

162 "On religious grounds...there is nothing" Charles Ellis Dickson, "Jeremiads in the New American Republic," 192–93.

162 "Millions will be" JA to AA, re: Continental Fast Day, 17 June 1775, *AFC* 1: 216.

162 "I mix religion" JA to BR, 12 April 1809, *SOF,* 155.

163 "All religious congregations" JA, Fast Day Proclamation, 23 March 1798; James H. Hutson, *Religion and the Founding of the American Republic*, 82.

163 "the people in America...virtues in particular" John Witte Jr., *Religion and the American Constitutional Experiment*, 249.

163–64 "Some sought for" David Hackett Fischer, *The Revolution of American Conservatism*, 92.

164 "this guilty age...will be ineffectual" Ashbel Green, "Obedience to the Laws of God," 9 May 1798 (Philadelphia, 1798), 15, 17–18, 46–47.

164–65 "Whosoever resisteth" Charles F. O'Brien, "The Religious Issue in the Presidential Campaign of 1800," 89.

165 "will sweep away" Joseph W. Phillips, *Jedidiah Morse and New England Congregationalism*, 74.

165 "our respected" Jedidiah Morse, "A sermon delivered....May 9, 1798" (Boston, 1798), 11.

166 "to destroy...against all good" Joseph W. Phillips, *Jedidiah Morse and New England Congregationalism*, 73–85.

166 "the disposition of" Carl J. Richard, *The Founders and the Classics*, 29.

166 "not of the opinion" Walt Brown, *John Adams and the American Press*, 29.

167 "I have no doubt"   JA to TJ, 30 June 1813, *AJL*, 347.

167–68 "Some of the young"   TJ to JM, 10 May 1798, *ROL* 2: 1047–48.

168 "The president received"   TJ to JM, 17 May 1798, *ROL* 2: 1049.

168 "Rogue's March"   Gary B. Nash, *First City*, 130.

168 "You should know"   TJ to Martha Jefferson Randolph, 17 May 1798, *ROL* 2: 1063

168 "Christian liberty"   Charles Crowe, "Bishop James Madison and the Republic of Virtue," 61.

168–69 "our bounden duty"   Page Smith, *John Adams* 2: 917; Charles Ellis Dickson, "Jeremiads in the New American Republic," 200.

169 "the sacred duties"   Page Smith, *John Adams* 2: 1004.

169 "evangelical character...well-being of communities"   James H. Hutson, *Religion and the Founding of the American Republic*, 81.

CHAPTER SIX

PAGE

170 "O happy State"   Timothy Dwight, "Greenfield Hill," *The Connecticut Wits*, Vernon Lewis Parrington, ed.; John R. Fitzmier, *New England's Moral Legislator*, 145.

170 "For God, a God"   David Humphreys, "A Poem," *The Connecticut Wits*, Vernon Lewis Parrington, ed., 405.

171 "This great continent"   Elwyn A Smith, "The Voluntary Establishment of Religion," 171.

171 "One blood"   Timothy Dwight, "Greenfield Hill," *The Connecticut Wits*, Vernon Lewis Parrington, ed., 183, 247; John R. Fitzmier, *New England's Moral Legislator*, 43.

171–72 "with order...with parent's hand"   Timothy Dwight, "Greenfield Hill," *The Connecticut Wits*, Vernon Lewis Parrington, ed., 190–92.

172 He dedicated "Greenfield Hill"   John R. Fitzmier, *New England's Moral Legislator*, 44.

173 "Do you know"   Emory Elliot, *Revolutionary Writers*, 148.

173–74 "dangerous to the peace...and malicious"   Merrill Peterson, *Thomas Jefferson and the New Nation*, 605–6; James Grant, *John Adams*, 405.

174 "a monster that"   Adrienne Koch, *Madison's "Advice to My Country,"* 124.

174 "The right of freely"   James Morton Smith, "Virginia and Kentucky Resolutions," 422.

174–75 "To preserve the freedom"   TJ to William Green Munford, 18 June 1799; Dumas Malone, *Jefferson and the Ordeal of Liberty*, 418.

175 "worthy of the eighth...a natural right"   Merrill Peterson, *Thomas Jefferson and the New Nation*, 604–6, 615.

175 "to sever ourselves"   TJ to JM, 23 August 1799, *ROL*, 1119; Dumas Malone, *Jefferson and the Ordeal of Liberty*, 421.

175 "Take care, John Adams"   Eugene Perry Link, *Democratic-Republican Societies*, 205.

176 "Trusting to a popular"   Andrew Burstein, *Jefferson's Secrets*, 9.

176 "an elegant, ingenious"   September 1775, *DAJA* 2: 182.

176 "a conversation that"   Manning J. Daver, *The Adams Federalists*, 54.

176 "as much a republican"   Page Smith, *John Adams* 2: 755.

177 "There have been many"   23 July 1806, *Old Family Letters*; Zoltan Haraszti, *John Adams and the Prophets of Progress*, 4.

177 "This country never appeared"   Walt Brown, *John Adams and the American Press*, 29.

177 "Philosophers, theologians"   John Patrick Diggens, "Introduction," *The Portable John Adams*, xv.

177 "until Congress passes"   Carl Sferrazza Anthony, *First Ladies*, 64.

177 "old, querulous, bald"   John Ferling, *John Adams*, 364; Phyllis Lee Levin, *Abigail Adams*, 375.

177 "as we would a TURK"   Walt Brown, *John Adams and the American Press*, 48.

177–78 "Perdition catch them"   Page Smith, *John Adams* 2: 961.

178 "without being curtailed"   Carl Sferrazza Anthony, *First Ladies*, 63, 65.

178 "They breathe one spirit"   AA to John Quincy Adams, 26 May 1798; Thomas M. Roy, "Not One Cent for Tribute," 391.

178 "awed into silence"   Walt Brown, *John Adams and the American Press*, 96–101.

178 "the most grotesque"   JM to TJ, 10 June 1798, *ROL* 2: 1058.

178 "patriotic addresses"   Walt Brown, *John Adams and the American Press*, 97.

178 "by any terrors"   JA, "A Dissertation on the Canon and Feudal Law," *PWJA*, 14.

178 "an abridgment…excuse that expression"   Jay Fliegelman, *Jefferson, Natural Language, and the Culture of Performance*, 150.

178 "Mobs are the trite"   JA to AA, 6 July 1774, *AFC* 1: 126.

178 "The great barrier"   *WJA* 6: 151; C. Bradley Thompson, *John Adams & the Spirit of Liberty*, 182.

179 "the balance of"   JA, "Discourses on Davila," *PWJA*, 360.

179 "I have seen many"   Vernon Louis Parrington, ed., *The Connecticut Wits*, xvi.

179 "the spitting Lyon"   Dumas Malone, *Jefferson and the Ordeal of Liberty*, 363.

179 "the wretch"   Page Smith, *John Adams* 2: 932, 949–50.

179–80 "When I shall…of every Jacobin"   James Morton Smith, *Freedom's Fetters*, 222–46.

180 "Penitence must precede"   James Morton Smith, *Freedom's Fetters*, 324.

181 "Col. Lyon has been…the Rev. Gaolbird"   Alan V. Briceland, "John C. Ogden: Messenger and Propagandist of Matthew Lyon, 1798–99," 103–21.

181 "Connecticut is more"   Robert Edson Lee, "Timothy Dwight and the Boston *Palladium*," 237.

182 "One great sin"   Alan V. Briceland, "John C. Ogden: Messenger and Propagandist of Matthew Lyon, 1798–99," 103–21.

182 *Age of Reason*   James Morton Smith, *Freedom's Fetters*, 258–68.

182 *"in terrorem"*   Gary Wills, *Under God*, 367; James Morton Smith, "The Federalist 'Saints' versus 'The Devil of Sedition': The Liberty Pole Cases of Dedham, Massachusetts, 1798–9," 215.

183 "truth as a defense"   Susan Dunn, *Jefferson's Second Revolution*, 113; Walt Brown, *John Adams and the American Press*, 102–3.

183 28 to 40 percent   John Ferling, *Adams vs. Jefferson*, 144.

183 *"The Republican Atlas... The Rights of Man"*   Susan Dunn, *Jefferson's Second Revolution*, 139.

183 "MAN IS MAN"   David Hackett Fischer, *Liberty and Freedom*, 201.

183 "sufferings in the cause"   Jenny Graham, *Revolutionary in Exile*, 40.

184 "steady attachment"   2 April 1778, *DAJA* 4: 35.

184 "It will get me"   JA to AA, 13 March 1796; John Quincy Adams and Charles Francis Adams, *John Adams* 2: 199.

184 "How deeply have"   Jenny Graham, *Revolutionary in Exile*, 143.

184 "It suffices for a"   TJ to Thomas Mann Randolph, 3 May 1798; cf. Dumas Malone, *Jefferson and the Ordeal of Liberty*, 386.

185 "chief juggler"   Dumas Malone, *Jefferson and the Ordeal of Liberty*, 467.

185 "the Demo Cooper"   James Morton Smith, *Freedom's Fetters*, 312; Phyllis Lee Levin, *Abigail Adams*, 375.

185 "poor Priestley"   JA to T. Pickering, 13 August 1799, *WJA* 9: 14.

185 "As far as it"   JA to Thomas Pickering, 18 August 1799, *WJA* 9: 24.

185 "criminal and malignant... conduct to us"   James Morton Smith, *Freedom's Fetters*, 324, 330.

186 "There is a latent"   JA, "Novanglus," *PWJA*, 26.

CHAPTER SEVEN

PAGE

187 "That man must have"   Thomas Green Fessenden, *Democracy Unveiled, or, Tyranny stripped of the garb of patriotism, By Christopher Caustic* (pseudo.) (New York, 1806).

187 "Equality of Right"   *Three Centuries of American Poetry*, ed. Allen Mandelbaum and Robert D. Richardson Jr. (New York, 1999), 74.

187 "a Turk, a Jew"   Morton Borden, *Jews, Turks, and Infidels*, 16.

187 "The minister put"   Charles F. O'Brien, "The Religious Issue in the Presidential Campaign of 1800," 82.

187–88 "THE GRAND QUESTION"   Susan Dunn, *Jefferson's Second Revolution*, 148.

188 "become the sport"   Harry S. Stout, "Rhetoric and Reality in the Early Republic," 72.

188 "no less than rebellion"   Merrill Peterson, *Thomas Jefferson and the New Nation*, 639.

188 "GREAT GOD... of your country"   Charles O. Lerche Jr., "Jefferson and the Election of 1800," 480, 489.

188 "great arch priest... vitals of your country"   Susan Dunn, *Jefferson's Second Revolution*, 1, 86.

188 "Are you prepared"   Charles F. O'Brien, "The Religious Issue in the Presidential Campaign of 1800," 86.

188 "It is proper" *Aurora*, 13 September 1800; James L. Golden and Alan L. Golden, *Thomas Jefferson and the Rhetoric of Virtue*, 271.

189 "The question is not" Stephen E. Berk, *Calvinism Versus Democracy*, 142–43.

189 "From all known infidels" Joseph W. Phillips, *Jedidiah Morse and New England Congregationalism*, 92.

189 "Let us hear" Stephen E. Berk, *Calvinism Versus Democracy*, 141–42.

189 "the heads of…almost inconceivable" Reverend John Smalley, "Election Day Sermon 1800," Hartford, CT, 1800; *Presidential Sermons of the American Founding Era, 1730–1805*, ed. Ellis Sandoz, 2: 1417–46.

190 "I would not" William Linn, "Serious Consideration on the Election of a President" (Trenton, NJ, 1800), 4.

190 "of various kinds…breaks my leg" TJ, *Notes on Virginia*, Frank Shuffelton, ed., 165.

190–91 "Let my neighbor…scale of being" William Linn, "Serious Consideration," 4–10.

191 "Dusky Sally" Charles O. Lerche Jr., "Jefferson and the Election of 1800," 489.

191 "The passages upon slavery" JA to TJ, 22 May 1785, *ALC*, 21.

191–92 "great convulsion…origin of mankind" (John Mitchell Mason) "The Voice of Warning to Christians, the Ensuing Election of a President of the United States," *Presidential Sermons of the American Founding Era, 1730–1805*, ed. Ellis Sandoz, 2: 144–76.

192–93 "Mr. Jefferson…bonds of society" William Linn, "Serious Consideration," 14, 19.

193 "They wish it" TJ to JA, 15 June 1813, *AJL*, 331.

193 "Can the Liberties" TJ, *Notes on Virginia*, Frank Shuffelton, ed., 169.

193 "I hate polemical" Jon Meacham, *American Gospel*, 17–18.

193 "a natural and almost" Joseph Ellis, *American Sphinx*, 259, 407, n.88.

193 "Every man should" "Discourses on Davila," *WJA* 6: 227; *ROL* 2: 669.

194 "Mr. Adams reads" Page Smith, *John Adams* 2: 832.

194 "a book that has" JA, "To John Taylor of Caroline" (1814), *PWJA*, 368.

194 "The Devil's Bible" "Thomas Paine's Apostles: Radical Emigres and the Triumph of Jeffersonian Republicanism," 677.

194 "I have no doubt" Dumas Malone, *Jefferson and the Rights of Man*, 357.

194–95 "I have always" David McCullough, *John Adams*, 430.

195 "contains the catholic faith" John Chester Miller, *The Wolf by the Ears*, 212.

195 "The Jacobins differ" Noah Webster, "The Revolution in France" (New York, 1794); *Presidential Sermons of the American Founding Era, 1730–1805*, ed. Ellis Sandoz, 2: 1263.

195 "popes in government" AH, "A Vindication of the Funding System, Number 1," 1 September 1790, *PAH* 7: 645.

195 "sect…blasphemies" Dumas Malone, *Jefferson and the Rights of Man*, 356–57.

196 "My good woman" Robert M. S. McDonald, "Was There a Religious Revolution of 1800?", 173.

196 "Being the only"   David Hackett Fischer, *The Revolution of American Conservatism,* 224.

196 "a wonder"   (Tunis Wortman) "Solemn Address in Answer to 'Serious Considerations'" (New York, 1800), 18.

196–97 "hearsay...to the whites"   "Grotius," "A Vindication of Thomas Jefferson in answer to Rev. Linn's "Serious considerations on the election of a President." (New York, 1800), 15, 28.

197 "If a national"   William G. McLoughlin, *New England Dissent* 2: 1020.

197 "It is one"   Martin Border, *Jews, Turks, and Infidels,* 17.

197 "good government"   Lance Banning, *The Jeffersonian Persuasion,* 212.

197 "How much has religion"   Frank Lambert, *The Founding Fathers and the Place of Religion in America,* 283–84.

198 "wandering stars"   Emory Elliot, *Revolutionary Writers,* 42.

198 insider or outsider   R. Laurence Moore, "Insiders and Outsiders in American Historical Narrative and American History," 199–221; William G. McLoughlin, *New England Dissent* 2: 1021–24.

199 "The clergy, who...all the nation"   William G. McLoughlin, *New England Dissent* 2: 784–85, 1013–14.

199–200 "To religious men"   Noble E. Cunningham, *The Jefferson Republicans in Power,* 219.

200 "[He is] a man"   "To the People of New Jersey," 30 September 1800, Noble E. Cunningham Jr., "Election of 1800," 1: 138.

200 "a follower of...am a Republican"   Martin Border, *Jews, Turks, and Infidels,* 25–26.

200–1 "female of a...of the Devil"   *The Connecticut Wits,* Vernon Parrington, ed., 264; Frank Lambert, *The Founding Fathers and the Place of Religion in America,* 280.

201 "In the year 1798"   Dumas Malone, *Jefferson and the Ordeal of Liberty,* 462.

201 "the other 'Hosanna.'"   8 October 1782, *DAJA* 3: 15.

201 "You can and you can't"   William G. McLoughlin, *Revivals, Awakenings, and Reform,* 101.

202 "factious, cutthroat, frog-eating"   John Ferling, *Adams vs. Jefferson,* 110.

202 "Assassination shall be"   Darren Staloff, *Hamilton, Adams, Jefferson,* 217–19.

202 *Vox populi vox Dei*   William Maclay, *The Journal of William Maclay,* 346.

202 "The Quakers were"   TJ to Samuel Kercheval, 19 January 1810, *Jefferson Writings,* Merrill Peterson, ed., 1214.

202 "noted and violent"   James Morton Smith, *ROL* 2: 1008-9.

203 Washington is said   Ellis Sandoz, *Presidential Sermons of the American Founding Era, 1730–1805,* 2: 1342.

203 "babyish and womanly"   John Ferling, *John Adams,* 378.

203 "Here lies John Adams"   John Ferling, *Adams vs. Jefferson,* 198.

204 "disgusting egotism...of chief magistrate"   James Roger Sharp, *American Politics in the New Republic,* 240; Darren Staloff, *Hamilton, Adams, Jefferson,* 226.

205 "a bastard brat"   JA to BR, 25 January 1806, *SOF,* 50.

205 "a proud-spirited"   JA to AA, 9 January 1797; James Roger Sharp, *American Politics in the New Republic,* 236; John Ferling, *John Adams,* 360–61.

205 "than be indebted"   James McHenry to JA, 31 May 1800, *PAH* 24: 552–65.

205 "The devil is no"   JA to TJ, 3 March 1814, *AJL,* 419.

205–6 "Although I have long"   *DAJA* 3: 434–35.

207 "AS THE GOVERNMENT"   *Treaties and Other International Acts of the United States of America,* Vol. 2, Hunter Miller, ed. (Washington, D.C., 1931), 349–85.

207 "Thomas Paine is not…and be respectable"   Vernon Louis Parrington, ed., *The Connecticut Wits,* xlv–xlviii.

208 "Now be it"   Forrest Church, *The Separation of Church and State,* 121–23.

208–9 "Our money, our commerce"   JA to TJ, 3 March 1814, *AJL,* 417.

209 "Elections to offices"   JA to TJ, 6 December 1787, *AJL,* 214.

209 "You and I shall go"   JA to TJ, 6 April 1796, *AJL,* 261–62.

209–10 "disgusted with the world…reconcile man to life"   Page Smith, *John Adams* 2: 1037–56, 1068.

210 "This summer is"   TJ to JM, 5 February 1799, *ROL,* 2.

211 "At length election"   James Morton Smith, *Freedom's Fetters,* 373.

211 "great castle"   Phyllis Lee Levin, *Abigail Adams,* 384.

212 "The old gentleman"   Louisa Catherine Adams, "The Adventures of a Nobody"; L. H. Butterfield, *The Adams Papers* 1: xx.

212 "I had no other"   Page Smith, *John Adams* 2: 1091.

212 "I love him too"   JA to AA, 16 March 1780, *AFC* 3: 305; David McCullough, *John Adams,* 237.

212–13 "I renounce him"   Page Smith, *John Adams* 2: 1015.

213 "Oh! That I had died"   Page Smith, *John Adams* 2: 1053.

213 "might have given"   JA to TJ, 24 March 1801, *AJL,* 264.

213 "her hawk's eyes"   Signora Catoni (Sally McKean) to DM, 3 August 1797, *The Selected Letters of Dolley Payne Madison,* David B. Mattern and Holly C. Shulman, eds., 32.

213 "one of the choice"   AA to Mary Cranch, 8 May 1785; Edith B. Gelles, *Portia,* 86.

213 "A patriot without religion"   AA to Mercy Otis Warren; Edmund Fuller and David E. Green, *God in the White House,* 23.

213 "no pretensions to"   Phyllis Lee Levin, *Abigail Adams,* 390.

214 "If ever we saw"   Lynne Withey, *Dearest Friend,* 279.

214 "one of the most"   Carl Sferrazza Anthony, *First Ladies,* 79.

214 "I wrote many things"   AA to JA, 22 October 1775, *AFC* 1: 310.

214 "they should take"   David McCullough, *John Adams,* 559.

214 "an Infidel President"   John Ferling, *Adams vs. Jefferson,* 199.

214 "Oh ye rascally ringers"   Dumas Malone, *Jefferson the President: First Term,* 16.

215 "Monarch of Stony Field's"   Lynne Withey, *Dearest Friend,* 282.

215 "He was terribly open"   Dumas Malone, *The Sage of Monticello,* 100.

215 "Such is the melancholy"   Peter Shaw, *The Character of John Adams,* 218–19.

215 "Having been the object"   *DAJA* 3: 253.

216 "prejudiced by the"   Peter Shaw, *The Character of John Adams*, 292; Zoltan Haraszti, *John Adams and the Prophets of Progress*, 3, 11, 41.

216–17 "I have attended"   JA to BR, 18 April 1808, *SOF*, 116.

217 "a little capillary"   JA to BR, 27 February 1805, *SOF*, 23.

217 "undermined the"   JA to BR, 26 March 1806, *SOF*, 55.

218 "the clergy this way"   JA to AA, 11 June 1775, *The Letters of John and Abigail Adams*, Frank Shuffelton, ed., 63.

218 "The national fast"   JA to BR, 12 June 1812, *SOF*, 244.

218 "Dr. Priestley and"   JA to BR, 21 August 1811, *SOF*, 208–09.

218 "Nothing is more dreaded"   JA to BR, 12 June 1812, *SOF*, 244.

219 "[make] themselves the"   Edwin S. Gaustad, *Faith of Our Fathers*, 95.

CHAPTER EIGHT

PAGE

223 "Let foes to freedom"   *Thomas Jefferson's Scrapbooks*, Jonathan Gross, ed., 20.

224 "Carelessly throwing...rank and order"   Margaret Bayard Smith, *The First Forty Years of Washington Society*, Gaillard Hunt, ed., 5–8.

224 "There are fanatics"   TJ to Joseph C. Cabell, 26 February 1818; Andrew Burstein, *Jefferson's Secrets*, 207.

224 "the Revolution of 1800"   TJ to Spencer Roane, 6 September 1819, James E. Lewis Jr., "What Is to Become of Our Government?", 3.

225 "We have only"   TJ to Philip Mazzei, 24 April 1796, *PTJ* 29: 82.

225 "as real a revolution"   TJ to Spencer Roane, 6 September 1819, *TJW* 15: 212.

225 "What an effort"   TJ to Dr. Joseph Priestly, 21 March 1801, *WTJ* 9: 217.

226 "This part of"   JA to TJ, 24 March 1801, *AJL*, 264.

226 "Drunken frolics is"   Merrill Peterson, *Thomas Jefferson and the New Nation*, 659.

226 "Our country should"   James H. Hutson, *The Founders on Religion*, 191.

226 "on too interesting"   TJ to BR, 23 September 1800, *JEG*, 320.

227 "are marked, like"   Garry Wills, *Henry Adams and the Making of America*, 141–42.

227 "In every country"   TJ to Horatio G. Spafford, 17 March 1814, *TJW* 14: 119.

227 "cannibals,...etc."   Fred C. Luebke, "The Origins of Thomas Jefferson's Anti-Clericalism," 344.

228 "I am a Christian"   TJ to BR, 21 April 1803, *PTJ* 10: 457.

228 "Reason and Nature"   Jon Butler, *Awash in a Sea of Faith*, 219.

228 "His precepts are"   To Bishop James Madison, 31 January 1800, *PTJ* 9: 109.

229 "the most self-consciously"   Edwin A. Gaustad, *Sworn on the Altar of God*, xiii.

230 "Give us this day"   Dumas Malone, *Jefferson the Virginian*, 22.

231 "Everyone had...disturbing the peace"   Bishop Meade, *Old Churches and Families in Virginia* 1: 428.

231–32 "rapacious harpies...subjects' obedience"   Forrest Church, *The Separation of Church and State*, 1–3.

232 "the destinies of"   Thomas Jefferson, *Autobiography*, *WTJ* 1: 6.

232 "Attic society"   Dumas Malone, *Jefferson the Virginian*, 53.

232 "At these dinners"   Paul K. Conkin, "The Religious Pilgrimage of Thomas Jefferson," 14.

233 "Jefferson's Church"   Dumas Malone, *Jefferson the Virginian*, 8.

233 "Theist," etc.   Robert T. Handy, "The Magna Charta of Religious Freedom in America," 301–17.

233 "I am of a sect"   TJ to Ezra Stiles Ely, 25 June 1819, *JEG*, 386–87.

234 "the wisest invention"   Darren Staloff, *Hamilton, Adams, Jefferson*, 298.

233–34 "struck him...well-administered republic"   Garrett Ward Sheldon, "Liberalism, Classicism, and Christianity in Jefferson's Political Thought," 96.

234 "Sure I am of"   Henry Adams, *History of the United States of America During the Administrations of Thomas Jefferson*, 94.

234 "less addicted...into decay"   Forrest McDonald, *The Presidency of Thomas Jefferson*, 14.

234 "We are an industrious"   Andrew Burstein, *Jefferson's Secrets*, 69.

235 "lordly ideal of"   Michael Harrington, *The Politics at God's Funeral*, 20.

235 "And for the support...sacred honor"   David McCullough, *John Adams*, 135.

235 "The God who gave"   "A Summary View of the Rights of British America," *Jefferson Writings*, Merrill Peterson, ed., 122.

235 "The will of the"   Noble E. Cunningham Jr., "Election of 1800," 103.

235–36 "inalienable...sacred and undeniable"   Edwin S. Gaustad, *Sworn on the Altar of God*, 48.

236 "Millions of innocent...of the Trinity"   TJ, *Notes on Virginia*, Frank Shuffelton, ed., 166–67.

236–37 "Be it enacted"   Forrest Church, ed., *The Separation of Church and State*, 45–46.

238 "The gospel wants"   Reuben Edward Alley, *A History of Baptists in Virginia*, 101–2.

238 "I am glad"   TJ to JM, 8 December 1784, *ROL* 1: 353–54.

238 "principles of public"   Forrest Church, *The Separation of Church and State*, 56–60.

239 "partial gratification"   JM to TJ, 9 January 1785, *ROL* 1: 361.

239 "A Memorial...of the Gospel"   John T. Noonan Jr., *The Lustre of Our Country*, 74; Rhys Isaac, "The Rage of Malice of the Old Serpent Devil," 154; Lance Banning, "Madison, the Statute, and Republican Convictions," *The Virginia Statute for Religious Freedom*, 135 n.46.

239–40 "The equal right"   "James Madison, Memorial and Remonstrance Against Religious Assessments," *The Separation of Church and State*, Forrest Church, ed., 60–71.

240 "The Virginia act"   TJ to JM, 16 December 1786, *ROL* 1: 458–59.

241 "the insertion"   Forrest Church, *The Separation of Church and State*, 72–74.

241 "the Eden of"   TJ to Count Volney, 9 April 1797; Dumas Malone, *Jefferson and the Ordeal of Liberty*, 199.

241 "May business and play"   Dumas Malone, *Jefferson the Virginian*, 159–60.

241 "mild and amiable…shade of hazel"   Andrew Burstein, *The Inner Jefferson*, 30; Merrill Peterson, *Thomas Jefferson and the New Nation*, 245.

241–42 "soothe and calm"   TJ to Anne Willing Bingham, 11 May 1788, *PTJ* 1: 16; Darren Staloff, *Hamilton, Adams, Jefferson*, 243.

242 "plans of comfort…shortly to make"   Andrew Burstein, *The Inner Jefferson*, 62–63.

CHAPTER NINE

PAGE

244 "Tell me what"   Philip Freneau, *A Collection of Poems on American Affairs and a Variety of Other Subjects Chiefly Moral and Political* (New York, 1815), 2: 97–98.

244 "A republican's picture"   *Thomas Jefferson's Scrapbooks*, Jonathan Gross, ed., 41.

244 "corduroy small-clothes"   Henry Adams, *History of the United States of America During the Administrations of Thomas Jefferson*, 127.

245 "She felt indignant"   Margaret Bayard Smith, *The First Forty Years of Washington Society*, 12.

245 "equality or pell-mell"   TJ, "A Memorandus (Rules of Etiquette)," *Jefferson Writings*, Merrill Peterson, ed., 705.

245 "Etiquette of the Court"   John Ferling, *Adams vs. Jefferson*, 201.

246 "kissed the book…to be administered"   Louise Durbin, *Inaugural Cavalcade*, 16–20.

246 "That prescribed"   John Marshall to TJ, 2 March 1801, *PTJ* 33: 120.

246–47 "The body of"   TJ to P. S. Dupont de Nemours, 18 January 1802, Dumas Malone, *Correspondence Between Thomas Jefferson and Pierre Samuel du Pont de Nemours: 1798–1817*, 39.

247 "who had got"   TJ to Moses Robinson, 23 March 1801, *JEG*, 324.

247 "I shall hope"   TJ to Horatio Gates, 8 March 1801, *WTJ* 9: 205-6.

247 "The republicans are"   TJ to William Duane, 28 March 1811, *TJW* 13–14: 29; Dumas Malone, *The Sage of Monticello*, 33.

247 "duty of the chief"   TJ to John Garland Jefferson, 25 January 1810, *PTJ* 2: 183; Malcolm Kelsall, *Jefferson and the Iconography of Romanticism*, 31–32.

247–49 "sacred preservation…public faith"   TJ, First Inaugural Address, 4 March 1801, *WTJ* 9: 195–99.

249 "We have now"   Henry Adams, *History of the United States During the Administration of Thomas Jefferson*, 152.

250 "Our Statesmen"   Abraham Bishop, "Oration Delivered in Wallingford, on the 11th of March, 1801"; G. Adolph Koch, *Republican Religion*, 264.

250 "turn about is"   Richard J. Purcell, *Connecticut in Transition, 1775–1818*, 152.

250 "detach politics"   Phillip Hamburger, *Separation of Church and State*, 124.

250 "the 'friends of order'"   G. Adolph Koch, *Republican Religion*, 263.

251 "this redeemed continent"   Phillip Hamburger, *Separation of Church and State*, 139; Frank Lambert, *The Founding Fathers and the Place of Religion in America*, 283–84.

251 "Moral light has"   Joyce Appleby, *Capitalism and the New Social Order*, 83.

251 "such a state"   Phillip Hamburger, *Separation of Church and State*, 135.

251 "those sentiments of"   Charles Crowe, "Bishop James Madison and the Republic of Virtue," 63, 66.

252 "since the mountain"   TJ to Moses Robinson, 23 March 1801, *JEG*, 325.

252 "Republican Festival"   David Waldstreicher, *In the Midst of Perpetual Fetes*, 198–99.

252 "the federal priesthood"   Phillip Hamburger, *Separation of Church and State*, 140–41.

253 "Joshua of the...elder brother"   Susan Juster, *Doomsayers*, 158.

253 "friends of order"   Phillip Hamburger, *Separation of Church and State*, 139.

254 "I therefore, Sir"   Jack McLaughlin, *To His Excellency Thomas Jefferson*, 40–50.

254 "the different denominations"   James H. Hutson, *Religion and the Founding of the American Republic*, 84–85.

254–55 "I have a mind"   Jack McLaughlin, *To His Excellency Thomas Jefferson*, 49–50.

255 "Father of the"   Jack McLaughlin, *To His Excellency Thomas Jefferson*, 136.

255 "Thomas Jefferson was"   Elias Smith, "The Whole World Governed by a Jew:...A Discourse on the Government of Christ, as King and President," 57; Michael G. Kenny, *The Perfect Law of Liberty*, 25.

255 "Mr. Page, we"   Joyce Appleby, *Inheriting the Revolution*, 27.

255 "the Oven"   Constance McLauglin Green, *Washington: Village and Capital, 1800–1878*, 27.

256 "The gay company"   Margaret Bayard Smith, *The First Forty Years of Washington Society*, 13–14.

257 "the Lord direct"   James H. Hutson, *Religion and the Founding of the American Republic*, 86.

257 "Is he known to"   "Serious Considerations on the Election of a President," 17.

257 "Mr. Jefferson never"   Frank Lambert, *The Founding Fathers and the Place of Religion in America*, 277.

257 "howling Atheist"   Robert M. S. McDonald, "Was There a Religious Revolution of 1800?" 182.

257–58 "it was very"   W. P. and J. P. Cutler, *The Life of Rev. Mannasseh Cutler* 2: 119.

258–59 "a poor, ignorant...country is felt"   W. P. and J. P. Cutler, *Life of Rev. Mannasseh Cutler*, 2: 66–67; L. H. Butterfield, "Elder John Leland," 226–27.

259 "Mr. Jefferson mingled...all Federalists"   Margaret Bayard Smith, *The First Forty Years of Washington Society*, 30–31.

259 "Courting popularity"   W. P. and J. P. Cutler, *The Life of Rev. Mannasseh Cutler* 2: 119.

260 "slavery is a violent"   Robert A. Rutland, "James Madison," 279.

260 "Here lies JOHN"   Ellis Sandoz, ed., *Political Sermons of the American Founding Era, 1730–1805*, 2: 1081–82.

260 "I raised up"   Phillip Hamburger, *The Separation of Church and State,* 166 n.41.

260 "Why should we"   Richard J. Purcell, *Connecticut in Transition: 1775–1818,* 52.

261 "the passion of…MAN IN AMERICA"   Dumas Malone, *Jefferson the President: First Term, 1801–1805,* 108.

261 "Rebellion to tyrants"   L. H. Butterfield, "Elder John Leland," 220–21.

261 "as big as"   Page Smith, *John Adams* 2: 923.

262 "can talk by the"   "Observations upon Certain Passages in Mr. Jefferson's 'Notes on Virginia' Subvert Religion and Establish a False Philosophy" (1804), 31.

262 "triumvirate of *atheism, deism*"   Dumas Malone, *Jefferson the President: First Term, 1801–1805,* 177.

262 "Science and government"   Merrill D. Peterson, *Thomas Jefferson and the New Nation,* 576–81.

262 "Of all the charges"   Merrill D. Peterson, *Thomas Jefferson and the New Nation,* 580.

262 "I think it will"   David Hackett Fisher, *The Revolution of American Conservativism,* 97.

263 "He never with a"   Linda K. Kerber, *Federalists in Dissent,* 70.

263 "mammoth priest…custards and cream"   Dumas Malone, *Jefferson the President: First Term,* 107.

263–64 "universally excited…next Thanksgiving Sermon"   L. H. Butterfield, "Elder John Leland," 221–28; Merrill D. Peterson, *Thomas Jefferson and the New Nation,* 722–23.

264 "mere usurpers of"   Garrett Ward Sheldon, "Eclectic Synthesis: Jesus, Aristotle, and Locke," 83.

265 "as favors granted"   Robert M. S. McDonald, "Was There a Religious Revolution of 1800?", 188.

265 "from the governor"   Levi Lincoln to TJ, 17 June 1806; Dumas Malone, *Jefferson the President: Second Term, 1805–1809,* 148.

265 "I know it will"   TJ to Levi Lincoln, 1 January 1802, *WTJ* 9: 347.

265 "into an abyss"   TJ to Levi Lincoln, 25 October 1802, *WTJ* 9: 401.

265–66 "Believing with you"   TJ to the Danbury Baptist Association, in the State of Connecticut, 1 January 1801, *Jefferson Writings,* Merrill Peterson, ed., 510.

266–67 "Among the various…of other denominations"   William G. McLoughlin, *New England Dissent* 2: 1004–11, 1065–70, 1113.

267 "I am informed"   G. Adolph Koch, *Republican Religion,* 217.

267 "junto of little"   Ellis Sandoz, *Political Sermons of the American Founding Era, 1730–1805* 1: 790.

268 "The Deistical idea"   Thomas Allen to TJ, 4 March 1805; Paul Goodman, *The Democratic-Republicans of Massachusetts,* 92.

268 "Their character must"   Dumas Malone, *Jefferson the President: Second Term, 1805–1809,* 12.

268 "the vile, the blasphemous"   Charles O'Brien, "The Religious Issue in the Presidential Campaign of 1800," 88.

268 "the government, morals"   Robert Edson Lee, "Timothy Dwight and the Boston *Palladium*," 229–39.

269 "The *Palladium* should"   John R. Fitzmier, *New England's Moral Legislator,* 63.

269 "If this project"   Joseph W. Phillips, *Jedidiah Morse and New England Congregationalism,* 94.

269 "Federal Religion"   John R. Fitzmier, *New England's Moral Legislator,* 64.

269 "be by degrees"   Joseph W. Phillips, *Jedidiah Morse and New England Congregationalism,* 101.

270 "I trust"   George Jackson (Virginia), 22 February 1803, *Circular Letters of Congressmen to their Constituents, 1789–1829,* Noble E. Cunningham Jr., ed., 1: 312.

271 "I know there"   Robert Williams (North Carolina), 28 February 1803, *Circular Letters of Congressmen to their Constituents, 1789–1829,* Noble E. Cunningham Jr., ed., 1: 312.

272 "God is taking"   Paul Goodman, *The Democratic-Republicans of Massachusetts,* 93.

272 "preached gospel"   Dumas Malone, *Jefferson the President: First Term, 1801–1805,* 207.

CHAPTER TEN

PAGE

273 "HAPPY the man"   *Thomas Jefferson's Scrapbooks,* Jonathan Gross, ed., 250.

273 "an abridgement of"   Eugene R. Sheridan, "Introduction," *JEG,* 28, n.87; Forrest Church, *The Jefferson Bible,* i–xxx.

274 "diamonds...dunghill"   TJ to JA, 12 October 1813. *AJL,* 384.

274 "Syllabus on the"   TJ to JA, 22 August 1813, *AJL,* 369; TJ to William Short, 31 October 1819, *JEG,* 389.

274 "ought to displease"   TJ to BR, 23 September 1800, *JEG,* 320.

274 "All truths are related"   BR to Reverend Jeremy Belknap, 6 June 1791, *Universalism in America,* Ernest Cassara, ed., 92.

274–75 "the result of"   TJ to BR, 21 April 1803, *JEG,* 331.

275 "I have performed"   TJ to JA, 12 October 1813, *AJL,* 384.

275 "What suspicions of"   James H. Hutson, *The Founders on Religion,* 26.

275 "In an age"   JA to BR, 2 February 1807, *SOF,* 82.

275 "women of rank"   JA, 2 April 1778, *DAJA* 4: 37.

276 "the general diffusion"   Linda K. Kerber, *Women of the Republic,* 210–11.

276 "Mrs. Adams says"   JA to BR, 13 October 1810, *SOF,* 170.

276 "The Jews, the Greeks"   Stacy Schiff, *A Great Improvisation,* 236n.

276–77 "It is not to be"   TJ to WS, 13 April 1820, *JEG,* 391–92.

277 "REVOLUTION after the"   Michael A. Bellesiles, "The Soil Will Be Soaked with Blood: Taking the Revolution of 1800 Seriously," 59.

277 "What can I do"   Ron Chernow, *Alexander Hamilton,* 658.

278 "frail and worthless"   Arthur Schlesinger Jr., *War and the American Presidency*, 149.

278 "In times like"   AH to John Jay, 7 May 1800, Walter Stahr, *John Jay*, 360–61.

278 "all lawful means...begin to slumber"   Nathan Schachner, *Alexander Hamilton*, 411–12.

279 "God called him"   John F. Berens, *Providence & Patriotism in Early America*, 134.

279 "It attacks every"   Manning Dauer, "Election of 1804," I: 181.

279 "nothing would be"   Joseph Ellis, *American Sphinx*, 246, 405 n.67.

280 "We have firmly"   Sean Wilentz, *The Rise of American Democracy*, 137.

280 "I consider the"   James Thomas Flexner, *George Washington: Anguish and Farewell*, 447.

280 "The whole commerce"   TJ, *Notes on the State of Virginia, Jefferson Writings*, Merrill Peterson, ed., 288.

282 "I am aware that"   William Choen, "Thomas Jefferson and the Problem of Slavery," 503–26.

282 "New-born infants"   TJ to Jared Sparks, 4 February 1824, *TJW* 16: 8–14; Peter S. Onuf, *Jefferson's Empire*, 227.

282 "abandoning children"   John Chester Miller, *The Wolf by the Ears*, 101.

282 "will probably never"   TJ, *Notes on Virginia*, Merrill Peterson, ed., *Jefferson's Writings*, 289.

282 "Nothing is more certainly"   TJ, "Autobiography," *Jefferson Writings*, Merrill Peterson, ed., 000.

283 "Can the liberties"   TJ, *Notes on Virginia*, Frank Shuffelton, ed., 169.

283 "We are not in"   TJ to JM, 6 September 1789, *ROL* I: 640–42; Adrianne Koch, *Jefferson and Madison: The Great Collaboration*, 62–96.

283 "tears and groans"   "Answers to Questions of Monsieur Jean Nicholas Démeunier," 24 January 1786; Charles B. Sanford, *The Religious Life of Thomas Jefferson*, 71.

284 "there is none...CHARITY (obsolete)"   Dumas Malone, *Jefferson the President: Second Term*, 371–77.

285 "Why are these libels"   Merrill Peterson, *Thomas Jefferson and the New Nation*, 714.

285 "a melancholy truth"   TJ to John Norvell, 14 June 1807, *WTJ* 10: 417.

285–86 "Lay Preacher...they cannot fall"   William C. Dowling, *Literary Federalism in the Age of Jefferson*, 1, 8, 15, 57.

286 "Ordered my horse"   Merrill Peterson, *Thomas Jefferson and the New Nation*, 721.

286 "Resume thy shells"   Dumas Malone, *Jefferson the President: First Term*, 231.

286 "a base...a liar, whoremaster"   Dumas Malone, *Jefferson the President: Second Term*, 378.

287 "interested aristocracy"   TJ to Thomas Seymour, 11 February 1807, *WTJ* 10: 369.

288 "republican throughout"   Susan Juster, *Doomsayers*, 134.

291–92 "Sinners dropping...of the lamb"   Paul K. Conkin, *Cane Ridge*, 93–95.

292 "We could not"   Jean V. Matthews, *Toward a New Society*, 31.
292 "Never did a"   TJ to P. S. du Pont de Nemours, 2 March 1809, *TJW* 12: 259–60; Dumas Malone, *Jefferson the President: Second Term*, 668.
292 "everything I love"   TJ to JM, 9 June 1793, *ROL* 2: 781.
293 "a general tavern"   Merrill Peterson, *Thomas Jefferson and the New Nation*, 729, 924.
293 "Not being apt"   Dumas Malone, *Jefferson the President: Second Term*, 528.
293 "My temperament is"   TJ to JA, 8 April 1816, *AJL*, 467.
293 "The storms roll"   Margaret Bayard Smith to Susan B. Smith, *Forty Years of Washington Society*, 60.
293 "an approaching wave"   Gordon S. Wood, "The Trials and Tribulations of Thomas Jefferson," 413.
294 "holy hill"   James L. Golden and Alan L. Golden, *Thomas Jefferson and the Rhetoric of Virtue*, 74.
294 "would a missionary"   TJ to John Page, 4 May 1786, *PTJ* 9: 446.
294 "I am fond"   TJ to AA, 25 September 1785, *AJL*, 70.
294 "eaten to a honeycomb"   Dumas Malone, *Jefferson and the Ordeal of Liberty*, 322.
295 "I am a *real*"   TJ to Charles Thompson, 9 January 1816, *JEG*, 365.
295–96 "I have received"   TJ to Margaret Bayard Smith, 6 August 1816, *Forty Years of Washington Society*, 126–27; *JEG*, 375–76.
296 "Mine, after all"   Andrew Burstein, *Jefferson's Secrets*, 81.
296 "pillow of ignorance"   TJ to JA, 12 October 1823, *AJL*, 601.
296 "made so soft"   TJ to the Reverend Isaac Story, 5 December 1801, *JEG*, 325.

CHAPTER ELEVEN

PAGE
299 "Tax all things"   James H. Smylie, "Protestant Clergy, the First Amendment and Beginnings of a Constitutional Debate, 1781–91," 140.
299 "It seems the mode"   JA to AA, 14 January 1797, *AFPEA*.
299 "I do believe that"   Margaret Bayard Smith, *Forty Years of Washington Society*, 63.
299–300 "The friendship of a"   James Morton Smith, *ROL* 1: 12.
301 "There was an attempt...and spoke audibly"   Margaret Bayard Smith to Susan B. Smith, March 1809, *Forty Years of Washington Society*, 59.
301–2 "To avoid the...are bound to express"   James Madison, First Inaugural Address, 4 March 1809, *PJMP* 1: 18.
302 "You must tell me"   Margaret Bayard Smith, *Forty Years of Washington Society*, 412.
302–3 "The room was so...be in bed"   Margaret Bayard Smith to Susan B. Smith, March 1809, *Forty Years of Washington Society*, 61–63.
303 "the crowd was"   Henry Adams, *History of the United States of America During the Administrations of James Madison*, 9.
303–4 "Truth is at...than my friend"   Margaret Bayard Smith to Susan B. Smith, March 1809, *Forty Years of Washington Society*, 58–59, 64.
304 "suspended his powers"   Alf J. Mapp Jr., *The Faiths of Our Fathers*, 43.

304–5 "A gloomy, stiff"   Andrew S. Trees, *The Founding Fathers and the Politics of Character*, 111.

305 "A grave air"   Virginia Moore, *The Madisons*, 27.

305 "gentleman of great"   Robert Allen Rutland, *James Madison: The Founding Father*, 18.

305 "modest even unto"   Adrienne Koch, *Madison's "Advice to My Country,"* 87.

305 "place to an expression"   Margaret Bayard Smith to Mrs. Boyd, 17 August 1828, *Forty Years of Washington Society*, 236.

305–6 "I never knew"   Richard N. Côté, *Strength and Honor: The Life of Dolley Madison*, 259–60.

306 "very sociable"   Ralph Ketcham, *James Madison*, 630.

306 "little Madison"   Edmund Fuller and David E. Green, *God in the White House*, 45.

306 "Mr. M.'s anecdotes"   Margaret Bayard Smith to Mrs. Boyd, 17 August 1828, *Forty Years of Washington Society*, 234.

307 "the respectable though"   Irving Brandt, *James Madison* 1: 32.

307 "James Madison his"   James Thomas Flexner, *George Washington and the New Nation*, 125.

307 "Deo Gratia"   Irving Brandt, *James Madison* 1: 36.

308 "long groaned under"   James Madison Sr. to John Leland, 23 August 1781; William Mead, *Old Churches, Ministers, and Families in Virginia* 2: 87.

308 "The magistrate ought"   John T. Noonan Jr., *The Lustre of Our Country*, 65.

308 "free and equal"   Ralph Ketcham, *James Madison*, 30; Drew R. McCoy, *The Last of the Fathers*, 102.

308–9 "explored the whole"   Virginia Moore, *The Madisons*, 41.

309 "I find them"   Irving Brandt, *James Madison* 1: 119.

309 "I have sometimes"   JM to William Bradford, 25 September 1773, *PJM* 1: 96.

309–10 "Clio's Proclamation"   Irving Brandt, *James Madison* 1: 87.

310 "Who could have"   Irving Brandt, *James Madison* 1: 115.

310 "lasting alienations"   Irving Brandt, *James Madison* 1: 89.

311 "little spirit…I do not meddle"   JM to William Bradford, 28 April, 25 September, 10 June 1773, *PJM* 1: 84, 89, 97; James Morton Smith, ed., *ROL* 1: 38.

311 "My sensations for"   James Madison to William Bradford, 9 November 1772, *PJM* 1: 75.

311 "with the prevailing"   Lance Banning, *The Sacred Fire of Liberty*, 77.

311–12 "That diabolical…mischievous projects"   JM to William Bradford, 24 January 1774, *PJM* 1: 105–6.

312 "publicly burnt…atrocious crimes"   Irving Brandt, *James Madison* 1: 163.

312–13 "If he does…and obsequious"   Irving Brandt, *James Madison* 1: 164–65.

313 "all men should"   George Mason, "Virginia Declaration of Rights," *The Separation of Church and State*, Forrest Church, ed., 26–29.

313 "devoutly…a holy zeal"   Lance Banning, *The Sacred Fire of Liberty*, 355.

314 "the overbearing and"   JM to William Eustis, 22 May 1823, *WJM* 9: 136; Lance Banning, *Jefferson & Madison*, 80.

314 "enthusiasm...restraint from it"   JM to TJ, 24 October 1787, *ROL* 1: 502.

314 "Mysteries belong to"   JM to the *National Gazette*, "Who Are the Best Keepers of the People's Liberties?", 20 December 1792, *PJM* 14: 427.

315 "the corrupting influence"   Ralph Ketcham, *James Madison*, 77.

316 "The Baptists are"   James Madison Sr. to JM, 30 January 1788, *PJM* 10: 446.

316 "The sentiments of"   James Gordon to JM, 17 February 1788, *PJM* 10: 516.

316 "friend of the rights"   James H. Smylie, "Protestant Clergy, the First Amendment and Beginnings of a Constitutional Debate, 1781–91," 120.

316 "absurd and groundless"   Paul Finkelman, "James Madison and the Bill of Rights: A Reluctant Paternity," 323–24.

316–17 "When the Constitution"   Forrest Church, *The Separation of Church and State*, 87–93.

317 "There is not"   Leonard W. Levy, "Establishment of Religion," 354–56.

318 "I hope you will"   Harry Ammon, *James Monroe*, 76.

318 "It is my sincere"   JM to George Eve, 2 January 1789, *PJM* 11: 404–5.

318 "a very spirited"   Richard Labunski, *James Madison and the Struggle for the Bill of Rights*, 166.

318–19 "unequivocal pledge"   Paul Finkelman, "James Madison and the Bill of Rights: A Reluctant Paternity," 336.

319 "Let me awaken"   Richard Labunski, *James Madison and the Struggle for the Bill of Rights*, 170.

319 "Service was performed"   Irving Brandt, *James Madison* 3: 241–42.

320 "Religion has much"   James H. Smylie, "Protestant Clergy, the First Amendment and Beginnings of a Constitutional Debate, 1781–91," 124–28.

321 "nauseous project...in criminal cases"   Leonard W. Levy, "Bill of Rights," 37–40.

321 "That all power"   Lance Banning, *Jefferson & Madison*, 17.

322 "Congress shall make"   John T. Noonan Jr., *The Lustre of Our Country*, 80–81.

322 "Thou must come...stranger"   Catherine Allgor, *A Perfect Union*, 28, 31.

322 "resorting to houses"   Richard N. Côté, *Strength and Honor*, 133.

323 "disregarded the wholesome...a great degree"   Virginia Moore, *The Madisons*, 48, 189.

324 "my age and"   Carl Sferrazza Anthony, *First Ladies*, 80.

324 "Accept and wear"   Richard N. Côté, *Strength and Honor*, 256.

325 "With respect to...nursing mothers"   Page Smith, *John Adams* 2: 1032.

325 "it might safely...no evil example"   Carl Sferrazza Anthony, *First Ladies*, 85.

325 "I was beaten"   Richard N. Côté, *Strength and Honor*, 251.

CHAPTER TWELVE

PAGE

326 "Ye ministers that"   *Three Centuries of American Poetry*, Allen Mandelbaum and Robert D. Richardson Jr., eds. (New York, 1999), 78–79.

326 "to include [Canada]"   TJ to JM, 27 April 1809, *ROL* 3: 1586.

327 "honorable to your"   Robert Allen Rutland, *The Presidency of James Madison*, 48.

327 "come forward with"   Dumas Malone, *The Sage of Monticello*, 115.

328 "An Appeal to"   Richard Buel Jr., *America on the Brink*, 106.

328 "under the guidance"   Richard Buel Jr., *America on the Brink*, 106, 143.

328–29 "As long as we"   Joseph W. Phillips, *Jedidiah Morse and New England Congregationalism*, 125.

329 "War is declared"   Donald R. Hickey, *The War of 1812*, 52.

329 "The spirit of"   Irving Brandt, *James Madison* 5: 24.

330 "Met Mr. Madison"   Irving Brandt, *James Madison* 4: 475.

330 "plain direct exhortation"   Irving Brandt, *James Madison* 5: 97.

330 "Sectarians [Baptists and Methodists]"   William Gribbin, *The Churches Militant*, 72.

330 "vote Christian"   Fred J. Hood, *Reformed America*, 111.

331 "Providence has given"   John Jay to Jedidiah Morse, 12 October 1816, "John Jay," faithofourfathers.net.

331 "duty to themselves...*which they preach*"   Richard Buel Jr., *America on the Brink*, 158, 175.

332 mosquito fleet   Donald R. Hickey, *The War of 1812*, 9.

332 "The seditious opposition"   JM to TJ, 17 August 1812, *ROL* 3: 1702.

333 "Ministers have the"   Phillip Hamburger, *The Separation of Church and State*, 152.

333 "from the pulpit"   TJ to P. H. Wendover, 13 March 1815, *TJW* 14: 279–82.

334 "Under the dominion"   Irving Brandt, *James Madison* 5: 27–28.

334 "their common vows"   JM, "First Fast Day Proclamation," 23 July 1813, *The Debates and Proceedings of the Congress of the United States of America*, Vol. 27, 13th Congress (Washington, D.C., 1854), 2674.

335 "Our two great"   Lynn W. Turner, "Elections of 1816 and 1820," 1: 301.

335 "Bible Christian"   Irving Brandt, *James Madison* 5: 199.

335 "With my persuasion"   William Gribbin, *The Churches Militant*, 21.

335 "stand fire"   Irving Brandt, *James Madison* 5: 340–41.

336 "ought to feel...against their country"   William Gribbin, *The Churches Militant*, 66, 71–72, 109.

336–37 "*Resolved,* as the sense"   Henry Adams, *History of the United States of America During the Administrations of James Madison*, 664.

337 "the sound of"   Timothy Pickering to E. Pennington, 12 July 1812; James Morton Smith, *ROL* 3: 1682.

337 "The rights which...repeated *French* orders"   Ralph Ketcham, *James Madison*, 537.

338 "Advice to a Raven"   Emory Elliot, *Revolutionary Writers*, 124–27.

338 "the wormwood"   William Gribbin, *The Churches Militant*, 16.

338 "more glorious than"   Richard Buel Jr., *America on the Brink*, 206.

339 "We are not"   BR to JA, 13 March 1809, *SOF,* 149.

340 "Fly, Monroe, fly!"   Anne Hollingsworth Wharton, *Salons, Colonial and Republican*, 205.

340 "It is vain"   Douglas R. Egerton, "Henry Clay," 70.

340 "Mr. Madison is perhaps"   Donald R. Hickey, *The War of 1812*, 302.

340–41 "I would rather"   Catherine Algor, *A Perfect Union*, 320.

341 "I have always"   DM to Edward Coles, 13 May 1813, *The Selected Letters of Dolley Payne Madison*, David B. Mattern and Holly C. Schulman, eds., 176.

341 "I insisted on"   DM to Lucy Payne Washington Todd, 23–24 August 1814, *The Selected Letters of Dolley Payne Madison*, David B. Mattern and Holly C. Schulman, eds., 193–94.

341–42 "made up in"…not among them   Margaret Bayard Smith, *Forty Years of Washington Society*, 16–17.

342 "rougher drastics"   TJ to JM, 29 June 1812, *ROL* 3: 1699.

342–43 "we can get…free or fearless"   TJ to William Short, 28 November 1814, *TJW* 13: 211–12; TJ to James Martin, 20 September 1813, *TJW* 13: 381–84; TJ to Henry Dearborn, 17 March 1815, *TJW* 14: 288–89; Peter S. Onuf, *Jefferson's Empire*, 124–27.

343 "is, under Providence"   Joseph W. Phillips, *Jedidiah Morse and New England Congregationalism*, 164.

343 "only twenty-three persons"   Henry Adams, *History of the United States of America During the Administrations of James Madison*, 1112.

343–44 "There is an alliance"   JR to BR, 10 July 1812, *SOF*, 251.

344 "The Christian religion"   JA to BR, 29 November 1812, *SOF*, 279.

344 "I believe that"   JA to BR, 3 July 1812, *SOF*, 249.

344–45 "I was seated"   Henry Adams, *History of the United States of America During the Administrations of James Madison*, 1121–22.

345 "And where is our"   Zoltan Haraszti, *John Adams and the Prophets of Progress*, 179.

345 "The Marats, the"   TJ to Marquis de La Fayette, 14 February 1815; Malcolm Kelsall, *Jefferson and the Iconography of Romanticism*, 9.

345 "this mad project"   George Dangerfield, *The Era of Good Feelings*, 86.

345 "A GREAT PAMPHLET"   Sean Wilentz, *The Rise of American Democracy*, 166.

345 "monarchists and traitors"   Donald R. Hickey, *The War of 1812*, 279.

346 "cruel, unnecessary"   *WJM* 8: 319n.

346 "Glory be to God"   Robert Allen Rutland, *The Presidency of James Madison*, 185.

346 "I believe"   Sean Wilentz, *The Rise of American Democracy*, 175.

347 "We have abundant"   William Gribbin, *The Churches Militant*, 133–34.

347 "Approach, ye Holy"   John F. Berens, *Providence & Patriotism in Early America*, 163.

347 "Our Mother who art"   William Gribbin, *The Churches Militant*, 133–34.

347 "We formed our"   Simon P. Newman, *Parades and the Politics of the Street*, 62–63.

348 "No people ought"   Barrett Ward Sheldon, *The Political Philosophy of James Madison*, 105–6.

349 "We have reason"   John Kerr (Virginia), 22 February 1815, *Circular Letters of Congressmen to their Constituents, 1789–1829*, Noble E. Cunningham Jr., ed., 2: 920.

349 "We are bound"   John Sevier (Tennessee), 3 March 1815, *Circular Letters of Congressmen to their Constituents, 1789–1829*, Noble E. Cunningham Jr., ed., 2: 950.

349 "The greater part"   Richard S. Alley, *James Madison on Religious Liberty*, 184.

349 "religious sects and"   David L. Holmes, *The Faiths of the Founding Fathers*, 95.

350 "I sincerely congratulate"   TJ to JM, 23 March 1815, *ROL* 3: 1764.

350 "notwithstanding a thousand"   JA to TJ, 2 February 1817, *AJL*, 508.

350 "A great object"   Lee Travers, *Celebrating the Fourth*, 205.

350 "The war has"   Robert S. Alley, "John Leland," 235.

351 "The letters and"   *WJM* 3: 19.

351–52 "The passage is…by the Bible"   Franklin Steiner, *The Religious Beliefs of Our Presidents*, 91–92.

352 "I hope my beloved"   David L. Holmes, *The Faiths of the Founding Fathers*, 96.

352 "scanty materials"   JM to TJ, 10 September 1824, *ROL*, 1898–1901.

353 "precedent for the"   Alf J. Mapp Jr., *The Faiths of Our Fathers*, 51.

353–54 "as distinctly as…human and divine"   JM, "Veto Messages, Feb 21 and Feb 28, 1811," *WJM* 8: 132–33.

354 "Among the various"   JM to the Baptists on Neal's Creek and on Black Creek, North Carolina, 3 June 1811, *WJM* 8: 511–12.

354–55 "Besides the danger…from small beginnings"   JM, "Detached Memoranda" [1819?] *Madison Writings*, Jack N. Rakove, ed., 761–62.

356 "They seem to imply"   Leonard W. Levy, *The Establishment Clause*, 122–24.

356–57 "an *advisory* Government…of Constitutional principles"   JM, "Detached Memoranda" [1819?], *Madison Writings*, Jack N. Rakove, ed., 764–66.

357 "It was not with"   *JMW* 3: 274.

357 "We are always"   JM, "Detached Memoranda," *Writings*, 762, 764.

358 "If one religion"   Robert S. Alley, *James Madison on Religious Liberty*, 191, 196 n.73.

358 "public strength with"   Robert Allen Rutland, *James Madison: The Founding Father*, 237.

358 "A government"   JM, Eighth Annual Address to Congress, 3 December 1816, "The American Presidency Project," John Woolley and Gerhard Peters, eds., www.presidency.ucsb.edu.

CHAPTER THIRTEEN

PAGE

361 "The moral beauties"   Philip Freneau, *A Collection of Poems on American Affairs* (New York, 1815), 20.

362–64 "black Venus…most bloody war"   Jonas Clopper, *Fragments of the History of Bahlfredonia*, Herman Thwackihs (Maryland, 1819).

367 "These are the times"   Thomas Paine, *The American Crisis I*, Philip Foner, ed., *The Complete Writings of Thomas Paine* 1: 50.

367 "Washington Crossing the"   David L. Holmes, "The Religion of James Monroe," *Virginia Quarterly Review* 79 (4): 589.

368 "So towering are…religion ends"   Harry Ammon, *James Monroe*, 17–18, 23.

368 "I very sincerely"   Harry Ammons, *James Monroe*, 27–28.

369 "Monroe is just"   Harry Ammons, *James Monroe*, 27.

369 "Believe me"   James Monroe to TJ, 9 September 1789, *PWJM*, 11.

369 "Turn his soul"   TJ to JM, 5 February 1787, *ROV* 3: 465.

370 "inviting confidence"   W. P. Cresson, *James Monroe*, 92, 282.

370 "Nature has given"   Noble E. Cunningham Jr., *The Presidency of James Monroe*, 34.

370 "Good old Col. Munroe"   Sarah Coles to DM, 31 July 1815, *The Selected Letters of Dolley Payne Madison*, David B. Mattern and Holly C. Schulman, eds., 202.

370 "Nothing is wanting"   W. P. Cresson, *James Monroe*, 85.

371 "I shall certainly"   W. P. Cresson, *James Monroe*, 149.

371 "fraterniz[ing] and"   Ron Chernow, *Alexander Hamilton*, 659.

371 "school for scandal"   Walt Brown, *John Adams and the American Press*, 25.

371 "winked at his"   James Monroe to JM, 5 July 1796, *PWJM*, 178.

372 "the whole of...they be, indifferent"   Thomas Paine, "Letter to George Washington" (1786), Philip Foner, ed., *The Complete Writings of Thomas Paine* 2: 689–723.

372 "For such a mongrel"   JA to Benjamin Waterhouse, 29 October 1805; Dumas Malone, *Jefferson the President: First Term*, 200.

372 "as if you stood"   G. Adolph Koch, *Republican Religion*, 134.

373 "Monroe will"   Daniel C. Gilman, *James Monroe*, 71.

373 "till all Virginians"   Lynn W. Turner, "Elections of 1816 and 1820," 1: 304.

373–74 "As to the style"   Louise Durbin, *Inaugural Cavalcade*, 28; Noble E. Cunningham Jr., *The Presidency of James Monroe*, 30.

374 "The Government has...in our favor"   James Monroe, First Inaugural Address, 4 March 1817, *PWJM*, 487–94.

375 "general absolution of"   Lynn W. Turner, "Elections of 1816 and 1820," 1: 312.

375 "The demon of party"   W. P. Cresson, *James Monroe*, 287.

375 "ERA OF GOOD"   George Dangerfield, *The Era of Good Feelings*, 95.

376 "eight millions of"   Lee Travers, *Celebrating the Fourth*, 208.

376 "to unite our"   James Morton Smith, *ROL* 3: 1760.

376 "The visit of"   Lee Travers, *Celebrating the Fourth*, 203.

376 "one people"   Ralph Ketcham, *Presidents Above Party*, 126.

377 "The people of"   "Address in Behalf of the Citizens of Hartford to President James Monroe," June 23, 1817; Lynn W. Turner, "Elections of 1816 and 1820," 1: 337.

378 "All the infidels"   *Autobiography of Lyman Beecher*, Barbara Cross, ed., 1: 394.

378–79 "Long have the...church and state"   William G. McLoughlin, *New England Dissent* 2: 1027–28.

379 "The Charter of"   Sean Wilentz, *The Rise of American Democracy*, 184–85.

380 "the ancient spirit"   Frank Lambert, *The Founding Fathers and the Place of Religion in America*, 284; Sean Wilentz, *The Rise of American Democracy*, 184–85.

380 "Why should this"   Sidney Earl Meade, *Nathanial William Taylor*, 133.

380 "What need we"   TJ to JA, 5 May 1817, *AJL*, 512.

382 "Benevolent Empire"   Marc L. Harris, "Revelation and the American Republic: Timothy Dwight's Civic Participation," 449–68.

382 "the best thing…gold-headed canes"   Lyman Beecher, *Autobiography of Lyman Beecher,* Barbara Cross, ed., 1: 60, 344, 392–406; Richard J. Purcell, *Connecticut in Transition, 1775–1818,* 264.

382 "The prevalence of…moral militia"   Jean V. Matthews, *Toward a New Society,* 39–40.

383 "A complete remedy"   James Monroe to JM, 20 March 1829, *PWJM,* 698.

384 "Bible Society of Salem"   W. P. and J. P. Cutler, *The Life of Rev. Mannasseh Cutler* 2: 320.

384 "I consider Unitarianism"   James King Morse, *Jedidiah Morse,* 71.

384 "half-reformation"   Stephen Prothers, *American Jesus,* 30.

385 "[New England] is now"   TJ to Horatio Spafford, 10 January 1816; James H Hutson, *The Founders on Religion,* 145.

385 "We have now"   JA to TJ, 4 November 1816, *AJL,* 493–94.

386 "I acknowledge the"   TJ to JM, 25 February 1822, *ROL* 3: 1837.

387 "There is a great…estimable man"   W. P. Cresson, *James Monroe,* 370.

388 American "court"   W. P. Cresson, *James Monroe,* 368.

388 "in the highest"   Carl Sferrazza Anthony, *First Ladies,* 103.

388 "Sun Beams May"   Linda K. Kerber, *Federalists in Dissent,* 19.

388 "splendid enough for"   Constance McLauglin Green, *Washington: Village and Capital,* 82.

389 "It is a mere…*fit accompaniment*"   Noble E. Cunningham Jr., *The Presidency of James Monroe,* 137, 140–41.

389 "ought not to"   Noble E. Cunningham Jr., *The Presidency of James Monroe,* 20.

CHAPTER FOURTEEN

PAGE

391 "Still one great"   *The American First Class Book,* John Pierpont, ed. (Boston, 1835), 164.

392 "the rights of"   JM, First Annual Address to Congress, 2 December 1817, "The American Presidency Project," John Woolley and Gerhard Peters, eds., www.presidency.ucsb.edu.

392 "the latitude of"   Noble E. Cunningham Jr., *The Presidency of James Monroe,* 48.

392 "The sons of"   R. Pierce Beaver, *Church, State, and the American Indian,* 67

392 "driving the wild"   GW to James Duane, 7 September 1783, *Washington Writings,* John Rhodehamel, ed., 536, 540–41.

392 "convince them that"   James Thomas Flexner, *George Washington and the New Nation,* 300.

393 "possess the lands"   GW to Arthur St. Clair, 6 October 1789, *Washington Writings,* John Rhodehamel, ed., 745.

393 "troublesome allies…connected with it"   Bernard W. Sheehan, *Seeds of Extinction,* 126, 208–9.

393 "gradually circumscribe"   Merrill D. Peterson, *Thomas Jefferson,* 1118.

393 "Indian men regard"   Walter Stahr, *John Jay,* 349.

394 "To promote this"   TJ to William Henry Harrison, 27 February 1803, *Jefferson Writings,* Merrill Peterson, ed., 1119.

394 "Tranquility between the" Irving Brandt, *James Madison* 4: 193.

394 "sanctimonious reverence" Joseph Ellis, *American Sphinx*, 238–40.

395 "had compelled us" JM, Seventh Annual Message to Congress, 5 December 1815, *Madison Writings*, Jack W. Rakove, ed., 711.

395 "no one could" Henry Adams, *History of the United States of America During the Administrations of James Madison*, 373.

396 "who come to" Bernard W. Sheehan, *Seeds of Extinction*, 127.

396–97 "to employ capable" R. Pierce Beaver, *Church, State, and the American Indian*, 68, 73–77.

397 "Considerations of humanity" JM, "To Congress—Removal of Indians," 30 March 1824, *PWJM*, 326.

397–98 "The distinction" JM, Second Inaugural Address, 4 March 1821, *PWJM*, 533.

399 "I know this scheme" P. J. Staudenraus, *The African Colonization Movement*, 17, 23–35, 86.

399 "might prove a" *PJM* 12: 438; Robert Allen Rutland, *James Madison: The Founding Father*, 70.

400 "for removing from" Drew R. McCoy, *The Last of the Fathers*, 285.

400 "regain the ascendancy" Sean Wilentz, *The Rise of American Democracy*, 224.

401 "Every man who…to be so" Glover Moore, *Missouri Controversy, 1819–1821*, 28, 292.

401 "Mr. President, the" *Annals of Congress*, 16(1): 269–70; George Dangerfield, *The Era of Good Feelings*, 221.

401–2 "would view with…pursuit of happiness" Glover Moore, *Missouri Controversy, 1819–1821*, 67–72.

402 "the illustrious authors" Noble E. Cunningham Jr., *The Presidency of James Monroe*, 91.

402 "all men are" Sean Wilentz, *The Rise of American Democracy*, 227.

402 "read in the North" Walter Stahr, *John Jay*, 372–73; Glover Moore, *Missouri Controversy, 1819–1821*, 74–79.

403–4 "The Bible itself…of the blacks" JA to Louisa Catherine Adams, 13 January 1820; James H. Hutson, *The Founders on Religion*, 206–7.

404 "This momentous question" TJ to John Holmes, 22 April 1820, *Jefferson Writings*, Merrill Peterson, ed., 1434.

404 "the pole-star" George Dangerfield, *The Era of Good Feelings*, 250.

405 "an effervescence among" Peter Shaw, *The Character of John Adams*, 314.

405 "to manifest before…wonderful Alliance" W. P. Cresson, *James Monroe*, 420–21.

405 "jihad" George Dangerfield, *The Era of Good Feelings*, 265.

406 "reactionary sovereigns" TJ to JA, 22 January 1821, *AJL* 2: 569–70.

406 "the bed of lies" Marquis de Lafayette to TJ, 10 December 1817; Malcolm Kelsall, *Jefferson and the Iconography of Romanticism*, 8.

406 "the state of" W. P. Cresson, *James Monroe*, 445.

406–7 "the most momentous…hemisphere of freedom" TJ to James Monroe, 24 October 1823, *PWJM*, 632.

407 "entangling alliances" TJ, First Inaugural Address, *Jefferson Writings*, Merrill Peterson, ed., 494.

407 "mere numbers" Joseph W. Phillips, *Jedidiah Morse and New England Congregationalism*, 180–81.

407–8 "Mr. Monroe has" JA to TJ, 10 October 1817, *AJL*, 522.

408 "the golden age" Gary Hart, *James Monroe*, 119, 125.

408 "a new act" Noble E. Cunningham Jr., *The Presidency of James Monroe*, 162.

408–9 "It has given" Harry Ammon, *James Monroe*, 490.

409 "easy conscience" George Dangerfield, *The Era of Good Feelings*, 97.

409 "a mind anxious" John Quincy Adams, "Eulogy on the Life and Character of James Monroe," 25 August 1831 (Boston, 1831), 92.

409–11 "the people and…have been subverted" James Monroe, *The People, the Sovereign, PWJM*.

411–12 "There behold him" Harry Ammon, *James Monroe*, 573.

412 "I am persuaded" GW to Presbytery of Massachusetts and New Hampshire, 23 October 1789, *WW* 30: 453.

EPILOGUE

PAGE

417 "You have been" TJ to JM, 17 February 1826, *ROL* 3: 1967.

417 "You cannot look" JM to TJ, 24 February 1826, *ROL* 3: 1967–68.

418 "decayed and in" Virginia Moore, *The Madisons*, 474.

418 "inexhaustible faith…heart and mind" Drew R. McCoy, *The Last of the Fathers*, 6, 192.

419 "deep feelings for" Kenneth O'Reilly, *Nixon's Piano*, 28.

419 "It was as painful" Drew R. McCoy, *The Last of the Fathers*, 308.

419 "Generally idle" Drew R. McCoy, *The Last of the Fathers*, 285.

419 "all the evils…do not see it" Irving Brandt, *James Madison* 5: 504.

419 "Why, this is bad" Irving Brandt, *James Madison* 5: 421.

420 "the genealogy of" Peter S. Onuf, *Jefferson's Empire: The Language of American Nationhood*, 144–45.

420 "Let the open" Irving Brandt, *James Madison* 5: 522–31.

421 "His head…dropped" Adrienne Koch, *Madison's "Advice to My Country*," 157.

421 "What's the matter" Virginia Moore, *The Madisons*, 478.

421 "but the hundred" Drew R. McCoy, *The Last of the Fathers*, 371.

421 "Every day or" David B. Mattern and Holly C. Shulman, eds., *The Selected Letters of Dolley Payne Madison*, 323.

422 "whenever it shall" DM to the House of Representatives, 9 January 1844, *The Selected Letters of Dolley Payne Madison*, 368, n.1.

422 "We had an excellent" DM to Richard D. Cutts, 16 July 1845, *The Selected Letters of Dolley Payne Madison*, 380–81.

422 "devoted relatives" David B. Mattern and Holly C. Shulman, eds., *The Selected Letters of Dolley Payne Madison*, 325.

423 "The tendency to" Adrienne Koch, *Madison's "Advice to My Country*," 43.

423 "The prevailing opinion...a decisive test"   JM to the Reverend Jasper Adams, *WJM* 9: 484–88; John F. Wilson, "The Status of 'Civil Religion' in America," 18–19; cf. David L. Dreisbach, *Religion and Politics in the Early Republic*, 117–21.

423–24 "That there has"   JM to F. L. Schaeffer, 3 December 1821; Ralph Ketcham, *James Madison*, 167.

425–26 "The undertaking in...were very deep"   David L. Holmes, "The Decline and Revival of the Church of Virginia," 53–109; John G. West Jr., *The Politics of Revelation & Reason*, 100.

426–27 "You and I"   JA to TJ, 13 July 1813, *AJL*, 358.

427 "the forest of"   TJ to JA, 27 June 1813, *AJL*, 335.

427 "thorns on the pillow"   TJ to JA, 12 October 1823, *AJL*, 601.

427 "corrected or revised"   Dumas Malone, *The Sage of Monticello*, 102.

427–28 "so great, so"   TJ to JA, 11 January 1816, *AJL*, 459.

428 "Are we to surrender"   TJ to JA, 12 September 1820, *AJL*, 574.

428 "one of the most"   JA to TJ, 2 February 1816, *AJL*, 461.

428 "For more than"   JA to TJ, 3 February 1821, *AJL*, 571.

428 "I have been"   JA to TJ, 18 June 1813, *AJL*, 362.

428 "I have read away"   JA to TJ, 20 June 1815, *AJL*, 445.

429 "Oh, Lord!"   JA to TJ, 18 May 1817, *AJL*, 515.

430 "made of Christendom"   TJ to Alexander Smyth, 17 January 1825; TJ to Thomas Whittemore, 5 June 1822; James H. Hutson, *The Founders on Religion*, 175.

430 "I set at defiance"   JA to TJ, 14 November 1813, *AJL*, 394; JA to Alexander B. Johnson, 22 April 1823; James H. Hutson, *The Founders on Religion*, 79.

430 "I assert the"   JA to Francis van der Kemp, 23 January 1813; James H. Hutson, *The Founders on Religion*, 134.

430 "the truth when"   JA to Caroline de Windt, 15 November 1821; James H. Hutson, *The Founders on Religion*, 79.

430 "Ask no such"   JA to Caroline de Windt, 24 January 1820; James H. Hutson, *The Founders on Religion*, 49.

430 "Then our grandchildren"   Page Smith, *John Adams* 2: 1078.

431 "I would trust"   JA to TJ, 25 June 1813, *AJL*, 334.

431 "If believing too"   JA to TJ, 3 December 1813, *AJL*, 403.

431–32 "the clergy will"   TJ to Jedidiah Morse, 6 March 1822, *Jefferson Writings*, Merrill Peterson, ed., 1455–56.

432 "laudable...or illicit object"   JM to TJ, 5 March 1822, *ROL* 3: 1838–39.

432–33 "The mulatto has"   Bernard W. Sheehan, *Seeds of Extinction*, 177; R. Pierce Beaver, *Church, State, and the American Indians*, 74–75.

433 "longing for opportunities"   Joseph W. Phillips, *Jedidiah Morse and New England Congregationalism*, 197.

433 "arduous and constant"   James King Morse, *Jedidiah Morse*, 160–61.

433–34 "providential substitutes...worship God"   Sidney E. Mead, *The Old Religion in the Brave New World*, 115–32.

434 "[Christianity] has survived"   Lyman Beecher, *The Memory of Our Fathers* (1827), 28; Elwyn A Smith, "The Voluntary Establishment of Religion," 180–81.

434 "The progress of...and civil trust"   Sidney E. Mead, *The Old Religion in the Brave New World,* 117.

434 "Republican of the...of Independence"   William G. McLoughlin, *New England Dissent, 1630–1833* 2: 1001–2.

435 "Your administration will"   JA to TJ, 3 July 1813, *AJL,* 349.

436 "manifested a sentiment"   TJ to Horatio G. Spofford, 11 May 1819, *TJW* 15: 189.

436 "ought to be frequently"   Jean V. Matthews, *Toward a New Society,* 21.

436 "There is not an idea"   JA to Timothy Pickering, 6 August 1822, *WJA* 2: 514.

436 "Mausoleusms...in brilliant colors"   Darren Staloff, *Hamilton, Adams, Jefferson,* 229.

437 "There is not an"   JA to AA, 3 July 1776, *The Letters of John and Abigail Adams,* Frank Shuffelton, ed., 192.

437–38 "portico...for its feast"   Malcolm Kelsall, *Jefferson and the Iconography of Romanticism,* 2–4.

438 "hallowed...these United States."   Gary B. Nash, *First City,* 7.

438 "the inherent and"   Stephen A. Conrad, "Putting Rights Talk in Its Place," 254.

438 "All eyes are"   TJ to Roger C. Weightman, 24 June 1826, *Jefferson Writings,* Merrill D. Peterson, ed., 1517.

438 "saddles on their"   Jonathan Gross, *Thomas Jefferson's Scrapbooks,* 16.

438 "This is the"   Andrew Burstein, *America's Jubilee,* 263.

439 "Lord, now lettest"   Michael Knox Beran, *Jefferson's Demons,* 197–98.

439 "the *nunc dimmitis*"   Merrill Peterson, *Thomas Jefferson and the New Nation,* 800.

439 "Never was a"   Margaret Bayard Smith, *Forty Years of Washington Society,* 315.

439 "I am answerable"   Edwin Gaustad, *Faith of Our Fathers,* 92.

440 "the old Roman"   Joseph J. Ellis, *Passionate Sage,* 202.

440 "In dogmatizing, laughing...unjust or cruel"   David McCullough, *John Adams,* 589, 612.

440 "a solemn"   Andrew Burstein, *America's Jubilee,* 235.

440 "Independence forever...the *human mind*"   Joseph J. Ellis, *Passionate Sage,* 206.

440 "Not a word"   John Quincy Adams and Charles Francis Adams, *John Adams* 2: 403.

440–41 "temple of liberty...purest faith"   Andrew Burstein, *America's Jubilee,* 237

441 "Do you know...Jefferson survives"   Andrew Burstein, *America's Jubilee,* 266–68.

441 "On our fiftieth"   Catherine L. Albenese, *Sons of the Fathers,* 192.

441 "holy purpose...perpetuate them"   Pauline Maier, *American Scripture,* 186.

441–42 "to describe...hovering near"   Margaret Bayard Smith, *Forty Years of Washington Society,* 230–31.

443 "We hold these"   "Declaration of Sentiments," *An American Primer,* Daniel J. Boorstin, ed., 378–79.

443 "I look forward"   Martin Luther King, Jr., "I Have a Dream," Taylor Branch, *Parting the Waters* (New York, 1988), 880.

443 "I have sworn"   TJ to BR, 23 September 1800, *JEG*, 320.

444 "All honor to"   Abraham Lincoln to Henry L. Pierce et al., 6 April 1859, in Lincoln, *Speeches and Writings: 1859–1865*, Donald E. Fehrenbacher, ed. (New York: Library of America, 1989), 19.

444 "When words cannot"   *Thomas Jefferson's Scrapbooks*, Jonathan Gross, ed., 59.

APPENDIX

PAGE

445 critics argue   e.g. Matthew Goldstein, "Myths of the Oath of Office," WASHline, May, 2006," www.wash.org.

445 "The chancellor"   Washington Irving, *George Washington: A Biography*, 651–52.

445 "well-researched"   Andrew Burstein, *The Original Knickerbocker: The Life of Washington Irving* (New York, 2007), 323.

446 "The scene was"   *Federal Gazette*, 8 May 1789; cf. Jedidiah Morse, *American Geography* (London, 1794) 2: 271–72.

447 "I rejoice in"   David Humphreys, *Pennsylvania Mercury*, 9 May 1789; reprinted in Philadelphia's *Federal Gazette*, 9 May 1789.

448 "I, _____, a Representative"   J. L. Bell, www.boston1775.blogspot.com/ 2006/10/swearing-into-office-so-help-me-god.html.

448 "I would pray"   TJ to John Marshall, 2 March 1801, *PTJ* 33: 119.

448–49 "That [oath] prescribed in"   John Marshall to TJ, 2 March 1801, *PTJ* 33: 120.

BIBLIOGRAPHY

Achenbach, Joel, *The Grand Idea: George Washington's Potomac and the Race to the West* (New York, 2004).

Adams, Henry, *History of the United States of America During the Administrations of James Madison* (New York, 1986).

———, *History of the United States of America During the Administrations of Thomas Jefferson* (New York, 1986).

Adams, James Luther, "The Voluntary Principle in the Forming of American Religion," *The Religion of the Republic,* Elwyn A. Smith, ed. (Philadelphia, 1971), 217–46.

Adams, John Quincy, and Charles Francis, *John Adams,* two volumes (New York, 2005).

Ahlstrom, Sydney E., *A Religious History of the American People* (New Haven, CT, 1972).

Albanese, Catherine, *Sons of the Fathers: The Civil Religion of the American Revolution* (Philadelphia, 1976).

Alley, Reuben E., *A History of Baptists in Virginia* (Richmond, VA, 1973).

Alley, Robert S., *James Madison on Religious Liberty* (Buffalo, NY, 1985).

———, "John Leland," *James Madison and the American Nation 1751–1836,* Robert A. Rutland, ed. (New York, 1994), 235.

———, *So Help Me God: Religion and the Presidency, Wilson to Nixon* (Richmond, VA, 1972).

Allgor, Catherine, *A Perfect Union: Dolley Madison and the Creation of the American Nation* (New York, 2006).

Altschuler, Glenn C., and Stuart M. Blumin, *Rude Republic: Americans and Their Politics in the Nineteenth Century* (Princeton, NJ, 2000).

Ammon, Harry, *The Genet Mission* (New York, 1973).

———, *James Monroe: The Quest for National Identity* (Charlottesville, VA, 1990).

———, "James Monroe and the Election of 1808 in Virginia," *The William and Mary Quarterly* (Third Ser.), Vol. 20, No. 1 (Jan. 1963), 40.

Andrewes, Launcelot, *Sermons,* G. M. Story, ed. (Oxford, 1967).

Anthony, Carl Sferrazza, *First Ladies: The Saga of the President's Wives and Their Power, 1789–1961* (New York, 1990).

Appleby, Joyce, *Capitalism and the New Social Order* (New York, 1983).

———, *Inheriting the Revolution: The First Generation of Americans* (Cambridge, MA, 2000).

———, "Jefferson and His Complex Legacy," *Jeffersonian Legacies,* Peter S. Onuf, ed. (Charlottesville, VA, 1993), 1–16.

———, *Thomas Jefferson* (New York, 2003).

———, "Thomas Jefferson and the Psychology of Democracy," *The Revolution of 1800,* James Horn, Jan Ellen Lewis, and Peter S. Onuf, eds. (Charlottesville, VA, 2002), 155–72.

Arnett, Ethel Stephens, *Mrs. James Madison: The Incomparable Dolley* (Greensboro, NC, 1972).

Baldwin, Neil, *The American Revelation* (New York, 2005).

Banner, James M. Jr., *To the Hartford Convention: The Federalists and the Origins of Party Politics in Massachusetts, 1789–1815* (New York, 1970).

Banning, Lance, *Jefferson & Madison: Three Conversations from the Founding* (Lanham, MD, 1995).

———, *The Jeffersonian Persuasion: Evolution of a Party Ideology* (Ithaca, NY, 1978).

———, "Madison, the Statute, and Republican Convictions," *The Virginia Statute for Religious Freedom,* Merrill Peterson and Robert C. Vaughn, eds. (New York, 1988), 109–38.

———, *The Sacred Fire of Liberty: James Madison & the Founding of the Federal Republic* (Ithaca, NY, 1995).

Beaver, R. Pierce, *Church, State, and the American Indian* (Saint Louis, MO, 1966).

Beliles, Mark A., "Christian Communities, Religious Revivals, and Political Culture," *Religion and Politcal Culture in Jefferson's Virginia,* Garrett Ward Sheldon and Daniel L. Dreisbach, eds. (Lanham, MD, 2000), 3–40.

Bellah, Robert N., *The Broken Covenant: American Civil Religion in Time of Trial* (Chicago, 1992).

Bellesiles, Michael A., "The Soil Will Be Soaked with Blood: Taking the Revolution of 1800 Seriously," *The Revolution of 1800,* James Horn, Jan Ellen Lewis, and Peter S. Onuf, eds. (Charlottesville, VA, 2002), 59–86.

Beran, Michael Knox, *Jefferson's Demons: Portrait of a Restless Mind* (New York, 2003).

Berens, John F., *Providence & Patriotism in Early America: 1640–1815* (Charlottesville, VA, 1978).

Berk, Stephen E., *Calvinism Versus Democracy: Timothy Dwight and the Origins of American Evangelical Orthodoxy* (Hamden, CT, 1974).

Berkhofer, Robert F. Jr., *Salvation and the Savage: An Analysis of Protestant Missions and American Indian Response, 1787–1862* (Lexington, KY, 1965).

Bernstein, R. B., *Thomas Jefferson* (New York, 2003).

Bestor, Arthur, "Thomas Jefferson and the Freedom of Books," *Three Presidents and Their Books* (Urbana, IL, 1955).

Birdsall, Richard D., "The Second Great Awakening and the New England Social Order," *Church History,* Vol. 39, No. 3 (Sept. 1970), 345–64.

Blakely, William Addison, ed., *American State Papers and Related Documents on Freedom of Religion* (Washington, DC, 1949).

Bloom, Sol, *George Washington the President: Triumphant Journey as President-elect* (Washington, DC, 1939).

Bodo, John R., *The Protestant Clergy and Public Issues, 1812–1848* (Princeton, NJ, 1954).

Boller, Paul F. Jr., *George Washington and Religion* (Dallas, TX, 1963).

Boorstin, Daniel J., *The Lost World of Thomas Jefferson* (Chicago, 1948).

Borden, Morton, *Jews, Turks, and Infidels* (Chapel Hill, NC, 1984).

Bowling, Kenneth R., "Congressional Election, 1788–90," *James Madison and the American Nation 1751–1836*, Robert A. Rutland, ed., 120.

Brady, Patricia, *Martha Washington* (New York, 2005).

Brands, H. W., *Andrew Jackson* (New York, 2005).

Brant, Irving, "Election of 1808," *History of American Presidential Elections 1789–1968*, Arthur M. Schlesinger Jr., ed. (New York, 1971), 1: 185–246.

———, *James Madison*, six volumes (Indianapolis, IN, 1941–61).

Briceland, Alan V., "John C. Ogden: Messenger and Propagandist of Matthew Lyon, 1798–99," *Vermont History: The Proceedings of the Vermont Historical Society*, Vol. 43, No. 2 (Spring 1975), 103–21.

Brockunier, S. Hugh, "Purcell's *Connecticut in Transition*," Richard J. Purcell, *Connecticut in Transition: 1775–1818* (Middletown, CT, 1963), vii–xvii.

Brodsky, Alyn, *Benjamin Rush: Patriot and Physician* (New York, 2004).

Brookhiser, Richard, *America's First Dynasty: The Adamses, 1735–1918* (New York, 2002).

———, *Rediscovering George Washington: Founding Father* (New York, 1996).

Brooks, John L., "Ancient Lodges and Self-Created Societies: Voluntary Association and the Public Sphere in the Early Republic," *Launching the "Extended Republic,"* Ronald Hoffman and Peter J. Albert, eds. (Charlottesville, VA, 1996).

Brown, Richard D., *Knowledge Is Power: The Diffusion of Information in Early America, 1700–1865* (New York, 1989).

Brown, Walt, *John Adams and the American Press* (Jefferson, NC, 1995).

Buel, Richard Jr., *America on the Brink: How the Political Struggle over the War of 1812 Almost Destroyed the Young Republic* (New York, 2005).

———, *Securing the Revolution: Ideology in American Politics, 1789–1815* (San Jose, CA, 2000).

Bullock, Steven C., *Revolutionary Brotherhood: Freemasonry and the Transformation of the American Social Order, 1730–1840* (Chapel Hill, NC, 1996).

Burns, James MacGregor, and Susan Dunn, *George Washington* (New York, 2004).

Burstein, Andrew, *America's Jubilee: July 4, 1826* (New York, 2001).

———, *The Inner Jefferson* (Charlottesville, VA, 1995).

———, *Jefferson's Secrets: Death and Desire at Monticello* (New York, 2005).

Butler, Jon, *Awash in a Sea of Faith* (Cambridge, MA, 1992).

Butler, Jon, and Harry S. Stout, eds., *Religion in American History: A Reader* (New York, 1998).

Butterfield, L. H., "Elder John Leland," *Proceedings of the American Antiquarian Society* 62 (1952).

Butterfield, L. H., Marc Friedlaender, and Mary-Jo Kline, *The Book of Abigail and John: Selected Letters of the Adams Family, 1762–1784* (Cambridge, MA, 1975).

Carwardine, Richard J., *Evangelicals and Politics in Antebellum America* (New Haven, CT, 1993).

Cassara, Ernest, ed., *Universalism in America: A Documentary History* (Boston, 1971).

Chadwick, Bruce, *George Washington's War* (Naperville, IL, 2005).

Chernow, Ron, *Alexander Hamilton* (New York, 2004).

Chitwood, Oliver Perry, *Richard Henry Lee: Statesman of the Revolution* (Morgantown, WV, 1967).

Choen, William, "Thomas Jefferson and the Problem of Slavery," *Journal of American History*, LVI (Dec. 1969), 503–26.

Church, Forrest, *The American Creed: A Biography of the Declaration of Independence* (New York, 2002).

——, *Jefferson's Bible* (Boston, 2000).

——, *The Separation of Church and State: Writings on a Fundamental Freedom by America's Founders* (Boston, 2004).

Clebsch, William A., *From Sacred to Profane America: The Role of Religion in American History* (New York, 1968).

Clopper, Jonas, *Fragments of the History of Bawlfredonia* by Herman Thwackihs (MD, 1819).

Cohen, I. Bernard, *Science and the Founding Fathers* (New York, 1995).

Commager, Henry Steele, *Jefferson, Nationalism, and the Enlightenment* (New York, 1986).

Conkin, Paul K., *Cane Ridge: America's Pentecost* (Madison, WI, 1990).

——, "The Religious Pilgrimage of Thomas Jefferson," *Jeffersonian Legacies*, Peter S. Onuf, ed. (Charlottesville, VA, 1993), 19–49.

Conrad, Stephen A., "Putting Rights Talk in Its Place," *Jefferson Legacies*, Peter S. Onuf, ed., 254–80.

Cord, Robert L., "Jefferson's 'Nonabsolute' Wall of Separation Between Chruch and State," *Religion and Political Culture in Jefferson's Virginia*, Garrett Ward Sheldon and Daniel L Dreisbach, eds., 167–87.

Côté, Richard N., *Strength and Honor: The Life of Dolley Madison* (Mt. Pleasant, SC, 2005).

Cresson, W. P., *James Monroe* (Chapel Hill, NC, 1946).

Cross, Barbara M., ed., *The Autobiography of Lyman Beecher*, two volumes (Cambridge, MA, 1961).

Cross, Malcolm L., "Washington, Hamilton, and the Establishment of the Dignified and Efficient Presidency," *George Washington and the Origins of the American Presidency*, Mark J. Rozell, William D. Pederson, and Frank J. Williams, eds. (Westport, CT, 2000), 95–115.

Crossen, Cynthia, "After U.S. Revolution, Country Was Split over France's War," *Wall Street Journal*, July 31, 2006, B1.

Crowe, Charles, "Bishop James Madison and the Republic of Virtue," *Journal of Southern History*, Vol. 30, No. 1 (Feb. 1964), 58–70.

Cunningham, Noble E. Jr., *Circular Letters of Congressmen to Their Constituents, 1789–1829*, three volumes (Chapel Hill, NC, 1978).

———, "Election of 1800," *History of American Presidential Elections 1789–1968*, Arthur M. Schlesinger Jr., ed. (New York, 1971), 1: 101–56.

———, *The Presidency of James Monroe* (Lawrence, KS, 1996).

———, *The Jefferson Republicans in Power: Party Operations, 1801–09* (Chapel Hill, NC, 1963).

———, *The Process of Government Under Jefferson* (Princeton, NJ, 1978).

Cutler, W. P., and J. P. Cutler, *Life, Journals and Correspondence of the Rev. Mannasseh Cutler* (Cincinnati, OH, 1888).

Dangerfield, George, *Chancellor Robert R. Livingston of New York, 1746–1813* (New York, 1960).

———, *The Era of Good Feelings* (New York, 1953).

Dauer, Manning, "Election of 1804," *History of American Presidential Elections 1789–1968*, Arthur M. Schlesinger Jr., ed. (New York, 1971), 1: 159–82.

———, *The Adams Federalists* (Baltimore, MD, 1953).

Dawidoff, Robert, "The Rhetoric of Democracy," *Thomas Jefferson and the Politics of Nature*, Thomas Engeman, ed. (South Bend, IN, 2000), 99–122.

Daynes, Byron W., "George Washington: Reluctant Occupant, Uncertain Model for the Presidency," *George Washinton and the Origins of the American Presidency*, Mark J. Rozell, William D. Pederson, and Frank J. Williams, eds. (Westport, CT, 2000), 3–36.

Detweiler, Philip F., "The Changing Reputation of the Declaration of Independence: The First 50 Years," *William and Mary Quarterly* (Third Ser.), Vol. 19 (Oct. 1962), 557–74.

Dickson, Charles Ellis, "Jeremiads in the New American Republic: The Case of National Fasts in the John Adams Administration," *New England Quarterly*, Vol. 60, No. 2 (June 1987), 187–207.

Diggins, John Patrick, *John Adams* (New York, 2003).

———, ed., *The Portable John Adams* (New York, 2004).

Dodds, Graham G., "George Washington: The Origins of Presidential-Press Relations," *George Washington and the Origins of the American Presidency*, Mark J. Rozell, William D. Pederson, and Frank J. Williams, eds. (Westport, CT, 2000), 187–201.

Dorrien, Gary, *The Making of American Liberal Theology: Imagining Progressive Religion, 1805–1900* (Louisville, KY, 2001).

Dowling, William C., *Literary Federalism in the Age of Jefferson: Joseph Dennie and The Port Folio, 1801–1811* (Columbia, SC, 1999).

Dreisbach, Daniel L., "Church State Debate in the Virginia Legislature: From the Declaration of Rights to the Statute for Establishing Religious Freedom," *Religion and Political Culture in Jefferson's Virginia*, Garrett Ward Sheldon and Daniel L. Dreisbach, eds. (Lanham, MD, 2000), 135–65.

———, *Religion and Politics in the Early Republic: Jasper Adams and the Church-state Debate* (Lexington, KY, 1996).

———, *Thomas Jefferson and the Wall of Separation Between Church and State* (New York, 2002).

Dunn, Susan, *Jefferson's Second Revolution: The Election Crisis of 1800 and the Triumph of Republicanism* (New York, 2004).

Durbin, Louise, *Inaugural Cavalcade* (New York, 1971).

Durey, Michael, "Thomas Paine's Apostles: Radical Emigres and the Triumph of Jeffersonian Republicanism," *William and Mary Quarterly* (Third Ser.), Vol. 44, No. 4 (Oct. 1987), 661–88.

Edmunds, R. David, *Tecumseh and the Quest for Indian Leadership* (Boston, 1984).

Egerton, Douglas R., "Henry Clay," *James Madison and the American Nation 1751–1836*, Robert A. Rutland, ed. (New York, 1994), 70–72.

Elkins, Stanley, and Eric McKitrick, *The Age of Federalism: The Early American Republic, 1788–1800* (New York, 1993).

Elliot, Emory, *Revolutionary Writers: Literature and Authority in the New Republic, 1725–1810* (New York, 1986).

Ellis, Harold Milton, *Joseph Dennie and His Circle: A Study in American Literature from 1792 to 1812* (Austin, TX, 1915).

Ellis, Joseph J., *American Sphinx: The Character of Thomas Jefferson* (New York, 1996).

———, "The Farewell," *George Washington Reconsidered*, Don Higginbotham, ed. (Charlottesville, VA, 2001), 212–49.

———, *Founding Brothers: The Revolutionary Generation* (New York, 2001).

———, *His Excellency George Washington* (New York, 2004).

———, *Passionate Sage: The Character and Legacy of John Adams* (New York, 1993).

Engeman, Thomas, ed., *Thomas Jefferson and the Politics of Nature* (South Bend, IN, 2000).

Ferling, John, *Adams vs. Jefferson: The Tumultuous Election of 1800* (New York, 2004).

———, *The First of Men: A Life of George Washington* (Knoxville, TN, 1988).

———, *John Adams: A Life* (New York, 1992).

———, *A Leap in the Dark: The Struggle to Create the American Republic* (New York, 2003).

Fielding, Howard Ioan, "John Adams: Puritan, Deist, Humanist," *Journal of Religion*, Vol. 20, No. 1 (Jan. 1940), 33–46.

Finkelman, Paul, "James Madison and the Bill of Rights: A Reluctant Paternity," *Supreme Court Review*, Vol. 1990, 301–47.

———, "Jefferson and Slavery: 'Treason Against the Hopes of the World,'" *Jeffersonian Legacies*, Peter S. Onuf, ed. (Charlottesville, VA, 1993), 181–221.

———, *Slavery and the Founders: Race and Liberty in the Age of Jefferson* (Armonk, NY, 1996).

Fischer, David Hackett, *Albion's Seed: Four British Folkways in America* (New York, 1989).

———, *Liberty and Freedom: A Visual History of America's Founding Ideas* (New York, 2005).

————, *The Revolution of American Conservatism: The Federalist Party in the Era of Jeffersonian Democracy* (New York, 1965).

————, *Washington's Crossing* (New York, 2004).

Fitzmier, John R., *New England's Moral Legislator* (Bloomington, IN, 1998).

Fleming, Thomas J., *First in Their Hearts: A Biography of George Washington* (New York, 1968).

Flexner, James Thomas, *George Washington,* four volumes (New York, 1965–72).

————, *Washington: The Indispensable Man* (Boston, 1974).

Fliegelman, Jay, *Declaring Independence: Jefferson, Natural Language, and the Culture of Performance* (Stanford, CA, 1993).

————, *Prodigals and Pilgrims: The American Revolution Against Patriarchal Authority, 1750–1800* (Cambridge, 1982).

Freeman, Douglass Southall, *Washington,* Richard Harwell, ed. (New York, 1968).

Freeman, Joseph F. III, "The Church of Virginia Before Independence," *Up from Independence: The Episcopal Church in Virginia* (Orange, VA, 1976).

Fuller, Edmund, and David E. Green, *God in the White House* (New York, 1968)

Furstenberg, Francois, *In the Name of the Father* (New York, 2006).

Gaustad, Edwin S., *Faith of Our Fathers: Religion and the New Nation* (San Francisco, 1987).

————, *Roger Williams* (New York, 2005).

————, *Sworn upon the Altar of God: A Religious Biography of Thomas Jefferson* (Ann Arbor, MI, 1996).

Gelles, Edith B., *Portia: The World of Abigail Adams* (Bloomington, IN, 1992)

Gilman, Daniel C., *James Monroe* (New Rochelle, NY, 1898).

Golden, James L., and Alan L. Golden, *Thomas Jefferson and the Rhetoric of Virtue* (Lanham, MD, 2002).

Goodman, Paul, *The Democratic-Republicans of Massachusetts: Politics in a Young Republic* (Cambridge, MA, 1964).

Gordon-Reed, Annette, *Thomas Jefferson and Sally Hemings* (Charlottesville, VA, 1997).

Graham, Jenny, *Revolutionary in Exile: The Emigrations of Joseph Priestley to America, 1794–1804* (Philadelphia, PA, 1995).

Grant, James, *John Adams: Party of One* (New York, 2005).

Green, Constance McLauglin, *Washington: Village and Capital, 1800–1878* (Princeton, NJ, 1962).

Green, Jack P., "The Intellectual Reconstruction of Virginia in the Age of Jefferson," *Jeffersonian Legacies,* Peter S. Onuf, ed. (Charlottesville, VA, 1993) 225–53.

Gribbin, William, *The Churches Militant: The War of 1812 and American Religion* (New Haven, CT, 1973).

————, "The Legacy of Timothy Dwight: A Reappraisal," *Connecticut Historical Society Bulletin,* Vol. 37, No. 2 (April 1972).

Grizzard, Frank E. Jr., *The Ways of Providence: Religion and George Washington* (Charlottesville, VA, 2005).

Gross, Jonathan, ed., *Thomas Jefferson's Scrapbooks* (Hanover, NH, 2006).

Hamburger, Phillip, *Separation of Church and State* (Cambridge, MA, 2002).

Handy, Robert T., "The Magna Charta of Religious Freedom in America," *Union Seminar. Quart. Review* XXXVIII, No. 3 + 4 (1984), 301–17.

Hanley, Mark Y., *Beyond a Christian Commonwealth: The Protestant Quarrel with the American Republic, 1830–1860* (Chapel Hill, NC, 1994).

Haraszti, Zoltan, *John Adams & The Prophets of Progress* (Cambridge, MA, 1952).

Harrington, Michael, *The Politics at God's Funeral* (New York, 1983).

Harris, Marc L., "Revelation and the American Republic: Timothy Dwight's Civic Participation," *Journal of the History of Ideas* (1993), 449–68.

Hart, Gary, *James Monroe* (New York, 2005).

———, *Restoration of the Republic: The Jeffersonian Ideal in 21st-Century America* (New York, 2002).

Hartmann, Werner, and Piers A. Vaughan, "The George Washington Inaugural Bible," www.stjohns1.org.

Hatch, Nathan O., *The Democratization of American Christianity* (New Haven, CT, 1989).

Henriques, Peter R., "The Final Struggle Between George Washington and the Grim King," *George Washington Reconsidered,* Don Higginbotham, ed. (Charlottesville, VA, 2001), 250–71.

———, *Realistic Visionary: A Portrait of George Washington* (Charlottesville, VA, 2006).

Hickey, Donald R., *The War of 1812: The Forgotten Conflict* (Urbana, IL, 1995).

Higginbotham, Don, "George Washington and Revolutionary Asceticism," *George Washington Reconsidered,* Don Higginbotham, ed. (Charlottesville, VA, 2001), 141–64.

———, ed., *George Washington Reconsidered* (Charlottesville, VA, 2001).

Hitchens, Christopher, *Thomas Jefferson: Author of America* (New York, 2005).

Holmes, David L., "The Decline and Revival of the Church of Virginia," *Up from Independence: The Episcopal Church in Virginia* (Orange, VA, 1976), 53–109.

———, *The Faiths of the Founding Fathers* (New York, 2006).

———, "The Religion of James Monroe," *Virginia Quarterly Review,* Vol. 79, No. 4 (Autumn 2003), 589–606.

Hood, Fred J., *Reformed America: The Middle and Southern States, 1783–1837* (University, AL, 1980).

Horn, James, Jan Ellen Lewis, and Peter S. Onuf, *The Revolution of 1800: Democracy, Race, and the New Republic* (Charlottesville, VA, 2002).

Howe, Daniel Walker, *The Unitarian Conscience: Harvard Moral Philosophy, 1805–1861* (Cambridge, MA, 1970).

Hudson, Winthrop S., ed., *Nationalism and Religion in America: Concepts of American Identity and Mission* (Gloucester, MA, 1978).

Humphreys, David, *Life of General Washington by David Humphreys,* Rosemarie Lagarri, ed. (Athens, GA, 2006).

Huntington, Samuel P., *American Politics: The Promise of Disharmony* (Cambridge, MA, 1981).

Hutchinson, Kay Bailey, *American Heroines: The Spirited Women Who Shaped Our Country* (New York, 2004).

Hutson, James H., *The Founders on Religion: A Book of Quotations* (Princeton, NJ, 2005).

———, "John Adams' Title Campaign," *New England Quarterly,* Vol. 41, No. 1 (March 1968), 30–39.

———, *Religion and the Founding of the American Republic* (Washington, DC, 1998).

———, "Thomas Jefferson's Letter to the Danbury Baptists: A Controversy Rejoined," *William and Mary Quarterly* (Third Ser.), Vol. 56, No. 4 (Oct. 1999), 775–90.

Irving, Washington, *George Washington: A Biography* (New York, 1994).

Isaac, Rhys, "The Rage of Malice of the Old Serpent Devil," *The Virginia Statute for Religious Freedom: Its Evolution and Consequences in America History,* Merrill D. Peterson and Robert C. Vaughan, eds. (New York, 1988), 139–70.

Jacoby, Susan, *Freethinkers: A History of American Secularism* (New York, 2004).

James, Sydney V., *A People Among Peoples: Quaker Benevolence in Eighteenth-Century America* (Cambridge, MA, 1963).

Jefferson, Thomas, *Notes on the State of Virginia,* Frank Shuffelton, ed. (New York, 1999).

———, *Thomas Jefferson: Writings,* Merrill D. Peterson, ed. (New York, 1984).

Johnson, Monroe, "James Monroe, Soldier," *William and Mary College Quarterly Historical Magazine* (Second Ser.), Vol. 9, No. 2 (April 1929), 110–17.

Johnson, Paul, *George Washington: The Founding Father* (New York, 2005).

Juster, Susan, *Doomsayers: Anglo-American Prophecy in the Age of Revolution* (Philadelphia, 2006).

Kaminski, John P., and Jill Adair McCaughan, *A Great and Good Man: George Washington in the Eyes of His Contemporaries* (Madison, WI, 1989).

Kaplanoff, Mark D., "Religion and Righteousness: A Study of Federalist Rhetoric in the New Hampshire Election of 1800," *Historical New Hampshire* 23 (Winter 1968), 3–20.

Kaye, Harvey J., *Thomas Paine and the Promise of America* (New York, 2005).

Kelley, Robert, *The Cultural Pattern in American Politics: The First Century* (Lanham, MD, 1979).

Kelsall, Malcolm, *Jefferson and the Iconography of Romanticism* (New York, 1999).

Kenny, Michael G., *The Perfect Law of Liberty: Elias Smith and the Providential History of America* (Washington, DC, 1994).

Kerber, Linda K., *Federalists in Dissent: Imagery and Ideology in Jeffersonian America* (Ithaca, NY, 1970).

———, *Women of the Republic: Intellect & Ideology in Revolutionary America* (Chapel Hill, NC, 1980).

Ketcham, Ralph, *James Madison* (Charlottesville, VA, 1990).

———, *Presidents Above Party: The First American Presidency, 1789–1829* (Chapel Hill, NC, 1984).

Ketchem, Ralph, and Nathaniel Stein, "Two New Letters Reveal Madison's Role, Unmask Ghost of Washington's Unused Inaugural," *Manuscripts* (Spring 1959), 1–15.

Kloppenberg, James T., "The Virtues of Liberalism: Christianity, Republicanism, and Ethics in Early American Political Discourse," *The Journal of American History*, Vol. 74, No. 1 (June 1987), 9–33.

Koch, Adrienne, *Jefferson and Madison: The Great Collaboration* (Old Saybrook, CT, 2004).

———, *Madison's "Advice to My Country"* (Princeton, NJ, 1966).

Koch, G. Adolf, *Republican Religion* (New York, 1933).

Kramnick, Isaac, "The 'Great National Discussion': The Discourse of Politics in 1787," *William and Mary Quarterly* (Third Ser.), Vol. 45, No. 1 (Jan. 1988), 3–32.

Kross, Peter, "Elias Boudinot, America's First President," *New Jersey History* (1987), www.flatrock.org/new_jersey/elias_boudinot.

Kurtz, Stephen G., *The Presidency of John Adams: The Collapse of Federalism, 1795–1800* (New York, 1961).

Labunski, Richard, *James Madison and the Struggle for the Bill of Rights* (New York, 2006).

Lambert, Frank, *The Founding Fathers and the Place of Religion in America* (Princeton, NJ, 2006).

Lee, Robert Edson, "Timothy Dwight and the Boston Palladium," *New England Quarterly*, Vol. 35, No. 2 (June 1962), 229–39.

Leibeiger, Stuart, *Founding Friendship: George Washington, James Madison, and the Creation of the American Republic* (Charlottesville, VA, 1999).

Lerche, Charles O. Jr., "Jefferson and the Election of 1800: A Case Study in the Political Smear," *William and Mary Quarterly* (Third Ser.), Vol. 5, No. 4 (Oct. 1948), 467–91.

Levin, Phyllis Lee, *Abigail Adams* (New York, 2001).

Levy, Andrew, *The First Emancipator: The Forgotten Story of Robert Carter* (New York, 2005).

Levy, Leonard W., *The Establishment Clause: Religion and the First Amendment* (Chapel Hill, NC, 1994).

———, "Establishment of Religion," *James Madison and the American Nation 1751–1836*, Robert A. Rutland, ed. (New York, 1994), 354–56.

Lewis, James E. Jr., "What Is to Become of Our Government?" *The Revolution of 1800*, James Horn, Jan Ellen Lewis, and Peter S. Onuf, eds. (Charlottesville, VA, 2002), 3–29.

Link, Eugene Perry, *Democratic-Republican Societies, 1790–1800* (New York, 1942).

Littell, Franklin Hamlin, *From State Church to Pluralism: A Protestant Interpretation of Religion in American History* (Chicago, 1962).

Litto, Fredric M., "Addison's *Cato* in the Colonies," *William and Mary Quarterly* (Third Ser.), Vol. 23 (July 1966), 431–49.

Longmore, Paul K., *The Invention of George Washington* (Berkeley, CA, 1988).

Loring, James S., *The Hundred Boston Orators* (Boston, 1852).

Luebke, Fred C., "The Origins of Thomas Jefferson's Anti-Clericalism," *Church History,* Vol. 32, No. 3 (Sept. 1963), 344–56.

Maclay, William, *The Journal of William Maclay* (New York, 1927).

Maier, Pauline, *American Scripture: Making the Declaration of Independence* (New York, 1997).

Malone, Dumas, *Jefferson,* six volumes (Boston, 1948–81).

———, *The Public Life of Thomas Cooper, 1783–1839* (New Haven, CT, 1926).

Mapp, Alf J. Jr., *The Faiths of Our Fathers* (Lanham, MD, 2003).

Marshall, John, *The Life of George Washington,* Robert Faulkner and Paul Carrese, eds. (Indianapolis, IN, 2000).

Marty, Martin E., *Righteous Empire: The Protestant Experience in America* (New York, 1970).

Marvick, Elizabeth W., "Family Imagery and Revolutionary Spirit: Washington's Creative Leadership," *George Washington and the Origins of the American Presidency,* Mark J. Rozell, William D. Pederson, and Frank J. Williams, eds. (Westport, CT, 2000), 77–91.

Mathews, Donald G., "The Second Great Awakening as an Organizing Process, 1780–1830: An Hypothesis," *American Quarterly,* Vol. 21, No. 1 (Spring 1969), 23–43.

Mattern, David B., and Holly C. Shulman, ed., *The Selected Letters of Dolley Payne Madison* (Charlottesville, VA, 2003).

Matthews, Jean V., *Toward a New Society: American Thought and Culture 1800–1830* (Boston, 1991).

McCollister, John, *So Help Me God: The Faith of America's Presidents* (Louisville, KY, 1991).

McCoy, Drew R., *The Elusive Republic: Political Economy in Jeffersonian America* (Chapel Hill, NC, 1980).

———, *The Last of the Fathers: James Madison & the Republican Legacy* (Cambridge, 1989).

McCullough, David, *John Adams* (New York, 2001).

———, *1776* (New York, 2005).

McDonald, Forrest, Novus Ordo Seclorum: *The Intellectual Origins of the Constitution* (Lawrence, KS, 1985).

———, *The Presidency of George Washington* (Lawrence, KS, 1974).

———, *The Presidency of Thomas Jefferson* (Lawrence, KS, 1976).

McDonald, Robert M. S., "Was There a Religious Revolution of 1800?", *The Revolution of 1800,* James Horn, Jan Ellen Lewis, and Peter Onuf, eds. (Charlottesville, VA, 2002), 173–98.

McGehee, Larry, *Bending the Twig: Pages from the Journal of a Pilgrim Parent* (Spartanburg, SC, 1998).

McGreevy, John T., *Catholicism and American Freedom* (New York, 2003).

McLaughlin, Jack, ed., *To His Excellency Thomas Jefferson: Letters to a President* (New York, 1991).

McLoughlin, William G., *Isaac Backus and the American Pietistic Tradition* (Boston, 1967).

————, *New England Dissent, 1630–1833: The Baptists and the Separation of Church and State,* two volumes (Cambridge, MA, 1971).

————, *Revivals, Awakenings, and Reform: An Essay on Religion and Social Change in America: 1607–1977* (Chicago, 1978).

McWilliams, John, *New England's Crises and Cultural Memory: Literature, Politics, History, Religion, 1620–1860* (Cambridge, 2004).

Meacham, Jon, *American Gospel: God, the Founding Fathers, and the Making of a Nation* (New York, 2006).

Mead, Sidney Earl, *The Lively Experiment: The Shaping of Christianity in America* (New York, 1963).

————, *Nathanial William Taylor, 1786–1858: A Connecticut Liberal* (Chicago, 1942).

————, *The Nation with the Soul of a Church* (New York, 1975).

————, *The Old Religion in the Brave New World: Reflections on the Relation Between Christendom and the Republic* (Berkeley, CA, 1977).

Meade, Bishop, and William Meade, *Old Churches, Ministers, and Families of Virginia,* Two volumes (New York, 1857).

Medhurst, Martin J., "From Duche to Medhurst: The Birth of Inaugural Prayer," *Journal of Church and State,* Vol. 24 (1982), 582–86.

Meyers, Marvin, *The Jacksonian Persuasion: Politics and Belief* (Stanford, CA, 1960).

Miller, John E., *The Federalist Era, 1789–1801* (Long Grove, IL, 1988).

Miller, Helen Hill, *George Mason, Constitutionalist* (Cambridge, MA, 2001).

Miller, Hunter, ed., *Treaties and Other International Acts of the United States of America,* Vol. 2. (Washington, DC, 1931).

Miller, John Chester, *The Wolf by the Ears: Thomas Jefferson and Slavery* (Charlottesville, VA, 1991).

Miller, William Lee, *The First Liberty: Religion and the American Republic* (New York, 1986).

Monroe, James A., *Hellfire Nation: The Politics of Sin in American History* (New Haven, CT, 2003).

Moore, Glover, *Missouri Controversy, 1819–1821* (Lexington, KY, 1966).

Moore, R. Laurence, *Religious Outsiders and the Making of Americans* (New York, 1986).

Moore, Virginia, *The Madisons* (New York, 1979).

Morgan, Edmund S., *The Genius of George Washington* (New York, 1980).

————, *The Genuine Article: A Historian Looks at Early America* (New York, 2004).

————, "John Adams and the Puritan Tradition," *New England Quarterly,* Vol. 34, No. 4 (Dec. 1961).

————, *The Meaning of Independence* (New York, 1976).

————, "The Puritan Ethic and the American Revolution," *William and Mary Quarterly* (Third Ser.), Vol. 24, No. 1 (Jan. 1967), 3–43.

Morison, Samuel Eliot, *The Young Man Washington* (Boston, 1932).

Morse, James King, *Jedidiah Morse: A Champion of New England Orthodoxy* (New York, 1967).

Nagel, Paul C., *John Quincy Adams: A Public Life, a Private Life* (Cambridge, MA, 1997).

Nash, Gary B., "The American Clergy and the French Revolution," *William and Mary Quarterly* (Third Ser.), Vol. 22, No. 3 (July 1965), 392–412.

———, *First City: Philadelphia and the Forging of Historical Memory* (Philadelphia, 2006).

Needleman, Jacob, *The American Soul* (New York, 2002).

Nelson, Craig, *Thomas Paine: Enlightenment, Revolution, and the Birth of Modern Nations* (New York, 2006).

Newman, Simon P., *Parades and the Politics of the Street: Festive Culture in the Early American Republic* (Philadelphia, 1997).

Noll, Mark A., *America's God: From Jonathan Edwards to Abraham Lincoln* (New York, 2002).

———, ed., *Religion and American Politics: From the Colonial Period to the 1980s* (New York, 1990).

Noonan, John T. Jr., *The Lustre of Our Country: The American Experience of Religious Freedom* (Berkeley, CA, 1998).

Nordham, George W., *The Age of Washington: George Washington's Presidency, 1781–1787.*

O'Brien, Charles F., "The Religious Issue in the Presidential Campaign of 1800," *Essex Institute Historical Collections,* Vol. 107 (1971), 82–93.

O'Brien, Conor Cruise, *The Long Affair: Thomas Jefferson and the French Revolution, 1785–1800* (Chicago, 1995).

Onuf, Peter S., *Jefferson's Empire: The Language of American Nationhood* (Charlottesville, VA, 2000).

———, ed., *Jeffersonian Legacies* (Charlottesville, VA, 1993).

O'Reilly, Kenneth, *Nixon's Piano* (New York, 1995).

Ovason, David, *The Secret Symbols of the Dollar Bill* (New York, 2004).

Parker, Theodore, *Historic Americans, Collected Works,* Vol. 13 (Boston, 1871).

Parrington, Vernon Louis, ed., *The Connecticut Wits* (Hamden, CT, 1963).

Pasley, Jeffrey L., "1800 as a Revolution in Political Culture," *The Revolution of 1800,* James Horn, Jan Ellen Lewis, and Peter S. Onuf, eds. (Charlottesville, VA, 2002), 121–52.

———, *"The Tyranny of Printers": Newspaper Politics in the Early American Republic* (Charlottesville, VA, 2001).

Peterson, Merrill D., *The Jefferson Image in the American Mind* (New York, 1960).

———, *Thomas Jefferson and the New Nation* (New York, 1970).

Peterson, Merrill D., and Robert C. Vaughan, eds., *The Virginia Statute for Religious Freedom: Its Evolution and Consequences in American History* (New York, 1988).

Phillips, Joseph W., *Jedidiah Morse and New England Congregationalism* (Rutgers, NJ, 1983).

Pierard, Richard V., and Robert D. Linder, *Civil Religion & the Presidency* (Grand Rapids, MI, 1988).

Price, Don K., *America's Unwritten Constitution: Science, Religion, and Political Responsibility* (Cambridge, MA, 1985).

Purcell, Richard J., *Connecticut in Transition, 1775–1818* (Middletown, CT, 1963).

Quitt, Martin H., "The English Cleric and the Virginia Adventurer," *George Washington Reconsidered,* Don Higginbotham, ed. (Charlottesville, VA, 2001), 15–37.

Rakove, Jack N., *James Madison and the Creation of the American Republic* (New York, 2002).

———, *James Madison: Writings* (New York, 1999).

Randall, Willard Sterne, *George Washington: A Life* (New York, 1997).

Rasmussen, William M. S., and Robert S. Tilton, *George Washington: The Man Behind the Myths* (Charlottesville, VA, 1999).

Remini, Robert V., *Andrew Jackson, Volume One: The Course of American Empire, 1767–1821* (Baltimore, 1977).

Rhodenhamel, John, ed., *George Washington: Writings* (New York, 1997).

Richard, Carl J., *The Founders and the Classics: Greece, Rome and the American Enlightenment* (Cambridge, MA, 1994).

Risjord, Norman K., "Election of 1812," *History of American Presidential Elections,* Arthur M. Schlesinger Jr., ed. (New York, 1971), 1: 249–72.

Roberts, Cokie, *Founding Mothers: The Women Who Raised Our Nation* (New York, 2004).

Roy, Thomas M., "'Not One Cent for Tribute': The Public Addresses and American Popular Reaction to the XYZ Affair," *Journal of the Early Republic,* Vol. 3, No. 4 (Winter 1983), 389–412.

Rozell, Mark J., William D. Pederson, and Frank J. Williams, ed., *George Washington and the Origins of the American Presidency* (Westport, CT, 2000).

Rutland, Robert A., "James Madison," *James Madison and the American Nation 1751–1836,* Robert A. Rutland, ed. (New York, 1994).

———, *James Madison: The Founding Father* (Columbia, MO, 1987).

———, *The Presidency of James Madison* (Lawrence, KS, 1990).

Sandoz, Ellis, ed., *Political Sermons of the American Founding Era,* two volumes (Indianapolis, IN, 1998).

Sanford, Charles B., "The Religious Beliefs of Thomas Jefferson," *Religion and Political Cultures in Jefferson's Virginia,* Garrett Ward Sheldon and Daniel L. Dreisbach, eds. (Lanham, MD, 2000), 61–91.

———, *The Religious Life of Thomas Jefferson* (Charlottesville, VA, 1984).

Schachner, Nathan, *Alexander Hamilton* (New York, 1946).

Schiff, Stacy, *A Great Improvisation: Franklin, France, and the Birth of America* (New York, 2005).

Schlesinger, Arthur Jr., ed., *The Cycles of American History* (New York, 1999).

———, *History of American Presidential Elections, Volume 1: 1789–1844* (New York, 1971).

———, *War and the American Presidency* (New York, 2005).

Schudson, Michael, *The Good Citizen: A History of American Civic Life* (Cambridge, MA, 1998).

Sharp, James Roger, *American Politics in the Early Republic: The New Nation in Crisis* (New Haven, CT, 1933).

Sharpe, James, *Remember, Remember: A Cultural History of Guy Fawkes Day* (Cambridge, MA, 2005).

Shaw, Peter, *The Character of John Adams* (Chapel Hill, NC, 1976).

Sheehan, Bernard W., *Seeds of Extinction: Jeffersonian Philanthropy and the American Indian* (New York, 1973).

Sheldon, Garrett Ward, "Eclectic Synthesis: Jesus, Aristotle, and Locke," *Thomas Jefferson and the Politics of Nature,* Thomas S. Engeman, ed. (South Bend, IN, 2000), 81–98.

———, "Liberalism, Classicism, and Christianity in Jefferson's Political Thought," *Religion and Political Culture in Jefferson's Virginia,* Garrett Ward Sheldon and Daniel L. Dreisbach, eds. (Lanham, MD, 2000), 93–105.

———, *The Political Philosophy of James Madison* (Baltimore, 2001).

Sheldon, Garrett Ward, and Daniel L. Dreisbach, *Religion and Political Culture in Jefferson's Virginia* (Lanham, MD, 2000).

Sheridan, Eugene R., *Jefferson and Religion* (Charlottesville, VA, 1998).

Shiels, Richard D., "The Second Great Awakening in Connecticut: Critique of the Traditional Interpretation," *Church History,* Vol. 49, No. 4 (Dec. 1980), 401–15.

Shuffelton, Frank, ed., *The Letters of John and Abigail Adams* (New York, 2004).

Silverman, K., *A Cultural History of the American Revolution* (New York, 1976).

Slaughter, Thomas P., *The Whiskey Rebellion: Frontier Epilogue to the American Revolution* (New York, 1986).

Smith, Elwyn A., ed., *The Religion of the Republic* (Philadelphia, 1971).

———, "The Voluntary Establishment of Religion," *The Religion of the Republic,* 154–82.

Smith, James Morton, "Alien and Sedition Acts of 1798," *James Madison and the American Nation 1751–1836,* Robert A. Rutland, ed. (New York, 1994), 10.

———, "The Federalist 'Saints' Versus 'The Devil of Sedition': The Liberty Pole Cases of Dedham, Massachusetts, 1798–9," *New England Quarterly,* Vol. 28, No. 2 (June 1955), 198–215.

———, *Freedom's Fetters: The Alien and Sedition Laws and American Civil Liberties* (Ithaca, NY, 1956).

———, "Virginia and Kentucky Resolutions," *James Madison and the American Nation 1751–1836,* Robert A. Rutland, ed. (New York, 1994).

Smith, Margaret Bayard, *The First Forty Years of Washington Society,* Gaillard Hunt, ed. (New York, 1906).

Smith, Page, "Election of 1796," *History of American Presidential Elections,* Arthur Schlesinger Jr., ed. (New York, 1971), 1: 59–98.

———, *John Adams,* two volumes (New York, 1962).

Smith, Richard Norton, *Patriarch: George Washington and the New American Nation* (New York, 1993).

Smylie, James H., "Protestant Clergy, the First Amendment and Beginnings of a Constitutional Debate, 1781–91," *The Religion of the Republic,* Elwyn A. Smith, ed. (Philadelphia, 1971), 116–53.

Spalding, Matthew, *A Sacred Union of Citizens: George Washington's Farewell Address and the American Character* (Lanham, MD, 1996).

Stahr, Walter, *John Jay: Founding Father* (New York, 2005).

Staloff, Darren, *Hamilton, Adams, Jefferson: The Politics of Enlightenment and the American Founding* (New York, 2005).

Staudenraus, P. J., *The African Colonization Movement, 1816–1865* (New York, 1961).

Stauffer, Vernon, *New England and the Bavarian Illuminati* (New York, 1918).

Steiner, Franklin, *The Religious Beliefs of Our Presidents from Washington to F.D.R.* (Amherst, NY, 1995).

Stout, Harry S., "Rhetoric and Reality in the Early Republic: The Case of the Federalist Clergy," *Religion and American Politics,* Mark Noll, ed. (New York, 1990), 62–76.

Stowe, Walter Herbert, ed., *The Life and Letters of Bishop William White* (New York, 1937).

Swanson, Mary-Elaine, "James Madison and the Presbyterian Idao of Man and Government," *Religion and Political Culture in Jefferson's Virginia,* Garrett Ward Sheldon and Daniel L. Dreisbach, eds. (Lanham, MD, 2000), 119–32.

Tabbert, Mark A., *American Freemasons: Three Centuries of Building Communities* (Lexington, MA, 2005).

Thompson, C. Bradley, *John Adams & the Spirit of Liberty* (Lawrence, KS, 1998).

Thompson, Thomas C., "Perceptions of a 'Deist Church' in Early National Virginia," *Religion and Political Culture in Jefferson's Virginia,* Barrett Ward Sheldon and Daniel L. Dreisbach, eds. (Lanham, MD, 2000), 41–58.

Todd, Charles Burr, *Life and Letters of Joel Barlow: Poet, Statesman, Philosopher* (New York, 1886).

Travers, Lee, *Celebrating the Fourth: Independence Day and the Rites of Nationalism in the Early Republic* (Amherst, MA, 1997).

Trees, Andrew S., *The Founding Fathers and the Politics of Character* (Princeton, NJ, 2004).

Turner, James, *Without God, Without Greed: The Origins of Unbelief in America* (Baltimore, 1985).

Turner, Lynn W., "Elections of 1816 and 1820," *History of American Presidential Elections,* Arthur Schlesinger Jr., ed. (New York, 1971), 1: 299–343.

Twohig, Dorothy, "The Controversy over Slavery," *George Washington Reconsidered,* Don Higginbotham, ed., 114–38.

Vidal, Gore, *Inventing a Nation: Washington, Adams, Jefferson* (New Haven, CT, 2003).

Waldstreicher, David, *In the Midst of Perpetual Fetes: The Making of American Nationalism, 1776–1820* (Chapel Hill, NC, 1997).

Weems, Mason L., *The Life of Washington* (Cambridge, MA, 1962).

Weintraub, Stanley, *General Washington's Christmas Farewell: A Mount Vernon Homecoming, 1783* (New York, 2003).

West, John G. Jr., *The Politics of Revelation & Reason: Religion and Civic Life in the New Nation* (Lawrence, KS, 1996).

Wharton, Anne Hollingsworth, *Salons, Colonial and Republican* (Philadelphia, 1900).

Wiencek, Henry, *An Imperfect God: George Washington, His Slaves, and the Creation of America* (New York, 2003).

Wilentz, Sean, *The Rise of American Democracy: Jefferson to Lincoln* (New York, 2005).

Wilkins, Roger, *Jefferson's Pillow: The Founding Fathers and the Dilemma of Black Patriotism* (Boston, 2001).

Wills, Garry, *Cincinnatus: George Washington and the Enlightenment* (Garden City, NY, 1984).

———, *Henry Adams and the Making of America* (New York, 2005).

———, *Inventing America: Jefferson's Declaration of Independence* (New York, 1978).

———, *James Madison* (New York, 2002).

———, *"Negro President": Jefferson and the Slave Power* (Boston, 2003).

———, *Under God: Religion and American Politics* (New York, 1990).

Wills, Gregory A., *Democratic Religion: Freedom, Authority, and Church Discipline in the Baptist South, 1785–90* (New York, 1997).

Wilson, Bird, *Memoir of the Life of the Right Reverend William White* (Philadelphia, 1839).

Wilson, Douglas L., ed., *Jefferson's Literary Commonplace Book,* The Papers of Thomas Jefferson, Second Series (Princeton, NJ, 1989).

———, "Jefferson and the Republic of Letters," *Jeffersonian Legacies,* Peter S. Onuf, ed. (Charlottesville, VA, 1993), 50–76.

Wilson, John F., "Jefferson and Bolingbroke: Some Notes on the Question of Influence," *Religion and Political Culture in Jefferson's Virginia,* Garrett Ward Sheldon and Daniel L. Dreisbach, eds. (Lanham, MD, 2000), 107–18.

———, "The Status of 'Civil Religion' in America," *The Religion of the Republic,* Elwyn A. Smith, ed. (Philadelphia, 1971), 1–21.

Wilson, John F., and Donald L. Drakeman, *Church and State in American History* (Boulder, CO, 2003).

Withey, Lynne, *Dearest Friend: A Life of Abigail Adams* (New York, 1981).

Witte, John Jr., *Religion and the American Constitutional Experiment* (Boulder, CO, 2000).

Wood, Gordon, *The Americanization of Benjamin Franklin* (New York, 2004).

———, *Creation of the American Republic 1776–1787* (Chapel Hill, NC, 1998).

———, "The Greatness of George Washington," *George Washington Reconsidered,* Don Higginbotham, ed. (Charlottesville, VA, 2001), 309–24.

———, *Revolutionary Characters: What Made the Founders Different* (New York, 2006).

———, "The Trials and Tribulations of Thomas Jefferson," *Jeffersonian Legacies,* Peter S. Onuf, ed. (Charlottesville, VA, 1993), 395–417.

Wright, Conrad, *The Beginnings of Unitarianism in America* (Boston, 1966).

Zacks, Richard, *The Pirate Coast: Thomas Jefferson, the First Marines, and the Secret Mission of 1805* (New York, 2005).

Zvesper, John, "The Madisonian Systems," *Western Political Quarterly,* Vol. 37, No. 2 (June 1984), 236–56.

INDEX